Athenic. [Murray Robinson]

Ceramic. [Murray Robinson]

SHAW SAVILL'S MAGNIFICENT SEVEN

Corinthic - Athenic - Ceramic – Gothic
Persic – Runic – Suevic

Andrew Bell and Murray Robinson

Ships in Focus Publications

Published in the UK in 2011 by Ships in Focus Publications
18 Franklands, Longton
Preston PR4 5PD
ISBN 978-1-901703-60-3

Front cover: HMRY *Gothic* alongside at Hobart, see page 113. *[Reg Wilson/Russell Priest collection]*
Above: *Ceramic* at Wellington, 7th October 1970, with the Union Steam Ship Company's tug *Tapuhi (232/1945)* (ex *Empire Shirley). [V.H. Young and L.A. Sawyer]*
Back cover, top: *Athenic* in the Royal Docks at London, 22nd March 1969. *[V.H. Young and L.A. Sawyer]*
Back cover, centre: *Suevic* in August 1968, about to berth at the Ocean Steamers' Wharf in Adelaide's inner harbour, where she will load for Britain. At her stern is the tug *Tusker. [Chris Finney/Russell Priest collection]*
Bottom: *Ceramic* steaming in Cook Strait New Zealand, having departed Wellington for the very last time, 9th January 1972. *[V.H. Young and L.A. Sawyer]*

FOREWORD

Right Honourable Sir Anand Satyanand, GNZM, QSO
Governor-General of New Zealand

Greetings in the languages of the realm of New Zealand in English, Māori, Cook Island Māori, Niuean and Tokelauan: Kia Ora, Kia Orana, Fakalofa Lahi Atu and Taloha Ni.

As Governor-General of New Zealand, it is with much pleasure that I provide this Foreword for this book by Murray Robinson and Andrew Bell, *Shaw Savill's Magnificent Seven.*

This comprehensive book recounts the history of seven vessels owned by the Shaw Savill shipping company: *Corinthic, Athenic, Ceramic, Gothic, Persic, Runic* and *Suevic.* The ships were designed as large cargo vessels plying the trade routes between New Zealand and London, although four of them, *Gothic, Ceramic, Athenic and Corinthic,* also had cabins for 85 first-class passengers. Of the ships, only the *Runic* remains, as a wreck on Middleton Reef in the Tasman Sea, which the ship struck in 1961 whilst on a voyage from Brisbane to Auckland.

While the ships were a familiar sight in New Zealand's ports in the 1940s, 1950s and 1960s, the ship with which many people will have the fondest memories is the *Gothic.* As the Royal Yacht *Britannia* had yet to be completed, it was that Shaw Savill ship, also laden down with cargo, that transported the Queen and Prince Philip on the coronation world tour. Waiting on the Auckland wharves to greet the Royal couple on 23rd December 1953 was my predecessor as Governor-General, Lieutenant-General Sir Willoughby Norrie, dressed in full ceremonial uniform.

Whilst much has been written about this royal tour, this book adds to that body of work by telling the story of the life of the *Gothic* and her sister ships. The *Gothic* had a sad end, catching fire shortly after leaving Bluff in 1968, the event claiming the lives of seven people. While the crew managed to extinguish the blaze and the ship was saved and temporarily repaired, she only undertook one more cargo run before being sent to the breaker's yard.

Ships like the *Gothic* no longer visit our ports. The marine steam turbines that drove them, and their ways of loading and stowing cargo and the form of sea travel they embraced, have long since passed into history. However, the refrigerated cargo of butter, cheese and meat they carried to markets in the Northern Hemisphere played a key role in New Zealand's prosperity in the 25 years after the end of the Second World War. When the *Gothic* departed New Zealand from Bluff on 30th January 1954 with the Queen aboard, she was also fully loaded with agricultural cargo destined for the British market.

I congratulate Messrs Robinson and Bell on writing this book. The publication of *Shaw Savill's Magnificent Seven* will help ensure that the contribution of these ships and their crews to our economy and way of life, is not forgotten.

No reira, tēnā koutou, tēnā koutou, kia ora, kia kaha, tēnā koutou katoa.

Right Honourable Sir Anand Satyanand, GNZM, QSO
Governor-General of New Zealand

INTRODUCTION

This book follows our literary maiden voyage in 2009 when 'A Tasman Trio *Wanganella, Awatea, Monowai*' was published in the UK by Ships in Focus Publications. For our second expedition into print we have turned to the British company of Shaw Savill and Albion, known as the Shaw Savill Line and famous for the many outstanding passenger and cargo ships it owned. The liners *Dominion Monarch, Gothic* and *Southern Cross* come immediately to mind. In 1947 Shaw Savill introduced the first of a septet of steam ships that, until the last of them was scrapped in 1974, sailed the great trade route from Great Britain to New Zealand and Australia via the Panama Canal. So distinctive in every respect were these ships that the seven are remembered today collectively as the 'Big Ics'. We have called them Shaw Savill's Magnificent Seven. This book is their story.

The *Gothic*, one of their number, belongs to a special group of ships that will always be celebrated in maritime history and by those who follow it. In 1951 she was selected for conversion to Great Britain's royal yacht and, as HMRY *Gothic*, took Queen Elizabeth II and Prince Philip, Duke of Edinburgh, to New Zealand and then Australia for the very first visit to those countries by a reigning British monarch. The *Gothic* and her Merchant Navy crew performed this role outstandingly well. Fourteen years later she caught fire with the loss of seven lives including an entire family with two children. Her life story offers a wealth of material for a book but the *Gothic* cannot be considered alone, for she was part of a quartet of sisters known as the *Corinthic* class, named after the *Corinthic* which, in April 1947, was the first of them to enter service. *Athenic* and *Ceramic* made up the four. Then in November 1949 the *Persic*, very similar in design to the *Corinthic* class but without passenger accommodation, was followed into Shaw Savill's fleet by the *Runic* and *Suevic*. Of all seven only the *Runic* still exists, a sea-battered wreck atop Middleton Reef in the Tasman Sea. Her story is told in full here, for the very first time.

With the single exception of the *Runic*, they led ordinary lives with none of the *Gothic's* lustre in the service of Her Majesty. Yet greatness and glory emanate from every steel plate, rivet and frame by which all of them were made, for they came from a marvellous era of ship building, cargo carrying and sea travel that today has gone forever from the oceans. During the first three-quarters of the Twentieth Century Great Britain was the world's leading builder of merchant ships. By the start of the 1970s that title had passed to others but, before it did, there occurred a brief but fabulous last hurrah as, with the return to peacetime commerce from 1945, ship owners ordered new vessels in their hundreds from British yards. As well as demanding ever-greater efficiency and profitability from their ships, these owners wanted them to *look good*, a criterion sadly absent from present-day successors. And so, in those halcyon nautical times of the 1950s and 60s you might walk the waterfront of any major port and see some of the finest, most beautiful, most awesome sea-going castles of steel and timber ever created. The best of them came from British shipyards.

The *Gothic, Corinthic, Athenic, Ceramic, Persic, Runic* and *Suevic* belong to this era and personify it. The four ships of the *Corinthic* class were big and majestic in appearance with their long promenade decks set in the centre of the ship, topped by derricks and samson posts high on the superstructure. The impression of size and power was even greater with the *Gothic* and *Ceramic's* towering domed funnels. They had accommodation for 85 first class passengers and vast refrigerated holds for the carriage of food produced by New Zealand and Australia for Great Britain. *Persic* and her two sisters had the same hold space while their lowered superstructures, denied passenger accommodation, made them just as handsome in looks. All of them were powered by steam, their boilers and turbines generating up to 17,000 horse power with none of the computers or automation on which today's ships depend. And they were labour-intensive, requiring crews large enough to create villages at sea and hierarchies from ship's boys to the god-like master in his suite of cabins aft of the bridge. The life of these villagers comprised an endless routine of tending machinery, washing and painting decks and hulls, rigging cargo gear, cleaning cabins, serving food and drink, keeping watch and avoiding trouble be it from storms or superiors. Navigation was by means of sextants, chronometers, gyro and magnetic compasses, and Admiralty charts. Engineers stripped and overhauled pumps, burners, valves, generators, fans and condensers while keeping the ship at 17 knots. Pursers sat at their desks typing menus and passenger lists, keeping the ship's account books and adding up wages, taxes and allotments for the portage bill at voyage end. Always a practised eye was kept on the sea and the weather. One of the seven Big Ics was lost to shipwreck but fire was the principal hazard. Four of the seven suffered destructive fires, most notably the *Gothic* and *Corinthic.*

Commencing a book-writing project can be likened to standing at the foot of a near-vertical mountain, its faraway summit hidden against a precipice of cloud. Fortunately, at the very outset we happened upon two excellent mountain guides to ease our trepidation and set us on the right path for the climb.

The first is an anonymous, long-forgotten worker at the old Marine Department within the Government of New Zealand. In 1969, when all proceedings had been completed following the fire aboard the *Gothic*, this person gathered up all relevant documents and carefully placed them on one file. The Marine Department, swept from existence by long-ago restructuring, has its records housed at Archives New Zealand in Wellington and it was there, in their reading room four decades later, that we accessed that same file. We needed to search no further; everything was provided for us: witness statements, official reports, radio logs, crew lists, deck plans, press clippings and, best of all, photographs of the burnt ship and the repairs made to her.

Our second angel of inspiration was Warwick Thomson, a retired master mariner of Whangarei, New Zealand. Thomson was a young able seaman aboard the *Gothic* when she served as royal yacht. His duties comprised painting, washing decks, overhauling cargo gear, rigging side gangways and awnings and, when members of the royal party were about on deck, keeping away from their sight. Like his shipmates Thomson spent off-duty time playing cards and throwing darts but he also kept a diary in which he meticulously described the progress of that entire royal voyage. To add lavish cream to this already luscious cake, he took photographs and mounted these in an album. It was, of course, not permissible for rough seamen to stand in front of their sovereign with a camera, so Thomson shot his photos discreetly. His most remarkable photos have as their border an open porthole inside the *Gothic's* poop deck where the seamen were accommodated. There in that circle is the Queen coming down a ladder or taking the air on the *Gothic's* promenade decks, white jacketed officers all in attendance.

[Warwick Thomson]

We can imagine the phalanx of minders and media people accompanying celebrities, politicians and heads of state today, bodily intervening to stop unauthorised filming of the great person. Not so in 1953-54. Warwick Thomson recalls one occasion when the Queen actually did see him behind a porthole with his camera, taking a photo of the royal barge leaving the *Gothic's* side gangway. She looked up at him and smiled; the 27-year-old sovereign and the 20-year-old seaman.

There is no single, comprehensive, centralised repository of all the papers, files and records of Shaw Savill and Albion, which went out of existence in 1984. As a result, a book like this receives its oxygen from the privately-held photos, documents and memoirs of the people who lived and worked on the Big Ics. It says much about the qualities of the seven ships that many of these former seafarers have preserved comprehensive records and memories of their time in them. We are indebted to the kind and willing access they have each given us. Captain Graham Pepper, founder of the Shaw Savill Society, provided answers to a near-constant stream of e-mailed queries as we wrote this book. His work in conserving old files, ledgers and material from Shaw Savill meant we were able to see the cablegrams, many bearing the pencilled initials of Lord Sanderson, Chairman of Shaw Savill, that give the hitherto untold story of the *Runic's* failed salvage in 1961. Neil Hamilton, officer on watch the night the *Runic* went ashore, never to be shifted, gave us his account which is published here for the first time. Jimmy Andrew, the *Runic's* engineer on watch when she struck, also let us have his account.

With much patience *Corinthic* engineers George Wood and Bruce Birnie initiated us into the mystique of a steam turbine engine room. They did likewise with the deeper complexities of the refrigerating systems that were at the heart of the Big Ics. Retired naval architect Sam Parker guided us through the lost world of British shipbuilding in the late 1940s. Vic Young recalled the very special link the *Corinthic*, *Athenic*, *Ceramic* and *Gothic* had with Pitcairn Island. Ian Farquhar opened his extensive files of newspaper clippings for our use, as did Vic Young. Frank Pickering, Adrian (Pat) Chandler, Ian Condie, Edward Buckle, Dick Ashford, Warwick Thomson, Neil Hudson, Peter Carr, Graham Pepper, Bill Ashton and Philip Griffin all gave us their written memoirs. From filing cabinets, sea chests and attics in New Zealand, Australia and Great Britain we received a treasure-house of colour slides and black-and-white photos showing the Big Ics. We salute the generosity of their owners: Vic Young, Ian Farquhar, Neil Hudson, Warwick Thomson, Barry Davis, George Wood, Bruce Birnie, Malcolm Cranfield, Russell Priest, Marc Piché, Ian Condie, Brent Riddell, Jeremy Theakston, Brent Chambers, Chris Howell and Graham Pepper. To them and to all the others whose names we give in the Sources and Acknowledgements for this book, we are sincerely grateful.

Because dates for the royal tour of 1953-54 vary in some publications, we have relied on those provided in Warwick Thomson's diary, as recorded by him aboard HMRY *Gothic* during the course of the tour. Gross register tonnages for Shaw Savill vessels used in this book are those stated in the Appendix to S.D. Waters' book 'Shaw Savill Line - One Hundred Years of Trading', published in 1961.

We thank our publishers John Clarkson and Roy Fenton of Ships in Focus Publications. His Excellency The Right Honourable Sir Anand Satyanand, GNZM, QSO, Governor-General of New Zealand has most kindly provided us with a foreword for this book, and for this we are most grateful.

Andrew Bell	Murray Robinson
Porthleven	Raumati Beach
Cornwall	Kapiti Coast
England	New Zealand

July 2011

This book is dedicated to the men and women who served on the Big Ics

CONTENTS

SOURCES

A diary of the 1953-54 Royal Tour, written aboard HMRY Gothic, Warwick Thomson (unpublished)
A History of Port Lyttelton, W. H. Scotter
All Hands and the Cook, Captain Barry Thompson
An Innocent Aboard, Warwick Thomson
Archives New Zealand, documents pertaining to the fire on the *Gothic*, July-August 1968: (1) copy of the *Gothic's* official log. (2) declaration of survey of the *Gothic's* safety equipment, 24th April 1968. (3) *Gothic's* crew list, July 1968. (4) radio logs. (5) preliminary report by Surveyor of Ships at Wellington, into the *Gothic's* fire damage, 9th August 1968. (6) New Zealand Police report into fire on board the vessel *Gothic*, 26th August 1968. (7) electrical inspector's report, 9th August 1968. (8) scientific report, 15th August 1968. (9) coroner's report, 30th August 1968. (10) Wellington Fire Board report, 23rd August 1968. (11) statements by the *Gothic's* master, officers, engineers and crew before the Superintendent of Mercantile Marine at Wellington, August 1968.
Bank Line, H.S. Appleyard
Bridge log of *Runic* for 26th-27th March 1961, held by the Shaw Savill Society
British Ocean liners - A Twilight Era, 1960-85, William Miller
Cablegrams regarding the stranding and loss of *Runic*, held by the Shaw Savill Society
Clyde Shipbuilding from Old Photographs, J.R. Hume and Michael S. Moss
Destroyer Weapons of World War 2, Peter Hodges and Norman Friedman
Development: The Journal of the Cable Price Downer Group, December 1968
Dreadnoughts in Camera 1905-1920, Roger D. Thomas and Brian Patterson
From Dungarees to Doeskin, Warwick Thomson (unpublished memoir)
Harland and Wolff's Empire Food Ships 1934-1948, Richard P. de Kerbrech
Heat and Heat Engines for Marine Engineers, W. Embleton
Ironfighters Outfitters and Bowler Hatters, George C. O'Hara
Last of the Steam-Powered Fleet article by Don Wright; published in the Otago Daily Times, 10th May 2010
Letter dated 11th March 1961 from Captain J.P. Williams, Salvage Master, to the Salvage Association, London regarding damage to, and salvage preparation for, SS *Runic* aground. Held by the Shaw Savill Society
Lloyds Register 1970-71
Mailships of the Union-Castle Line, C.J. Harris and B.D. Ingpen
Merchant Fleets Royal Mail Line and Nelson Line, Duncan Haws
Modern Marine Engineering, A.C. Hardy
Modern Shipfitter's Handbook, W.E. Swanson
New Zealand Marine News, journal of the New Zealand Ship and Marine Society Inc. Various issues including Vol. 20 No. 3 Summer 1968-69
New Zealand Naval Vessels, R.J. McDougall
Pix magazine 11th March 1961
Radio Log from ZLW Wellington Radio, *Runic* stranding
Royal Standard Red Ensign, Sir David Aitchison
Shaw Savill and Albion : the Post-War Fortunes of a Shipping Empire, Richard P. de Kerbrech
Shaw Savill Line: Athenic Ceramic Corinthic Gothic publicity brochure dated March 1951, kindly loaned to the authors by Ian Condie
Shipbuilding and Shipping Record
Shipbuilders to the World, M. Moss and J.R. Hume
Ships and Sealing Wax, Basil Lord Sanderson
Ships In Focus Record 24th June 2003; Shaw Savill's Big ICs, Captain Edward Buckle and Roy Fenton
Ships that Serve New Zealand, I.G. Stewart
Shipwreck on Middleton Reef, Bill Belcher and Aileen Belcher
Splendid Sisters, Alan Mitchell
Steam Ship Runic, John M. House (unpublished memoir)
Terence Williams Collection; Voyager New Zealand Maritime Museum. ID [15799]
The Book of the Ship, A.C. Hardy
The Cunard White Star Quadruple-Screw Liner Queen Mary, The Shipbuilder and Marine Engine-Builder
The Empire Ships, W.H. Mitchell and L.A. Sawyer
The Flag of the Southern Cross 1939-1945, Frank C. Bowen
The History of North East Shipbuilding, David Dougan
The Last Blue Water Liners, William H. Miller
The Royal Yacht Britannia : The Official History, R. Johnstone-Bryden
The Running and Maintenance of Marine Machinery, the Institute of Marine Engineers, London
The Second Mauretania 1939-65, The Shipbuilder and Marine Engine-Builder
The Shipbuilder and Marine Engine Builder
The Shipping World
The Tyser Legacy, Ian Farquhar
Tropical Cyclones in the Northeastern Australian Region – 1960/61 Season, Government of Australia
Union Fleet, Ian Farquhar
Verbal Notes and Sketches for Marine Engineer Officers Vols 1 and 2, J.W.M. Sothern
Voyage Record Cards, the Guildhall Library, London
Warships of Australia, Ross Gillett
Warships of World War II, H.T. Lenton and J.J. Colledge
Where Giants Dwell – A Sailor's Tale, Gerry Evans
White Star, Roy Anderson

ACKNOWLEDGEMENTS

In addition to those mentioned in the Introduction, we thank sincerely the following:
Julia Holmes of the Wirral Archives Service, Birkenhead; Antony Paltridge of Government House, New Zealand; Mike Pryce, Peter Newall, Martin Cahill, James Howden, John House, Harry Hignett, Mike Downes, David Green, Cornelis Balk, Ron Ingledew, Roger Beckett, Barry Davis, Brent Chambers, Brian Smith, Marshall Meek, Avril Loughlin of the Public Record Office of Northern Ireland, Brian Mountjoy, John MacMillan, Gerry Wright, Ambrose Greenway, Dexter Fry of TRANZ International Image Library Ltd., Auckland; Anna Sussmilch of the Royal New Zealand Air Force, the Royal New Zealand Air Force Museum of Wigram, New Zealand; Steve Roscoe, Marleene Boyd of the Bill Laxon Maritime Library, Voyager New Zealand Maritime Museum, Auckland; Rhonda Field of the Bluff Maritime Museum; Derek Ion, the Archives Office of Tasmania, John Smith of the Naval Historical Society of Australia, James Macrae at the Library of the Institute of Marine Engineering, Science and Technology, London; Ben Smith of The Times Archive, London; David Berry of Kodak Express, Paraparaumu, New Zealand; Peter Kiernan, Prue Bell, Louise Robinson.

The *Corinthic* at anchor off Southend waiting for a berth in the Royal Docks where she will top off her cargo prior to departure for New Zealand. Note the unusual athwartships stow of the derricks serving Numbers 3 and 4 hatches. As built, these were doubled up with two derricks off each samson post. This allowed working of two cargo hooks simultaneously but made for difficulties not only with complicated rigging but also because of the very limited space on top of the bridge and accommodation houses. The advantage was the wonderfully clear deck space over and around the hatches, for use by passengers. *[V.H. Young and L.A. Sawyer]*

CORINTHIC, THE LEAD SHIP

Genesis

When Basil Sanderson took over as Managing Director of Shaw Savill in April 1945, the company had already obtained licences from the British Admiralty to build two large cargo vessels as replacements for war losses. A tender from Cammell Laird and Co. Ltd. of Birkenhead had been accepted for building the first of the two. In his letter dated 29th January 1945 John Macmillan, Shaw Savill's Managing Director, confirmed the company's order. A contract was signed on 20th February 1945. Both ships were to resemble closely the design used for Shaw Savill's pre-war refrigerated ships. Five of these had been built for the company with just one of them, the *Waipawa* (10,727/1934), surviving the Second World War. Two of the five were larger, improved versions of the original three and it was the plans for these, the *Waimarama* (12,843/1938, lost in 1942) and the *Waiotira* (12,823/1939, lost in 1940) that were used as the basis for the two new ships.

The war in Europe ended on 8th May 1945. John Macmillan retired at the end of the following month, whereupon his successor decided it was essential to go to Australia and New Zealand as soon as the war against Japan was won. His purpose was to assess how trading conditions in Australia and New Zealand had changed since 1939, and what Shaw Savill must now do to successfully resume business with these two countries. Basil Sanderson left England by air on 13th November 1945 and was away for just over 15 weeks. Amongst other matters, he determined that the two new ships must be reconfigured to provide accommodation for some 80 first class passengers in addition to their cargo payload. Also, they must be supplemented by two further ships to provide the necessary sailings once every four weeks between London and New Zealand. Not knowing whether it was still possible to modify the plans for the first two ships, both of which were now under construction, Sanderson cabled London from Wellington and was advised in reply that there was still time for this to be done. Following his return to London on 28th February 1946 Sanderson quickly gained all the formal approvals needed from his director colleagues and from the British Admiralty. In this way the first of the ships that came to be known as the Big Ics was conceived.

It had been 1921 when Shaw Savill last ordered a steam ship, moreover no vessel had ever previously been built for the company by Cammell Laird. Shaw Savill's preference certainly would have been Harland and Wolff Ltd., from whose Belfast yard the war-built *Wairangi* (12,804/1942 ex *Empire Grace*) and the *Waiwera* (11,286/1944) had come. But Harland and Wolff had responsibility for the second of the two new ships and, under the circumstances of the time, it would not have been advisable to have two large vessels coming simultaneously from the same builder. Separating the orders meant much greater probability of delivery times being met. When the war ended in 1945 and licensing restrictions on construction of new merchant ships were eased, the British ship building industry fell into a state of turmoil. There were acute shortages throughout Great Britain both of skilled workers and of all the resources needed for building passenger and cargo ships. Steel in particular was desperately lacking; in 1947 only 60% of shipyard orders for steel were met. This, set against huge demands from ship owners wanting new tonnage to replace war losses, produced a formidable rise in prices. In 1946 a new ship cost between 70% to 100% more than in 1938. Meanwhile ship builders who had specialised in naval vessels now, in the face of cancellations for large numbers of warships at war's end, had quickly to re-adapt their works and their employees to the planning and fabrication of merchant vessels. During the nine and a half month period from VE Day to the beginning of March 1946 the British Admiralty terminated orders for 727 naval vessels amounting to £125 million.

Waimarama docking at Liverpool. The design of the *Corinthic* was based on the plans of this ship and her sister *Waiotira*. Both had very short lives. The four-year-old *Waimarama* under the command of Captain R.S. Pearce DSC was bombed, set on fire and sunk during the famous 'Pedestal' Malta convoy of August 1942. *Waiotira* had been in service just 13 months when she was torpedoed in the North Atlantic on Christmas Day 1940. Her master was Captain A.V. Richardson who went on to command the *Ceramic* and the *Gothic*. *[J. and M. Clarkson]*

Top: Guests crowd the launch platform in front of *Corinthic's* bow while, above them, shipyard workers get a much better view from a roof at the head of the slipway. The wine bottle, having just been released by Mrs Gwen Douglas, is in mid-flight and an instant away from disintegration. On Mrs Douglas's right, standing next to the lady with the bouquet of flowers, is the tall figure of 51-year-old Basil Sanderson, Shaw Savill's managing director. *[Captain Graham Pepper, Shaw Savill Society]*

Above: The *Corinthic*, first of the Big Ics, going down the ways. She was launched into the Mersey on the top of a flood tide. Note the absence of drag chains, unnecessary because of the great width of the river opposite Cammell Laird's shipyard. Captain Arthur Jones, the *Corinthic's* first chief officer and later to become her longest-serving master, is in the crowd lining her forecastle rails. *[Captain Graham Pepper, Shaw Savill Society]*

Launch and lunch

The keel of Yard Number 1175 was laid down on Slipway Number 3 at Cammell Laird's south yard on 14th May 1945. Just over one year later, at 11 o'clock on the morning of Thursday 30th May 1946, Mrs Gwen Douglas named her *Corinthic* and launched the first of the Big Ics into the Mersey by releasing a bottle of South African wine against her bow. Conditions were fine, warm and sunny with a light southerly wind. She dropped off the way-ends and into the river without a hitch, to then be picked up by waiting tugs. The new ship was the largest built on Merseyside since the end of the war and so a big, festive crowd was present. Standing beside Basil Sanderson at the front of the launch platform was W.J. Jordan, New Zealand's High Commissioner to London. Mrs Douglas was his daughter. Sponsor for the *Corinthic* was originally to have been the High Commissioner's wife, Winifred Jordan, but she was unwell and unable to perform the launching ceremony.

Once afloat, the *Corinthic* was towed to Cammell Laird's fitting-out basin. The launch party meanwhile repaired to the Woodside Hotel, outside the shipyard's main gate, for a gala luncheon hosted by Sir Robert Johnson who was Chairman of Cammell Laird. Prominent at this occasion was High Commissioner Jordan. He had begun his life in New Zealand 42 years earlier as a labourer, having arrived from England in 1904 as an assisted immigrant aboard the White Star liner *Corinthic* (12,367/1902). A man who enjoyed telling listeners of his prodigious rise up the social ladder, Jordan led at least one newspaper man to report that the new ship's name had been chosen by Basil Sanderson in tribute to the old *Corinthic's* role in bringing Jordan to the land of his fortune. When it came Mr Sanderson's turn to rise from his seat and toast the new ship he instead set upon a theme to which he would return at the launchings of other Big Ics. Three fast cargo ships ordered by Shaw Savill in 1933 had, he said, cost £1 million in total. Fourteen years later at 1947 prices, this same amount would be needed to duplicate just one of those same ships. There would, Sanderson believed, be no end to this until the spirit of private enterprise again became the working man's hallmark, unhampered by 'soul-deadening' interference from the State.

Design origins

The design of the *Corinthic* class evolved from the plans of the last two refrigerated cargo vessels built for Shaw Savill prior to the outbreak of war in 1939. Like the company's three earlier ships, the *Waimarama* and the *Waiotira* were big, fast, three island-type refrigerated cargo liners. Each had a raised forecastle, a forward well deck containing Numbers 1 and 2 hatches, and a raised centre island with Number 3 hatch separating the bridge and funnel.

Numbers 4 and 5 hatches were on the aft well deck ahead of a raised poop incorporating Number 6 hatch. The superstructure on the raised centre island comprised one deck running its full length. Above this was a bridge house forward of Number 3 hatch that was two decks in height. With the *Corinthic* ships required to berth a minimum of 80 passengers all in one class, it was simply a matter of extending the lower of the two decks comprising this bridge house so that it too ran the full length of the centre island. Number 3 hatch was thereby moved up one level. Immediately aft of it was added a new deckhouse with two lifeboats at either side. On top of this deckhouse was placed the elliptical funnel along with engine room ventilators and skylight, plus four winches and two samson posts with their derricks for working Number 4 hold. Its base partially hidden by lifeboats outboard of it, the funnel seemed lower and squatter than it actually was.

In the new design the centre island, with this enlarged superstructure, was extended aft over the well deck space that aboard the *Waimarama* and the *Waiotira* was occupied by Number 4 hatch. This hatch was now raised three decks so that, like Number 3, it sat flush with the deck planking on the top of the superstructure. Forward of Number 3 hatch was a single-level deckhouse containing the navigating bridge, the master's suite and accommodation for the deck officers and cadets. There were winches and samson posts with their derricks on the roof of this deckhouse as well. A further set of samson posts was added later, bringing the total to six posts on the top of the superstructure. No attempt was made at streamlining, unlike the Port Line's flagship *Port Brisbane* (11,942/1949) whose keel was laid one year later at Wallsend by Swan, Hunter and Wigham Richardson Ltd.

Her bow was raked at approximately 11 degrees and she was given a handsome cruiser stern. The overall result was a square-cornered, box-like profile framed by near-vertical masts fore and aft; the rake of the funnel was half an inch per foot. Overall the effect might have been ponderous and displeasing to the eye but it was not. When viewed from fine off the bow or from astern when loaded down to her marks, the *Corinthic* had a graceful power and beauty all of her own. There was a solid, functional, magisterial bearing to her that, became much admired.

Passenger comfort

All the accommodation for the *Corinthic's* passengers was located in the centre superstructure, above the hull. There were three levels: the Boat and Games Deck, the Promenade Deck and, lower-most, the Bridge Deck. The deckhouse situated on the Boat and Games Deck, between Numbers 3 and 4 hatches, contained a total of 22 cabins. Eighteen of these, to port and starboard, were single-berth cabins while along the rear of the deckhouse were four twin-berth cabins. Two of these latter cabins had private bathrooms, all the others used shared facilities. There was a children's play room at the forward end while centrally inside the deckhouse were the tops of two big, vertical shafts running deep into the ship: the boiler or funnel casing, and the engine casing.

There were no coamings to Numbers 3 and 4 hatchways. Hatch boards and tarpaulin covers were placed over the hatch tops just below deck level and then, over this, removable slabs of timber decking was laid flush with the surrounding deck. The result was a huge games-playing area for use by the passengers, all of it liberated of fittings such as ventilators, stanchions, rigging, lockers and companionways. It was for the time, and especially for a working cargo ship, a quite remarkable feature. Such fittings as were needed had all been banished to the roof of the deckhouses: samson posts, funnel stays, awning spars, cargo winches, the engine room skylight, fans and machinery for the Thermotank air ventilation system (air conditioning was not fitted to the *Corinthic* or her sisters) and two very large cowl ventilators mounted ahead of the funnel.

The *Corinthic* was fitted with four galvanised-steel lifeboats on Welin-Maclachlan gravity davits. Three of them were hand-propelled with Fleming T-type gear (vertical levers which each boat's occupants moved back and forth to activate the propeller) and the fourth had a diesel motor. The two larger boats, mounted on the forward davits, could take 90 people and they measured 30 feet in length by 10 feet six inches width and four feet seven inches depth. The two smaller boats, on the aft davits either side of the funnel, were 26 feet long, 9 feet 1.5 inches wide and four feet in depth. One of these was the motor boat, which could accommodate 50 people while the other could accommodate 64 people.

One level below the Boat and Games Deck, the *Corinthic's* Promenade Deck was devoted entirely to spacious rooms and genteel recreation for her 85 passengers. Forward on this deck was the purser's bureau, main passenger entrance and stairway, while at its aft end was the smoking room and, opening from this, the veranda cafe with views over the ship's after decks. Along the port and starboard sides - there were no inboard passenger cabins - were 18 single-berth rooms 10 of which had private bathrooms, and 10 twin- or three-berth rooms all of which had their own bathrooms except for two twin-berth cabins right forward on the port side. Many adjoining cabins had connecting doors, thereby allowing flexibility when booking family groups. A suite comprising bedroom, bathroom and private sitting room was located right forward on the starboard side, adjacent to the purser's bureau. An additional five bathrooms for general use were provided for those cabins on the Promenade Deck that had none. These public facilities were all attended to by bathroom stewards. If the two private and four public bathrooms on the Boat and Games Deck were factored in, this made a total of 32 bathrooms both public and private, for the use of just 85 passengers. Unremarkable today, this ratio of bathrooms to users was, by immediate post-war standards, quite exceptional and a mark of great luxury. The baths ran salt water with each also having a fresh water shower. As fitted, the *Corinthic* was provided with two babies' cots which could be placed in cabins as needed.

A wide stairway opposite the purser's bureau led down to the Bridge Deck where the dining saloon and lounge, the latter's forward windows looking towards the bow of the *Corinthic*, were both situated. The décor of these and all the passenger rooms followed that so successfully used in 1938 aboard the *Dominion Monarch*, Shaw Savill's flagship: colours, tones and finishes of the most refined quality yet solid and practical, with all adornment kept to a minimum. Panelled and polished Empire woods were very much the dominant fashion both pre- and post-war for the public rooms of British liners: the *Corinthic's* lounge is recorded as done out in 'lay vertical figure avodire' (African white mahogany; a lightweight tropical wood from the Ivory Coast) 'with cross bandings of sapele' (African reddish-brown wood) and 'door and feature panels being in pommeli' (or pommele: any exotic wood that has a dappled or highly figured grain). Deep upholstered armchairs alongside mahogany furniture with table-tops 'in fine figured veneer' completed the look. All of it was made by Cammell Laird's craftsmen. Chair coverings were a mix of bright green leather along with brown and rust-coloured tapestries, while the window curtains were in rose and gold. Fluorescent lighting tubes, a major innovation for the time, were fitted inside glazed metalwork casings to otherwise plain-painted deckheads; these lights were supplied by the British Thomson-Houston Co. Ltd. of Rugby. Underfoot was a polished birchwood floor set off with Persian rugs. Bookcases housed the *Corinthic's* library; there were also writing desks and a small grand piano. With the huge shortages of materials and tradespeople in Britain during the post-war years, putting together this princely décor was a very considerable achievement for the *Corinthic's* builders.

In the 66-seat dining saloon, aft of the lounge and 1,660 square feet in area, was one of two murals by Peter Scott, both of which were commissioned for the *Corinthic.* Entitled 'Wild Geese Rising from a Marsh on the Severn Estuary', it was hung centrally on the after bulkhead of the dining saloon, above the main sideboard. The other mural, 'Morning Flight on the Norfolk Coast', hung in the smoking room.

The floor of the dining saloon was covered in a product called Ruboleum. This was a more pliable form of linoleum and

Above: The *Corinthic's* dining saloon, looking aft and to starboard. Above the sideboard is Sir Peter Scott's mural 'Wild Geese Rising from a Marsh on the Severn Estuary.' In the foreground is the captain's table with seating for eight. *[Captain Graham Pepper, Shaw Savill Society]*

Below*:* The smoking room with the second of the two Peter Scott murals commissioned for the *Corinthic*. Sir Peter Scott, who lived between 1909 and 1989, was the only child of Antarctic explorer Captain R.F. Scott RN. *[Captain Graham Pepper, Shaw Savill Society]*

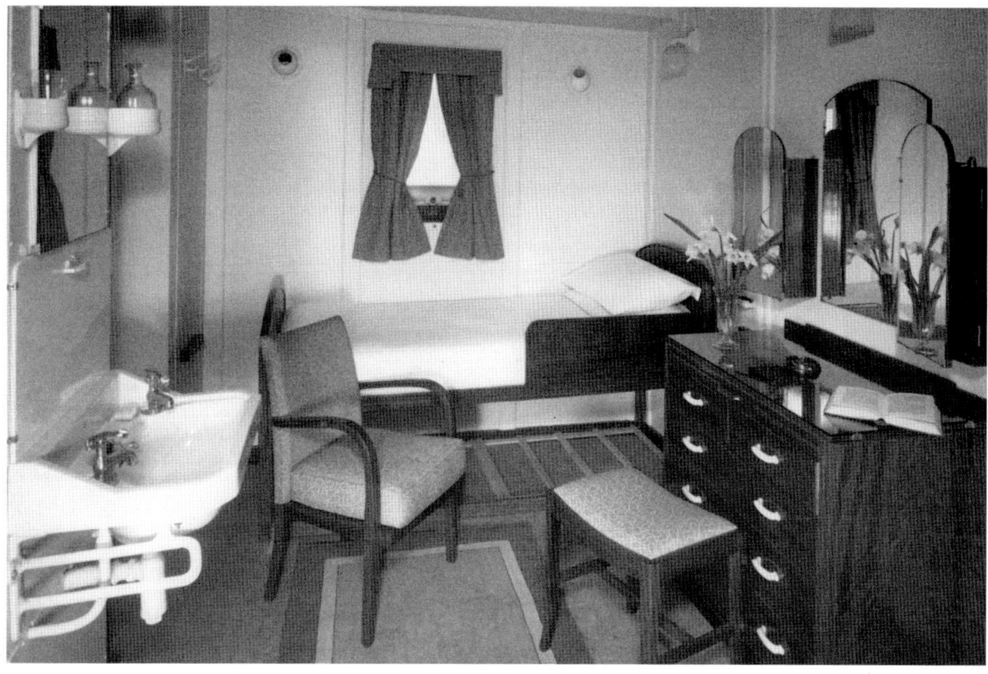

Top: A single-berth passenger cabin. The outlets on either side of the window provide warmed or cooled air from the *Corinthic's* Thermotank punkah-louvre system. *[Captain Graham Pepper, Shaw Savill Society]*

Middle: The lounge, looking across to starboard. The photographer is standing beside the entrance lobby that led out to the alleyway on the port side of the *Corinthic's* Bridge Deck. Behind the bookcase are the stairs leading up to the purser's bureau and passenger cabins on the Promenade Deck. The lounge floor is in polished birchwood with Persian rugs. Note the flourescent lighting. *[Captain Graham Pepper, Shaw Savill Society]*

Bottom: A two-berth cabin. The chest of drawers with bedside cabinets is made of mahogany. *[Captain Graham Pepper, Shaw Savill Society]*

came in panels of differing shades. It was also to be found in the main entrance, on the passenger stairways and in the corridors and cabins.

No liner from those times was complete without a smoking room, that august sea-going institution where gentlemen passengers could ease back in leather chairs and enjoy their cigars, card games, liquid comforts from the bar and conversation of a manly disport, all without the intrusion of wives and mothers. The *Corinthic's* smoking room was aft on the Promenade Deck and larger in size than her lounge. Its central feature, below the Peter Scott mural, was a large wall-mounted electric radiator with bronze grille, a black marble hearth step and surrounds in Clipsham stone. For many of the smoking room's occupants the words 'central feature' were perhaps better applied to the bar in the after port corner, with its attentive bevy of white-jacketed, tray-proffering stewards. Wall panelling was Nigerian cherry with cross bandings in walnut; the windows were framed in sycamore with heavy tapestry curtains. There were ample chairs finished in jade hide coverings. Fluorescent lighting and Persian rugs on the ruboleum floor completed the décor.

Perhaps the *Corinthic's* most attractive room on a warm sunny afternoon out at sea was the veranda cafe, right aft on the Promenade Deck. Extending across the full width of the ship, it had peach-coloured walls and cane furniture in bright fabrics. Seated here, the smoking room bar just through the doors, passengers could enjsoy sea air and panoramic views out over the *Corinthic's* wake. If the weather became pesky, shelter was gained from glazed Essavian sliding screens that could be pulled across the wrought iron balustrade fitted along the veranda cafe's aft edge. With no more than 85 passengers aboard there was neither competition for seats nor disruption from others less inclined to relax.

At the forward end of the deckhouse on the Boat and Games Deck was a children's playroom. This facility appears not to have been made great use of, and was subsequently done away with during a 1950s refit. The space was converted into the ship's radio room which was moved from its original location down on the Bridge Deck.

Frozen food

Official Number 167909, *Corinthic* was, at the time of her building, 15,264 grt and 8,812 nrt. Her length overall was 561 feet exactly while between fore and after-most perpendiculars she was 530 feet exactly. Moulded breadth was 71 feet exactly and the *Corinthic's* draught fully loaded was 29 feet 7 7/8 inches. The ship was divided into eight watertight compartments by seven transverse bulkheads that rose up as far as the Shelter Deck. Refrigerated cargo capacity in her six holds amounted to 524,703 cubic feet with an additional 170,250 cubic feet for general cargo. Numbers 1 and 2 holds were devoted entirely to frozen or chilled cargo, as was Number 3 hold except for general cargo carried at Bridge Deck level in Number 3 (and also in the forecastle). Each of the three after cargo holds had main and upper 'tween decks only, there was no lower 'tween deck as in the forward three holds. In Number 4, both the lower hold and main 'tween deck took frozen or chilled cargo, with general cargo in the upper 'tween deck spaces. The same applied to Number 5 hold but with frozen or chilled cargo in the upper 'tween deck. Number 6 hold was entirely for general cargo.

There were three electrically-driven refrigerating machines aboard the *Corinthic*, supplied by the British firm of J. and E. Hall Ltd. of Dartford and all located in one room, starboard side amidships on the Upper Deck. Three refrigerating engineers were carried on the ship, looking after the refrigerating plant with its system of compressors, brine pumps, evaporators, condensers, carbon dioxide storage bottles and cold air circulating fans. Twenty two steel derricks (later increased to 24) with lifting capacities of five, seven and 12 tons were rigged to the masts and samson posts for working the six holds. In addition, a 50-ton heavy lift derrick was mounted at the fore end of Number 2 hold, and there was a seven-ton derrick on the starboard side of the engine room skylight, abaft the funnel, for lifting heavy gear inside the engine room. As built, the *Corinthic* had 21 electric cargo winches manufactured by Laurence, Scott and Electromotors Ltd. of Norwich. All of them had a five-ton maximum lifting capacity except for the two winches on the poop deck, aft of the mainmast. As well as lifting cargo, these were designed for use in warping the ship when manoeuvring on and off the berth, and thus had a larger seven-ton capacity. On the forecastle, the *Corinthic's* electric windlass was manufactured and supplied by Clark, Chapman and Co. Ltd. of Gateshead. The electro-hydraulic steering gear for turning the *Corinthic's* semi-balanced, streamlined, double-plate rudder came from Brown Brothers and Co. Ltd. of Edinburgh.

Burning

Cammell Laird's huge fitting out basin had a water surface of 15 acres and it was here the *Corinthic* lay for the remainder of 1946 while she was completed. In June 1946 a joiners' strike brought all work to a halt but by the start of 1947 she was nearly ready, acceptance trials and delivery to her owner having been scheduled for mid-February. She was berthed alongside the fitting out basin's west wall, beside Cammell Laird's boiler shops and it was here, some time around 5 a.m. on Saturday 4th January 1947, that a fire began inside her Number 5 hold.

The source was later found to have been an electrical short-circuit in temporary lights that had been rigged inside the hold while it was fitted out. This ignited a tarpaulin cover that had been spread over the hatchway, which in turn fell into the bottom of the hold where it set alight a quantity of cork insulation and timber lying there. Smoke escaping from the open hatchway alerted a night watchman, who had local fire brigades to the *Corinthic* almost immediately. But the fire took hold, flames leaping out of the hatch beneath heavy clouds of smoke and steam. Six hours after its discovery, the steel bulkheads of Number 5 hold were white-hot, the fire was advancing and the *Corinthic* had taken on a starboard list of up to 20 degrees towards the quayside. Some 30 fire appliances and 150 fire fighters from Birkenhead, Liverpool, Wallasey and Port Sunlight were engaged or standing by.

Sixty Cammell Laird employees volunteered to go down into the smoke-filled Numbers 4 and 6 holds, adjacent to the fire. Working in gangs of up to 12, they stripped the varnished timber linings and the cork insulation from the bulkheads using sledge hammers and crowbars. Their labour continued for over four hours from 7.30 a.m. in dense smoke and searing temperatures. Undoubtedly it was this that saved the ship. At one point the men were driven out on deck as timber insulation spontaneously burst into flames. Other shipyard workers used oxy-acetylene torches to cut holes in the bulkheads so that fire fighters could direct water jets at the seat of the fire in Number 5 hold. Two fire fighters were injured during this work. More holes were cut so that water in the burning holds from the fire hoses, causing the list, could drain into the *Corinthic's* double bottom tanks from where it was pumped overboard.

Just a short distance aft of the *Corinthic* was Ellerman Lines' *City of Pretoria* (8,450/1947) also fitting out and nearly complete. With the likelihood of the fire spreading to engulf the *Corinthic's* stern, Cammell Laird staff began preparing to move the *City of Pretoria*. But once the fire fighters were able to reach the base of the fire with their hoses, it soon came under control. By 1 p.m. the fire was retreating and the *Corinthic* was being brought upright by pumps. Not until 8 p.m. was the fire declared to be out.

Miraculously, the *Corinthic's* engines and passenger accommodation were untouched. The after part of the ship in way of Numbers 4, 5 and 6 holds had, however, been extensively damaged and would have to be refitted from scratch. Perhaps the greatest loss, in that time of acute shortages, were the 80 sets of tools belonging to 150 joiners and plumbers who had been working in Numbers 4 and 5 holds. Work started immediately on clearing debris from the fire. On 13th January 1947 the *Corinthic* was placed in Cammell Laird's Dry Dock Number 7. Here, heat-twisted frames were straightened and buckled plating was cut away and renewed. The entire insulated linings of Number 4 and and 5 holds, along with all

Top left: Just six weeks away from her trials, smoke from the fire raging in her Number 5 hold obscures the after decks of the *Corinthic* as she leans against the fitting-out berth. *[Ian J. Farquhar collection]* Fire damage to the hold's insulated lining and brine piping grids is shown in the two right-hand views, while repair work inside the hold's 'tween decks is partially complete at lower left. *[Captain Graham Pepper, Shaw Savill Society]*

their refrigerating plant, similarly were replaced. Mindful of the significance of this ship not only for themselves but for the entire British shipbuilding industry as it re-adjusted to peacetime needs, Cammell Laird's managers spared no effort in getting the *Corinthic* ready for her trials. Astonishingly, these were delayed by only a few weeks, the fully repaired *Corinthic* putting to sea on 25th March 1947, 80 days after the fire, for trials in the Firth of Clyde.

These trials were successful in all respects and she was classified by Lloyds Register of Shipping as 100A1. The *Corinthic* was accepted by Shaw Savill as soon as she returned to Liverpool. For the company's staff ashore and afloat it was a momentous event, a rare moment of celebration and great prestige amid all the drab hardship of post-war Britain. She was Shaw Savill's first new liner since the *Dominion Monarch,* eight years and a world war ago. Brand-new and immaculate at a time when British and Commonwealth ports were filled with old, war-weary liners still under requisition or offering basic, austerity fare, the *Corinthic* was a wonderful symbol of the long-awaited return to the mystique of peacetime sea travel.

On her upper-most deck, immediately aft of the *Corinthic's* funnel, was a deckhouse that, given her near loss by fire, was of much greater significance than its small, unobtrusive dimensions might suggest. It was the known as the foamite house. Inside was a large tank for storage of a fire-fighting foam product called foamite. The tank's outlets were connected to the ship's fire-fighting mains.

An uneventful life

The *Corinthic's* first Master was Captain T.V. Roberts. He had commanded Shaw Savill's *Arawa* (14,462/1922) and *Largs Bay* (14,182/1921) during the Second World War, and was known as 'Gentleman Roberts' because of his habit of showing great courtesy even towards the humblest of ship's personnel. At Liverpool the new vessel loaded a full general cargo and then, after embarking 85 passengers at Princes Landing Stage, she sailed on the afternoon of Saturday 12th April 1947 to begin her maiden voyage. Aboard was a crew numbering 124. One day later the *Corinthic* steamed into Carrick Roads off Falmouth, stopping engines at 12.30 p.m. to disembark a party of shipyard workers. These men from Cammell Laird had accompanied the *Corinthic* for the very first night of her working life to ensure all her machinery, particularly the boilers and turbines, were working to specification with the vessel underway fully loaded. Once they had been taken off, the *Corinthic* departed for the South Atlantic and Cape Town, following the route to Australia for this inaugural voyage that her old namesake the White Star liner *Corinthic* had used. Sydney was reached on 3rd June, then she crossed to Wellington. After loading chilled and frozen cargo on the New Zealand coast, the *Corinthic* departed Auckland with passengers for London at the end of July.

She proved to be a very comfortable sea-boat with a slow, even rolling motion in rough weather, but both the *Corinthic* and *Athenic* were judged not to have a sufficient margin of stability. For this reason, the *Corinthic's* breadth of 71 feet was increased by one foot in the *Ceramic* and *Gothic,* final two ships of her class. After disaster having been so closely averted when she caught fire at Birkenhead, a grounding not quite six years later appears to have been the only other mishap in her career. In October 1952, while coming up the Thames to berth at the King George V Dock, the *Corinthic* stranded on the mud off Stone Ness Lighthouse at the junction of St Clements Reach and Long Reach, a few miles above Gravesend. There were no passengers aboard at the time. The *Corinthic* was floated off on the next high tide, without damage.

When the *Corinthic* class first entered service Shaw Savill placed the liners on a round-the-world route that took them from London on an outward leg to New Zealand via Curacao and the Panama Canal. On departing either Wellington or Auckland they crossed the Tasman Sea to Australia with calls at Brisbane, Sydney, Melbourne, Adelaide and Fremantle, then from Western Australia they sailed for London via South Africa (the homeward leg). As an alternative to this, on some voyages the liners followed the same track home as on the outward leg, via Curacao and Panama instead of Australia and South Africa. Occasionally they diverted to Port-of-Spain on the island of Trinidad, instead of Curacao. Sailings schedules show them still operating the Australia-to-South Africa route in 1953 but by 1958 the *Corinthic* and her sisters had discontinued this; Curacao and either Balboa or Cristobal in the Panama Canal Zone were the only ports of call on both the outward and homeward legs. Also by this time, the *Corinthic* was no longer name-ship of the class, that distinction having passed to the *Gothic*.

A complete round trip to and from London took three and a half to four months with the voyages out to, and back from, New Zealand each taking 30 to 32 days at a speed of 17 knots. *Corinthic's* Voyage Number 24 of 1957 typifies her schedule. She commenced this voyage on the morning of Thursday 28th March when she departed Tilbury with 76 passengers. Willemstad on the Caribbean island of Curacao was reached on Monday morning 8th April. Eight to ten hours was usually spent there taking on fuel oil. The *Corinthic* would steam through Santa Anna Bay, the long, natural channel that divides the town of Willemstad and leads into the Schottegat. In this large, land-locked harbour she would tie up at one of the bunkering jetties at Royal Dutch Shell's oil refinery. That same afternoon, Monday 8th April, the *Corinthic* left Curacao steaming for Cristobal and the Atlantic entrance to the Panama Canal, where she arrived on Wednesday afternoon 10th April 1957. She moored there overnight, followed by a dawn sailing to transit the canal. Passenger ships such as the *Corinthic* were given preference ahead of other vessels and the transit would normally be completed by around 2 p.m. the same day, if there were no holdups. On this voyage she transited the Canal the following day, 11th April, the ship passing Balboa on the Pacific side of the canal that afternoon. After crossing the Pacific and calling at Pitcairn Island she berthed at Princes Wharf, Auckland on the morning of Monday 29th April 1957. Passengers left the ship there (or, on

Corinthic at London early in her career. Her hull has been sullied by weeks at sea on the long voyage home; it will be touched up and made perfect in time for next sailing day. Shaw Savill's flagship *Dominion Monarch* can be glimpsed at far left. *[J. and M. Clarkson collection]*

SHAW SAVILL LINE

PLAN OF FIRST CLASS ACCOMMODATION

s.s. CORINTHIC
(OIL BURNING TWIN-SCREW TURBINE—15,682 TONS)

s.s. ATHENIC
(OIL BURNING TWIN-SCREW TURBINE—15,187 TONS)

BOAT & GAMES DECK

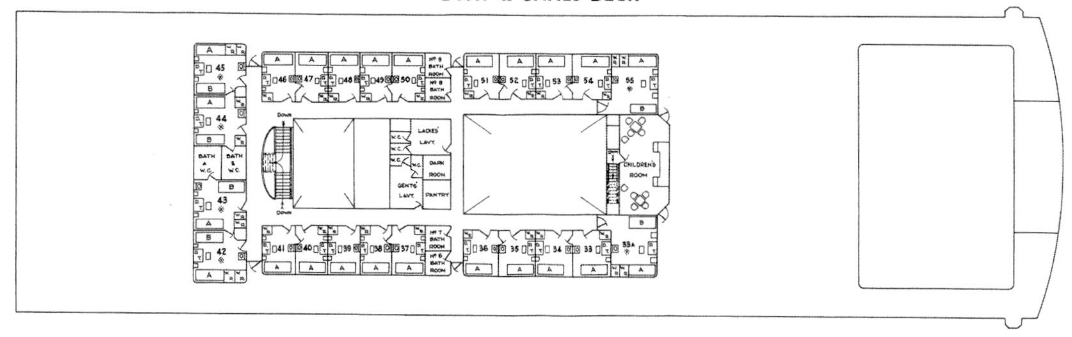

PROMENADE DECK

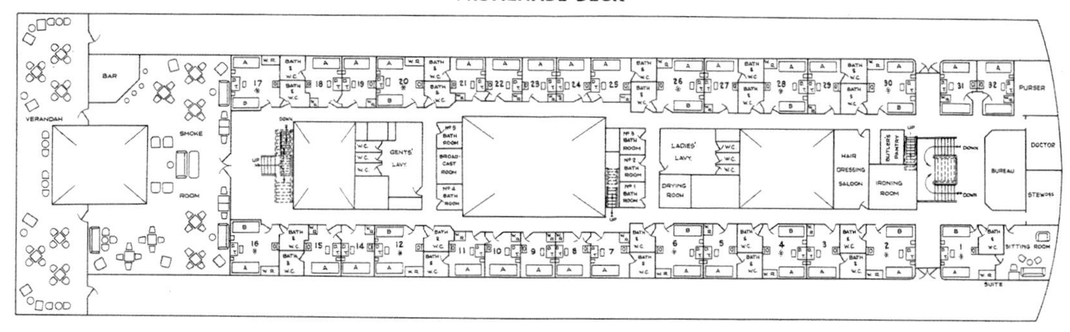

⊞ – WASHBASIN	D.T. – DRESSING TABLE
A – BEDSTEAD	ROOMS MARKED ※ CAN BE FITTED WITH A PORTABLE PULLMAN BERTH
B – BEDSTEAD	
W.R. – WARDROBE	

BRIDGE DECK

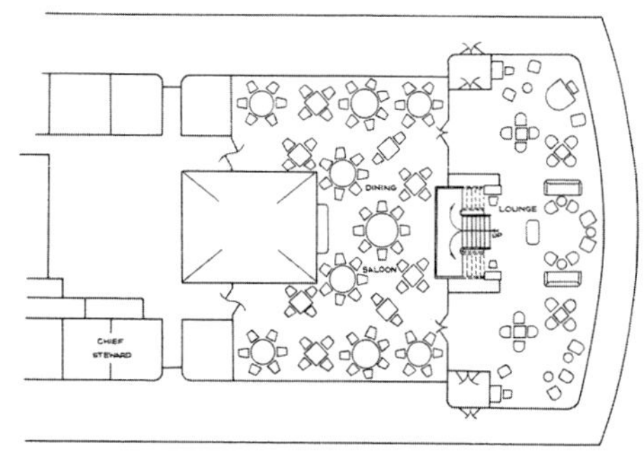

SHAW SAVILL LINE
(SHAW SAVILL & ALBION CO. LIMITED)
PASSENGER OFFICE:
11A. LOWER REGENT STREET, LONDON, S.W.1

[Andrew Bell collection]

some voyages, at Wellington if this was the first port of call). A leisurely six to eight weeks was then spent on the New Zealand coast, working cargo. Ports visited included Opua in the Bay of Islands, Gisborne, Napier, New Plymouth, Lyttelton, Timaru, Port Chalmers and Bluff, sometimes twice on the same trip to discharge and then load. Down to her marks with refrigerated and general cargo, the *Corinthic* sailed from Wellington on the homeward leg of the voyage, again transiting the Panama Canal and arriving at London on 14th July 1957.

London was Shaw Savill's home port. The *Corinthic* and her sisters seldom went to any other British port; if they did, it was most likely Liverpool. First landfall on the homeward leg after crossing the Atlantic was usually the lighthouse atop Bishop Rock at the western-most tip of the Isles of Scilly. She then made for Start Point on the south side of Start Bay in South Devon. Having rounded Start Point, the *Corinthic* headed for Brixham in Tor Bay. Here a Trinity House channel pilot came aboard, bringing with him newspapers and mail for the ship. With 'helm and engines to master's orders, pilot's advice' entered in the bridge log, the vessel now steamed up the English Channel through the Downs, round North Foreland and into the Thames Estuary, going as far as Gravesend on the River Thames. Arrival here was usually on a Tuesday. At Gravesend a launch from the Port Health Authority met the ship and uplifted her Bill of Health, certifying whether there was infectious disease aboard. A river pilot now took over from the channel pilot, coming aboard with his own helmsman.

From Gravesend the *Corinthic* next disembarked her passengers at the Tilbury Landing Stage, just up-river. With all passengers gone she would then anchor off to await that night's tide, before moving to the Royal Docks. Each liner company, including

Shaw Savill, had regular berths in these docks. Having manoeuvred the ship into the lock and with the outer gates closed against the river, the river pilot and his helmsman then went ashore, their place being taken by another man called the dock pilot. That was his proper title but he was more usually known as the mud pilot. His was a jealously guarded role handed down through families, their members belonging to ancient guilds and societies of watermen. Few had been to sea, working their entire lives instead in the Royal Docks and on the River Thames where they demonstrated the greatest skill in moving, turning and berthing large ocean-going ships inside the crowded, confined waters of the docks with the aid of Port of London Authority tugs.

Captain Ian Condie witnessed their abilities while on the bridge of the *Corinthic's* sister ship *Ceramic*, where he was serving as a cadet, 'Our mud pilot was Mr Langman who, when I knew him, had to stop at the top of the pilot ladder to regain his breath, for he was an old man. He would stand there wheezing and say to the cadet whose duty it was to meet the pilots, 'You go on ahead laddie and put the kettle on, I'll be up in a minute'.

'Mr Langman had one son and a son-in-law. The latter manned a small rowing boat and was responsible for ferrying the first ropes ashore at the berth. The former went down aft to where the second mate was stationed on the *Ceramic's* docking bridge, where his job was to pass information and orders to and from his father. The son was 50 or 60 years old but his father on the bridge would order the cadet manning the telephones: 'Tell my boy down aft to let go the tug.'

After two to three weeks spent discharging cargo while alongside at the King George V Dock, the *Corinthic* would then be moved to the Royal Albert Dock to load. The Shaw Savill Dock Office, which housed all the company's superintendents and the Crewing Department, was located at the north-west corner of the peninsula between the Albert and the King George V Docks, near where the eastern end of the City of London Airport runway is today. As the *Corinthic's* sewage discharged straight overboard, in common with all vessels of that time, the toilets aboard the ship could not be used while she was alongside. This despite the utterly filthy, reeking condition of the water in the docks. Crew members had to go ashore and use the Port of London Authority's toilets on the wharf; *Corinthic* engineer George Wood recalls none of them were ever clean.

Fully loaded, paintwork immaculate and back at the King George V Dock, the *Corinthic* would depart for New Zealand on the night's tide, usually on a Thursday. Passengers were embarked on sailing day, having been taken to the ship by coach from either Fenchurch Street or Liverpool Street stations. With three Port of London Authority tugs in attendance, and with the ship's engineers careful about making too much smoke as the boilers were flashed up, the *Corinthic* moved through the locks and out into the river, where bigger tugs took over.

Some notable visitors trod her decks during the *Corinthic's* life. On Monday 30th October 1950, while berthed at the Royal Docks in London, she was inspected by King George VI and Queen Elizabeth. Princess Margaret accompanied her parents. Planning was, at the time, underway for a royal visit by the King, Queen and Princess Margaret to New Zealand and Australia. George VI, who was not in robust health, had expressed a desire that a suitable merchant vessel be found (the royal yacht *Britannia* was not yet built) aboard which the royal party could make this tour. The task of choosing a vessel was given to the Permanent Secretary of the British Ministry of Transport, Sir Gilmour Jenkins. He decided that the *Corinthic* class, specifically either the *Gothic* or *Ceramic*, fastest of the quartet at 19.5 knots, provided exactly what was needed. Having assented to this choice, the King then asked to see the actual ship. Neither the *Gothic* or *Ceramic* were in home waters at the time, but the near-identical *Corinthic* was. The guests were conducted over the ship by Basil Sanderson, His Majesty appearing entirely delighted with what he was shown.

Among the biggest celebrities of film and stage in post-war Britain were the actors Vivien Leigh and her husband, Sir Laurence Olivier. At the request of the British Council they made a tour of Australia and New Zealand in 1948, departing from Liverpool aboard the *Corinthic* on 14th February along with their party, numbering 40, who called themselves the Old Vic Touring Theatre Company. Travelling aboard the *Corinthic* with them were all the costumes, props and scenery needed for the plays they were to perform during the tour. The *Corinthic* sailed from Liverpool via Madeira and Cape Town, Sir Laurence using the dining saloon for rehearsals every day and pausing only to allow the saloon to be laid for lunch, then moving to the lounge late in the afternoon when the saloon was needed to prepare for dinner. At Fremantle, which the *Corinthic* reached on 15th March, the company disembarked to open its tour in Perth five days later. Six months was spent in Australia, the Oliviers then flying from Brisbane to Auckland, New Zealand for a further five weeks. They reboarded the *Corinthic* at Glasgow Wharf, Wellington at 7.30 a.m. on 16th October 1948 after the very final performance of their tour at Wellington's St. James Theatre the night before. Sir Laurence was, at the time, recovering from surgery on his knee carried out in Wellington the previous week, after suffering an injury while at Sydney. With his leg in plaster he was brought to the ship's side in an ambulance accompanied by two nursing sisters. Despite the rain his stretcher was placed in a canvas sling with an ambulance officer at each end, and then lifted 30 feet into the air using one of the ship's after derricks. Sir Laurence was then swung aboard the *Corinthic*, the spectacle watched by passengers lining the *Corinthic's* rails. She sailed for London at 8 a.m.

In 1967 an engine room greaser hid his 19-year old New Zealand bride aboard the ship for the voyage home to England. He accomplished this by knocking the bottoms out of a chest of drawers in his cabin, the lady hiding therein while being supplied with food taken from her husband's messroom. Family members in New Zealand, suspecting what had happened, notified the police who contacted Shaw Savill, who in turn radioed the *Corinthic's* master with orders to search his ship. Sprung from her hideout after three weeks' incarceration, the couple were assigned an officer's cabin for the balance of their honeymoon. At the London law courts they were fined a total of £34.00 and sent on their way.

Another story is told of a certain British seafarer in Auckland, New Zealand who wished to return to the Old Country but without the nuisance of having to pay or work his passage. He had a near-relative working as a seaman aboard the *Corinthic*, then berthed at Auckland. The seaman was persuaded to embark the traveller and conceal him. All went well until the vessel was approaching Panama. A Pacific-themed dance evening was held for the passengers and from the *Corinthic's* veranda cafe, aft on the Promenade Deck, the stowaway heard music while deep in his hideaway. His relative meanwhile went up to the bridge just prior to midnight, where he was wheelman for the first hour of the 12 to 4 a.m. watch under the second officer. Unable to resist, the stowaway borrowed a set of going-ashore clothes from an empty crew cabin and headed up to the veranda cafe. Being a man of great social charm, he was soon dancing with a attractive young lady passenger. But, unbeknown to our intrepid stowaway, the *Corinthic's* third officer had earlier appraised himself of this particular lady's comeliness. Joining the dance after coming off watch at midnight, the officer saw a man in her arms who bore an alarmingly close resemblance to the seaman supposedly on the bridge steering the ship. A quick telephone call to the second officer on the bridge confirmed that the seaman was, indeed, at his post on the grating behind the wheel. The stowaway's ruse was quickly uncovered. He was landed at Cristobal and from there flown back to Auckland and the attentions of the New Zealand Police. Shaw Savill recovered the cost of the flight by way of deduction from the seaman's pay.

Engines

Matakana (8,048/1921) was the last steam-powered vessel built for Shaw Savill prior to the Second World War. A number of steamers were acquired in various ways during that period but, from then on until 1946, Shaw Savill embraced the technology of marine

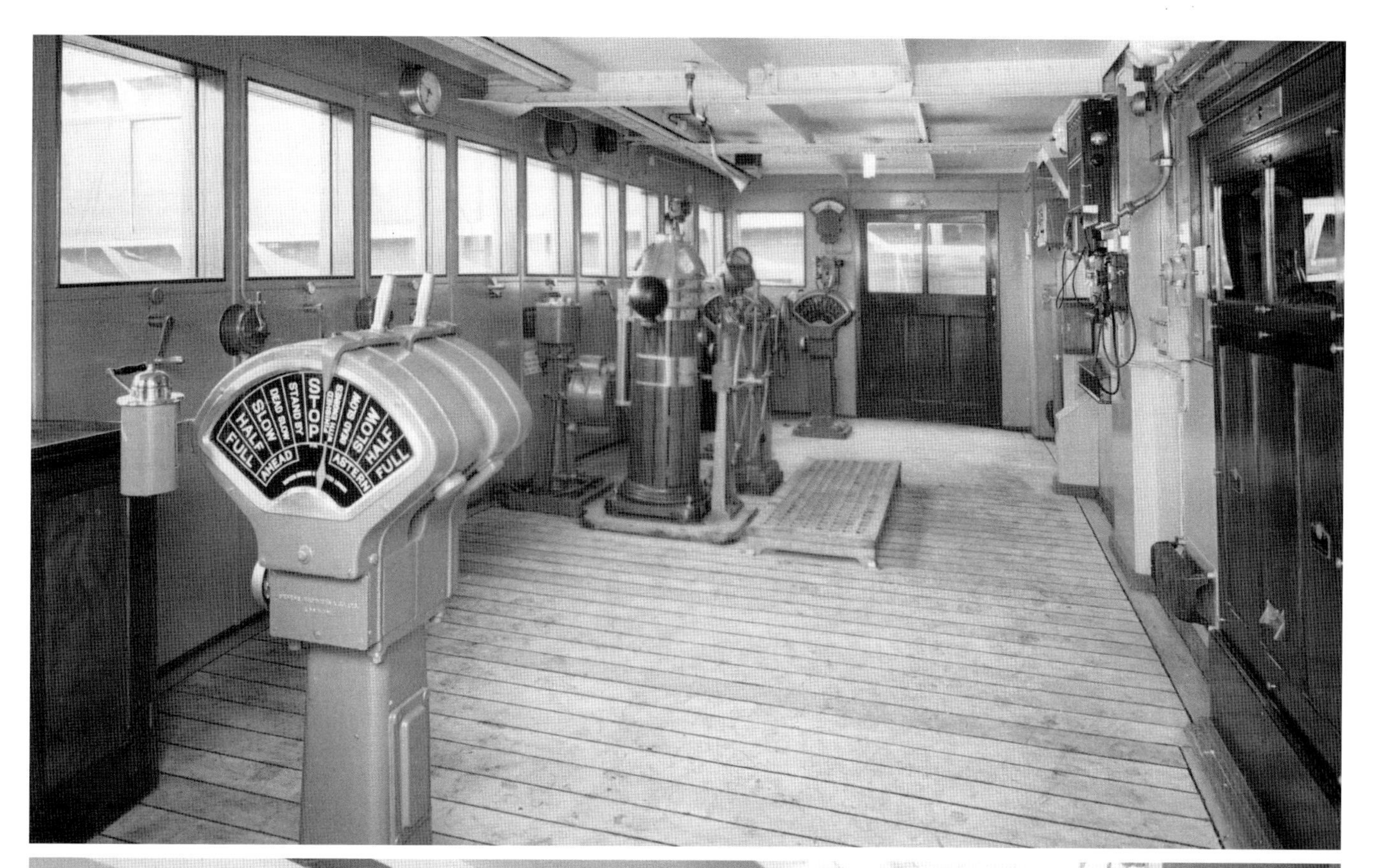

Wheelhouse and chart room of the *Corinthic* when new. The skills of Cammell Laird's tradesmen are fully displayed in these photos. No water-resistant carpets here; cadets or seamen on day work were detailed to wash and scrub the timber planking most mornings before breakfast. Inside the large varnished cabinet with glass panels (top right) are the smoke detection indicators. Note the skylight in the chart room deckhead and the brass rail with moveable lights over the highly polished chart table. The chart room windows have patterned black-out curtains to avoid light seeping into the wheelhouse at night. At left on the chart table is the apparatus controlling the ship's radio direction finder. The chart room settee has a decidedly non-ergonomic look; no self-respecting watch officer would ever be caught sitting on it. At right, out of the picture, is a door leading to the master's day room. *[Captain Graham Pepper, Shaw Savill Society]*

diesel propulsion for its new ships. A total of 10 motor vessels were ordered, with the war-built *Wairangi* and *Waiwera* bringing the number to 12. Among them was the outstanding *Dominion Monarch.* When delivered at the end of January 1939 this vessel, with her four Doxford oil engines each producing 8,000 brake horse power, was among the world's largest motor liners.

For the *Corinthic* and her sisters it was decided to go back to steam power. The long, round-the-world voyages on which they would be employed demanded machinery that gave the most economic fuel consumption. Diesel-engined ships were always better in this respect. However, following the major strides achieved during the war with high-pressure water-tube boiler technology and also with reduction gearing for steam turbines, this option was seen by Shaw Savill as offering a comparable fuel efficiency. Advantages of greater reliability and much less vibration also weighed in steam turbines' favour.

She was a twin-screw ship with a normal service speed of 17 knots. All of the *Corinthic's* machinery was located in her engine room, referred to as 'the pit'. There was no separate boiler room or generator room. At the engine room's fore end, behind a tall screen, lay the boilers while outboard of the turbines were the four electricity generators, two per side. Auxiliaries comprised air compressors, lubricating oil coolers, salt water evaporators, oil purifiers, heat exchangers, a steam generator, filter tanks, circulating pumps, feed pumps, transfer pumps, bilge pumps, water service pumps, general service pumps, lubricating oil pumps, sanitary pumps, extraction pumps, refrigeration circulating pumps and ballast pumps. All of this gear was mounted on the horizontal steel plates known as the tank tops – the upper level of the ship's double bottom – which formed the floor of the engine room.

The *Corinthic* was fitted with two sets of single-reduction geared steam turbines of the reaction type, manufactured by her builders, one to port and one to starboard. They occupied the after half of the engine room. Each set drove one of two propeller shafts and comprised three turbines: high-, intermediate- and low-pressure. The turbines were each inside a heavy metal case and each had a central rotating shaft or rotor. Turbine blades were mounted in rings on this rotor and in corresponding rows on the inside of the case (the stator). The blades on the rotor were grouped in stages of increasing length so that, as the steam passed through the turbine and its pressure dropped, it met with longer blades.

Superheated steam from the boilers entered the high-pressure turbine, where the fixed blades of the stator directed it onto the moving blades of the rotor. As the steam expanded and accelerated through the rotor blades, it produced a reaction force which caused the rotor to turn, hence the term 'reaction turbine'. The steam expanded over every pair of fixed and rotating blades in each of the three separate turbine cases, causing the rotor in each to turn. Inducing a vacuum in the low-pressure case increased the pressure drop from the high-pressure inlet to the steam's exhaust at the condenser, thereby increasing the turbine's capacity to extract the maximum power from the steam and thus improving its efficiency.

Below each set of turbine cases and forming their support and attachment to the hull of the ship, was a condenser. This collected the exhaust steam from the turbines and, using seawater to cool it, converted the steam to water which was then pumped back into the boilers. The steam side of the condenser was kept under vacuum that had to be monitored carefully by the engineers, as even a small rise in pressure would cause a loss of thermal efficiency and a sharp increase in fuel consumption.

The three turbine cases in each set were positioned side-by-side, each delivering equal power with their separate pinions engaging a common gear wheel, which in turn was fixed to each propeller shaft. Positioned directly aft of each turbine, the reduction gearing was inside massive cast-iron gear cases whose tops were festooned with oil lubricating lines. The gearings' function was to reduce the very fast rotation of the turbines to the much slower rate at which the propeller shafts turned. The combined output of the turbine sets gave the *Corinthic* 14,000 shaft horse power at 120 revolutions of the propeller shafts per minute. Made of solid manganese-bronze and manufactured by the Manganese Bronze and Brass Co. Ltd. of Birkenhead, the two Scimitar propellers were each 16 feet in diameter. Their shafts were enclosed in bossings right aft to the propellers themselves. This meant that instead of protruding from the hull near the vessel's stern and then being attached to the hull by brackets, the hull itself was moulded so that it housed and 'internalised' the shafts.

It was not possible to reverse the main turbines when manoeuvring a ship astern. Separate astern turbines revolving in the opposite direction were needed for this. A high-pressure astern turbine was fitted inside the casing of the intermediate turbine in each set, along with a low-pressure astern turbine inside the casing of the low-pressure turbine. These astern turbines generated approximately 60% of the power of the ahead main turbines, and were used only when coming alongside or departing the wharf.

Starting the turbine sets from cold was a lengthy and delicate process. They had to be warmed by bleeding steam into the sets at low pressure while the turbines were rotated, so that all surfaces heated gradually and evenly. Moving the turbines slowly in this way was done with turning gear, one for each turbine set. This gear comprised a worm screw driven by an electric motor, acting on a worm wheel fitted to the propeller shaft. Without this even warming process, the rotors and blades would bend out of their precise alignments, a calamitous event that required lifting of the heavy turbine cases and replacement of all the damaged parts. Similarly, once they were fully warmed, and with high-pressure steam about to be put to the turbines, the turning gear had to be disengaged. Otherwise it would be destroyed once the propeller shafts were revolving at speed. For this reason, signs that read 'Turning Gear IN' or 'Turning Gear OUT' were displayed on the manoeuvring platform to warn and remind the engineers.

The engine manoeuvring platform, from where the turbines were controlled, was located in the centre of the engine room at the forward end the *Corinthic's* turbine sets. Each turbine set had its own separate, identical controls such that the manoeuvring platform was divided to port and to starboard. On each side, horizontal manoeuvring wheels made of polished chrome were linked by shafts running up to valves on the big, asbestos-lagged steam lines passing overhead from the boilers. There were three of these wheels; one for ahead working, one for astern working while the third opened and closed the astern turbine isolating valve. By turning the first two manoeuvring wheels, the quantity of steam entering the turbine set could be changed, thus determining the speed at which the turbines revolved. The third wheel was used to isolate the astern turbines when the ship was not manoeuvring. In this way the speed of the ship, and the ahead or astern direction in which she was travelling, was governed.

There was no direct control of the engines from the bridge (which was disparagingly referred to by engineers as 'the greenhouse' because it had many windows and was occupied by vegetables – the deck officers). Very careful handling was required; the turbines could not be stopped as if applying a brake nor could they be quickly switched from ahead to astern. When the ship was steaming 'full away' at 17 knots, at least 10 to 20 minutes warning was needed for the engines to go to manoeuvring mode from this cruising mode. Bled steam had to be shut off from the high and intermediate turbines, and these had to be allowed to gradually decelerate. Next, the turbine rotors had to be manually wound back from the turbine stators. This was done to increase the clearances between the moving blades on the rotors and the fixed blades on the stators. Doing so prevented them touching when the blades expanded and contracted as steam put to the turbines was changed with manoeuvring of the ship.

When manoeuvring was underway, converting a telegraph order from the bridge into an actual movement of the engines was always a slow process; pilots more familiar with diesel ships would often have to be reminded of this. Sometimes with a flurry of engine orders from the bridge - slow ahead, half ahead, full astern - the engineers at the wheels on the manoeuvring platform would find

Part of the engine manoeuvring platform inside the *Corinthic's* engine room, showing the 'ahead' manoeuvring wheels along with telegraphs, counters, dials and inclinometer on the gauge boards. To port and starboard through the central passageway are the main turbine sets with their whitewashed, asbestos-lagged steam lines. The ladder in the distance leads up to the switchboard flat. On each side of this ladder are Sharples oil purifiers. *[Captain Graham Pepper, Shaw Savill Society]*

themselves several movements in arrears. All engine movements ordered from the bridge were written in the engine room log book, along with the time. They were then carried out in the order received. Those on the bridge soon got the message: with steam ships such as the *Corinthic* there could be no instant response to a barrage of hasty, ill-considered engine orders.

Just behind the wheels, also on each side of the manoeuvring platform, was a gauge board on which were mounted a variety of instruments: an electric telegraph showing engine orders from the bridge, electric gongs which sounded whenever the telegraph pointers moved, revolutions-per-minute indicators, revolutions counters along with dials showing steam inlet pressures, temperatures, main condenser vacuum, forced lubrication pressures plus other readings. There were also alarm indicators. Centrally between the two gauge boards was a passageway opening and above this was another gauge board, this one having an inclinometer showing the angle of the ship as she rolled or listed, a barometer and a clock. On either side of the manoeuvring platform were air vents that supplied cool air; temperatures inside the engine room were, of course, very high and so the engineers spent as long as they could standing under these vents. When the *Corinthic* was being manoeuvred in harbour, one engineer would be at the manoeuvring wheels for each turbine set, with a senior engineer standing behind them in case anything went wrong. A junior engineer would be given the job of answering the bridge to engine room telegraph each time it rang; he was known as 'Dings'. The second engineer would be in overall charge on the manoeuvring platform, with the chief engineer usually nearby. All the manoeuvring wheels and gauge boards faced aft but by turning round the engineers could see forward to where the boilers were located.

Generating superheated steam for the turbines at 375 pounds per square inch (p.s.i.) and 750 degrees Fahrenheit were two oil-fired Yarrow-type, five-drum, water-tube boilers. Manufactured by Cammell Laird, they were in the forward part of the *Corinthic's* engine room, one to port and one to starboard, and they operated under the Weir closed feed system via two steam turbine-driven main feed pumps. Each pump was capable of supplying all the feed water needed by the boilers. The Weir Closed Feed System 'secured boilers and feed lines against corrosion due to gases in solution in the feed water'. This feed water, pure and distilled, was made by the salt water evaporators. Both main feed pumps were located immediately forward of the engine manoeuvring platform, on the starboard side. Next to them, just aft of the starboard boiler, was a steam generator which supplied steam taken from the main boilers at 4,000 pounds of steam per hour and 125 p.s.i. This steam was used for domestic needs, for oil fuel heating and for making the purified water needed to replenish the boiler feed water supplies. Each boiler had one furnace and six burners. The function of the burner was to inject the heated fuel oil into the airflow supplied to the furnaces by the forced draught fans. If more steam was required, more burners were fired. This was done manually unless an adjacent burner was already ignited.

Oil fuel was injected from the tips of the burners and, for this purpose, there was a range of different-sized tips with which they could be fitted. For manoeuvring, all burners were fitted with the maximum-sized tips. Once manoeuvring was completed and 'full away' was ordered, with the ship working up to her normal 17 knots cruising speed, all burners would still be in use but the tips could be varied depending on the steam flow required for the turbines.

Each boiler was served by two large fans: a forced draught fan bringing air *in* for combustion of oil in the boiler furnaces, and an induced draught fan to draw the burnt exhaust gases up through the funnel uptakes and *out* the top of the funnel. This was known as a balanced draught system. Air came into the engine room through the two big cowl vents directly ahead of the *Corinthic's* funnel. Electrically driven, the forced draught fans sucking air through these vents were located in the fan flat, an area

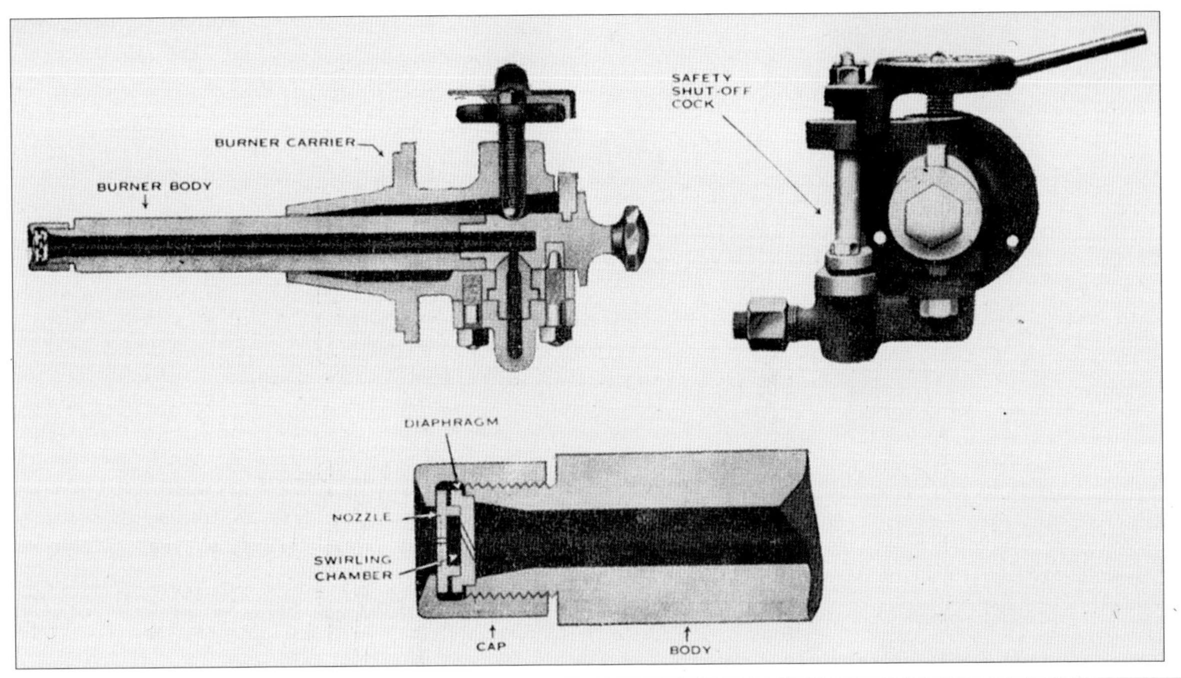
SAFETY SHUT-OFF COCK
BURNER CARRIER
BURNER BODY
DIAPHRAGM
NOZZLE
SWIRLING CHAMBER
CAP
BODY

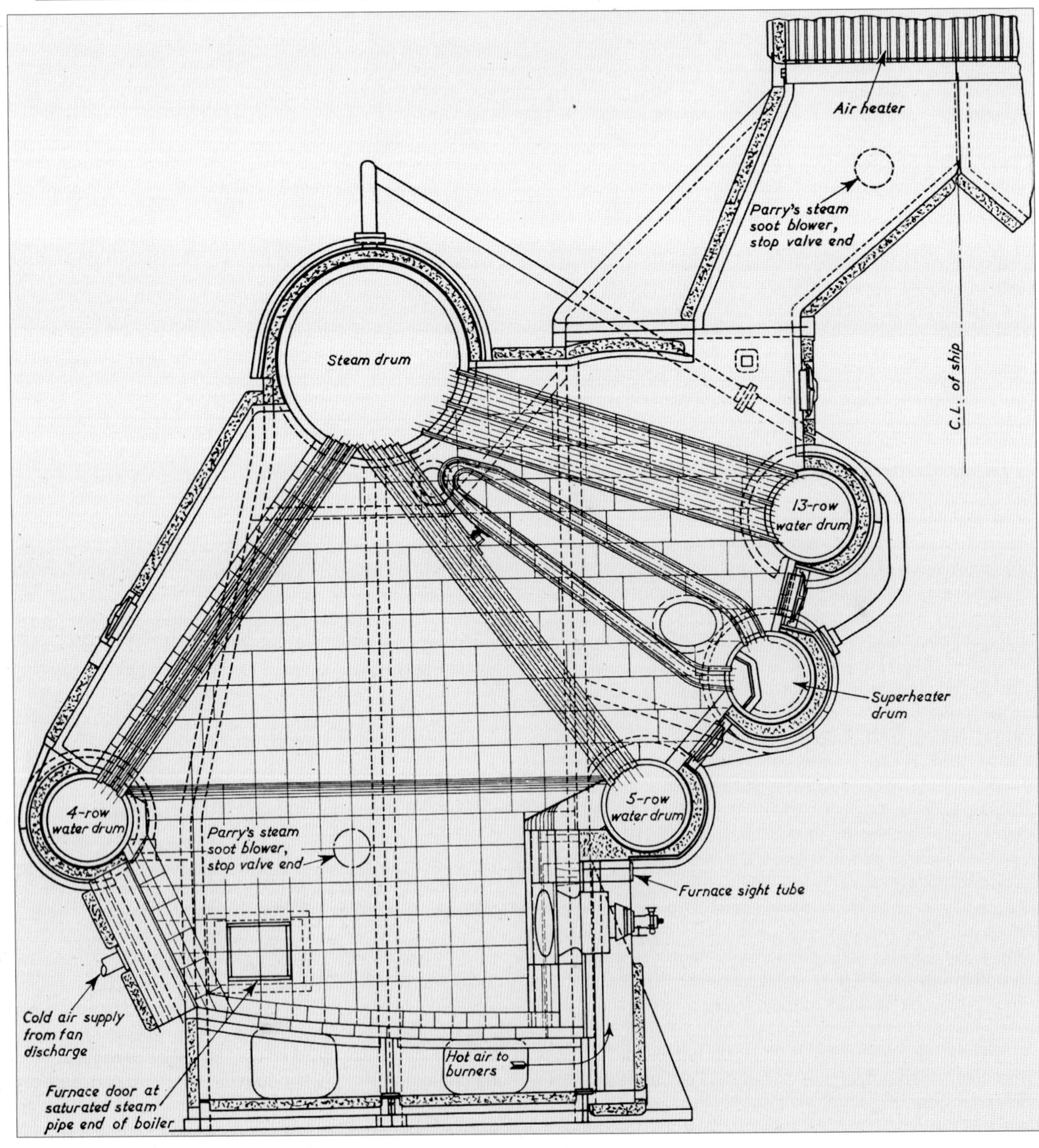
Air heater
Parry's steam soot blower, stop valve end
C.L. of ship
Steam drum
13-row water drum
Superheater drum
4-row water drum
5-row water drum
Parry's steam soot blower, stop valve end
Furnace sight tube
Cold air supply from fan discharge
Hot air to burners
Furnace door at saturated steam pipe end of boiler

Opposite page: Diagrams showing (top) the Wallsend-Howden oil fuel burners used aboard the *Corinthic* along with an enlargement of the burner's inner workings. Also (bottom) a five-drum, single-flow Yarrow marine boiler of the type fitted to the *Corinthic*. A burner can be seen under the boiler's furnace sight tube at right. The furnace is the central area in the lower section of the boiler; the funnel uptakes for the exhaust gases are at top right. The diagram shows the boiler looking from aft to forward; the firing alley is the unmarked area at lower right. Aboard the *Corinthic* this would have been the port boiler, with the starboard boiler across the firing alley to the right.

above the engine room on the Upper Deck. The induced draught fans, also electrically driven, were located in the funnel casing much higher in the ship, at Promenade Deck level. All the fan equipment was manufactured and supplied by James Howden and Co. Ltd. of Glasgow.

The *Corinthic's* double bottom tanks could hold a maximum 4,000 tons of oil fuel, lubricating oil and diesel fuel, along with 600 tons of fresh water and 250 tons of boiler feed water. Tanks below the three forward holds and the boilers were used to store oil fuel (these tanks could be used for water ballast once the fuel had been expended). Wing tanks along both sides of the engine room gave further capacity for oil fuel, along with spaces between and at the sides of the shaft tunnels under Number 4 hold. Diesel oil was stored in the aftermost sections of the engine room wing tanks. Lubricating oil was stored in the double bottom tanks below the turbines. Feed water was also held here. The *Corinthic's* fresh water tanks were in the double bottoms under Number 5 hold and around the shaft tunnels below this hold.

Forward of the boilers and mounted amidships was a Cochran oil-fired vertical boiler. This auxiliary boiler or donkey boiler was used when the *Corinthic* was in harbour or whenever the main boilers were off-line. It produced 2,800 pounds of steam per hour at a pressure of 125 p.s.i. On either side of the Cochran boiler were oil fuel settling tanks while along the sides of the engine room were fuel tanks for diesel oil and boiler oil.

There was no watertight bulkhead separating the boilers from the remainder of the engine room. Instead the area occupied by the boilers - the stokehold or boiler flat - was divided off from the turbines by a thin metal screen that ran athwartships. A central opening in this screen allowed the engineers to look through to the manoeuvring platform. Both boilers were kept on-line at all times when the *Corinthic* was at sea. Along with the Cochran vertical boiler, they were operated from a common firing alley which ran fore-and-aft between the boilers. Although the boilers were usually problem-free, nothing about them was automated and all depended on the skill of the engineers, particularly when the vessel was being manoeuvred in harbour. There was an engine telegraph repeater in the stokehold for each of the turbine sets; if, for instance, full ahead was ordered when the ship was at a lesser speed, more burners had rapidly to be fired to keep up the steam pressure as the turbines began to revolve faster. This firing was done manually by the engineers. With the boilers' superheater drums located directly above, there was very little headroom for them in front of the burners. Conversely, if stop engines was ordered from the bridge when the turbines were at full speed, the engineers had to 'pull' (or shut off) the burners just as quickly, to avoid excess steam pressure and lifting of the safety valves.

When operating the boilers it was necessary to keep the induced draught air pressure at a slightly higher level than that for the forced draught, so as to keep the boiler furnaces under a slight negative pressure. If this was not done, flames in the boilers could blow back into the stokehold. Balancing the fan pressure to avoid smoke was always vital, especially when entering or leaving port. Bruce Birnie, who sailed on the *Corinthic* for two years from June 1962, rising from junior to fifth engineer, recalls one departure with passengers from Auckland when a forced draught fan stopped. This caused a solid plume of dense black smoke to emit from the *Corinthic's* funnel in front of hundreds of on-lookers packing the wharf.

If there was too much smoke, complaints were sure to rapidly follow. George Wood was on the engine manoeuvring platform on another occasion in Auckland when a forced draft fan suddenly stopped. The P&O liner *Canberra* was berthed at an adjacent wharf. 'Thick black smoke literally boiled off the top of our funnel and climbed up the *Canberra's* white-painted side, smothering passengers on her sun decks and swimming pools. I didn't have a life from the chief engineer for ages after that!'

The *Corinthic* coming alongside in Wellington harbour on Monday 12th January 1953. No passengers are aboard as she is working cargo on the New Zealand coast. Smoke pours from her funnel; engineers on the manouevring platform can expect their chief's verbal displeasure. *[V.H. Young and L.A. Sawyer]*

Inside the *Corinthic's* engine room, looking aft and to port in the direction of the switchboard flat. In front of the switchboard are the tops of the reduction gear cases with their oil lubricating lines. Turbine cases can be seen at lower right and centre right, along with their steam lines and valves. *[Captain Graham Pepper, Shaw Savill Society]*

Electricity for the ship and for the host of engine room auxiliaries was provided by four 350 kW diesel generators located two on each side of the engine room, outboard of the turbine sets and in line fore and aft. The slow-running diesels, made in Glasgow by the British Polar Engine Co. Ltd. operated at 375 revolutions per minute, driving the 220 volts direct-current generators which were manufactured by the Sunderland Forge and Engineering Co. Ltd. They ran on diesel and not the heavy oil fuel consumed in the boiler furnaces. Power was distributed to the ship from the *Corinthic's* main electrical switchboard, housed on a platform known as the switchboard flat. This platform ran athwartships against the after bulkhead of the engine room, level with the tops of the reduction gear cases. The *Corinthic's* electrical wiring was supplied by British Insulated Callender's Cables Ltd. of London. Directly above the switchboard flat, at Main Deck level, was the engineers' and electricians' store rooms and workshops. Above this again, on the Shelter Deck, was the refrigerating plant.

Also on the Shelter Deck, inboard of the stewards' accomodation on the port side and the petty officers' quarters to starboard, was the emergency generator room. This housed a big, six-cylinder, Paxman Ricardo diesel motor driving an electricity generator capable of powering the *Corinthic's* emergency lighting, her steering gear and the air compressors used for charging the air-start systems on the four diesel generators in the engine room. As with most ships having an emergency generator room, it was on a deck completely separate from the engine room so that it would not be affected should the engine room be incapacitated by fire or flooding.

The walls of the engine room were painted white and everything was always kept scrupulously clean, with brass and chrome highly polished. During the month-long voyage home from New Zealand the cleaning and repainting intensified in preparation for arrival at London. Here the ship was inspected in detail by Shaw Savill's marine and engineer superintendents. Senior officers who failed to meet the company's very high standards in this respect would have the superintendents' displeasure made abundantly clear to them.

Lighting in the engine room was by way of tungsten bulbs in big circular shades with white insides, hung from the deckheads. All engineers on watch carried torches with which to read thermometers and gauges in awkward places, or to peer into the bilges and other unlit areas. As for noise, the *Corinthic* and her sisters were distinctly quieter compared to motor ships. The turbines emitted a humming sound while from the boilers came the noise of large volumes of air being moved at high speed. Burning oil in the furnaces produced a roaring effect but the loudest noise source was the clattering of the four British Polars driving the generators. This went on constantly. Up in the fiddley - the space above the boilers - there was only the low rumble from the electric fans. Higher still, inside the funnel, near-silence prevailed. Engineers could disappear up there on the pretext of checking all was in order, for a quiet smoke.

The engineers

What was it like to work in the *Corinthic's* engine room? It was certainly an ideal place to learn about operating and servicing heavy machinery. Marine engineers usually began their careers with a five-year apprenticeship on leaving school, either in a shipyard or as a shipping company cadet at sea. Having completed this, and having satisfactorily finished 21 months sea time and watch keeping, a young engineer could then sit for his ticket - the British Ministry of Transport examination for a second class engineer (steamship) or second class engineer (motorship) certificate. This was the minimum qualification to sail as a second engineer. Chief engineers were required to hold first class steam or motor certificates, depending on which type of ship they were serving aboard. Many chiefs held both certificates - the were known as combined chiefs or double-header chiefs - and these were highly valued and respected qualifications. The words ticket and certificate might suggest they were of a lesser status when compared to the plethora of diplomas and degrees available today, but obtaining these certificates required years of study and sea time. The oral examinations alone could be particularly daunting, lasting up to three hours at first class level. Because Shaw Savill was one of a diminishing number of companies operating steam-powered cargo vessels, this meant Big Ics such as the *Corinthic* were sought after by engineers wanting to get their combined first class engineer's certificate. Marine engineers who, in later life, came ashore having only the motor qualification, found their employment options severely limited.

George Wood sailed as an engineer on the *Corinthic* between June 1961 and August 1964, by which time he had risen from Ninth to Fifth Engineer. He was aboard her again from June to September 1965 as Third Engineer, then finally in February 1966 as Extra Second Engineer. Wood remembers the *Corinthic* carried a staff of eleven engineers including the chief engineer, along with three electricians (known as 'leckies') and two refrigerating engineers ('freezers'). Engineers were ranked in decreasing seniority from second down to eleventh, the most junior. Officers below the rank of fifth were all classed as junior engineers, with promotion determined on time spent in the company's employ. The fifth, fourth, third and second engineers all had seniority to take charge of watches in the engine room.

Accommodation for the engineers was all in single-berth cabins occupying the after half of the Bridge Deck. Between them and the passenger lounge and dining saloon at the forward end of the Bridge Deck was the *Corinthic's* galley. The chief engineer had a suite of three rooms: day room, bedroom and private bathroom on the starboard side right aft on this deck, while the second engineer had similar quarters to port but with his day room half the size. He also kept a large lockable store for consumables used in the engine room: torches, hand-cleaner, metal polish, paint brushes. A separate lounge was provided for the engineers; here they ran their own bar while the vessel was in port in New Zealand waters. They also had their own dining mess where the engineers ate from the same menu as the passengers. Three stewards were assigned to look after them: waiting at tables, cleaning the dining mess and the engineers' lounge, making beds and cleaning the engineers' bathrooms. Because of their senior status, the chief and second engineers took their meals in the first class dining saloon where they hosted their own passenger tables.

The engineers did not consider themselves to be officers. 'Why do you not allow *me* to be served first?' demanded a female passenger of a uniformed engineer at one of the *Northern Star's* lounge bars. 'You're supposed to be an officer and a gentleman!' 'Madam', replied the man in uniform, 'I am not an officer, I'm an engineer. And I'm not a gentleman, I'm an Irishman!'

F.H. (Frank) Papworth was the *Corinthic's* longest-serving chief engineer, remembered as a fine leader who performed his job with great thoroughness. He was addressed by his engineers as 'Chief'; he in turn called the fifth engineer and those ranked above by their first names, while the sixth engineer and below were referred to only by surname. The chief had complete authority for running the engine room and for the discipline and efficiency of all its personnel. It was a separate kingdom from the remainder of the ship; the master, chief officer and purser never ventured there. If and when he had any concerns, the master took them to the chief engineer in his day cabin and left him to deal with it. Deck officers often were actively discouraged from mixing with the engineers. During the two years from June 1962 that Bruce Birnie sailed as an engineer on the *Corinthic*, he never visited the deck officers' accommodation and never spoke with the *Corinthic's* master. On joining the *Corinthic* as a 21-year-old, Birnie was introduced to Second Engineer Doug Miller but it was some time before he met the chief engineer. Contact between the engineers and the passengers was almost non-existent, perhaps an occasional foray into the passenger lounge to take part in a dance.

Born at Maryport on the Solway Firth in Cumbria on 28th October 1902, Frank Harvey Papworth served at the *Corinthic's*

Engineers in their mess uniform at a dance for passengers in February 1964. From left: A. Nolan, Supernumerary Second Engineer; J.L. Pace, Junior Second Engineer; B.S. Birnie, Fifth Engineer; F.H. Papworth, Chief Engineer; M. Smith, Eighth Engineer; M. Rankin, First Electrician; B. McElhinney, Third Electrician; J. Welsh, Second Electrician; A. Marsh, Sixth Engineer. *[Bruce Birnie]*

Chief Engineer for almost 11 unbroken years, a quite remarkable length of time. He was appointed the *Corinthic's* Second Engineer in October 1946 while she was still fitting out, returning as her Chief Engineer in July 1954. Chief Papworth stayed with the *Corinthic* until he retired from the sea on 1st May 1965.

New engineers taken on by Shaw Savill usually spent their first six months working on company vessels in dock, under refit or on short coastal voyages between British ports. They were then considered sufficiently experienced with ships' machinery and shipboard routine to go deep sea. Hazards in the engine room were also brought to their notice; perhaps the most dangerous were superheated steam leaks from the steam pipes. These leaks could be heard but, unlike saturated steam they could not be seen. Great care was therefore needed never to get in front of a superheated steam leak. Another source of risk, not recognised as such in those times, was the asbestos with which all the steam pipes and parts of the boilers were lagged so as to minimise heat loss. This lagging was of great thickness and, whenever it had to be dismantled by the engineers so as to repair a steam pipe, there would be clouds of asbestos particles in the air and on the decks around them. Only since the 1970s has the often fatal condition we know as asbestosis, from inhalation and retention of asbestos fibres, been fully understood.

In addition to the engineers the *Corinthic* had two engineer petty officers (the title petty officer was, however, not used by Shaw Savill): the Donkeyman (known as 'donks') and the Engine Room Storekeeper ('stores'). Accommodation for both was in the petty officers' quarters, starboard side on the Shelter Deck just forward of the *Corinthic's* hospital. Three firemen and three greasers were carried; they had two berth cabins aft under the poop on the same deck, also starboard side.

Frank Papworth, the *Corinthic's* Chief Engineer from July 1954 to May 1965, at Auckland. *[George Wood]*

As well as checking water levels, bearing temperatures, valve settings and monitoring the gauges on the manoeuvring platform, there was a constant schedule of maintenance work to be carried out during each of the four-hour watches. These watches usually comprised a senior, an intermediate and a junior engineer along with one greaser and one fireman. During manoeuvring the watches would be doubled up, with twice the number of engineers on duty. The Donkeyman and the Engine Room Storekeeper were day workers; they did not stand watches.

The second engineer was the senior watch-keeping engineer and also in charge of the day-to-day work in the engine room. He kept the 4 to 8 watch, having the fifth and eighth engineers with him. Normally the second was very busy with administrative work – stores and spares lists, reports, survey arrangements – so in practice his watch was run by the fifth engineer. He also assigned tasks to day workers in the engine room: these men worked 6 a.m. to 5 p.m. each day and slept the night without being woken to go on watch ('all night in', as this was called). The fourth engineer kept the 8 to 12 watch, assisted by the seventh and tenth engineers; he had responsibility for the oil fuel bunkers so major pumping of oil fuel between tanks would take place on this watch. The third engineer kept the 12 to 4 watch with the sixth and ninth engineers; his particular responsibility, along with the donkeyman, was the British Polar diesel generators.

These were one of the biggest sources of work in the engine room, as they required constant maintenance. A story is told of a nameless engineer who 'fried the Polar'. 'He had been overhauling the aft port diesel generator and had forgotten to open individual cocks for the cooling water at the back of each cylinder. He started the diesel on test just before the end of his watch and left it running when the watch changed. We realised something was wrong when we went round there to find smoke pouring off the engine. I couldn't open the cocks as the sudden cooling would have cracked something, so we could only slow the engine to the minimum speed and crack the cocks open to cool her gradually, while screaming for the culprit to come back down and carry the can. Fortunately, we did no serious damage.'

Junior engineers spent most of their watches in the stokehold, where their job was to remove and clean burners on the work benches there. The turbines themselves were running constantly and needed no maintenance work while the ship was at sea, but there was always plenty for the engineers to do elsewhere: stripping and overhauling pumps and compressors, repairing faulty inlet and exhaust valves, attending to leaking pipes or keeping an eye on the two Howden-Ljungstrom air pre-heaters. These devices along with their electric motors were positioned in the boiler uptakes inside the funnel casing at Shelter Deck level. Hot exhaust gases from the boiler furnaces flowed into the pre-heaters via the boiler uptakes and the induced draught fans. Here, it warmed the cold air that was being simultaneously drawn into the stokehold from outside the ship by the forced draught fans. George Wood recalls the Ljungstrom pre-heaters were 'bitches' of machines because they were liable to catch fire due to the heat and build-up of oily soot carried into the boiler uptakes from the furnaces. This soot was blown overboard each night using Howden steam blowers, which employed dry steam to clear accumulated soot from the Howden vortex soot collectors. The process was known as 'blowing tubes'. A phone call would be made to the bridge during the 12-4 watch at night, when no passengers were out on deck, asking that the ship be turned across the wind. This ensured that the soot, vented out the top of the funnel, would be carried away from the decks and not down onto them. Once done, the ship would return to her course.

The eleventh, junior-most, engineer was a day worker, kept occupied in the engine room during the outward leg of each voyage, then becoming third refrigerating engineer when the vessel was loaded with frozen cargo on the homeward leg. The three refrigerating engineers each stood four hourly watches on this leg, doing so in the refrigerating machinery flat on the Upper Deck. All the electricians were day workers, their time spent servicing the myriad of electrical gear in the engine room and all over the ship.

When the *Corinthic* was in port with her main boilers shut down, reduced watches were manned in the engine room. Between them, the eighth, ninth and tenth engineer each stood 12-hour generator watches: 12 hours on, 24 hours off. In addition to the diesel generators they kept an eye on the Cochran auxiliary boiler if it was in use. The fifth, sixth and seventh engineers took turns sleeping one night in three aboard, in case anything should go wrong.

Each day at noon when the *Corinthic* was at sea the 8-12 intermediate engineer, usually the seventh, had to deliver the engine room log to the chief in his day cabin. This log book detailed all the readings and workings for the previous 24 hours. Some chief engineers took only a mild interest, delegating all to the second engineer who, as the *Corinthic's* sisters grew older and wear and corrosion increased his workload, would often be assisted by the appointment of an extra second engineer. Frank Papworth, however, was a man who knew his engines intimately. Examining the log, he would rapidly pick up errors or inconsistencies to the detriment of the poor engineer standing in front if him. Bruce Birnie remembers these frequent interrogations. There was no point in denial; Chief Papworth was always right. As chief engineer he

The *Corinthic's* 4-to-8 engine room watch, June 1962. From left: Fifth Engineer George Wood, Second Engineer Doug Miller and Tenth Engineer Bruce Birnie. *[George Wood]*

wrote up the main copy of the engine room log; at the end of each voyage this would go ashore to Shaw Savill's engineering superintendents for their perusal.

Unless he specifically wished to, a chief engineer did not take part in the day-to-day manual work in his engine room. Usually mid-morning, Chief Papworth would appear amongst his boiler-suited and be-grimed engineers in his uniform with four gold lace rings edged with purple on his sleeve ends, keen to see what they were up to. Nothing escaped his view. George Wood tells of an extra second engineer who had been seconded temporarily to the *Corinthic* from another shipping company, getting in his time with steam engines before sitting for his combined first class engineer (steam and motor) certificate. He was dismantling one of the two centrifugal pumps located on the stokehold floor that supplied salt water to cool the bearings in the Howden-Ljungstrom air pre-heaters. These pumps had cast-iron bodies which the salt water tended to soften, and thus they had to be handled very carefully. Finding that the pump was resisting his attempts to dismantle it, the extra second made use of a hammer. Promptly the machine fell apart under his hammer blows, leaving him covered in black sludge. At this point Chief Papworth walked into the stokehold. Nearby engineers decamped as fast as they could but not before seeing the extra second looking up haplessly at the glowering Papworth: 'It just came to bits in my hands, Chief!'

When the *Corinthic* was transiting the Panama Canal the watches in the engine room were reduced from four to two hours each, because of the workload from the constant manoeuvring and also because of the fierce humidity. Having left Panama, the ship passed into the Pacific Ocean's Humboldt current where a dramatic lowering of the sea temperatures always took place. As a result, there was a constant slowing down of circulating pumps and adjusting of valves. Slip-ups with this would bring a summons to Papworth's day cabin, to explain why the temperatures recorded on the daily logs were fluctuating. Conversely, on the homeward leg between Panama and the island of Curacao there was a very warm current which, depending on the time of year, could play havoc with the ship's carbon dioxide refrigerating system. Seawater passing through the condenser in the refrigerating plant would not be cool enough to convert the carbon dioxide gas to liquid.

Temperatures in the engine room, even under the ventilation fans, often reached 120 degrees Fahrenheit (49 degrees Celsius). In the stokehold fiddley, which had to be inspected every two hours, the temperatures averaged 145 degrees F (63 degrees C). On one occasion, with the ship alongside at Balboa on the Pacific side of the Panama Canal, George Wood and Bruce Birnie were told by the second engineer to repack a boiler stop valve on top of one of the boilers. The temperature there was up to 184 degrees F (85 degrees C). On completion of the task both men emerged onto the *Corinthic's* Boat Deck, where they were each rewarded with a cold beer by the chief engineer. Both then promptly collapsed with heat exhaustion. Amused passengers had to step around their slumped bodies but the *Corinthic's* master, observing the fuss, was not sympathetic.

Sadly the arts of marine steam boilers and turbines, together with the prodigious skills needed to make and operate them, have largely gone. Without the aid of the computer technology upon which we depend today, these men created and ran machinery that could propel a fully-laden 15,000 grt vessel such as the *Corinthic* around the world in all weathers at a consistent 17 knot speed, stopping only to take on more fuel and water. Breakdowns and accidents occurred but they were seldom. George Wood recalls one on the *Corinthic* which serves to well illustrate the complexity and the power of the machines the engineers dealt with: 'The drains from the main boiler safety valve waste pipes ran down and across the tank tops to the hot well, but over the years the horizontal pipes had filled with gunge and rust-flakes. This had not been spotted. So the waste pipes were not being properly drained and, it is assumed, had filled with water. On this particular occasion, when manoeuvring the ship in the Thames, something got in our way and the pilot on the bridge reduced speed by ordering slow ahead on the engines. In the stokehold, the junior engineer was not fast enough in getting the burners pulled (to reduce steam pressure as the slowing turbines stopped taking steam). So the boiler pressure rose to the point where the safety valves lifted. But the excess steam could not move the water sitting in the waste pipes. The steam took the next best course, splitting the waste pipes which were about nine inches in diameter with four inches thickness of asbestos lagging on them. Steam under very high pressure, along with hot water and disintegrating asbestos, suddenly began venting into the engine room from the ruptured pipes, accompanied by an ear-splitting roar.

The second engineer, at the manoeuvring platform, did not know what had happened so he shut the bulkhead stops. These were the remotely-operated valves isolating the boilers from the turbines. The result was even more bedlam, with the turbines no longer getting any steam and all of it instead discharging into the engine room. The split in the pipes was right above the passage between the manoeuvring platform and the stokehold, so hot water was pouring down and stopping anyone getting from the platform to the stokehold. The junior engineer in the stokehold was new to the job, but had enough sense to pull all the burners so that the boilers were no longer making steam. On the manoeuvring platform, the second engineer rang the engine telegraphs to stop, thereby alerting the bridge that further engine orders could not, for the moment, be complied with. Meanwhile a fireman, thoroughly rattled, headed up the ladders into the fiddley on his way to the boat deck and his muster station. Here, a huge plume of steam was shrieking from the front of the funnel but this cut off abruptly as soon as the bulkhead stops were re-opened and the turbines were getting steam again. It took us days to get that asbestos cleaned up, by which time we'd all had several lungfuls.'

Another memory from George Wood well illustrates the camaraderie and pride of purpose that bonded the engineers. During a visit to Curacao for bunkering the *Corinthic*, under pilot's orders at Willemstad, was being manoeuvred at double full astern when she inadvertently ran across an underwater bank. A very large quantity of shell was sucked through the main injection valves and dumped inside the condensers and coolers. All of it had to be removed but the *Corinthic*, scheduled to transit the nearby Panama Canal, could not be delayed. The engineers turned-to and stayed in the engine room until the job was finished. Such an event, with all engineers working without relief because of a major emergency, was called a Paddy's watch. Bruce Birnie remembers being down in the engine room for some 30 hours. Normal watches also had to be kept as the ship was underway. Chief Engineer Papworth donned a boiler suit - the only time he is ever remembered as having worn one - to relieve the second engineer. One turbine set was kept running while the other was shut down and its condenser dismantled. Each condenser tube - there were over 1,000 of them - had to be individually cleared of shell debris by pushing rods through them; 'punching tubes' as this task was known. With both condensers fully operational again, the same then had to be done to all the generator and auxiliary coolers. The *Corinthic* successfully reached the Canal on time for her transit.

The life of a sea-going engineer could also have its dramas outside the engine room's confines. On one occasion with the *Corinthic* mid-Atlantic, she diverted at night to the assistance of a Greek tramp ship with a seaman needing surgery for appendicitis. The man was transferred to the *Corinthic* aboard her motor lifeboat, with Bruce Birnie as the boat's engineer: 'It would be the most frightening event I experienced while at sea. Being dropped and retrieved in total darkness down and then up the side of a rolling ship in a 10 metre swell is something I don't ever want to repeat'. Captain H.O.V. Andersen was the *Corinthic's* Master at the time, a fine seaman who had been Chief Officer of the *Gothic* for the 1953-54 royal tour of New Zealand and Australia. Bruce Birnie recalls Captain Andersen manoeuvring the *Corinthic* to get the lifeboat back alongside. 'Once the boat had been hoisted from the sea, Captain Andersen was there to greet us. He gave the boat's crew a bottle of rum to share.'

The engine room ratings

Bill Aston served as a fireman and as a greaser in the *Runic's* engine room, near-identical to that of the *Corinthic*, from 9th April 1954 to 3rd October 1960. He was her Engine Room Storekeeper for 14 voyages, coming ashore at the end of the voyage immediately prior to the *Runic's* loss. One fireman was assigned to each of the watches and, like the engineers, he stood a four-hour watch followed by eight hours off duty. The fireman looked after the boilers: 'It was a hot and not-too-clean a job', remembers Aston. When coming on duty he changed the burners in the boilers, 12 in total on the *Corinthic*, cleaning the ones just removed so that they were ready for use again during the next watch. The junior engineer on watch carried out this same task which was done once during every four hour watch, and he also did the burner changing when the ship was being manoeuvred in port. Most important of the fireman's duties was monitoring the water levels in the main boilers. He did this by hawk-like observation of the water levels in the indicator glasses, a difficult task when the ship was pitching and rolling. By manipulating pumps and valves the fireman ensured the

The liner beautiful, away to sea. *Corinthic* leaving Waitemata harbour, Auckland, for London. Her gear is stowed, the holds are full and one or two passengers can be seen on deck. For their protection against the wind, canvas screens have been rigged along the rails of the *Corinthic's* Promenade and Boat Decks. On the ship's left hand is North Head. Rangitoto Island lies hidden in the mist ahead. *[V.H. Young and L.A. Sawyer]*

correct boiler steam pressures, water levels and steam temperatures were always maintained. Losing water in the boilers for as little as 30 seconds could result in very serious damage.

It was also the fireman's responsibility to keep the stokehold meticulously clean. This part of his job demanded constant attention. The bulkheads were washed and wiped, as were the exterior surfaces of the boilers along with all other fixtures in the stokehold. Paintwork was renewed where necessary. The greaser on watch in the engine room did the same. Grubbiness or deterioration of any sort was not tolerated and quickly spotted by the prowling chief engineer. 'I was just about to get it done' never cut any ice with Chief Papworth as he pointed accusingly at rust or dirt that was not there five minutes before. Especially treacherous in this respect were the plates comprising the floor of the stokehold and engine room. On the *Corinthic* they were laid in the form of steel chequer plate with a diamond pattern, and each diamond depression had to be washed with paraffin and a wire brush to remove grease and dirt. In particular this was done after departure from London, shore staff having trampled all manner of grime until it lay caked between the plates. Once cleaned, the paraffin generally kept the plates from rusting, but rust could appear with the speed of a burglar, especially if there was a hot water leak nearby. It had to be eliminated immediately, as did any spillage of boiler oil or lubricants.

The greaser oiled and lubricated bearings and moving parts throughout the auxiliary machinery in the engine room, ensuring that none were running hot. He kept all the pumps, machinery cases and all surfaces clean. When the ship was coming into port, and with the fireman fully occupied with the main boiler fires, it was the greaser's job to flash up the Cochran auxiliary boiler and start its feed pump so that steam was available once finished with engines was telegraphed from the bridge and the main boilers were shut down. At sea during the watch, the greaser made the tea for the engineers and ratings. He climbed the ladders and went aft to the crew galley located in the deckhouse on the Poop Deck. The chance to go up on deck and have a quiet smoke while the tea brewed in its big aluminium teapot was something of a perk for the greaser. He brought the teapot back and the engineers and ratings helped themselves; sometimes during the watches at night the greaser was able to score a plate of toast.

The firemen and greasers also worked alongside the engineers in the heavy labour needed for major overhaul tasks, sometimes working day shifts on overtime rates. Assisting the greaser was a wiper, as junior greasers were called. This was the lowest rank in the engine room. At the other end of the scale were two senior engine room ratings: the Donkeyman and the Engine Room Storekeeper - the ERS. Both men were highly experienced through long service, having worked their way up from fireman and greaser, and both reported directly to the chief engineer and the second engineer. Many of these senior men spent years living and working on the same ship; George Wood recalls a very long-serving donkeyman on the *Corinthic* who the junior engineers addressed as Mister Montague. The primary job of the donkeyman was maintaining the generators and the steering gear. The ERS ran the engineers' and electricians' store rooms and workshops. A large inventory of stores and spare parts was always carried, along with numerous engineering tools. All of it had to be accounted for, and at the beginning of each overhaul or repair job the ERS issued the parts and tools needed, then ensured the tools were properly returned. A cablegram dated 29th March 1961 from Shaw Savill's Sydney office to the company's London Head Office, concerning the *Runic* stranded on Middleton Reef, gives an idea of the comprehensive range of engineering stores and spares aboard these vessels:

'Generator armatures wet also spares stowed (in the) funnel casing, main switchboard, with various spares (for) refrigerated pumps and motors, various pump and motors for main engines and auxiliaries, boiler room pumps and motors, motor starters and boxes (of) starter spares, steering motors and pumps complete with spares (for) winch motor controllers and contactors, induced and forced draft fan motors with starters and contactors, windlass motors and contactors, diesel and turbo generators with mechanical spares, evaporator and steam generator coils, boiler mountings spares, refrigeration plant spares, spare gear engine room stores, boiler spares comprising tubes, plugs, starters, engine room telegraphs and all gauges and instruments (for) main panel.' All of this was left behind on the *Runic* when she was abandoned.

The ERS also ran a small business on the side, cleaning the white boiler suits worn by the engineers. Those availing themselves of this service paid the storekeeper, but the chief and second engineer had theirs laundered at the expense of the company. Engineers always wore white whereas the boiler suits worn by engine room ratings were blue. Usually the whiter and cleaner the boiler suit, the higher the seniority of the engineer wearing it.

While the ship was alongside in port there were numerous additional duties. The bilges were cleaned, the lagging on the high pressure steam lines was cleaned and then whitewashed. With the main boilers shut down the boiler furnaces were attended to. The interiors of the funnel and boiler casings were washed and repainted. If the main boilers were shut down for a lengthy period of time, the firemen and greasers would close the funnel covers. This involved climbing the ladders inside the funnel and, once out on the funnel top, swinging each of the boiler flue covers on its hinges and bolting them down over the smoke exhaust hole. There were two covers, one for each boiler uptake; each cover measured approximately six by eight feet and was elliptical in shape. Getting them closed could be a vile job as the nearby diesel exhausts on the funnel top would be belching out fumes as would the uptake from the Cochran auxiliary boiler.

Corinthic and the Commodore

For more than half her life the *Corinthic* was commanded by one man, Captain A.C. Jones, known variously as 'Pitcairn Jones' and 'the Uncrowned King of Pitcairn'. Arthur Conway Jones was appointed Master of the *Corinthic* on 15th September 1951 and remained so until 22nd August 1963, a few months before his retirement. His long association with the *Corinthic* began when Shaw Savill assigned Chief Officer Jones to stand-by her at Cammell Laird shipyard in May 1946. He was up on her forecastle the morning she was launched in May that year. When Captain John Hart, Master of the *Iberic* (11,100/1960) retired on 21st March 1962 Captain Jones became Commodore of Shaw Savill, a position he held until he left the *Corinthic*, and the sea, on 22nd August 1963. Captain L.J. Hopkins then took over from him as Fleet Commodore.

Captain Jones was a remarkable master because of the very strong interest he took in the professional development of cadets and deck officers aboard the *Corinthic*. Masters in those days were under no obligation to bother with any of this, but Captain Jones was an exception. Polite and never abusive, he believed in getting involved with junior deck officers and in setting the highest standards for his crew. Drilling officers in how to react to sudden emergencies was a favourite topic. In late April 1941 Captain Jones had been watch officer on the bridge of the *Dominion*

Aboard the *Iberic* at London, 21st March 1962. Captain John Hart, Master of the *Iberic* and Shaw Savill's Fleet Commodore, is handing over to his successor on the eve of his retirement. The new Commodore, Captain A.C. Jones of the *Corinthic*, is at left with his wife. Mrs Hart is third from left. *[Captain Graham Pepper, Shaw Savill Society]*

Life in the fast lane aboard the *Corinthic* late at night and somewhere at sea. Captain A.C. Jones arm-in-arm with a lady passenger and a merry ship's officer. The lady is Ina Williamson, a frequent Shaw Savill passenger during post-war years. *[Captain Graham Pepper, Shaw Savill Society]*

Captain Jones and a passenger judging a children's fancy dress competition. *[Captain Ian Condie]*

Monarch when she collided with the Royal Mail line's *Highland Chieftain* (14,131/1929). Filled with troops, the *Dominion Monarch* was sailing in a large convoy at the time. From this experience and other near-mishaps during his long career, Captain Jones had learned the value of crew training. Never content to simply pass the time in his day cabin during each voyage, Captain Jones knew every part of the *Corinthic* and was immensely fond of her. As Fleet Commodore, he could have asked for transfer to any of Shaw Savill's newer ships but chose instead to remain with the *Corinthic* which, at the time of his appointment, was 15 years old.

When he first saw Pitcarin Island in 1933 from aboard Shaw Savill's *Akaroa* (15,182/1914), Jones noted the desolate condition of much of the island's terrain, stripped of forests and eroded by winds. A keen gardener, once appointed Master of the *Corinthic* Captain Jones resolved to fix this. Along with her sisters, the *Corinthic* always made regular calls at Pitcairn Island when crossing the Pacific to and from New Zealand. While hove-to in Bounty Bay, always treacherous because of the heavy ocean swell, the islanders would come out in their longboats to trade with the passengers and crew. Mail and cargo was off-loaded into the boats as they surged alongside the ship, her derricks lowering drums of oil, sheets of iron and baulks of timber. The Pitcairn Islanders were magnificent boatmen, exceptionally skilled at manhandling large, heavy cargoes into their boats while keeping station alongside a big ship in a running sea.

Pride of place in these cargoes were consignments of tree plants and seedlings which Captain Jones purchased with his own money and brought out from New Zealand. At his urging, the islanders used these to re-forest their lands. The *Corinthic's* wheelhouse became a de facto greenhouse, filled with vegetation all destined for Pitcairn with the watch officers and quartermasters conscripted as Captain Jones's assistant gardeners in caring for this plant life. On one voyage, a beehive for Pitcairn Island was transported on the *Corinthic's* bridge, much to the consternation of her officers. Also at Captain Jones's instigation a much larger deck cargo in the form of a bulldozer was shipped to Pitcairn so the islanders could improve their roads, drainage and food gardens. Two of the islanders' longboats were lashed together so the bulldozer could be lowered on the ship's derricks and taken ashore.

Pitcairn Islanders always received a most friendly welcome aboard the *Corinthic,* Captain Jones keen to give them every possible help. Their longboats would be hoisted onto the well decks by her derricks and taken to nearby Henderson Island, where the boat crews would harvest Miro for their carvings. Islanders were carried to and from New Zealand most probably for very little if any charge, berthed either in the crew accommodation or, if it was not in use, in the ship's hospital. On Pitcairn, Captain Jones is commemorated by the rocky point in Bounty Bay that is named in his honour. On his very final voyage aboard the *Corinthic*, prior to retirement, Captain Jones went ashore on Pitcairn Island having received permission from Shaw Savill to leave his ship for a brief visit. It is said he returned very subdued and dismayed by the primitive living conditions he found on the island.

Captain Ian Condie sailed as the *Corinthic's* Fourth Officer under Captain Jones, who was over 60 at the time. He remembers him as 'a pleasure to serve under, an old fashioned gentleman with a sense of humour and a courteous manner that extended to his officers. He had an antique habit of addressing every officer, even the most junior, as 'sir'.' In addition to his devotedness to Pitcairn, among his other interests was constant searching for some new, unnamed geographical feature - a rock, headland or shoal - that would get his or the *Corinthic's* name printed on a chart. For this purpose he became what was known as a 'rock dodger', taking his ship much closer to land than other masters would consider advisable. Captain Condie: 'Pitcairn was the high point of his voyage as he took the *Corinthic* into Bounty Bay little more than a ship's length from the rocky shore at the foot of the island cliffs. The water was very clear and Jonesy always stopped over a shoal patch which had a large rock fully visible in the middle of it. Triumphantly a passenger would see the rock and call out in alarm to the Master, who would be leaning out over the bridge wing. Captain Jones would smile in delight, salute and bow slightly. His officers could almost hear him saying 'thank you, thank you, and now for my next trick...'

The second officer as ship's navigator laid off prudent courses taking her several miles away from the land but that was not good enough for Captain Jones, who took the *Corinthic* well inside the allotted track. Officers on watch spent their time trying to convince themselves to have every faith in their Captain while wondering where exactly their life jackets were stowed as the jagged trace on the echo sounder paper showed the sea floor rising to the same depth as the ship's bottom, leaving no time to stop the ship or take evasive action. Luck, or the gods that watch over seafarers, were always with Jonesy. He never put his ship aground but he did make one discovery that should have put his name on the relevant chart.

'It happened one voyage just after the ship had passed Rapa Island in the south-eastern Pacific while homeward bound for London via Panama. The island was receding astern and Captain Jones, show-time over after having taken the ship very close, had retired to his day room for a refreshing beer with a passenger guest. There was nothing now but open ocean until the *Corinthic* reached Pitcairn, several days away. The solitary sounding marked on the chart said 1,500 fathoms, nine thousand feet of water. Time to relax.

The second officer knocked at the open door of the captain's day room. 'Excuse me, sir', he said. 'You know you are always looking for something to add to the charts'. 'Yes?' replied the Master, puzzled. 'Would you like to come and look at it?' asked the second mate politely.

Corinthic off Bounty Bay, Pitcairn Island on a fine, near windless day in 1957. Note the awning spread over Number 4 hatch to keep the verandah cafe and the smoking room a little cooler in the Pacific's equatorial latitudes. An islanders' whaleboat has been towed out by another whaleboat, equipped with a motor, from which this photograph was taken. Both boats are waiting for the *Corinthic* to turn and create a lee, after which her engines will be kept at dead slow ahead. Only if the ship was further out from the island would engines be stopped. The whaleboat will then use oars to come alongside the liner, with the motor whaler rafting up outboard of it. *[V.H. Young and L.A. Sawyer]*

Jonesy came out onto the bridge wing where the second officer pointed over the side. There, quite visible in the clear sea, were lumps of coral over which the ship was steaming at 17 knots. The echo sounder made it clear this was no mistake; the depth of water was not 1,500 fathoms as declared on the chart, but 15 fathoms – 90 feet, and the *Corinthic* was occupying 30 of them.' As it was not marked on the chart, there was no way of telling the extent or the shoal water, whether it was rising and whether the ship was going to suddenly run out of ocean and go aground.

Most fortunately the shoal soon terminated and the depth of water plunged back to the ocean abyss. Ian Condie continues: 'Captain Jones stood calmly on the bridge until the echo sounder trace suddenly dropped off the scale, then he went back to finish his beer as if nothing had happened. That is what he was paid for. Needless to say, the shoal was carefully documented and, on arrival at Panama, the necessary information was handed to the Hydrographic Service. Warnings were swiftly promulgated in Admiralty Notices to Mariners, but to Captain Jones's great fury the discovery was credited to the United States Hydrographic Department. His anger did not abate until a new second mate discovered another, far less dangerous shoal and persuaded the Royal New Zealand Navy to give credit where it was due. Captain Jones did, however, keep well clear of Rapa Island thereafter.'

Rock dodging, where courses are laid off on the chart so as to intersect with the land and not to a point well clear of it, required not only luck but very steady nerves and a very sharp lookout on ships like the *Corinthic* that could not be stopped or turned quickly. Another memory of Captain Jones from Ian Condie: 'About six hours steaming north east of Pitcairn was Henderson Island. It is a very small, very flat, low-lying place, uninhabited and covered with vegetation. There is one beach, otherwise the cliffs fall more or less straight into the sea. When I was Fourth Mate of the *Corinthic* one voyage outward bound, we were due to pass Henderson Island shortly after sunrise. The night had been overcast so I had not been able to get star sights at twilight, but I was not worried. The previous evening's stars had been a good fix and it was a bright sunny morning with extreme visibility, marred only by a few scattered rain showers. The radar was not only switched on but appeared to be working well since it showed all the rain.

Captain Jones came on the bridge wearing his distinctive self-designed dressing gown, to assess the situation. He asked if I had sighted Henderson Island and I replied that I had not but that it should be in sight a point or two to port. I added there was nothing showing on the radar except rain squalls. He suggested one of them might be obscuring the land and that it should come in sight after the squall passed over it. We stayed on the port wing talking while both keeping a lookout.

There was one particular rain shower right ahead that appeared to be moving only very slowly and increasing in size as we approached, and the radar indicated it was a heavy one. I began to wonder whether we should alter course around it but there was still no sign of the island and it was more important to sight the land. We were both using binoculars to search, casting an occasional look at the approaching rain.

Then the same thought occurred simultaneously to the Master and myself, respectively the most senior and the most junior officers on the *Corinthic's* bridge. We were both increasingly suspicious of that rain cloud we were approaching, and both of us were drawn to look more closely at it. To our horror, at each edge to the rain, two points on each bow, land began to appear. Our navigation had been too exact and we were headed right at the middle of Henderson Island! It took the rapid application of a significant amount of helm to steer her clear.'

Left: Captain Jones outside his day cabin aboard the *Corinthic* with Pitcairn Islanders. From left: Bernice Christian, Captain Jones, John Christian, Helen Young, Ruth Christian.
Right: A whaleboat from Pitcairn Island being lifted over-side at Henderson Island from the *Corinthic's* forward well deck using her derricks and winches; March 1963. *[V.H. Young and L.A. Sawyer; Bruce Birnie]*

Arthur Conway Jones was born in 1898 at Shepton Mallet, a town in Somerset where his father was rector of the Anglican parish. He served his apprenticeship with Ellerman Lines before joining Shaw Savill as a junior deck officer in 1925. After 38 years with the company, the final 17 months as Fleet Commodore, Captain Jones officially retired on 1st December 1963 aged 65, and was awarded the CBE in the January 1964 New Year's Honours List. He lived at his home in Hythe, Kent, dying on 21st December 1987 at the age of 89.

Cargo only

By the mid-1960s, although the *Corinthic* was still taking near-full complements of passengers on peak-season voyages, Shaw Savill was finding it no longer economic to operate her and her sisters as passenger-carrying vessels. During the many weeks spent discharging then loading on the New Zealand coast, with no passengers aboard, cooks and stewards had little if anything to do while still on full wages. Also, regardless of whether full cargo consignments had been loaded, passenger sailing schedules always had to be adhered to. Delays caused by labour troubles on the wharves or failure of cargoes to reach the ship on time, meant she often sailed without full holds. It was therefore seen as much more efficient to split the passenger and cargo business. The *Corinthic* and her three sisters were downgraded to cargo-only ships, their passenger clientèle being handled by the liners *Southern Cross* and *Northern Star*, neither of which took cargo. She departed London on her last passenger voyage on 18th February 1965 with Captain H.O.V. Andersen as her Master.

Corinthic under the meat loaders at Bluff, New Zealand. These were lowered into the holds where they delivered meat carcasses using conveyor belts enclosed against the weather. Watersider gangs still had to carry and stow each carcass as it came off the loaders. Note the *Corinthic* has temporarily lost her white hull band. *[Ian J. Farquhar collection]*

For the *Corinthic*, another problem was addressed during this conversion. Because of their height, lifting cargo in and out of Numbers 3 and 4 hatches had always been a slow job, located as they were on the top of her superstructure three decks higher than the neighbouring hatchways. In an effort to speed matters up for Number 3 at least, an extra pair of samson posts and derricks had been added just ahead of the *Corinthic's* funnel during an early 1950s refit. Now, with passenger cabins on the promenade deck no longer needed, it was decided to cut down her superstructure above Numbers 3 and 4 holds by one deck.

The tender for the conversion was awarded to Wilton Fijenoord at Schiedam in Rotterdam. Work began on 5th July 1965 and was completed on 13th February 1966. The after part of the deckhouse on the Boat and Games Deck, inboard of the after port and starboard boats, was removed along with these two boats and their davits. One deck lower, the Promenade Deck was cut away outboard of the trunking above Numbers 3 and 4 hold, leaving this area open. This allowed the hatchways to be relocated one deck below. Samson posts, derricks, winches and ventilators were all repositioned. The engineers' quarters were moved to the former passenger cabins in what remained of the Promenade Deck, and the crew accommodation was moved from the poop to the space previously occupied by the engineers. The interior of the poop was stripped for extra cargo stowage. On the Bridge Deck, the old passenger lounge became a combined officers' and engineers' lounge, as did the dining saloon. Her gross register tonnage prior to the conversion was listed at 15,682; it now decreased to 14,282 (net register tonnage reduced from 9,060 to 7,659 after the conversion).

The result of these amputations was not altogether dissatisfying to the eye, but it clearly signalled the *Corinthic* was no longer the prestige liner she had once been. George Woods was one of three engineers sent to Schiedam in early February 1966 to raise steam and bring her to Southampton, where the *Corinthic* arrived on 14th February. During the conversion, cracks had been found in the superheater drums of both boilers. New drums had to be manufactured and fitted. Had the company known of this major defect prior to the conversion, and the great expense involved in rectifying it, the *Corinthic* would instead probably have been sent for scrapping. Shaw Savill hoped to get another five to ten years

Reduced to cargo-only duties, the *Corinthic* in Lyttelton harbour on 26th October 1967. Behind her, Mount Herbert is covered in low cloud. *[N.J. Kirby]*

out of her, but it seems that boiler troubles persisted. In August 1967 she was moored on the River Fal in Cornwall with the *Suevic* alongside, while heavy repair work was carried out on her boilers.

She had in fact three years and eight months left after her return from Schiedam. While still employed on the UK-New Zealand refrigerated cargo trade, the *Corinthic* was also used for other one-off refrigerator cargoes among them a 1969 charter to the Dolphin Line to load apples at Hobart and, in 1968, taking meat and dairy cargoes to Montreal for the Montreal Australia New Zealand Line Ltd. (MANZ Line). Running costs must have been colossal by that time. After discharging the last of a British cargo at Sydney from 2nd to 10th September 1969, orders were received for the *Corinthic* to proceed from there direct to Kaohsiung in Taiwan for breaking up. There were no farewells or plaudits. At the conclusion of a slow passage north, the *Corinthic* reached the yard of the China Steel Corporation at Kaohsiung on 23rd October 1969. Her sister ship *Athenic* arrived two days later. Demolition commenced the following month.

The *Corinthic* in August 1967, laid up in the King Harry Passage on the River Fal, a location that offers very good protection from the weather. The *Suevic* is alongside; both vessels are undergoing boiler repairs. *[Captain Graham Pepper, Shaw Savill Society]*

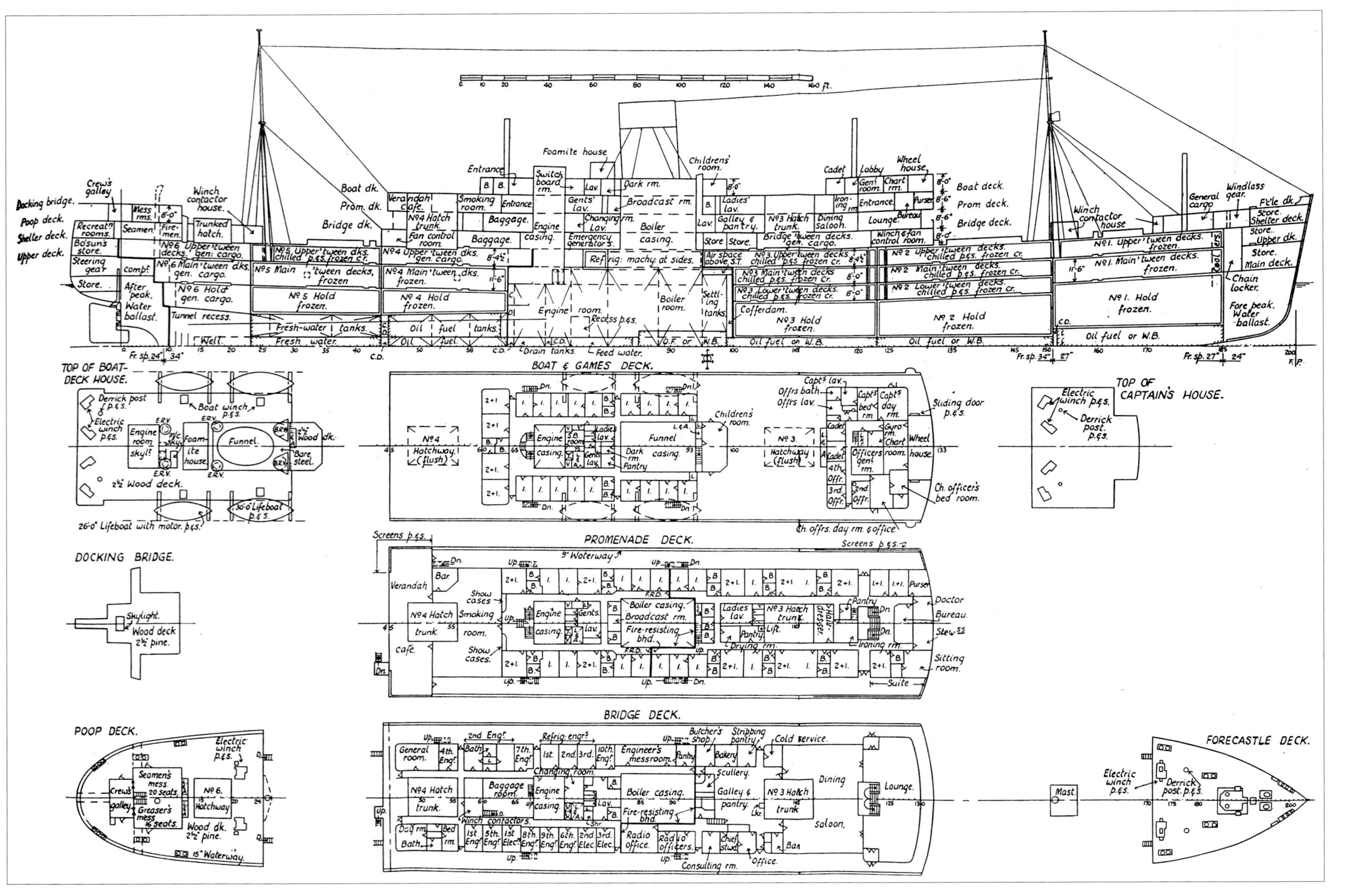

Docking bridge.
Poop deck.
Shelter deck.
Upper deck.
Crew's galley
Winch contactor house.
Trunked hatch.
Boat dk.
Prom. dk.
Bridge dk.
Foamite house
Entrance
Switch board rm.
Childrens' room.
Wheel house.
Boat deck.
Prom deck.
Bridge deck.
Windlass gear.
General cargo
Fc'le dk.
Nº 5 Hold frozen.
Nº 4 Hold frozen.
Engine room.
Boiler room.
Nº 3 Hold frozen.
Nº 2 Hold frozen.
Nº 1. Hold frozen.
Fore peak. Water ballast.
Chain locker.
After peak. Water ballast.
Tunnel recess.
0 10 20 40 60 80 100 120 140 160 ft.
TOP OF BOAT-DECK HOUSE.
BOAT & GAMES DECK.
TOP OF CAPTAIN'S HOUSE.
26'-0" Lifeboat with motor. p.&s.
30'-0" Lifeboat p.&s.
DOCKING BRIDGE.
Skylight.
Wood deck 2½" pine.
PROMENADE DECK.
9" Waterway
Verandah
Bar.
Cafe.
Smoking room.
Show cases
Doctor
Bureau.
Sitting room.
POOP DECK.
Seamen's mess. 20 seats.
Greaser's mess 16 seats.
15" Waterway.
BRIDGE DECK.
Engineer's messroom.
Dining saloon.
Lounge.
Consulting rm.
Office.
FORECASTLE DECK.
Mast.

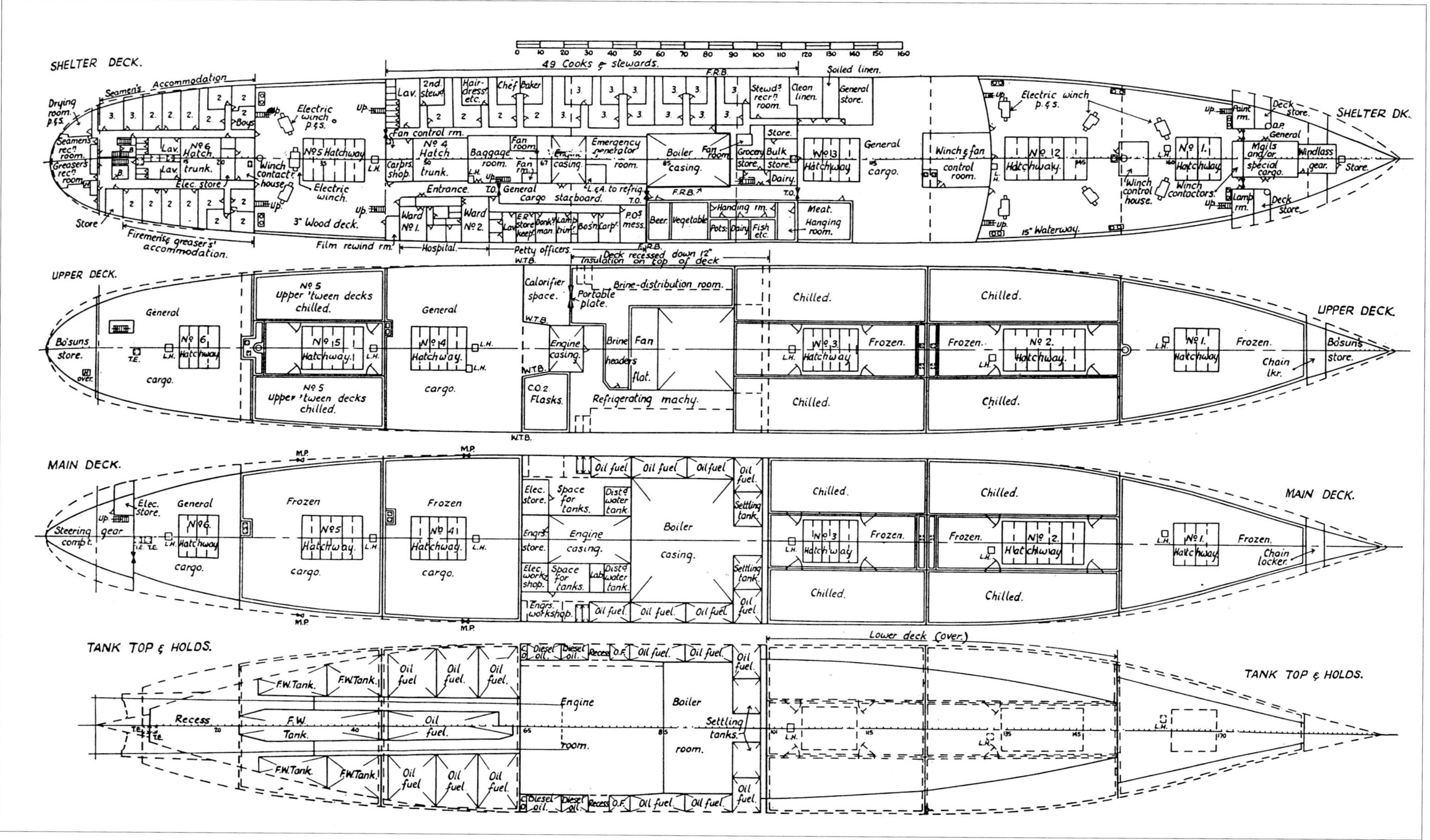

General arrangement plans for *Corinthic*. [Andrew Bell collection]

This page upper: *Corinthic* in the Jubilee Floating Dock at Wellington. *[V.H. Young and L.A. Sawyer]*
This page lower: At Port Chalmers with the Union Steam Ship Company's *Waitemata* (7,364/1946) in the foreground, June 1963. *[Bruce Birnie]*
Opposite page, top left and right: At sea, February 1964. Note the horse box at left in the photo looking towards the *Corinthic's* stern. *[Bruce Birnie]*
Middle: A quite lovely study by Vic Young of the *Corinthic* in Wellington harbour, April 1965. *[V.H. Young and L.A. Sawyer]*
Bottom: Underway in the St Lawrence Seaway with pilot aboard, July 1968. Despite the removal of much of her Boat and Promenade Decks, the *Corinthic* remains a fine-looking ship. At her next port of call the bosun will have seamen over-side to bring the boot-topping up to the same immaculate standard as her hull and decks. *[Marc Piché]*

CORINTHIC

Brand-new, the *Athenic* in Waitemata Harbour, Auckland for the very first time, September 1947. The Auckland Harbour Board's steam tug *William C. Daldy* (346/1935) is partially in view under her port bow, while to starboard a line-handling boat waits to assist with mooring ropes. *[V.H. Young and L.A. Sawyer]*

ATHENIC ASCENDANT

Liner most lovely

Ahh...the beautiful *Athenic*! Finest of the Seas! Embodiment of a now-vanished style of ocean travel that flourished in the middle decades of the twentieth century: ships taking refrigerated cargo plus first class passengers around the world in the most select comfort. Second of the *Corinthic* class and second ship for the UK to New Zealand service to be named *Athenic*, she was delivered at Belfast on 16th July 1947 four and half months after the *Corinthic*. *Athenic* was an exact repeat of the earlier ship: same dimensions, engines, internal and external layout and the same cargo and passenger capacity. But she came from a different shipyard: Harland and Wolff at Queen's Island in Belfast. Harland and Wolff Ltd. had built all of Shaw Savill's refrigerator ships from whose successful design the *Corinthic* class had been fashioned. Like the *Athenic* and her many consorts, the methods by which she was put together have long disappeared. *Athenic's* keel was laid down within six weeks of the ending of the war in Europe; the war against Japan was then at its height and anticipated to continue well into 1946. Ship Number 1326, as she was known until her launch, began as just another war-built austerity merchant ship, expected to go to sea painted all in grey and with nothing of the finish and refinements of a peace-time cargo liner.

Building ships by hand

British shipyards at the time of the *Athenic's* building in 1945-46 were still the same as they had always been: vast, bleak sprawls of factories, cranes, chimneys and tenements along the edges of great rivers. Armies of workers lived and laboured in and around these yards, segregated rigidly into roles, following tradition-based methods and practices with the ships they created. These same methods were applied to the *Athenic* and her sisters. Major changes that came with the introduction of welding, automation and prefabrication were just a few years ahead; during the late 1940s and 1950s Britain's merchant shipbuilding industry led the world but not for much longer.

The process for constructing the *Athenic* began with Shaw Savill receiving a licence during the last months of the Second World War from the British Admiralty. This licence, part of a regime for controlling the use of Britain's shipbuilding resources during the war, specified the yard in which she was to be laid down. The same had occurred with the *Corinthic*. When the licensing system was relaxed after the war's end, shipping companies resumed the procedure of calling for tenders for new vessels they wanted built. Each shipyard interested in bidding would then submit a tender setting out how it proposed to best answer the company's needs along with the price, warranties and how soon the new vessel would be ready.

Once the successful tenderer had been decided, negotiations took place for the writing of a contract that stipulated every aspect of the ship's design, capacity, machinery and performance at sea. As part of this, plans that showed the appearance of the ship were made by the company's and the shipyard's naval architects. Located in the shipyard's design office, the naval architects did all the engineering calculations regarding the new ship's speed, engine power and endurance, draught, displacement, hull shape, trim and stability, types and volumes of cargo to be loaded and numerous like factors. Once the contract was agreed to and signed, the new ship was allocated a yard number: 1326 in the the *Athenic's* case. Her name would not be announced until the day of her launch.

A key role at this stage of drawing up a contract was played by the estimators. These men had first-hand knowledge of the myriad costs of everything their shipyard produced and procured. Forecasting the costs of building a ship right down to the last rivet meant they combined the talents both of economists and soothsayers. The management had to have full confidence in the estimators' reasoned calculations.

Blueprints or working drawings were next prepared, incorporating all the requirements of both the classification society and the flag state. Classification societies - in the *Athenic's* case Lloyds Register of Shipping in London - are impartial bodies that set the rules concerning the strength of ships, the thickness and type of steel plates and frames with which they are built, and the spacing of rivets holding the plates and frames together. Depending on the way in which these rules have been applied for each ship, certificates of classification are issued by the society. This assures the underwriters that the ship is correctly and soundly built and worth the risk of insuring her against mishap. The 'flag state' is the country in which the ship will be registered and by whose laws her design and construction must comply. Port of registry for the *Athenic*, like all her sisters, was Southampton, so she had to meet all the requirements for design and construction that were set out in British legislation at the time including internal subdivision, freeboard height, fire protection and extinguishing, and life saving appliances. If and when these have all been met satisfactorily, a Certificate of Survey is issued to the vessel, in the *Athenic's* case by the British Board of Trade.

Work now started on producing the thousands of individual drawings giving the shape, layout and measurements of every aspect of the new ship. This work was done in the shipyard's drawing office, a large room illuminated by high windows and skylights beneath which rows of long, flat tables were set up. Draughtsmen stood bent over these tables working with stiletto-sharp pencils, ink pens, curves and rulers; their drawings were done on long lengths of linen cloth and tracing paper. During the post-war years printing machines were introduced for making copies of the drawings that had to be submitted for approval to the ship's owners, the classification societies, and to surveyors from the flag states. Copies were also made this way for distribution to the various departments within the shipyard that would be making parts for the ship.

There was also the tracing office, usually located near the drawing office and staffed by women. They produced drawings of the finest accuracy that were traced from the originals of ships' plans, showing her as fitted - in other words, when the vessel was fully completed and ready for sea. These tracings, called general arrangement plans, would later be supplied to the vessels' owners for their use.

The scale lines plans and accompanying tables of data, all prepared in the design office, were next sent to the shipyard's mould loft. This was another huge, window-lit room up to 400 feet in length and 75 feet across, smooth timber-floored and free of pillars or subdividing walls. Here, in a process known as laying off, the lines of the hull were meticulously scrieved or cut into the floor using scrieving knives or sharp, heavy pencils. By this process a full-sized image of the ship was created. Usually made of yellow pine, the mould loft's floor, or scrieve board, was planed afresh after every ship had been laid off. Wooden curves, battens and angles were kept in their hundreds on racks or in the roof trusses; these were cut and fitted together by the loftsmen to match the exact scrieved outlines. Carpentry benches lined the walls of the mould loft for this purpose. The task was immensely complex, a skilled loftsman having to visualise in three dimensions the precise form of every piece of steel needed for the ship, doing so by taking exact measurements from the scrieve board. He then created an accurate, full-sized replica in wood. The resulting templates, or moulds, one for each steel component of the new ship beginning with the keel and frames, were next sent to the shipyard's plate shops.

In the plate shop lengths of steel plate, delivered to the yard from foundries and steel rolling mills, were sheared, bent, rounded, formed, punched, flanged and pressed into the required lengths and shapes for the new ship. Plate-bending rolls and hydraulic presses were used to do this, working the steel to the exact curve and lines of the ship's hull. Rows of rivet holes were made with pneumatic drills, this work being done before shaping of the plates took place. The skilled men who operated these machines, as was the case throughout the shipyard, were demarcated into specific trades each with their own fiercely unionised identity. Also in the plate shop or in a separate framing shop, lengths of steel for frames and angles were heated in long furnaces then bent to the required shape on a bending table. This consisted of large iron plates laid horizontally together on a concrete floor, all exactly level. The plates were drilled with extensive rows of holes into which iron pins and wedges were placed. Using the templates from the mould loft, the precise shape and curve of the frame or angle was marked out with chalk on the bending table, then steel pins known as plugs were placed in holes along the chalk line. Meanwhile the steel was heated to a bright orange then moved to the bending table by crane. Using sledgehammers, levering tools and wedges, the ironsmiths worked as quickly as they could to push, bend and turn the steel to the shape delineated by the pins. As soon as the frame or angle was shaped, it was dogged down and its edges bevelled to the proper angle. It was then left to cool. Each completed piece of steel had instructions and identification numbers painted on it, in accordance with the drawings and templates. They were then moved by cranes to store yards ready to be taken to the building berths.

It was here that the steel pieces were put together to become a ship. The job was done by armies of skilled men with a host of different trades working with steel. The ship was erected on a building berth or building slip - open spaces that inclined down to the water's edge flanked on both sides by gantries, railways and tall cranes or derricks. The *Athenic* was built on Number One Slip at Harland and Wolff's Queen's Shipyard beneath the immense 230 feet high, 840 feet long Arrol gantry that had been constructed between 1907 and 1909 by Sir William Arrol and Co. Ltd. of Glasgow for the White Star liners *Olympic* and *Titanic*. Work on the building berth commenced with the laying down of the new ship's keel. For the *Athenic* this took place on 12th June 1945, on the same slip where the keel of *Titanic* had been laid 36 years earlier on 31st March 1909. The keel comprised a series of long, flat, bottom plates laid end-to-end on top of massive wooden blocks stacked one above the other. Shipwrights sighted or positioned these blocks so that their tops were in an absolutely straight line descending in height to the water. With the keel plates laid and joined by riveting, a centre keel girder four feet one inch in height for the *Athenic* was riveted on top of them. Projecting outwards on either side from this girder, vertical and horizontal plates were riveted together by means of angle bars to form the vessel's double bottom. This consisted of the external, rounded bottom of the ship and, four feet one inch above this in the case of the *Athenic*, a horizontal watertight floor so that the vessel thereby had an inner and an outer skin. The space between them was divided into tanks. These were used for storage of fuel oil, lubricating oil, fresh water and for carrying seawater ballast when the ship was at sea. Immensely strong, the upper horizontal floor was known as the tank tops and on this the ship's engines and boilers were mounted on their foundations. The tank tops also formed the bottom of the ship's holds.

With the double bottom completed from bow to stern, the vertical frames were next lifted into place by the derricks or hammerhead cranes positioned along the sides of the building berth. Like tall pillars, these frames marched down each side of the ship 34 inches apart. Each frame was given a number, beginning with frame 0 right aft. Frame 0 was defined as the centreline of the rudder stock, or the after side of the rudder post, depending on the particular style of rudder fitted to the ship. The frames then advanced numerically towards the bow, frame 200 being at the very point of the *Athenic's* bow. From frame 151, which was at the bulkhead separating the *Athenic's* Numbers 1 and 2 holds, the frame spacing was reduced from 34 inches to 27 inches. The spacing was further reduced to 24 inches at the bulkhead separating Number 1 hold and the forepeak. This was the collision bulkhead. A similar reduction in spacing was made with the stern frames; the purpose was to give more strength to the vessel at her bow and stern. Each frame was fixed to the sides or margin plates of the double bottoms. Special steel castings were made for the stern where the frames had to be shaped to accommodate the propeller shafts and rudder. Horizontally within the ship, the frames were braced by transverse steel beams forming the decks, also by longitudinal girders and by the watertight bulkheads.

The *Athenic* was fully framed by 28th February 1946. With framing completed, timber staging was put up along the outboard and inboard sides of the frames, together with rows of horizontal planks. This scaffolding gave access for the gangs of five to six platers under a foreman who fitted the individual steel plates making up the vessel's shell plating (on her hull) and her deck plating. Each plate was lifted by crane then manhandled into its correct position so that it lapped over or under the plates immediately ahead and astern of it. This was called joggling. A plate overlapping beneath its neighbour had an in-joggle, while overlapping on top of its neighbour was an out-joggle. If a plate was not already formed exactly to the right size and shape, a wooden template called a lath was made and sent back to the plate shop. Here the lath was used to cut, plane and bend the plate to the required form. Bolts were used to temporarily secure the plates; a completed row of plates running horizontally along the frames from bow to stern was called a strake.

Now came a process of hanging up - riveting the plates to each other and to the hull frames. Building berths rang constantly to the sound of hammers on steel, a vessel like the *Athenic* taking millions of rivets each one individually heated and hammered. Suspended from cranes, hydraulic riveting machines battered the rivets into place and shaped their heads. In parts of the ship not accessible to these machines, the work was done manually. The riveters worked in gangs of four to six men, each having his own speciality. Hole-borers made the rivet holes with pneumatic drills, reamers smoothed the sides of the holes, heaters - usually boys - worked the small portable, coke-burning furnaces or braziers that heated the rivets. When each was at the required shade of red-hot, the heater tossed the glowing rivets one by one up to the heavily-gloved catcher boy. Grabbing the rivet as it flew towards him, the catcher shoved it into the rivet hole where the holder-on, standing on the other side of the plate, held it in place with a long claw-hammer known as a dolly. Now the two strikers, also called formers, got to work; one left-handed the other right-handed, one on either side of the plate. Fifteen alternate blows from each striker with his 1.8 kilogram hammer was usually enough to knock the rivet down against the plate's surface. As it cooled, a series of aimed blows rounded its edges. Lines of rivets were hammered not just around the margins of each steel plate but in rows down their centres, securing them to the joggled or overlapping plates beneath.

Riveting work, dangerous, monotonous yet requiring great physical strength and skill, was carried out in all weathers often high up on the hull. Gangs worked as fast as they could for they were paid by the numbers of rivets seated. Each gang left chalked symbols on the plates assigned to them, identifying their tallies of rivets completed. Work continued at night if the ship was behind schedule, the building berth illuminated by electric searchlights or by lucal lamps. Pressurised and kerosene-burning, the latter emitted a six-feet-high yellow flame like a blow torch. From 1945 hand-held pneumatic riveting guns had taken over from manual hammering in most shipyards, but these also required great physical strength. Shipyards had nothing of the health and safety precautions required in industrial workplaces today, and injuries were not infrequent.

When a plate had been riveted, along came the caulker. His job was to make the riveted edges of each plate watertight; doing so by grooving the plate edges with specialised power tools so that they were tightly in contact. In the case of the *Athenic* electric arc welding, introduced into British shipyards during the Second World War, was used alongside riveting and in place of the traditional caulking. Every joint between neighbouring plates was filled with a welded seam along the plate's longitudinal edges, and with a welded butt along its vertical edges. These welded butts and seams created a smooth, continuous watertight join that avoided the need to shape each plate where it met the next one. Welding of plates was soon entirely to supercede riveting as the preferred method for building ships, but it was greeted with fierce resistance from some British shipyard workers who saw any introduction of change as an assault by yard owners on their hard-won skills and pay rates.

Within the labyrinth of staging, heavy timber logs called shores were braced against the hull to keep it upright as its weight grew. Once the shell plating of the hull was finished - on 30th September 1946 for the *Athenic* - platers and riveters got to work installing the horizontal steel plates that made up each deck, also the vertical trunkings for the holds, the engine rooms and boiler rooms. Following them up onto the staging were the painters, applying thick anti-fouling paint to the hull below the waterline then coating the above-water steel in the gleaming livery of the vessel's owners.

The launch

Now she was ready for the most critical, the most stress-filled event in every ship's life: her launching. The task was carried out by shipwrights and required very great skill and preparation. As the plating advanced and the vessel's superstructure was built, the shipwrights started work on the floor of the building berth around the stacked timber blocks on which she was resting. These consisted of keel blocks beneath her keel, and bilge blocks under her sides. Here the shipwrights constructed two parallel tracks inclining down to the water, one on either side of the keel, together known as the sliding ways. These were heavily greased with melted tallow. Beneath them, the sliding ways rested on a massive timber support structure called the standing ways. Huge white-painted timber baulks called poppets, reinforced with steel, were erected on the sliding ways under her bow on both sides of the ship (the fore poppets) also at her stern (the after poppets). Their function was to brace and support the vessel like a cradle as she was launched.

As launch day approached, setting up began: transferring the weight of the ship's hull from the keel and bilge blocks to the sliding ways and the poppets. Hundreds of shipwrights lined up along the sides of the hull, each with a sledgehammer or a long ramming pole. To the tolling of a bell they hammered long timber wedges under the hull, their hammer strikes all in unison, to raise the ship off the keel and bilge blocks. Once the hull was on the sliding ways most of the keel blocks were removed. Another contingent of shipwrights checked and adjusted the timber shores to keep her firmly braced as her weight settled onto the sliding ways. Tumbler shores, designed to support the vessel but fall away as she started to move when launched, were placed around the after hull. All the staging around the vessel had gone by this time while, at her bow, the shipwrights built the launch platform and adorned it with flags and colourful bunting. Enormous bundles of heavy steel drag-chains were ranged each in the form of horseshoes along the sides of the building berth, the rounded portion of each horseshoe away from the water and its ends fixed to the hull by wire hawsers. These chains would act as a brake as the ship went down the sliding ways, arresting her momentum so that she did not collide with the opposite shore. Because of the great width of the Mersey at Birkenhead, drag-chains had not been necessary when the *Corinthic* was launched.

Launches usually were timed to occur about half an hour before slack water at a spring high tide, allowing a short margin in case of any last minute delay. If there was too strong a wind, if there was fog, or if the high tide did not produce sufficient depth of water off the building berth, the launch would have to be postponed. During the final hours beforehand, shipwrights used their sledge-hammers and ramming poles to knock away the remaining keel blocks, all the bilge blocks and the final wooden shores. Once gone, electro-mechanical counter-weights called launch triggers were applied and these were all that restrained the ship from slipping prematurely down the inclined ways. She was watched constantly to make sure no movement occurred. The counter-weights in turn were held in position by small timber shores known as daggers.

As the appointed hour of 12 noon drew near on Tuesday 26th November 1946, the top men of Harland and Wolff and Shaw Savill climbed the stairway to the launch platform at the bow of Ship 1326, accompanied by their wives and guests. Foremost among them all was the lady sponsor to whom the honour had been given of breaking a bottle of champagne across her lower bow. Sponsor for Ship 1326 was Mrs J.A. Beasley, wife of the Australian High Commissioner to the United Kingdom. When the sponsor arrived at the building berth it was traditional for one of the shipyard's youngest apprentices, carefully selected and groomed, to step forward and present her with a bouquet of flowers. Below the launch platform, crowds of shipyard workers and their families jostled for the best vantage points from which to see the new ship go down to the water. A clergyman intoned prayers to bless the ship, his voice drowned by the festive hubbub until all was suddenly

Launch day, 26th November 1946 and Mrs Alma Beasley, the *Athenic's* sponsor, is presented with flowers by a youthful apprentice at the foot of the launch platform steps (left). In front of Yard Number 1326's bow (right) she pauses for the camera with bottle in hand, a minute or so before announcing the new ship's name. Bowler-hatted Basil Sanderson, Shaw Savill's Managing Director, is immediately to her left. At far left of the picture, adjusting his coat, is Sir Frederick Rebbeck, Chairman of Harland and Wolff. *[Captain Graham Pepper, Shaw Savill Society]*

hushed by the loud ringing of a bell. On the floor of the building berth the bell's peal set in train a carefully rehearsed procedure. Warning lights at each of the dagger stations told the shipwrights to knock clear the timber daggers on each of the launch trigger counter-weights, and then take out their securing pins. Electro-magnets were all that now held the counter-weights in position. Teenage apprentice shipwrights - dagger boys - then ran as fast as they could from each of the dagger stations, up the building berth to the launch platform. Here, each dagger boy held up the pin and the timber shore that he brought with him, to the yard manager and his assistants responsible for the launch. This was to verify that all the counter-weights were free of their daggers and securing pins. This was known as the dagger race.

All of them had reached the launch platform by the time the clergyman was finished. The yard manager, having confirmed all was now ready, turned to Mrs Beasley who had meanwhile been given the champagne bottle. Decorated with Harland and Wolff and Shaw Savill flags, the bottle lay in a small ornamental cradle suspended on twin wires. Pulling the bottle right back, she spoke the time-honoured words 'I name this ship *Athenic*' and then let go the bottle from her gloved hands so that it swung forward and disintegrated against the *Athenic's* bow. Simultaneously, a button was pushed to cut the electrical circuit to the electro-magnets, thereby releasing the counter-weights. Her bow moved away from the launch platform as down the sliding ways the *Athenic* went. Had she failed to move, hydraulic rams positioned on the floor of the building berth would have been fired by the shipwrights to deliver the necessary push to the fore poppets cradling the ship. Use of these rams was very rarely needed. As she dropped off the way-ends and entered the waters of the River Lagan, the heavy drag-chains attached to the *Athenic's* sides leapt in the air amid showers of rust, slowing and then stopping her sternwards movement. The poppets broke free from the hull and floated clear, as they were intended to, their job done. On shore, the crowds cheered and ran forward, hats were waved and the band played 'Rule Britannia' (or some other appropriate tune.)

The just-launched *Athenic* being placed alongside her fitting out berth. *[Ulster Folk and Transport Museum 9722B]*

Fitting out

Tugs immediately picked up the ship and towed her the short distance to Harland and Wolff's Abercorn Basin, where the *Athenic* was tied-up alongside a fitting out jetty. Work now began on transforming her bare steel interior spaces into cabins, kitchens, alleyways, holds, lounge and dining spaces, bathrooms, machinery rooms and store rooms. Heating, electricity, plumbing, ventilation, fire detection and telephone services all had to be installed. Masts, funnel, samson posts and rigging, anchors, the lifeboats, rails, ventilators, the deck planking, the navigating bridge, radio equipment, cargo gear and a host of other fixtures were put aboard.

One of the *Athenic's* two boilers, manufactured at Belfast, being lifted aboard on 13th January 1947. *[Ulster Folk and Transport Museum 10098]*

Receiving her foremast, 17th April 1947. *[Ulster Folk and Transport Museum 10102]*

Nearly complete but with her funnel still to be painted in Shaw Savill's colours, the *Athenic* is pulled ahead by the tugs *Meadow* (242/1942) and *Southampton* (227/1910) on 12th June 1947. She is passing the Royal Mail liner *Andes* (25,688/1939) undergoing her post-war refit at Belfast while on the *Athenic's* starboard bow, the aircraft carrier fitting out is probably HMS *Bulwark* or *HMS Centaur*. *[Ulster Folk and Transport Museum 10105]*

The work was done by battalions of skilled tradesmen: joiners, pipe-fitters, electricians, locksmiths, coppersmiths, cabinet-makers, glaziers, plumbers, blacksmiths, sheet metal workers, riggers, french polishers, upholsterers, labourers, painters and redlead-ers.

The biggest task was installing the ship's engines. Some vessels were launched with these already on board; the *Athenic* was not. Her turbines, reduction gearing and boilers were all manufactured by Harland and Wolff at their Queen's Island foundry and engine works. Having been fully completed, tested and then dismantled, the machinery was taken to the *Athenic* and hoisted aboard by the shipyard's 1908 German-built floating crane, which was capable of lifting 150 tons weight to a height of 134 feet. Each component was lowered down to the tank tops via the boiler casing and, once there, moved using the overhead lifting beams inside the engine room and placed on its foundations. Installing the myriad of steam pipes, valves, electrical circuits, boiler uptakes, switchboards, auxiliary gear, steering gear, fuel lines, air vents, sea-water cooling, store rooms and workshops was done next. Prior to launch both the *Athenic's* propellers had been fitted to the shaft ends at her stern. From the engine room the propeller shafts extended through the lower after holds to the stern gland, with each shaft enclosed in a narrow tunnel to permit access for inspection and lubrication.

During the fitting out, which would take seven months to complete, the *Athenic's* master, chief engineer and their respective senior officers arrived at Belfast to stand-by the ship. This meant observing every part of her completion, itemising all defects and then reporting to the management of Shaw Savill that the vessel was fully sound and seaworthy. In June 1947 steam was raised in the *Athenic's* boilers for the very first time, closely watched by T.H.K. White, her Chief Engineer. Turbines, generators and auxiliaries were all run and tested with the ship alongside her fitting-out berth. This was a prelude to the next major event in the new ship's life: her sea trials. At 8 a.m. on 15th July 1947 the *Athenic* was taken to sea in Belfast Lough. Her engines were worked up to full power and her speed calculated over a specific distance run. She was turned, stopped, run full ahead and full astern, then steamed at full power for an endurance test all before the critical eyes of representatives from Shaw Savill and Lloyd's Register of Shipping. All the systems and services on the ship were tested. When the master, chief engineer and the superintendents from Shaw Savill declared themselves satisfied that all particulars of the contract with Harland and Wolff had been met, the *Athenic* was handed over. This took place at Belfast at 10 p.m. on Wednesday 16th July 1947. The flag of Harland and Wolff was hauled down from the *Athenic's* mainmast, and the

The *Athenic* berthed in the Musgrave Channel, Belfast on 11th July 1947, a few days before the commencement of her sea trials. *[Ulster Folk and Transport Museum 10437]*

Steaming her trials and picture-perfect. The *Athenic* at full speed on Belfast Lough, July 1947. *[Ulster Folk and Transport Museum 4843]*

house flag of Shaw Savill hoisted in its place for the very first time. A certificate of survey and an international load line certificate were issued by Lloyd's Register of Shipping. The flag state, in the *Athenic's* case Great Britain, issued the most important document of all: her passenger certificate. This authorised the ship to carry no more than a specified maximum number of passengers. Framed behind glass, these certificates were displayed on the *Athenic's* chart room bulkhead, with the passenger certificate hung outside the purser's bureau for all to see. *Athenic*, Official Number 167927, of 15,187 grt, signal recognition letters GBLS, was now ready to begin her working life.

She sailed that evening in ballast for Liverpool under the command of 54-year-old Captain David Aitchison. For the previous four years Aitchison, destined to become Shaw Savill's most famous post-war seafarer, had been Master of the company's motor cargo vessel *Wairangi* (ex *Empire Grace,* 12,804/1942, renamed *Wairangi* on 6th February 1946). Loading of the *Athenic* commenced at Liverpool and was finished at London by the end of July. At both ports the new ship created wide interest just as the *Corinthic* had. In the Royal Albert Dock the *Athenic* took aboard 1,300 cars, 50 tractors and 6,000 tons of bridge-building materials. The cars came by Thames River lighters from the Ford Motor Company's Dagenham

Left: Looking along the side of the *Athenic's* bridge house towards her port wing. The door to the master's day cabin, aft of the wheelhouse, is open at right. An awning has been rigged over the deck space above Number 3 hatch where the photographer is standing. Note the davit structure for the *Athenic's* accommodation ladder. *[Brent Riddell]*
Right: August 1962 in the southern Pacific, approaching the coast of New Zealand and finish of the voyage's outward leg. Derricks have been topped in readiness for opening the hatches. *[Brent Riddell]*

Works. Having embarked a full complement of 85 passengers at Tilbury, the *Athenic* sailed from London on Friday 1st August 1947 to begin her maiden voyage to New Zealand.

The passage via Panama to Auckland, where her passengers left the ship, took one month. From Auckland the *Athenic* called at Wellington and then was berthed at the George Street Wharf in Port Chalmers by 21st September to complete unloading. Some 60,000 frozen beef and lamb carcasses and 11,000 sacks of grain were next taken aboard, the *Athenic* then sailing for Wellington for final loading. Passengers boarded the ship at Queens Wharf.

The pursers and their two legged cargo

Because they were first class ships the clientèle aboard the *Athenic* and her three *Corinthic* class sisters was very different from the immigrants and younger people to be found on Shaw Savill's tourist class *Mataroa* (12,390/1922), *Tamaroa* (12,405/1922) and the four Bay class ships. Passengers aboard the *Corinthic* class ships were generally older and from well-to-do backgrounds: diplomats, civil servants, military officers, politicians, company executives, academics, judges, professional people - many of them travelling with their spouses and families. During the busiest seasons (October to November for the outward leg, March to early May for the homeward leg) the ships always commanded near-full passenger lists but rarely did they number more than 70 to 80. The *Athenic* and the *Corinthic* stayed popular right up until the time when Shaw Savill announced, at the end of April 1964, that they were no longer economic in this role and that, from March the following year, no further passenger bookings would be accepted. Much disappointment was expressed by long-term regulars at this news. There were, of course, numerous other liners on the UK to New Zealand route, including Shaw Savill's *Southern Cross* and *Northern Star*, but none of them had quite the ambience of the *Athenic*. She was fitted with simple yet strikingly elegant interiors that still look every inch as tasteful and attractive as they did in 1947. The dining saloon on her Bridge Deck was a beautiful room painted in two shades of French grey with panelling and columns in banded walnut, maple and sycamore. Fluorescent light tubes, a big innovation for the time, were mounted in wide circular recesses above the tables while long mirrors gave the room an added spaciousness. Nothing resembling the superb Peter Scott mural in the *Corinthic's* dining room seems to have been commissioned for the *Athenic*, but this did not detract from her plushness. Seating was for 68 diners so that, with a full complement of passengers, two sittings were required: 8.15 and 9 a.m. for breakfast, 12.30 and 1.30 p.m. for lunch, and 6.30 and 7.30 p.m. for dinner. Timings were adjusted to 8.30 a.m., 1 p.m. and 7 p.m. if there was just one sitting needed.

The passenger experience aboard the *Athenic* was a delectation of fine hotel pampering and quiet relaxation for which the modern sea traveller, shouldering his or her way through the hordes aboard today's cruise ships, might well yearn. Seasickness was the only drawback; the *Athenic* and her sisters were not fitted with stabilisers. With seldom more than 70 passengers and a long sea voyage of up to 30 days aboard a big ship, there was plenty of space, plenty of time and plenty of attention from the officers and stewards. During the off-peak seasons the *Athenic* and her sisters were often half-full and sometimes nearly empty of passengers, carrying as few as ten.

Key responsibility for passenger care and well-being lay with the purser, whose office (the purser's bureau) and adjoining cabin was right forward on the Promenade Deck. When the *Corinthic* class first entered service the purser also did the job of chief steward on each ship, and he was assisted by a crew member known as the purser's writer. This man dealt with the passenger and crew administration. Then in the 1960s the roles were separated; a chief steward (later known as the catering officer) and a purser were appointed to each of the four liners. Subordinate to the purser was an assistant purser and junior assistant purser. These two men ran the purser's bureau where a host of routine paperwork was done: typing of menus and daily news bulletins, end-of-voyage accounts, all customs and port documentation, varying from port to port; passenger lists, crew lists, allocation of cabins, cashing of passengers' travellers cheques, bar accounts and liquor stock takes, sale of stamps and memorabilia, depositing of money and valuables, forward reservations for passengers, typing up the master's correspondence, distribution of mail, receipt and filing of memoranda from head office and liaison with shore office staff at each port visited. They also handled telegrams that passengers wanted sent by radio from the ship, taking the completed message forms to the radio office and charging the passenger for the number of words to be transmitted.

A tranquil morning in Wellington Harbour as the *Athenic* arrives to load cargo, circa 1956. Note in this view she has the additional samson posts and derricks in front of her funnel, making for faster working of cargo at Number 3 hatch. *[V.H. Young and L.A. Sawyer]*

Voyaging on the *Athenic,* 1962. Top left: Off Pitcairn Island in the southern Pacific Ocean. The island was named in honour of Midshipman Robert Pitcairn who, on 3rd July 1767, sighted the island from aboard the British sloop HMS *Swallow.* Twenty three years later in 1790, mutineers from another British ship, HM Armed Transport *Bounty*, famously settled there. *[Brent Riddell]*

Lower left: Rapa Island, another remote way-point on the Pacific crossing 1,074 km (666 miles) south east of Tahiti. Also known as Rapa Iti ('little Rapa' in Tahitian) and about 4.5 miles in diameter, this volcanic island, part of the Bass Islands of French Polynesia, has a population of about 500. It was first sighted by Captain George Vancouver RN aboard HMS *Discovery* in 1791. *[Brent Riddell]*

Right: A Pitcairn Islander descending the *Athenic's* side by rope ladder to waiting boats. Note the jacket sleeve of the liner's chief officer at upper left. *[Brent Riddell]*

Originally from Bristol, Dick Ashford sailed on the *Athenic* for six voyages from 1952. For the first three of those trips he was Junior Assistant Purser under Eric Scales, the *Athenic's* Assistant Purser. Ashford was then promoted to Assistant Purser for his last three voyages on the *Athenic*, with a junior assistant purser under him. On one of those voyages the then Prime Minister of Australia, Robert Menzies, took passage aboard the *Athenic* from Capetown via Fremantle to Melbourne, where he disembarked. Travelling with his family and a small party of staff, Dick Ashford remembers the ship being met by noisy protests against Mr Menzies and his government from the waterfront unions at both Fremantle and Melbourne.

The chief steward-purser did not involve himself in any of the daily office work, all of which was done by the two assistant pursers. They would pull up the screen door over the purser's bureau at 9 a.m., working at their desks and attending to passengers as they came and went from the counter. The screen came down again at lunch time and remained down until 4 p.m., when passengers could again seek the guidance of the pursers until the bureau closed for the day at 5.30 p.m. Dick Ashford and Eric Scales shared a forward-facing cabin on the Promenade Deck with upper and lower bunk berths. The cabin door was right beside the purser's bureau. Next to theirs, in the port fore corner of the Promenade Deck, was the doctor's cabin while immediately above was the port wing of the bridge. Both assistant pursers took their meals with the passengers in the dining saloon and, following dinner, they organised social amusements in the lounge.

President of the horse race meetings; a willing *Athenic* passenger got up in fancy dress for one of many social events during long, leisured afternoons and evenings at sea. *[Brent Riddell]*

In addition to ship's administration, the purser and his staff performed the role that entertainment directors carry out on cruise ships today. They devised a programme for each evening at sea except the last one, when passengers were expected to repair early to their cabins for packing of luggage. There were themed dances, film shows, treasure hunts, Sunday church services, horse race meetings with jockeys in fancy dress, housey-housey, presentations by gramophone in the lounge of orchestral music plus quiz nights with lists of witty, informative questions to be prepared. Aboard the *Corinthic* Captain Jones would usually give a presentation of colour slides taken at Pitcairn Island. This and the films would be screened under awnings on the Boat and Games Deck, or the veranda cafe would be used. A scrubbed-white canvas screen was rigged above Number 5 hatch directly aft of the veranda cafe, from whose balcony seated passengers viewed the film. Off-duty crew would gather at the aft end of the Bridge Deck, immediately below the veranda cafe and out of sight of passengers, where they also watched the screening. On the second-to-last night at sea, a gala dinner, prize presentation and dance would be held in the smoking room. By day, deck golf, quoits and deck tennis were played on the Boat and Games Deck if the weather was favourable, tournaments being arranged for the more athletic. Listening agreeably to the conversation and complaints of passengers was also a skill essential for the purser, necessary lest any unremedied grumbles find the ear of the captain.

If they were up to date with their work, the assistant pursers could expect a few hours off in the afternoon before reopening the purser's bureau at 4 p.m. Young men in their twenties, they usually socialised late of an evening with the cadets and the second, third and fourth officers, visiting each other's cabins to talk and relax. They rarely mixed with the engineers. But as the homeward leg of each voyage neared its conclusion, any thoughts of leisure disappeared under a mountain of paperwork that had to be finished by the time the ship reached London.

One of the biggest jobs remembered by Dick Ashford was drawing up the portage bill. This was a very large, multi-columned document on which the wages earned by each individual crew member for the full voyage was itemised and calculated. Overtime, pay for night watchman duties, income tax, union fees, deductions and allotments made to family members, wages paid in advance - subs, as these were called; national insurance, fines imposed, payments to officers' tailors: all this had to be calculated for each officer, engineer and rating. Only the master and chief engineer were excluded from the portage bill; their pay was by separate arrangement direct from Shaw Savill's head office. In the right-hand column the sum owed to each crew member when paying off the ship was pencilled in. All the column totals had to add up to the final figure at the bottom right-hand corner. The work was done while the ship was coming up the English Channel, in-bound for the Thames Estuary. Crew pay-off usually took place when the ship tied up in the Royal Docks to commence her cargo discharge, after disembarkation of passengers at Tilbury. Because the portage bill needed to be fully completed and signed off by the master ready to be sent ashore at Tilbury, the assistant pursers had to anticipate the date and hour when the voyage ended. If by chance the *Athenic* was delayed because of fog, tides or some unforeseen problem, thereby lengthening the voyage by one or two days, all calculations making up the portage bill would have to be re-done. And often under severe time pressure. Dick Ashford recalls it as a nightmare job, with total accuracy vital as the portage bill determined the cash handed to each seaman, steward, fireman and greaser.

With the portage bill taken ashore at Tilbury, Shaw Savill staff would board the ship at the Royal Docks with suitcases filled with £30,000 to £40,000 in notes and coin. On pay-off day each crew member stood in line at the purser's bureau and was handed what the portage bill stated; deductions by way of subs paid and fines owed meant that for some there was very little cash-in-hand to show for a three to four month voyage. Discharge books were also issued; these had been held in the purser's safe. Some ratings who had proved troublesome during the voyage got their discharge books back with conduct stamped as DR - declined to report. This meant they would be unlikely to get employment with Shaw Savill again. They got no sympathy as often these men had added to the assistant pursers workload, especially on the New Zealand coast. Deserters, signing on of replacement crew members, men who breached discipline aboard ship, men taken into police custody while ashore, others who were still ashore when the ship left port; all of this occupied both men typing up the requisite forms with endless carbon copies to be filed and distributed.

Highlight of the voyage was always the day-long transit of the Panama Canal, especially for passengers who had not seen it before. Wide shade awnings were rigged by the seamen on the Boat and Games Deck, fore and aft of the funnel, and a buffet lunch was served on deck if the weather was suitable. With no more than 85 passengers there was plenty of room on deck. Aboard the *Athenic* the buffet table served a second, macabre purpose whenever a death occurred among the passengers.

Philip Griffin attended two burials at sea aboard *Corinthic* class ships: 'The lamp trimmer (a deck petty officer) sewed up the body in canvas and the last stitch went through the deceased's nose; if there was life in the body, that stitch would make it kick. The body was then laid on a polished hatch board at Number 5 hatch in the after well deck and covered with the flag of the country the body came from. The ship's company mustered for the service; passengers could attend if they wanted to, most did as it broke the monotony of a Pacific crossing. Cameras and cine cameras were definitely in evidence. The captain read the burial service and then the bridge was signalled to stop the engines; when the propellers ceased turning two quartermasters lifted the inboard end of the hatch and the body slipped from under the flag. A couple of heavy shackles inside the canvas shroud carried the body straight to the bottom. The burial was duly entered in the ship's log book.'

Each day at sea there was a mileage sweep, with passengers invited to calculate the distance run by the ship every 24 hours. Tickets for this cost a shilling, obtainable from the purser's bureau except on Sundays. Passengers devoted much effort into calculating the number of miles steamed and the daily sweep was always well subscribed. All proceeds went to the ship's sports and entertainment fund which could have anything up to £100 or more salted away. Horse race meetings also fomented good revenues and great interest with passengers, their minds agreeably sharpened by the sea air, inventing droll names for their equine mounts: '*Stolen Kisses* by *Philanderer* out of *Sight*', '*Forever Amber* by *Traffic Light* out of *Control*' (Captain Jones's horse) and '*Hopeful* by *Broke* out of *Funds*'. Winners were decided by throws of a dice.

The ship's two Marconi radio officers also played their part in keeping passengers amused. Every day in the radio office they tuned to the broadcasts in morse of world news items from AAP-Reuters that were transmitted from Portishead Radio Station in England. A Radio News sheet comprising two foolscap pages was then prepared. Copies were printed using a Gestetner printing machine and distributed to the lounge and smoking room every morning (from where passengers were asked not to remove the news sheets to their cabins).

At sea, daily visits to the engine room were arranged for passengers willing to confront the heat and the descent by ladders to the very lowest level inside the ship. Engineer George Wood, who sailed aboard the *Corinthic*, remembers they were known as the Cook's Tours. Always at 11 a.m. Chief Engineer Frank Papworth would conduct a small group of passengers, never more than four, around the *Corinthic's* engine room and attempt to explain what was happening beneath the turbine cases and inside the boilers. Opening the spy or sight tube looking into the boiler furnaces was always of interest to the passengers: they could see the oil burning amid swirling flames. Engineers on watch would ensure they looked suitably engrossed in their work as the passengers were ushered past.

The ship's surgeon also came within the purser's realm. He attended to the medical needs of the crew and the passengers for which a fee -10 shillings in 1961- was payable for each consultation. When in port, with crew members free to go ashore after work, the surgeon could expect to treat all repercussions arising from 'drinking saloons, hotels and gaming houses' as ships' articles phrased it. Drunkenness, venereal disease, injuries from fighting or falling, stomach disorders, lice; each time the *Athenic* and her sisters sailed for the homeward leg there would be a queue outside the hospital dispensary, located starboard side aft on the Shelter Deck. The surgeon was also expected to perform operations at sea for casualties both from aboard ship and from nearby vessels with no doctors that had radioed for help. Many surgeons were competent in every respect, others seemed to have been little more than a disgrace to their profession. Drinking, laziness and eccentricity were the principal faults in this respect. Bruce Birnie, who sailed on the *Corinthic* as an engineer, recalls a surgeon who was a former Indian Army officer more interested in washing and grooming any horses the ship happened to be carrying. On one trip, when the *Corinthic* was on the New Zealand coast, the third engineer became seriously ill. Examined by this so-called surgeon, the engineer was mis-diagnosed for three weeks as having gout. Only when Chief Engineer Frank Papworth insisted on getting a second opinion - from the Otago Medical School in Dunedin, where the *Corinthic* was berthed - was it found that the third engineer had rheumatic fever. He was invalided off the ship.

Under the chief steward or the catering officer was the chef (the chief cook), the second cook, baker and the second steward, all of whom had petty officer rank. The ship's hotel services - her victualling department - was run by the second steward who had some 44 male stewards and two stewardesses under his control. They were divided into bedroom stewards, who cleaned and attended to the passenger cabins, bathroom stewards who took care of the bathrooms, the dining room waiters and the bar stewards who served tea, coffee and drinks in the smoking room and refreshments in the lounge. Bedroom stewards were each assigned about eight cabins to look after – known as 'a set of sheds'. There were also the stewards assigned to the officers and engineers. The second steward - a very busy man when the *Athenic* was carrying a full passenger complement - was also in charge of stewards' stores, clean and dirty linen, and the ship's laundry.

The master and the senior officers - the chief engineer, the chief officer, the chief steward and the purser - were required to mix socially with the passengers while exercising discretion in making sure this did not interfere with their duties. They could come and go from the lounge, the smoking room (also known as the bar) and the veranda cafe but all other officers and engineers were not permitted to do so except by invitation. Each evening the master, the chief engineer, usually the chief officer and always the chief steward and purser would be in the lounge for pre-dinner drinks, wearing their mess kit uniforms. Then at the appointed time they led the way through the glazed double doors into the adjacent dining saloon. Dinner was by silver service attended to by white-gloved and starched-jacketed waiters all under the critical eye of the head waiter. Individual dining tables were each hosted by one of the vessel's senior officers and also the second dfficer. On the bridge the fourth officer would take over the 4-8 p.m. watch for the chief officer. The other deck officers, the nursing sister, assistant pursers and the radio officers had their own table in a corner of the dining saloon. In its centre was the largest of all the tables: round in shape and seating eight – the captain's table. Those considered to be in life's higher stations amongst the passengers could expect to dine here with the master. At this table they were served by the captain's tiger, the master's personal steward. He was always a very senior man who could be relied upon for attentiveness and discretion. The captain's tiger cleaned and maintained the master's cabin, served his meals and organised the various receptions, afternoon teas and the like that were hosted by the master for his guests and passengers.

Prior to the commencement of each voyage the purser scanned the list of passengers about to embark and selected those who might join the master at his dining table: bishops, politicians, military officers, company directors, university professors, socialites; anybody considered to have rank or importance. He then submitted the list to the master for his perusal. Some masters detested having to mix and ingratiate themselves with passengers, others relished it. For 12 years Captain G.H. Heywood was Master of the *Athenic*, joining her on the first day of July 1957 and leaving only for holiday entitlements until, in October 1969, the ship was finally withdrawn from service. He thrived on hearty social immersion with his travelling public.

George Halliley Heywood was born 25th August 1907 and joined Shaw Savill on 29th November 1932. Senior masters of that era were seldom well disposed towards their junior officers or cadets. There was very little encouraging or nurturing of junior officers; it was a matter of either performing to the master's total satisfaction or not. In the latter instance, an angry reprimand often would follow. The surest way to offend Captain Heywood and receive the blunt force of his tongue was to make a mistake in full view of the *Athenic's* passengers. He demanded that they see nothing other than a totally efficient, highly trained, spotless ship. Neil Hamilton remembers arriving at Curacao on his first voyage aboard the *Athenic* after joining her in May 1961: 'The cadet and quartermaster were trying to lower the gangway but could not put inside turns on the winch drum. Passengers were lining the

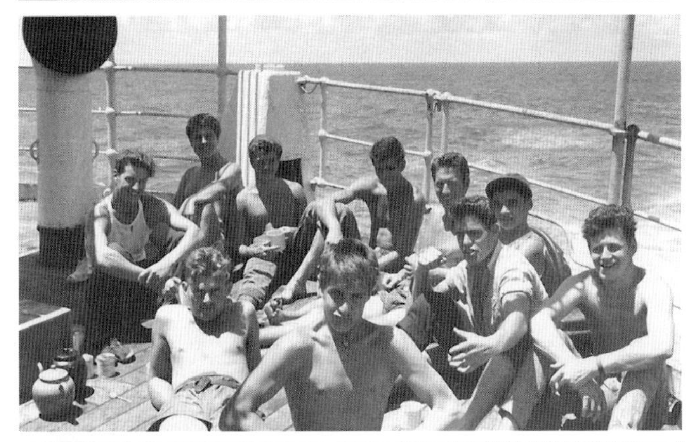

Top to bottom: looking aft from the forecastle head past the windlass and anchor cables, with the front of the *Athenic's* superstructure neatly framed by her forward sampson posts *[Neil Hudson]*. The view from the poop deckhouse, looking towards the veranda cafe with its wrought iron balustrade. An awning shades the starboard side of the Boat Deck aft *[Neil Hudson]*. *Athenic's* seamen knocked-off for smoko, with teapot and cups at left. Behind them, the liner's wake spreads below the stern rails as she crosses the Pacific *[Neil Hudson]*. Sports events for children passengers in 1962, supervised by the *Athenic's* assistant pursers. *[Brent Riddell]*

Clockwise from top left: Inside the *Athenic's* lounge, smoking room, children's playroom, a two-berth cabin, veranda cafe, ladies' hairdressing saloon, private sitting room for the suite, and the dining saloon. The furnishing of the sitting room in particular is exquisite; add a television screen and larger windows leading to a private balcony, and it would be as good as anything found on a cruise ship today. *[Captain Graham Pepper, Shaw Savill Society]*

rails watching. I was sent from the bridge by the master to show them how to do it. When everything was right I went back to the bridge. The chief officer told me that if I had not been able to sort the problem out, especially in front of passengers, I would have been finished as far as Heywood was concerned.'

When the *Athenic* was on the New Zealand coast she was made available as a venue for organisations raising funds, celebrating local events or promoting their business links with the sea. Receptions by Shaw Savill were also held on board; all of it at Captain Heywood's instigation. He delighted in public functions of this sort and expected his officers and crew to prepare and perform meticulously for them. With the ship empty of passengers the *Athenic's* cooks and stewards often had little else to do except contemplate another night's run ashore. The master made full use of this opportunity. From formal dinners and balls to galas and gracious afternoon teas, the great and the good from all walks of New Zealand society were welcomed aboard with Captain Heywood as their ever-convivial host. Regulars were the Meat Marketing Board, the Dairy Board, the Apple and Pear Board, Federated Farmers, the New Zealand Country Women's Institute, various branches of the Honourable Company of Master Mariners, and local Rotary Clubs. There were tours of the bridge and the engine room, visits by school children, sailing lessons for boy scouts, ladies' flower-arranging and book clubs, card evenings and reunions for veterans. As a direct result of all this, the *Athenic* and her sisters became extremely well-known and well-liked, an affection that remained long after they had all made their final sailings from New Zealand's waters.

No further passengers

Captain Heywood was Master when on 28th January 1965 the *Athenic* departed from London on her very last round voyage carrying passengers. Following her return, a fire occurred aboard the ship on 15th May 1965 while she was alongside in the Royal Albert Dock. She put to sea a few days later, sailing for Wallsend on the Tyne and the shipyard of Swan, Hunter and Wigham Richardson Ltd. Here, between 23rd May and 14th August 1965, the *Athenic* was converted to a cargo-only vessel, having all her passenger facilities removed. In the same way as the *Corinthic* part of the *Athenic's* Promenade Deck was demolished to allow the hatches for Numbers 3 and 4 holds to be lowered by one deck, so that working of cargo from these holds was speeded up. Winches, samson posts and derricks serving the two holds were repositioned, the after two lifeboats vanished as did the deckhouse inboard of them, and the crew accommodation was reorganised so that their quarters right aft on the Shelter Deck, under the poop, was turned over to cargo stowage. Her gross register tonnage prior to the conversion was listed at 15,187; it now decreased to 14,248 (net register tonnage was reduced from 8,722 to 7,622 after the conversion). Captain Heywood resumed command of the *Athenic* in her new guise. Former officers recall that, with no further passengers to entertain, he became increasingly morose and withdrawn.

Down in the freezer

Earnings from passengers, even when the *Athenic* and her sisters were fully booked, made only a minor contribution to the ships' profitability. It was the cargoes of refrigerated New Zealand foodstuffs plus, to a lesser degree, general cargoes carried out to New Zealand and brought to Great Britain, that generated the profits for Shaw Savill. The *Athenic's* capacity plan drawn up in August 1965 shows her having 517,903 cubic feet of insulated cargo space throughout five of her six holds (Numbers 1, 2, 3, 4 and 5). This insulated space comprised the lower holds and the area above each lower hold, just as large but divided vertically into layers called 'tween decks. Basically, two types of refrigerated cargo were carried: frozen, where the goods needed to be refrigerated to a temperature below freezing point, and chilled where they travelled best when cooled to specific temperatures above freezing point. All the insulated lower holds and 'tween decks were designed to carry either frozen and chilled cargoes, or a combination of both. Each of the 'tween decks was subdivided into big insulated rooms, known as meat lockers. Chilled lockers were usually in the wings of the 'tween decks, at the ship's sides and outboard of the hatch squares. Frozen lockers were inboard, fore and aft of the hatch squares. They could be used either for frozen or chilled cargoes, depending on the specific nature of cargoes loaded for each voyage. All the lockers had wide insulated doors for easy access; when closed these doors were gas-tight. The *Athenic* was identical to the *Corinthic* in the arrangement of her holds.

The *Athenic* as she looked after having her superstructure cut down to improve cargo handling at Numbers 3 and 4 hatches. Removal of her Promenade Deck in way of Number 3 allows us to better see the big ventilator cowls ahead of her funnel, through which air was supplied by forced draft fans to the *Athenic's* boilers. *[Chris Howell]*

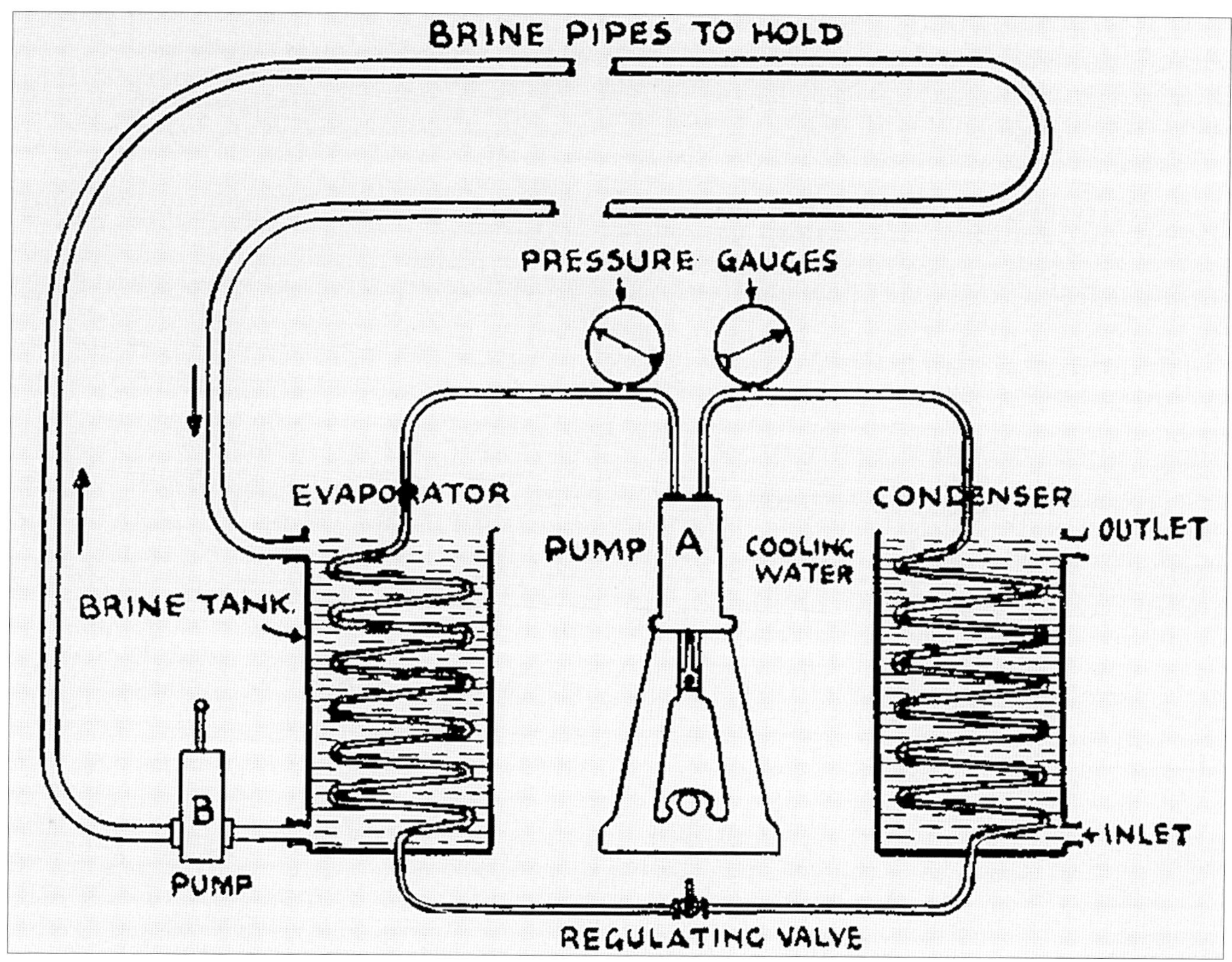

The refrigerating system aboard the *Athenic* and her sisters, taken from and acknowledged to 'The Book of the Ship' by A. C. Hardy (1949). Pump 'A' is the compressor, Pump 'B' is the brine header.

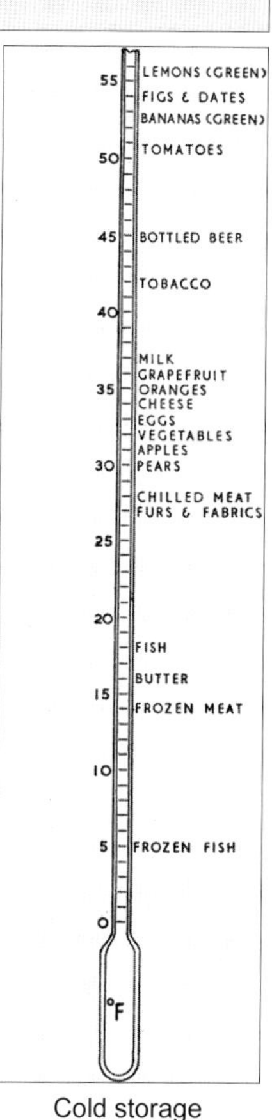

Cold storage temperatures for various foodstuffs and other products. The freezing point of water is 32° F

The *Athenic's* refrigerating plant was housed on the Upper Deck in a series of insulated and non-insulated rooms built around the boiler casing. Largest of these was the refrigerating engine room, housing three big carbon dioxide refrigerating machines of the horizontal enclosed type, each machine having two single acting, forged steel compressors running at 200 to 300 r.p.m. Manufactured by J. and E. Hall Ltd. of Dartford, the refrigerating machines were positioned in-line with each coupled directly to a variable speed, 160 h.p. electric motor.

Carbon dioxide (CO_2) was used as refrigerant. The CO_2 was supplied to the ship as a gas in steel cylinders; these were housed in the CO_2 bottle room which was immediately aft of the refrigerating machinery room on the *Athenic's* starboard side. The refrigerating process involved compressing the CO_2 gas in the compressors and then piping it through coiled copper pipes inside condensers. Seawater was pumped through these condensers, acting as a coolant. This lowered the temperature of the CO_2 gas to a point at which, because of the great pressure exerted by the compressors, the gas liquefied as it passed down through the condenser coils.

The liquid CO_2 then flowed through a regulating (or expansion) valve as it was next piped into evaporators. Like the condensers, these were pressure vessels and the *Athenic* had three of them, housed in their own separate room. Inside the evaporators, the liquid CO_2 passed through evaporating coils that were surrounded by brine. This was calcium chloride dissolved in fresh water, preferably distilled; the denser the mixture, the lower its freezing point. The pressure of the liquid CO_2 was then reduced sufficiently to allow it to boil and change back into a gas, extracting heat from the surrounding brine. The lower the pressure in the coil, the lower the boiling point was and the greater the amount of heat extracted. By regulating the pressure in the evaporators, the boiling point of the liquefied CO_2 could be raised or lowered so that more or less heat was removed from the brine. Thus the temperature of the brine could be adjusted up or down, depending on the temperature required for a particular cargo.

When the CO_2 reached the end of the evaporator coil, it was pumped back to the compressors to begin the cycle again: re-compressed, re-cooled, re-liquefied. The cycle went on continuously, using the same CO_2 gas. Any slight leakage could be made good by injecting gas from the CO_2 reserve cylinders into the suction side of the compressors.

Meanwhile, having been cooled in the evaporators, the brine was pumped into brine headers which distributed it through a system of piping grids around the sides and under-floors of the insulated holds where frozen cargo was stowed. Through use of separate brine headers, the temperature in each lower hold and in each 'tween deck locker was regulated independently of all the other refrigerated spaces. The piping grids formed a circuit, sometimes comprising up to 1,000 feet of 1.5 inch diameter galvanised pipe, taking the brine back to the evaporators for re-cooling. Such were the quantities of brine used that if a breakdown in the refrigerating machinery occurred, the temperatures in the holds would not alter for many hours afterwards.

A different method was employed for chilled cargo: beef, fruit and dairy produce, where the temperature was maintained above freezing point. Brine was pumped from the evaporators to spaces known as air cooling batteries in each 'tween deck. There were 29 of these batteries aboard the *Athenic*, each lined with brine pipes. Air drawn into the batteries, chilled by contact with the pipes, was then blown through the 'tween decks by electric fans. Circulation of cold air prevented stagnant pockets of CO_2, produced naturally as fruit ripens, from forming around the fruit cargo.

A refrigerated cargo from New Zealand comprised a variety of meat, fruit and dairy products, firstly: frozen butter in the lower holds, where its weight helped with the ship's stability. Butter boxes were made of New Zealand native Kahikatea wood, used because it was lightweight, clean and odourless, until these were replaced later by cardboard cartons as the Kahikatea forests became exhausted. Cheese was crated - two rounds of cheddar per wooden crate - and transported as chilled cargo either in the lower holds on account of its weight, or in the 'tween decks. Because it was chilled and not frozen, cheese could not be carried in the same lower holds as butter. Cardboard cartons were also used later for cheese, which was then no longer shipped in rounds but in blocks. Apples and pears in pine boxes were similarly carried in the 'tween decks. Boxed or cartoned fruit had to be kept separate as the gases released from one type of fruit could prematurely ripen and spoil other fruit. Frozen lamb and mutton carcases wrapped in muslin mutton cloth were stowed fore-and-aft in the lower holds and in the 'tween decks lockers, the temperatures inside of which were lowered for frozen cargo when they were not being used for chilled beef.

Offal such as liver and kidney along with chilled beef quarters were also loaded; the chilled beef, if carried, was hung from steel hooks in the chilled meat lockers. The length of the voyage to Britain meant there were some risks in transporting meat as chilled, not frozen if because of hold-ups the ship exceeded the time for delivering chilled beef in best condition. Lamb and mutton were always carried frozen, never chilled. Towards the end of their lives the *Athenic* and her sisters loaded cartoned meat, either chilled or frozen, for markets other that Britain.

There was no refrigeration in Number 6 hold, Number 4 hold at Upper Deck level (the upper 'tween deck of this hold) or in Number 3 at Shelter Deck level. All of these spaces held general cargo, amounting to 172,004 cubic feet in total: bales of wool, sacks of grain and seeds, tins of milk powder, casein, hides, pelts and skins, boxes of canned meat and drums of tallow.

Three refrigerating engineers were carried on the *Athenic*, ranked according to seniority and known as the chief freezer, second freezer and third freezer. They led very busy lives for it was vital that exact and even temperatures be maintained in each area of the insulated holds, depending on the particular refrigerated cargo and the temperatures necessary to keep it in best condition. For instance, prime beef was carried chilled so that its appearance was not degraded. Chilled beef commanded a much higher price when it reached Smithfield Market and thus it received special attention when unloaded, having to be rushed up to the market unlike the frozen meat which could lie in storage for years. Inferior beef would be frozen, as was all mutton, lamb and pork. Perishable cargoes such as fruit had to be kept at specific temperatures without fluctuation.

Throughout the homeward voyage, with insulated holds full and the refrigerating plant in continuous operation, the freezer engineers each stood a four-hour watch every 12 hours. During their watches they routinely checked the lower hold and 'tween deck temperatures, unscrewing the caps to sounding pipes on the weather deck and hauling up mercury thermometers from where they had been positioned while the cargo was being loaded. Only in exceptional circumstances might the engineers go into a refrigerated hold fully stowed to the deckheads, while at sea. Access to the holds was via booby hatches, small lockable openings separate from the main hatchways either out on deck or inside the mast houses or nearby superstructure. Ladders bound with rope led down into the refrigerated depths of the hold; those interconnecting the 'tween decks were usually at a 45 degree angle or thereabouts but in the polar darkness of the lower holds they were generally vertical. To suffer an accidental fall in there was to risk freezing to death or serious injury along with a very difficult rescue.

At the watch desk in the refrigerating engine room the refrigerating engineers kept detailed records of temperatures in each part of the lower holds and 'tween decks. Temperature and CO_2 content in the meat lockers were particularly delicate as they had to be maintained within very narrow limits throughout the voyage. A distinction needs to be noted here between the CO_2 used as refrigerant, CO_2 that had to be injected into the chilled beef lockers, and the CO_2 given off naturally by fruit. Chilled meat stored in an atmosphere containing 10 per cent of carbon dioxide would keep sweet and free from mould or bacterial growth for extended periods. Along with the constant monitoring of temperatures the freezers had to keep every part of the refrigerating machinery in full working order. A chief engineer might consider his turbines and boilers to be the heart of the ship; the master would see his navigating bridge as the ship's brain, but it was this refrigerating machinery that was the vessel's true source of economic life. It kept in prime condition merchandise worth an enormous amount of money and the backbone of Shaw Savill's profits. Ultimately it did not matter if navigation on the bridge was faulty or if the main engines stopped. As long as the refrigerating plant continued operating, the ship could still be towed to port and her cargo landed for payment.

Carbon dioxide was one of the three industrial refrigerants used during the period when the *Athenic* and her sisters were built, methyl chloride and ammonia being the other two. Because it was the cheapest and being an inert gas, non-poisonous, odourless, and non-corrosive, CO_2 was the favoured marine refrigerant. It had, however, two disadvantages. The first was that the natural boiling point of CO_2 is very low, which means that it had to be compressed to very high pressures (over 1,000 lbs per sq. ins) to bring it to the conditions where it would vaporise and condense at the normal temperatures of a refrigerating machine. The second disadvantage is that its critical temperature is about 88 degrees Fahrenheit which falls well within the range of seawater temperatures. At its critical temperature and above, it is impossible to liquefy the gas no matter what pressure it is subjected to, and as part of the circuit depends upon condensing the gas in a condenser cooled by circulation of seawater, great difficulty was experienced when in tropical waters with their higher temperatures. For the *Athenic* and her sisters this was particularly evident in the Caribbean Sea between Panama and Curacao.

The holds themselves were heavily insulated with granulated cork and fibreglass. Some 185 tons of fibreglass was fitted as hold insulation aboard the *Athenic* and *Corinthic*. It was packed between two layers of tongue-and-groove wooden boards that lined the sides, floors and deckheads of each lower hold and 'tween deck. On the outward leg from London, the insulated holds were used for carrying general cargo, with the refrigerating plant deactivated. The London dockers were masters at shifting and fitting heavy boxed items of cargo of varying sizes into tight spaces, so that all of the hold space was filled. Lengths of timber known as tomming were nailed up to secure the cargo in place for the long voyage out to New Zealand, against the movement of the ship. Additional timber dunnage was laid as flooring underneath cases in the holds and 'tween decks to facilitate access for slings and strops owned by the respective stevedoring companies. These slings and strops were removed after loading and then, at the end of the voyage, re-inserted for discharge. All this wood had to be replaced in New Zealand each time the cargo from Britain and the Continent was discharged and before refrigerated cargo could be loaded for the return voyage. Local carpenters were engaged to rip out the used timber; with this having to be done every voyage the labour and the quantities of timber needed were prodigious. Some of the wood was employed again in general cargo spaces but a good part of it, despite strenuous controls imposed by government authorities, found its way into a lucrative black market trade especially during the post-war years when there were major shortages of building materials in New Zealand. Sawdust from the carpenters' work, supplemented by large quantities brought aboard in bags, was laid as insulation in the 'tween decks beneath the timber flooring where general cargo was to be stowed above spaces filled with refrigerated cargo.

On the waterfront
Along with other major shipping companies Shaw Savill had a large shore-based infrastructure in both New Zealand and Australia. Head Office in New Zealand was at No. 1 Brandon Street, Wellington, Shaw Savill also having branch offices at Auckland and Christchurch. Their job was to handle the myriad practical and administrative details of ship operations: obtaining cargoes, getting them to the wharves for loading, passenger bookings, mid-voyage repairs and refits, crewing, services needed by ships in each port, supply of food, water and other consumables, compliance with customs, marine, health and other government departments. At smaller ports where the company had no shore staff, ships' agents did this work.

In port, stowing the refrigerated cargo in the lower holds was the responsibility of the deck officers and cadets under the chief officer. In overall charge of loading operations for all Shaw Savill ships on the New Zealand coast were the head stevedores, each of whom was a certified master. In smaller ports where there was no head stevedore, the role was performed by the local agent. Beneath the head stevedore was a hierarchy of men: stevedores, responsible for loading the company's ships berthed at each of the ports while aboard each ship, answering to the stevedores, were the foremen-in-charge. The chief officer usually liaised with the stevedore or, in his absence, the foreman-in-charge regarding day-to-day loading work.

The job of the chief officer was to ensure the different types of produce coming aboard were all stowed in their correct places in the holds, with all space utilised fully and efficiently and all goods stowed tightly against the motion of the ship at sea. This necessitated deck officers clambering over piles of boxes and cartons coming aboard to ensure the stowage was being properly carried out by the New Zealand watersiders. In addition to rigging temporary lights and rope guardrails in the holds, it was the job of the cadets to keep a record of where cargo was being stowed. This was for the second officer's master cargo plan. Cadets also assisted the officers to measure up the amounts of space remaining in the lower holds and 'tween decks as cargo loading progressed. Thermometers in hand, the refrigerating engineers were also in attendance, moving constantly about the cargo as it was unloaded from rail wagons alongside the ship, testing to make sure it was frozen or chilled right through and in good condition.

Other than setting up the cargo gear and opening the hatches prior to the commencement of discharge or loading, the seamen were not involved in cargo work. While in port they carried on with usual maintenance jobs around the vessel. The most common task was painting the hull of the ship on the side outboard from the wharf. Cargo handling was the exclusive fiefdom of the watersiders - the wharfies and their union leaders. There was no love lost between them and a ship's crew; the very well-paid wharfies aroused such enmity that generally the seamen and watersiders kept to themselves. Whatever the stevedores might aim

Chilled cheese rounds in their timber crates coming off a rail wagon on the Wellington wharves, ready to be hoisted aboard for stowing in a ship's refrigerated holds.

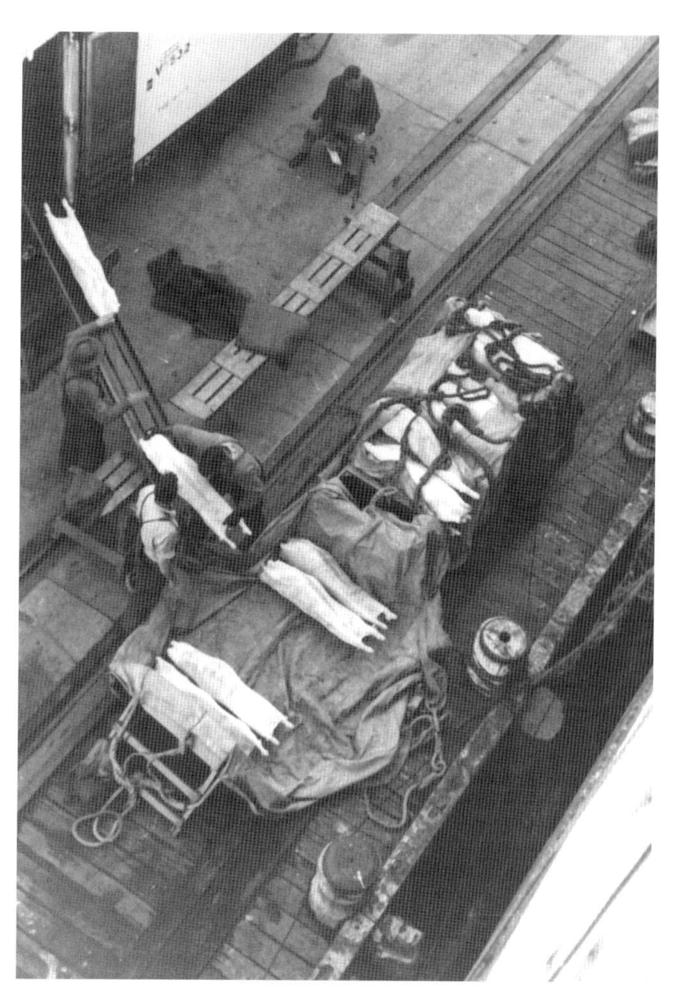
Frozen meat carcasses exiting the rail wagon that has delivered them to the wharf. They are being placed in canvas slings ready for lifting aboard by the ship's derricks.

for in terms of loading timetables, the pace was set by the wharfies. Working in gangs, they did the heavy physical labour in the holds, lifting, carrying, heaving and stacking individual pieces of break bulk cargo. They also operated the ships' derricks and winches for lifting the cargo, they opened and closed the hatches at the start or finish of each working day, and they rigged tarpaulin rain covers known as tents over the open hatchways. At the first hint of rain all loading work ceased; rainwater frozen between stacked carcases and boxes meant the refrigerated cargo could not be unloaded in Britain without damage.

The work in the lower holds and 'tween decks was back-breaking and tedious; it was also very cold for the vessel's refrigerating plant would be running as the freezer cargo came aboard. Each box of butter weighed 56 pounds (25.5 kg). Some 200 to 300 wharfies laboured deep in the holds stacking these boxes: with 11-hour days the job took up to three weeks. Under their notorious spelling system, only half to two-thirds of these men would be working at any one time; the rest would be on 'ups' - out of the holds having a quiet smoke in the sun (or elsewhere, their prolonged absence deliberately unnoticed). This meant that the gangs in the holds and 'tween decks typically had double the number of men required for the job.

After the butter boxes came the frozen lamb and mutton carcasses. These were brought to the ship's side in insulated rail wagons and pushed out of the wagon doors onto the wharf via steel rails. Each carcass in its mutton cloth wrapping was then picked up and manhandled by the wharfies into a cargo net which, loaded with approximately 50 carcasses, was lifted aboard and down into the hold by the wharf cranes or ship's derricks. The wharfies in the lower holds and 'tween decks had to race to clear the net of its load, lifting and moving the carcasses on their shoulders, before the crane or derrick hook once again appeared overhead, lowering the next net filled with carcasses down to them. When lockers in the wings of a hold or 'tween deck were being filled, the carcasses often had to be moved a considerable distance from the net. Working to keep ahead, the wharfies described their lot as 'under the hook'. Big reefer ships like the *Athenic* and *Corinthic* took many tens of thousands of carcasses. In the 1960s the New Zealand ports of Bluff and Timaru installed all-weather meat loaders - mechanical conveyor systems which replaced the nets, cranes and hooks but the wharfies still had to move and stow carcasses individually. Lamb carcasses invariably were big and heavy: *Corinthic* engineer George Wood recalls Chief Engineer Frank Papworth watching the loading one day at Bluff: "If that is lamb, they must be cross-breeding the sheep with elephants now!'

The *Athenic* and her sister liners had one particular drawback when working cargo, and that was the limited deck space in which to stow hatch beams, tarpaulins, plugs and wooden hatch slabs while working the lower holds. The insulated lockers on each side of the 'tween decks, with clear access needed to their wide doors, severely restricted the available space. At Numbers 3 and 4 hatches the problem was worse as the flush timber decking had to be removed and stowed before these hatches could be opened, adding to the general clutter.

If there was a shortage of wharf labour, a ship's crew would be offered work. Neil Hudson, who sailed as a seaman aboard the *Athenic* from October 1956 to January 1957, recalls: 'We were able to spend a number of days loading frozen lamb carcasses while the ship was alongside at Queen's Wharf West at Auckland. She had brought a large quantity of steel out from the UK for building the Auckland Harbour Bridge. Casual wharf workers like us were known as seagulls and we worked from 9 a.m. to 9 p.m each day, for which we received four pounds, four shillings and eight pence for a day's labour.'

Membership of the watersiders' trade union was compulsory and the unions were ferociously led and highly militant. Work slowed or stopped frequently as the men exercised their considerable powers to disrupt and delay when the higher wages and improved conditions they sought were not forthcoming. Strikes, walk-outs, picket lines and go-slows - many of them in sympathy with other New Zealand labour unions - were commonplace. Industrial labour troubles filled the newspaper headlines during the 1950s, 1960s and 1970s. The employers were just as determined; responding with lock-outs and use of scab labour. 'Scabs' were men not belonging to the unions employed to work cargo during strike action. They aroused the most vociferous hatred and protests.

Alongside this were the many tricks and scams contrived by the wharfies for hitting back at the despised employers and shipowners. Typical of these involved wharfies suddenly slowing down the final loading of a ship's cargo on sailing day, with pilot and tugs standing by to get the ship off the berth and out of harbour. As departure time approached and work in the holds reduced to a crawl, threatening to prevent the vessel from sailing, the master and stevedore became more and more frantic. Then, once payment of overtime to the wharfies had been agreed to and guaranteed so as to get the ship away, the pace of work miraculously accelerated. Loading would be completed faster than normal with plenty of time before sailing. The wharfies still got their full overtime.

In addition to assisting the officers, ships' cadets were posted around the holds to watch for cargo pilfering. Standing and watching was about as much as they could do; the cadets had no means of stopping them should the thieves be careless enough to allow their activities to be spotted. Pilfering and broaching the cargo was widespread. *Corinthic* engineer George Wood remembers a Shaw Savill stevedore in Auckland known as The Hood. A big, larger-than-life ex-seaman, he had a special hatred for pillagers. Despite his vigilance, potential for crime abounded. As well as ships' crews and the armies of wharfies, numerous carpenters and their labourers worked in the holds tomming off the cargo stows. This involved temporarily bracing and wedging the stacked boxes, casks, sacks, drums and bales in partially-filled holds as the ship moved from port to port around the coast of New Zealand, loading her cargo for Britain.

It was Shaw Savill's usual practice that, before appointing an engineer as chief, he sailed at least one voyage as first or chief refrigerating engineer. The refrigerating engineers came under the command of the *Athenic's* chief engineer. For just over eleven years from 27th July 1955 to 1st September 1966, this position was held by Francis William White who was born in England on 14th October 1904. His remarkable tenure, surpassing that of Chief Engineer Frank Papworth on the *Corinthic* (July 1954 to May 1965) came after a distinguished 29-year record with Shaw Savill.

The London docks

Shaw Savill's home port was London. The Royal Docks were completely surrounded by high walls and fences with entrances guarded by the Port of London Authority's own police force. By day thousands of men worked there, the roads on the landward side of the big cargo sheds choked with lorries. At night the docks were near-deserted. Seafarers had to walk long distances from their ships to the nearest gate from where they could catch buses. Most of the dock workers lived around the docks in North Woolwich, Canning Town, Silvertown and East Ham. They formed a community and had a way of life the richness and mannerisms of which have now disappeared forever. Captain Ian Condie, who sailed as a cadet aboard the *Ceramic*, recalls: 'Everywhere there were little sheds, cubby-holes and hideaways containing, as they had for generations, people important in their own little ways. These places were generally known as cribs and if a young officer needed some plumbing done aboard ship, for example, it was wonderful what could be achieved if he were to drop in on the plumbers' crib and stay for a mug of tea. Any attempt to abuse or short-circuit the system in this respect would definitely bring offence and prove counter-productive. As soon as the ship tied up in the docks, having arrived fully-laden from New Zealand, the shore labour and repair personnel would swarm aboard, each trade taking over an empty cabin as their crib. It was definitely worthwhile finding out where they all were if you were left to stand-by a ship in port.'

The dockers in London and the United Kingdom were equally militant and ran a closed shop, resisting outsiders, interference and change. Ian Condie: 'Cargo was worked by gangs of workers most of whom were called casuals but each company had some gangs called perms who were kept on a retainer and paid piece-work on the company's ships. These men, very well paid in comparison with the casuals, could move an astonishing amount of cargo in an astonishingly short time. Cargo was handled by shore cranes either into or from lighters alongside, and from the quay sides. Hygiene was not a priority; it would have broken a New Zealand meat inspector's heart to watch New Zealand meat being landed on a filthy wharf then thrown into vans to be driven away.'

Final fluster

In late January 1969 the *Athenic* was in the North Pacific, homeward bound with refrigerated cargo from New Zealand. On Friday 24th January a radio call was heard from Sitmar Line's *Fairsea* (13,433/1942) asking for assistance after her engines had been disabled by fire on 23rd January. She had been some 900 miles west of Panama, nine days into a voyage from Sydney to Southampton with 985 passengers. The *Athenic* diverted to the *Fairsea's* position and reached her on the morning of Saturday 26th January. After standing by the crippled liner until a tug arrived later the following day, the *Athenic* resumed her voyage. Eventually the *Fairsea* was towed to the port of Balboa by the US freighter *Louise Lykes* (10,954/1965). The *Fairsea's* old Doxford oil engines could not be repaired and she was later towed to La Spezia for breaking up.

When the *Athenic* berthed at London at the end of that same voyage, it would be her penultimate arrival there. After discharge in New Zealand in May 1969, she loaded a meat and dairy cargo at New Plymouth and Auckland for the Montreal Australia New Zealand Line Ltd. (MANZ Line). Departing Auckland on 3rd July never to return, the *Athenic* sailed for the Texas port of Galveston in the Gulf of Mexico where she arrived on 27th July

1969. Discharge of her refrigerated cargo continued at New Orleans, Charleston South Carolina, Philadelphia, New York and Boston. The very last items of cargo were taken out of her holds at Montreal in mid-September 1969 and she left that port of the 19th. Captain Heywood was still her Master and by this time he had been notified of the *Athenic's* sale for demolition. He was given orders to steam at slow speed for Taiwan. During this last voyage upkeep of the ship was continued at the same high standard as always, even on her very final day at sea. Empty, the *Athenic* transited the Panama Canal on 28th September, arriving at Kaohsiung on 25th October 1969. Her sister ship *Corinthic* was already there, having been handed over two days earlier. Breaking of the *Athenic* by the Haw Zon Iron and Steel Company commenced on 5th November 1969. She was just 22 years and four months old.

The *Athenic* in U.S. coastal waters, showing the modifications made to her in 1965. Numbers 3 and 4 hatches are one deck lower, with their samson posts and derricks repositioned. The engine room skylight and ventilators aft of the funnel are also one deck lower. Former passenger cabins in what remains of the Boat and Promenade Decks are now occupied by the engineers, while seamen, firemen and greasers have been moved to the engineers' former accommodation on the Bridge Deck. Aft, the old crew accommodation under the poop is now cargo space. With no further passengers, the two after lifeboats and their davits are gone. *[V.H. Young and L.A. Sawyer]*

Above: Two views of the *Athenic* transiting the Panama Canal in January 1957. Left: The canal viewed ahead from the mainmast crosstrees. Right: In the Gaillard Cut with off-watch seamen enjoying the sun and scenery from the poop. *[Neil S. Hudson]*

Below: Two nostalgic views of the *Athenic* in the Caribbean, October 1956, taking on bunkers at Royal Dutch Shell's oil refinery in the Schottegat, Curacao. *[Neil S. Hudson]*

Above: The *Athenic* berthed at Gladstone Pier on the eastern side of the inner harbour at Lyttelton, New Zealand. At top right is the Lyttelton Harbour Board's suction hopper dredge *Peraki* (1,896/1960) while berthed ahead of the *Athenic* is the Board's grab suction dredge *Tewhaka* (324/1910). The grassed and forested peninsula behind the *Athenic* is Diamond Harbour. *[Neil Hamilton]*

Below: September 1963 and still carrying passengers though in this photo she is minus one of her aft lifeboats. It may possibly have been been landed for repairs and survey. *[World Ship Society Ltd. 35056]*

Below: Cargo-only and in her dotage, the *Athenic* at Sydney in 1966. She is lying at Dalgety's berth No 1 in Darling Harbour, which was exclusively reserved for Shaw Savill vessels including all the company's passenger liners. This photo shows clearly how her Promenade Deck was reduced outboard of Numbers 3 and 4 hatches. Her hull's plating in the wind and water area is primed with red lead paint and awaits a coat of black. *[Neil Hamilton]*

Below: A farewell view of the *Athenic*, shown here at the beginning of her very last voyage. She is in the St. Lawrence Seaway, flying the Canadian flag and with her holds empty, having departed Montreal on 19th September 1969. On 28th September the *Athenic* will transit the Panama Canal one final time, then spend four weeks crossing the Pacific before arriving at Kaohsiung and oblivion. *[Marc Piché]*

The deck crowd: youthful seamen on the *Athenic* attending to the ceaseless round of upper deck maintenance. This page: Rigging shade awnings aft on the Boat Deck, and painting the bridge front. Opposite page: Scrubbing the deck planking, rigging the passengers' swimming pool, stripping off old paint ready for new, and knocked-off from work. *[All: Neil S. Hudson]*

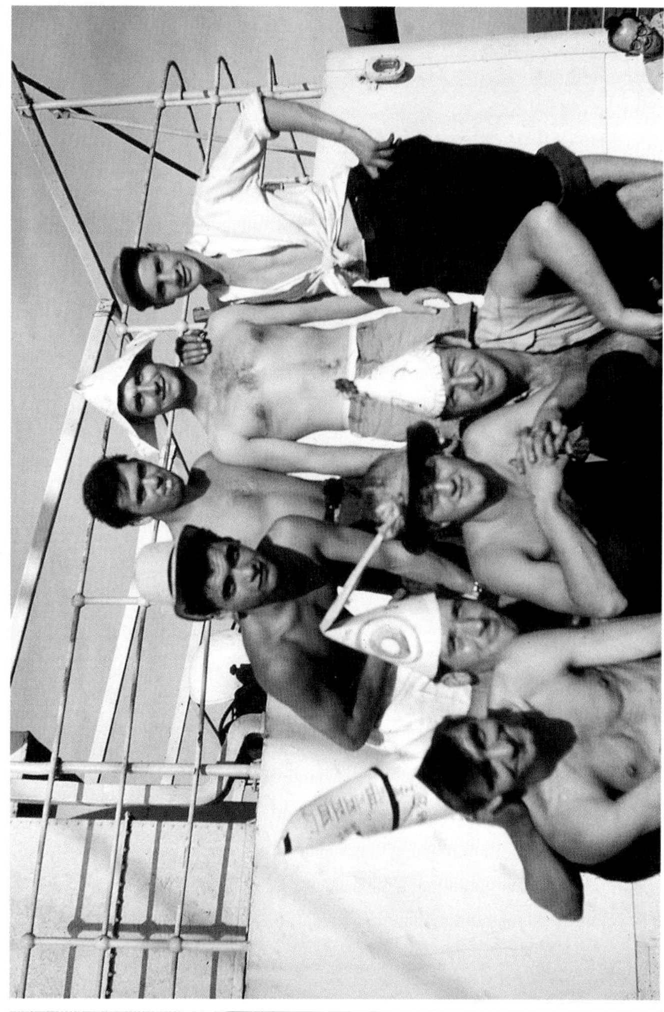

Maritime majesty: the *Ceramic* clears Wellington Heads on Sunday 9th January 1972. This photograph, taken by Vic Young from a small boat, beautifully captures the grace, size and power of the Big Ics. Bound for Liverpool, she looks as tidy as ever but the *Ceramic* will not be returning. Stowed in her holds is her final refrigerated cargo from New Zealand, and this is her last departure from the ports of that country. *Ceramic's* three sisters are long gone, adding greater poignancy to the occasion. Cutting torches will begin their work just eight and a half months from the date of this photo. *[V.H. Young and L.A. Sawyer]*

A *CERAMIC* CELEBRATION

Fairest of them all

In February 1951, having completed discharge in London at the end of Voyage Number 6, the *Ceramic* was sent round to Merseyside and the shipyard of Cammell Laird at Birkenhead, arriving on 14th February. It was her first return to the place of her construction since she departed Liverpool on her maiden voyage in November 1948. This time she went to Cammell Laird's ship repair division, at the northern end of the yard. There her hull was painted white with green boot-topping, for she was to be the stand-by royal yacht for the planned visit by King George VI and Queen Elizabeth later that year to New Zealand and Australia. Rail wagons were shunted to the vessel's side bringing large wooden crates from the firm of John I. Thornycroft and Co. Ltd. of Woolston, Southampton. Inside these crates were steel components for modifications to the top of the *Ceramic's* funnel. Cranes hoisted the fin-like structure with its domed centre into position and the riveters got to work. Variously known as the Thornycroft funnel top or bonnet, or smoke and fume raising device, it added 12 feet to the height of *Ceramic's* funnel. Square intakes in front and horizontal louvres on each side were designed to create an airflow across the top of the funnel, propelling smuts and gases from the boiler uptakes out over the stern of the vessel instead of down onto her decks.

The date when the funnel top was hoisted into place is not known but when the *Ceramic* emerged from Cammell Laird's yard in mid-April 1951 she was a transformed ship. It was not so much the white hull; many consider her to have looked much better in black. Her white paint soon became disfigured when she commenced loading her next cargo for New Zealand. Previously just another of Shaw Savill's *Corinthic* class, simply by the addition of this funnel top she now gained a quite remarkable power and grandeur of appearance. It marked her out immediately from the *Corinthic* and *Athenic*, which were never given Thornycroft funnel tops and visually became less noble as a result. The *Gothic*, to be inducted as royal yacht two years later, also received this extension to her funnel. Having come from a different shipyard, she lacked the *Ceramic's* neat, pleasing rows of identical stanchions evenly spaced along both her Promenade and Bridge Decks. Arguably the *Ceramic* was the best-looking, most eye-catching of all the passenger-carrying Big Ics, a distinction given to her in large part by that one modification to her funnel.

Cammell Laird and Co. Ltd. was the only shipbuilder to produce two of the *Corinthic* class, the *Ceramic* following the *Corinthic*, first of the quartet, by some 19 months. Shaw Savill had been very pleased with the *Corinthic* and had no hesitation in accepting the tender submitted from Cammell Laird for building the third member of the class. The order for her was by letter dated 18th January 1946 from John Macmillan, Shaw Savill's Managing Director, and the contract was signed on 31st December 1946. Keel laying for Yard Number 1185 occurred on 12th November 1946 at Slipway Number 6 situated in Cammell Laird's south yard at Birkenhead. She benefited from all the experience gained with the *Corinthic,* in particular having one foot of width added to her beam

In Wellington harbour, 3rd March 1950. No passengers are aboard; the *Ceramic* is working cargo on the New Zealand coast. Note the labyrinth of awning spars above her bridge house. Two samson posts, each rigged with two derricks, occupy the limited space on top of this deck house at its aft end along with ventilation fans and four big electric winches side-by-side. The awning spars must have greatly constricted the operation of this gear serving Number 3 hatch. *[V.H. Young and L.A. Sawyer]*

Ceramic with white hull in Gladstone Dock, Liverpool, loading outwards. *[World Ship Society Limited]*

for improved stability. Another distinguishing feature was the *Ceramic's* rounded, soft nose bow as opposed to the straight bar type of the *Corinthic* and *Athenic*. Launch into the Mersey took place on the high tide at 12 noon on Tuesday 30th December 1947. The day was recorded as fine, sunny and cold with a slight mist and no wind. Mrs Isobel Keville, wife of William Errington Keville CBE, Director and General Manager of Shaw Savill, performed the launch ceremony. At the celebratory luncheon held afterwards in Liverpool, Mrs Keville was presented with 'a pearl necklet and ear studs, gifts of her own choosing' by Sir Robert Johnson, Chairman of Cammell Laird, in appreciation for her role as the *Ceramic's* sponsor.

The name selected for the new ship commemorated an earlier Shaw Savill liner lost in an especially brutal torpedoing during the Second Word War. Under the command of Captain H.C. Elford, *Ceramic* (18,713/1913) had been on passage from Liverpool to Sydney via Durban when, around midnight on 6th-7th December 1942 in mid-Atlantic, west of the Azores, she was sunk by the German submarine U 515. Six hundred and fifty four lives were lost, a toll so horrendous that, when it was announced in 1947 that the new ship would be named *Ceramic*, letters were published in 'The Times' both for and against the decision. Basil Sanderson, Chairman of Shaw Savill, replied that the company's only intention was to honour the memory of the *Ceramic* and all those aboard her who had perished. The new ship would indeed prove a fine and distinguished successor.

After fitting out and successfully running trials, the *Ceramic* began her maiden voyage from Liverpool on Tuesday 16th November 1948. She was under the command of one of Shaw Savill's veteran masters, Captain A.V. Richardson. An Australian by birth, Arthur Victor Richardson was 60 at the time and had been a passenger liner master for almost 20 years. He joined the *Ceramic* at Birkenhead on 8th October 1948, three weeks before her sea trials, and remained with her until transferring to the *Gothic* on 9th October 1951. Captain Richardson was to have been the *Gothic's* Master for the royal tour that was cancelled following the death of King George VI on 6th February 1952. The *Gothic* proved to be Arthur Richardson's final ship. He retired on 30th April 1953, aged 65, and was awarded an OBE in the Coronation Honours List of that year.

The *Ceramic* berthed at Auckland on Friday 17th December 1948 after a 31-day passage from Liverpool via Panama. During the first seven days of her maiden voyage the new liner had been caught in a particularly severe Atlantic storm. Spray was recorded as going over her bridge to a height of 60 feet above the sea. Speed had to be reduced so that during one 24-hour period she steamed 206 miles compared to her best day's run of 445 miles. Aboard the ship were 80 passengers who disembarked at Auckland, after which the *Ceramic* sailed immediately for Wellington where she arrived the following day. Here, discharge of her cargo commenced, most of it British-made cars. Captain Richardson, in New Zealand for the first time in two years, was interviewed by a reporter from 'The Dominion' newspaper: 'She is exceptionally steady, and there is remarkably little vibration with the new type of impulse turbine with which she is equipped. She differs slightly from her sister ships, her beam and horsepower being slightly greater – and when run-in will be capable of more than 20 knots'. From Wellington the *Ceramic* went to New Plymouth to load her very first refrigerated cargo.

Ceramic, Official Number 182344, was a steam ship of 15,896 grt. Her general arrangement plans, showing her as built, state that she was 530 feet exactly in length between perpendiculars, with a 72 feet moulded breadth and a moulded draught of 43 feet 4½ inches. These same plans show the anti-aircraft weaponry that was to be fitted to the *Ceramic's* Boat and Games Deck should the expected sequel to the just-finished world war become reality. Twin Oerlikon guns would occupy circular tubs at the outboard end of each bridge wing. Aft of these, outboard of Number 3 hatch on the Boat and Games Deck, were to be twin 40mm Bofors STAAG mountings, one to port and one to starboard. Each weighed an extraordinary 17 tons, was radar controlled and hydraulically powered, and each came with its own stand-by diesel generator. STAAG was short for stabilised tachymetric anti-aircraft gun; such was its size, complexity and temperamental nature that it was also known as 'the antlered beast'. Another set of Bofors guns each with its own director was to be positioned at the aft end of the Boat and Games Deck. None of this stability-destroying arsenal was ever put aboard the ship.

'Lloyd's Register' for 1970-71 states that the *Ceramic's* draught when fully loaded was 29 feet seven inches. Her length overall is given as 561 feet, with her length between perpendiculars as 530 feet 11 inches. She had 514,386 cubic feet of insulated cargo space and 147,656 cubic feet of non-insulated space.

Design and layout for the *Ceramic* was near-identical to that of the *Corinthic* but, in addition to the Thornycroft funnel top, the wider beam and the soft-nosed bow, she could be recognised from the the *Corinthic* and *Athenic* firstly by an extra deckhouse above the passenger accommodation on the Boat and Games Deck, inboard of the lifeboats. The funnel was positioned on this new deck house, thus giving it added height. At the forward end of the passenger accommodation on the Boat and Games Deck was the *Ceramic's* radio room, plus cabins for her radio officers. They had been transferred to this new position from where they were aboard the *Corinthic* and *Athenic*: two decks lower on the starboard side of the Bridge Deck, just aft of the galley. Secondly, there were no big cowl ventilators just forward of the funnel, four tall mechanical ventilators being fitted instead around the engine room skylight abaft the funnel. A further pair nestled on either side in front of it, making six in total.

The *Ceramic* accommodated 85 first class passengers and the furniture and decor chosen for them also varied from the earlier ships. Spaciousness and sumptuousness were the keynotes and this is clearly reflected in the writings of journalists who were shown over the ship when she reached New Zealand on her maiden voyage. Their reports do not bear the writers' names but, whoever they were, there could be no more eloquent a tribute to the *Ceramic* and the Birkenhead craftsmen who produced her interiors. From the 'Evening Post' of 7th January 1949: 'The most charming in Old World and modern furnishings combines to make the new Shaw Savill liner *Ceramic* a palatial and comfortable home afloat. Satin-finished sycamore, panelled with beams of deep brown, and beige and blue parquet-patterned floors beneath rose persian rugs give the lounges, smoking and dining rooms an air of spacious coolness. This is further carried out in the clean-cut lines of modern armchairs upholstered in beige, pencil-blue, and blonde rose leathers and piped in contrasting shades and seen to advantage beneath soft amber lighting.

Grouped around a wide fireplace, of which the dominant feature is a delightful mural depicting Epsom race-goers of 1820, are winged armchairs upholstered in saxe blue and rose tapestry. Another fine mural in the dining room is a green-toned scene of Thames-side London before the Great Fire. Wide windows are hung with modern curtains of beige tapestry worked in a classic flower design and china cabinets which are set attractively in lounge corners display beautiful pieces of pottery including reproductions of Wedgwood pieces presented to Princess Elizabeth as wedding gifts. Peach-pink walls and green and white waved striped upholstery adorn the verandah cafe with its unstained wooden occasional tables.

Cabins, even single-berth ones, are built in roomy proportions that give the unusual comfort of [ample] walking room. Carried out in the palest pink, green and cream tints, they have highly polished furniture with ample drawer and wardrobe space. Well-sprung single beds replace bunks throughout the ship and most cabins have their own beautifully fitted bathrooms adjoining. Single berths range from £150 to £200 and the one double deluxe suite, priced at £480, can accommodate a family of three. Carpeted in soft green, it is upholstered in honey-coloured satin tapestry with curtains of lime and honey ottoman striped damask. An inset wall radio, writing desk and tables are in golden sycamore. Green and honey with palest green quilted silk bedspreads have been chosen for the two-berth state room. As is usual in ships of this line, special attention has been given to the designing and equipping of quarters for children and the nursery is one of the most pleasant places on board.'

From 'Notes for Women' published in the 'Otago Daily Times' on 15 January 1949: 'Quilted maple, Nigerian cherry, pommele, weathered sycamore, French walnut, and African mahogany are only a few of the rare and lovely woods used for the striking panelling which is an outstanding feature of the interior decoration of RMS *Ceramic*, at present berthed at Port Chalmers. Every section of this lovely ship is perfectly appointed, from the stainless steel galley, with everything of the latest in kitchen equipment, to the spacious lounge, perhaps the most attractive room on board.

Features of the ship that at once capture the eye are glass-fronted bookcases filled with books forming a passengers' library, china cabinets set cunningly in curved corners of the room, and a table-grand piano, standard lamps and huge wine-coloured rugs on a floor of natural-toned wood, smooth and ideal for dancing when the rugs are rolled back in the evenings. Leather tub chairs in a rich jade green are perfectly contrasted with others in wine or figured tapestry, while hydrangeas in tubs contribute a note far removed from any association with the sea. The collection of Wedgwood pieces in the china cabinets is of sentimental and historic, as well as intrinsic value. Those of the greater sentimental value, at least at the moment, would probably be two blue and white jasper vases which had stood on Princess Elizabeth's wedding cake, and historical pride of place would possibly be awarded to a dull green Nelson vase created upon the centenary of the famous admiral.

The outstanding feature of the dining room, a handsome room decorated in shades of rust and reseda green, is a mural of London Bridge as it appeared at the beginning of the Seventeenth Century, when buildings occupied the entire length of the bridge. The smoking room and, opening off it the verandah cafe are a study in contrasts, the former furnished with solid leather chairs in different shades and having a non-skid floor of inlaid patterned rubber, and the cafe, a cool spot during tropical days, with its cane chairs, pale walls and easily opened windows.

Every one of the 85 passengers which this one-class vessel accommodates is assured of a luxury cabin, usually with private bathroom. These cabins, decorated and finished in attractive colour schemes, are roomy and provided with every conceivable comfort, including heaters, writing desks, ample wardrobe space, large dressing tables with wing mirrors, and lavish lighting arrangements, to mention only a few. One luxury suite boasts a private sitting room with loose covers in beige damask, wall-to-wall dull green in both bedroom and sitting room, walls panelled in avodire, a light honey coloured wood with a beautiful grain, and draw curtains of brown and green striped tapestry - a charming room'.

Impulse turbines and Foster Wheeler boilers

Like the *Corinthic* and *Athenic*, the *Ceramic* and her sister ship *Gothic* were twin-screw vessels. Although the product of different shipyards, *Gothic* and *Ceramic* had identical machinery. It was more powerful than that of the earlier two liners, making both the *Ceramic* and *Gothic* two to two-and-a-half knots faster in speed. Two sets of geared turbines, supplied with steam from two high-pressure, oil-fired water tube boilers, gave a maximum 18,400 shaft horse power with propeller revolutions at 125 per minute. Service speed was 17 knots but when new the ships could attain 19.5 knots. It was this capacity for additional speed that resulted in their selection as royal yachts in preference to the *Corinthic* and *Athenic*. The *Ceramic* happened to be in overseas waters at the time when conversion for royal duties was needed, while the *Gothic* was in home waters. She got the nod instead, *Ceramic* becoming the stand-by yacht.

Ceramic and *Gothic's* impulse steam turbines rotated faster compared to the reaction type fitted to the *Corinthic* and *Athenic*. In an impulse turbine the total pressure drop between the initial high-pressure and the exhaust is divided into several stages. Each stage consists of a fixed diaphragm in the turbine case that contains nozzles, followed by a wheel on the rotor with a single row of blades fixed to its periphery. The nozzles direct the high-pressure, superheated steam simultaneously at all the turbine blades, in the form of very high velocity steam jets. The nozzles and blades increase in size at each stage to accommodate the greater volume of the steam as the pressure falls. The turbine blading was made of 13% chromium stainless steel.

The *Ceramic's* turbines were manufactured by Cammell Laird. Each ship had two turbine sets comprised of one high- and one intermediate-pressure cylinder having impulse blading, and a low-pressure reaction-bladed cylinder, with each cylinder rotor driving individual pinions in the gear case. The high- and intermediate-pressure gearing was double-reduction while the low-pressure was single-reduction. For astern running, impulse turbines giving 70% of the ahead power were fitted to both the intermediate- and low-pressure cylinders.

The *Ceramic* manoeuvring at Liverpool on 23rd August 1952. She had received her Thornycroft funnel top the year before at Cammell Laird's yard, where she was built. Note the dark-painted Essavian sliding screens pulled across the aft rails of the veranda cafe. A cargo vessel of the Federal Steam Navigation Company lies ahead of the *Ceramic's* starboard bow. *[John McRoberts/J. and M. Clarkson]*

The turbines in the *Corinthic* and *Athenic* had single-reduction gearing driving the twin screws. Single-reduction means that a relatively small gearwheel (a pinion) is attached directly to the turbine rotor end, driving a much larger gearwheel which is attached by a line of shafting to a tailshaft. In turn, the tailshaft passes out through the ship's side in a sterntube and has the propeller fastened at its end. Double-reduction is applied where the turbine rotor is of a type which rotates at much higher speed, as was the case with the *Ceramic* and *Gothic*. Because of this faster speed, it becomes impractical to reduce it to a usable propeller speed in one step. So a second pinion and gearwheel are fitted between the rotor and propeller shaft wheel to provide a second stage of reduction.

Instead of the Yarrow-type boilers fitted to the *Corinthic* and *Athenic*, steam was supplied to the turbines in *Ceramic* and *Gothic* by two Foster Wheeler water tube marine boilers. They delivered superheated steam at a pressure of 500 pounds per square inch and a temperature of 800 degrees Fahrenheit. Their oil fuel burning system was of the pressure jet type. The boilers were manufactured by the engine builders: Cammell Laird in the case of the *Ceramic* and the Wallsend Slipway and Engineering Co. Ltd. for the *Gothic,* under licence from Foster Wheeler Ltd. Each of two turbo-driven feed pumps supplied all the feed water needed by the boilers, operating on a closed feed system. The feed water was heated to a final temperature of about 310 degrees Fahrenheit using steam bled from the turbines. A steam generator of Caird and Raynor design was also fitted; it took bled steam from either the high or intermediate turbines and provided 6,000 pounds of steam per hour at 125 p.s.i. for oil fuel heating, ship's domestic services and for making the purified water needed to replenish the boiler feed water supplies.

Centrally between the two main boilers at the forward end of the engine room was a Cochran oil-fired vertical boiler. Known as the donkey boiler or auxiliary boiler, it supplied steam to the ship when she was in port with main boilers and the steam generator shut down. The donkey boiler's output was 3,600 pound of steam per hour at a pressure of 125 p.s.i.

Electrical power was provided by two British Thomson-Houston turbo generators driven by high-pressure steam from the main boilers, each with an output of 500 kW at 220 volts DC. They were located one to port and one to starboard on the dynamo flat, a raised platform set athwartships against the after bulkhead of the engine room, 22 feet above the engine room plates. Immediately below the dynamo flat were the tops of the cast-iron gear cases, aft of the turbines. In the centre of the dynamo flat, between the turbo generators, was the main electrical switchboard while along the port side of the dynamo flat were the steam generator and two evaporators. For harbour use when there was no steam for the turbo generators, electricity for the ship came from two Allen's diesel-driven generators each rated at 480 kW at 220 volts DC when running at about 333 r.p.m.

While leaving Auckland for Wellington on 30th December 1953 during the royal tour, the *Gothic* suffered a major engine breakdown when the rotor of her starboard high-pressure turbine bent out of its correct alignment. She was able to continue the New Zealand leg of the tour with the turbine disconnected from the starboard intermediate- and low-pressure turbines, which remained fully operational. The *Ceramic* meanwhile was berthed at the Royal Docks in London. In response to urgent cablegrams her starboard high-pressure turbine was uncoupled, landed and then immediately flown out to Australia. During her 15-day stay at Sydney following arrival with the Queen and Duke of Edinburgh on 3rd February 1954, the *Ceramic's* turbine was installed amid great secrecy by engineers from Cockatoo Dockyard. Four hours of high power steaming trials were conducted outside Sydney Heads, the turbine performing faultlessly as it did for the remainder of the royal tour. Thus did the *Ceramic* share in her sister ship's glory.

Or did she? Captain Sir David Aitchison, the *Gothic's* Master during the 1953-54 Royal Tour, describes the turbine surgery in his book 'Royal Standard Red Ensign' where he states: 'By a most fortunate coincidence the *Ceramic*, sister ship, happened to be in London. She was promptly robbed of her starboard high-pressure turbine, which was flown out to await us in Sydney...' But an examination of the voyage cards for the *Ceramic*, held in the Guildhall Library in London, reveals she sailed from Cape Town for Fremantle on 31st January 1954, just 32 days after the *Gothic's* breakdown. It is debatable whether the *Ceramic* would have been sent into the Atlantic for Cape Town, minus her starboard high-pressure turbine. Or indeed whether there was sufficient time for the turbine to have been extracted from her, then for the *Ceramic* to get from London to Cape Town at reduced speed and be ready to leave the Cape on the last day of January. The *Ceramic* was in Fremantle from 13th to 18th February 1954, and both ships were in Melbourne when the *Gothic* was berthed there, without the royal party aboard, from 24th February to 7th March. It is possible the high pressure turbine was a spare that, fortuitously, Shaw Savill had on hand for a contingency such as this.

Ceramic's chief engineer

Like Frank Papworth of the *Corinthic* and F.W. White of the *Athenic*, the *Ceramic* had a very long-serving, exceptionally capable Chief Engineer. Charles Simpson was born in Aberdeen on 8th December 1902, the son of a marine engineer foreman. At the age of 15 he began a fitter and turner's apprenticeship with Alexander Hall (Shipbuilders and Marine Engineers) in Footdee, Aberdeen, remaining there until 31st October 1923 when he went to sea with the Aberdeen White Star Line. After three years as Chief Engineer on the *Runic* Charles Simpson joined the *Ceramic* in 1955 and stayed with her for the next decade.

Peter Carr was appointed Third Officer of the *Ceramic* on 8th July 1964 when her Master was Captain N.S. Milne and the Chief Officer was C.A.S. Borthwick. He recalls Charles Simpson as 'our delightful and passenger-popular Scottish chief engineer. The Chief was a true artist at deck golf when playing against the passengers. He was a slight, ruddy-faced man, of slim build with a twinkling eye and great charm. The blue-rinse lady passengers adored him especially if he was their deck golf partner. He had a very neat trick of pushing his opponents' wooden pucks into the scuppers meanwhile guarding his partner's puck against attack!'

When he left the *Ceramic* in 1965, until he came ashore on 28th November 1967, Charles Simpson was Chief Engineer of the *Gothic*. He retired from Shaw Savill on the last day of 1967 after 44 years of continuous and exemplary service. Most unfortunately his retirement lasted only a short time as he died on 25th September 1969 as the result of complications during minor surgery.

The deck crowd

Although they came from different shipyards, in all practical respects the *Ceramic* and the *Gothic* were identical. Both had a complement of 22 seamen who lived in two- and three- berth cabins right aft under the Poop Deck on the port side. Firemen and greasers had their cabins to starboard. Each side had its own separate bathrooms and messrooms, the seamen and the engine room ratings following the tradition of keeping to themselves. Their cabin accommodation was quite inferior to that for seamen and engine room ratings aboard the *Persic*, *Runic* and *Suevic*. Space in some of the cabins was reasonable but others shared by two or three men were cramped and prison-like. They had metal bunk beds, small metal wardrobes, a wooden chest of drawers and a fixed slat seat with small table. Warwick Thomson sailed on the *Gothic* as an able seaman during her service as the royal yacht; on seeing for the first time the cabin he had been allocated, he wrote in his diary that it was 'shockingly barren...compared with *Runic's* nice neat cabins. There are three of us in this one, I think the dimensions are about 20 by 8 feet. The three bunks are on the after bulkhead while the three lockers (steel) and drawers are on the forward one. If you can picture a narrow corridor sealed off at both ends with furniture on both sides, then that's our cabin. The deck is composition, not lino, and this makes everything seem so dismal.' The 22 seamen shared four wash basins, two showers and one bath. Always tradition-bound and superstitious of change, the older mariners especially would have noted that many of the bunks in their cabins were fitted athwartships, so as to make best use of limited space, instead of the usual and much more comfortable fore-and-aft (which was the case with all the passenger, engineer and officer beds).

On the Poop Deck immediately aft of Number 6 hatch was a large deck house containing separate messrooms for the *Ceramic's* seamen and engine room ratings. Each was the same size; that for the seamen had two tables for six and two tables for four. A deck boy was assigned to clean and maintain the seamen's messroom and also the seamen's bathroom. Aft of the messrooms, almost right at the stern rails of the ship, was the crew galley. A recreation room was provided for the seamen, another for the firemen and greasers plus a third, minute area for ship's boys. There seems no memory of these facilities amongst *Gothic* and *Ceramic* veterans, most probably because the recreation rooms were so small, cheerless and isolated that they were never used. The seamen's recreation room is shown on the *Ceramic's* general arrangement plans as having only two tables each with four chairs, a writing table for one, and nowhere for the compulsory dart board. The boys' recreation room was just big enough for one four-seater table. The men inhabited their messrooms instead, located up on the Poop Deck with ease of access and plenty of light and ventilation.

Neil Hudson sailed on the *Athenic* as an able seaman from October 1956 to January 1957, signing on at the Connaught Road Shipping Office in London on 10th October 1956. He writes of those times: 'When wanting to join a ship in the UK, a seaman goes into the shipping office and looks the board over to see what ship requires how many crew. These are written up as, for example, 'two able seamen, one deck boy, SS *Athenic* for New Zealand, signing on 10th October 1956'. Once you have selected a ship or run that you fancy, you approach the clerk behind the counter and tell him the ship you are interested in, as well as your rating position. He enters your name in a book and hands you a chit to take to the relevant ship where you present this to the mate. If he thinks you are suitable after scanning your papers showing your previous discharges, he will sign the chit for you.

Then it's back to the shipping office, clutching your signed paper which you return to the clerk. For some reason these clerks, at least most of them that I struck, seemed as miserable as sin, having forgotten to smile from the instant they were born. With an absolute

(From left) Chief Engineer Charles Simpson, at his table in the *Ceramic's* dining room *[George Wood]*. Second officer Ted Buckle *[Peter Carr]*. Chief Officer Arthur Borthwick *[Peter Carr]*. Second Officer Peter Carr *[Peter Carr]*.

At Wellington on 13th September 1970: one of the *Ceramic's* five-ton maximum lift capacity electric winches (left) on the port side of her fore well deck between the Numbers 1 and 2 hatches. Part of the mast house with derrick heels can be seen at left. [*Russell Priest*]. Looking along the portside alleyway of her Bridge Deck (right). Note the double teak doors into the forward lounge, also the lounge windows at left that have been blanked out. The three windows further aft belong to the officers' dining saloon. Under them is the base to one of the ventilators that provide air to the cargo spaces in the 'tween decks below. *[V.H. Young and L.A. Sawyer]*

minimum of words you'd be told 'signing Monday tenth, 1030 hours', as I was in the case of the *Athenic*, and that was it. You left the office and didn't come back until that stated day and hour when, once again, you approached the counter, its pasty-faced occupant still there. He appeared never to have been outdoors into the sun, or to have changed his dark pinstriped suit with beer stains from last Christmas's office party. You waited for him to speak: 'Wot Ship?' '*Athenic*, for New Zealand', I reply. 'I know where's she's for!' he comes back, his face near cracking through the effort of speaking.

Next he bangs down a small glass bottle on the counter and says 'union, doctor, back to me'. You move away and head for a nearby door labelled 'The National Union of Seamen', with 'Enter' written below. Inside the door is another sullen, sour-faced individual reeking of stale tobacco. 'Book!' he demands. You hand over your four by five inch union book whereupon he licks his nicotine-stained fingers and fumbles to the page with the square showing the current date: 8th October 1956 - 41st week. He picks up a hand-held stamping device, slams it down on an ink pad and then onto my union book. Repeatedly he bangs the stamp on the page, as if not quite sure he's successfully thumped it to death. After the banging stops he states, almost with an inkling of glee on his face: 'That'll be forty-four shillings and three pence'. 'Christ!' I exclaim, 'is that a year's subscription?' 'That be the Union entrance fee and subs paid up to today', he informs me, sneering now. Although the signing-on date for the *Athenic* was a Wednesday, the Union official slyly backdates the amount I have to pay to the start of that week. I was to find the union next to useless, making damn-all effort for its members. After recovering myself from having to surrender my money to him, he hands back my well-stamped book and I move to another door, this one with 'Doctor' printed in white letters.

Here I'm confronted with yet another scowling ancient mariner. 'Got yer bottle, mate?' he asks with an accent never heard at the Royal College of Surgeons. 'Right, go in there and fill it, then come back here an' see the doc'. I comply. The doctor appears and rams a chunk of wood into my mouth. 'Say arr', he commands. 'Arr' I say, to which he declares 'OK, you can go and sign on'. Whether he saw anything of concern in my mouth or whether that filled bottle went straight into the trash can, I do not know. Back at the main counter again, I put my signature to number fifteen on the ship's articles as an able bodied seaman. I am now a member of the *Athenic's* crew, she is lying in the Royal Albert Dock and off I go aboard with my gear.

My cabin mate was a Scotsman named John McLean and we were allocated the largest of the seamen's cabins, located right aft and shaped rather like a wedge because of the ship's plating coming round to form the stern proper. Our bunks were two separate units so there was no climbing into an upper berth as in some of the other cabins. The accommodation wasn't too bad but it was certainly not up to the standard of New Zealand ships.'

The seamen, known as the deck crowd, the deck crew or the herd, were generally all young men 16 years to late 20s in age. There were various ratings: first in seniority was the bosun, an older, highly experienced man with many years of seafaring behind him. He was the foreman in charge of the deck crew, taking his directions from the chief officer and supervising all the endless maintenance tasks around the external decks. The bosun, the deck storekeeper (known by the term lamp trimmer or lampie) and the carpenter (chippie or chips) were petty officers (POs) though this term was not used by Shaw Savill. Aboard the *Ceramic* they had their cabins and messroom in the centre superstructure at Shelter Deck level. Next the quartermasters (QMs) also senior and very experienced. They served on the bridge as helmsmen and, when in port, as gangway watchmen. Below them in rating were the able seamen (ABs) who had qualified by time worked at sea – three or four years. The efficient deck hands (EDH) were younger seamen who had sat the Merchant Service examination in seamanship but were not yet qualified by time at sea to be rated as able seamen. Men not yet efficient deck hands were known as ordinary seamen (OS).

To further complicate the picture, there were also men rated as deck hand uncertificated (DHU). This was a designation usually but not always given to seamen who had done their training in the Royal Navy or in the Commonwealth navies, and who had been enticed back to sea during a time of manpower shortage. They were senior in age and status to ordinary seamen. Once they had sufficient sea time and had passed the examinations, they would eventually acquire their AB qualification. Youngest of all aboard the ship, 16 or 17 years, were the deck boys. They functioned as messmen or peggies, bringing food to the messrooms from the galley, setting tables and washing dishes after meals, cleaning the messrooms and crew bathrooms, making the petty officers' beds and cleaning their cabins and bathrooms.

The seamen wore no uniform; typical dress was dungaree trousers and jersey or, in the tropics, bare-chested. On their belts or through a cord round their waists they usually carried a sheath knife and a marlin spike. They were either watch keepers or day workers (day men). Each watch usually comprised three seamen: two ABs and a senior OS and their jobs were lookout, wheelman and standby man. The latter was called 'the farmer', and they rotated these three jobs each hour as the watch progressed. The wheelman stood on the grating in front of the steering wheel and kept the ship to her course or, if the auto pilot was engaged, watched to ensure she maintained her correct heading. At night the lookout would be stationed on the forecastle head unless sea conditions meant this was too hazardous. He then stood lookout on one of the bridge wings, with a cadet as

Aboard the *Ceramic* at Wellington,13th September 1970. Clockwise from top left: The emergency steering position inboard of the docking bridge wings on the roof of the *Ceramic's* poop deckhouse. A magnetic compass stands on its pedestal in front of the steering wheel, with a gyro compass repeater at right and engine telegraphs under their canvas cover at left. The voice pipe connects to the steering gear compartment five decks below on the *Ceramic's* Main Deck.

The view forward from the roof of the poop deckhouse towards the veranda cafe, with the *Ceramic's* mainmast bisecting the picture.

The aft well deck, where Number 5 hatch was located. Hatch beams can be seen at lower right, along with a five-ton maximum lift capacity electric winch. Behind the winch, which was manufactured by Laurence Scott and Electromotors Ltd., is the door to the seamen's cabin accommodation. Above the door is the poop deck with its deckhouse containing the seamen's messroom, the firemen and greasers' messroom and the crew galley. The port docking bridge wing is at upper right.

Looking up at the *Ceramic's* foremast showing the crosstrees, lookout post, part of the topmast with its signal yard, mast shrouds, steel ladders, two flood-lights and topping lifts for the derricks. At rear of the mast can be seen part of the *Ceramic's* heavy lift derrick, which had a 50-ton maximum lift capacity.

Right up in the bow of the ship, looking back at the *Ceramic's* bell and electrically-powered windlass, with sampson posts on either side. Left and right in the foreground are the cable stoppers.
[All Bruce S. Nicol/Russell Priest collection]

lookout on the other bridge wing or in the wheelhouse. The farmer stayed in the seamen's messroom on standby until the first hour of the watch was completed, whereupon he took over as wheelman or lookout. At sunrise the forecastle lookout was stood down in clear weather, but he stayed there as lookout if the ship was steaming in reduced visibility.

Every morning at 6.30 the day men and petty officers asleep in their cabins were called by the standby man. Half an hour later the day routine began with day men and the watch seamen other than the wheelman rigging hoses and washing down the decks with seawater. Breakfast was at 8 a.m. Day work continued from 9 a.m. with 'smoko' in the messroom an hour later. This was supposed to last just 15 minutes but often went on until the bosun arrived and drove the seamen back to their tasks.

At midday it was time for dinner, served by the peggies. This was the main meal of the day. Work resumed at 1 p.m. but there was a general rule that, even on cargo ships, the hours between two and four were sacrosanct with only quiet duties usually performed. The ancient art of siesta was observed by those having the rank and privilege to do so. Afternoon smoko was at 3 p.m., then normally at 5 p.m. all labour ceased with day men and unoccupied watch-keepers knocking off for the day. Tea was at 5.30 p.m. A system of reliefs was worked so that all but the man who had the second two-hour trick at the wheel was fed. At 8 p.m. this last man enjoyed what was called a blackpan - usually a mixed grill prepared by the cook as his final duty of the day. It probably

Ceramic in the dry dock located at the western end of King George V Dock, where Shaw Savill held three appropriated berths. The dry dock was in frequent use for short stays between voyages with ships having marine growth removed and anti-fouling paint applied. Work like this was often scheduled over weekends so as not to interrupt cargo handling. *[V.H. Young and L.A. Sawyer]*

got its name from the alleged state of the frying pan at day's end. The day workers could, of course, be kept working to any hour past knock-off, or roused out of their bunks at any time of night, if there were urgent tasks that needed to be completed. Overtime was paid for this.

Day work was an endless round of manual labour. Ship owners like Shaw Savill took a very determined pride in the appearance of their ships, particularly on sailing day and when arriving in port at the end of a voyage. Neatly painted hulls, spotless masts, derricks and samson posts along with gleaming white superstructures were all achieved only through constant effort on the part of seamen against the depredations of rust, funnel smuts and salt corrosion. Warwick Thomson: 'In port all hands would most probably be painting, keeping clear of cargo work. With the ship at sea after final departure from port, the day men would be set to work sending down all the topping lifts and guys, then stripping down and overhauling all the cargo blocks and cargo runners. Some runners would have to be replaced and the discarded ones saved for creating preventer guys. These preventers or 'lazy guys' were so-called as they were redundant to the outboard guys on the derricks when working cargo, in the event of a guy failing under the strain of union purchase working. In all my time, I never saw one being needed. All the overhauled gear (except cargo runners which were greased and left on the winch barrels) was then stowed away in the forecastle for the long passage to or from New Zealand. The lamp trimmer was charged with this stowage and ensuring that all gear was correctly accounted for.

Once the cargo gear was all stowed, our days were spent washing inboard paintwork with fresh water, and holystoning or barberising which was scrubbing the decks with sand and stiff brooms. The work was drudgery and monotonous, especially unpleasant in cold weather. Hardest of all was washing deckheads where you'd be working with arms up-raised and water running down your sleeves. Each seaman's area of responsibility was called a fleet and if it happened to be a complicated one with pipes, vents, lockers and other protrusions, it was called a banjo fleet. A wise sailor worked with his head to avoid getting one of these! Similar headworking was evident when seamen were called to draw holystones for scrubbing the timber decks. A well-worn holystone was lighter than a new one and so the old hands aimed for these; woe betide the ordinary seaman who presumed to pre-empt them by taking a worn holystone.

We used a variety of chemicals to make sugi-mugi for washing paintwork, a task known as sugiing or soogying. Sugi-mugi, shortened to 'sugi', was usually a mixture of caustic soda powder, soft soap and water, put together in a bucket into which you dipped your rag. It was very hard on the skin of your hands. A sailor in those days only reluctantly wore gloves when handling ropes and wire but he wouldn't be caught dead using them to sugi. Basol - orange crystals and caustic - was used in conjunction with holystoning to remove stains from the decks. A very early detergent called Teepol was also used sometimes to remove light grease from paintwork.

When the sugiing was done, it was on to the delights of chipping and rust removal. I was fortunate to spend most of my time as a seaman in relatively new and well-maintained ships but the limited amount of non wood-clad, black-painted steel decks on the forecastle head, over the general hatches and poop, the latter on the cargo-only sisters, required attention from time to time. As did the red-painted scuppers. During my time as a seaman Shaw Savill never extended to mechanical scaling machines; we always used hammers. To remove old paint and rust from railings, light chains were used. And I remember a simple way to paint rails was to use wads of cotton waste instead of brushes. It guaranteed a complete cover without any 'holidays' or missed-a-bit patches! We coated our hands in tallow first which helped them to come clean later. It was, like the sugi, very hard on the hands.

Nearing the end of a voyage the seamen would be put to work blacking down mast and funnel stays. A pungent mixture of the bosun's or lamptrimmer's own recipe, but predominantly comprised of Stockholm tar, was used for this. As with painting rails, we pre-coated our hands with tallow and employed cotton waste to apply the mixture. The method was simple. We were hoisted aloft in a bosun's chair then, attached by a free running large shackle around the stay, you were lowered by a shipmate (who literally held your life in his arms!). Using both hands clasped around the stay with a wad of cotton waste dipped in the mixture, each stay was treated in turn.

A week or so out from our first UK port, by which time all derricks, masts and samson posts were painted, it was the funnel's turn. The chief officer endeavoured to choose a day when a following breeze matched the ship's speed, before issuing his order through the bosun for the traditional (at least in Shaw Savill) 'job-and-finish'. This meant as soon as you completed the assigned painting tasks, you knocked off for the rest of the day. Men worked unusually fast rigging bosun's chairs and getting the job done as quickly as possible with the prospect of the balance of the day free. It was amazing how quickly the job was completed. If necessary, meals would be forgone in the overall interests of time off!

All the derricks would be re-rigged in that final week too, along with any last minute touching-up of paintwork preparing the ship for inspection by the steely-eyed company marine superintendents on arrival at our first UK port. It was always depressing to see that within an hour or two of docking in London or any other UK port, the ship looked as if it had never been cared for as she was invaded by the shore labour! Our messroom, instantly taken over by dock workers, became virtually inaccessible to us as soon as we came off docking stations. But then for most of the seamen, they couldn't have cared less. And I suppose I too was more interested in paying off and going on leave. The only difference was that I usually returned for the following voyage when it would all start again.'

In addition to the dreariness and repetitiveness of the work, there were masters and senior officers who could unnecessarily make life vile for hard-worked seamen. Many ships' masters when exercising their god-like powers were considerate and reasonable towards the well-being of crews, others were not. A story is told of a master who, during the long passages at sea, set up a carpentry bench on the upper deck just abaft the bridge where he occupied his time cutting and fashioning lengths of timber. The deck crowd had been stripping and varnishing the teak woodwork of the bridge house. With the varnish still drying, the master decided to resume planing and sawing at his workbench. Sawdust and wood chips were blown by the wind into the sticky varnish. The entire structure had to be stripped and varnished again, the master blithely shrugging it off.

Occasionally there were diversions to interrupt the tedium of painting, chipping and sugiing. Neil Hudson recalls: 'We arrived at the island of Curacao in the West Indies on 23rd October 1956 for bunkers, and went into the oil refinery at the back of the town of Willemstad. To get to the refinery the *Athenic* entered a narrow waterway passing through the town. Just inside the entrance was a floating bridge which was pulled aside to allow the ship to pass through and proceed between two high cliffs to the refinery. Bunkering commenced as soon as we were tied up, and took all day. I managed to get ashore with several of the crew for a few hours, which we spent in Willemstad town.

On sailing that evening, we noticed that part of the town of Willemstad was abruptly plunged into darkness as we got under way and steamed out of harbour. Our starboard anchor, which had been used while manoeuvring the ship into her berth that morning, had not been hauled up and restowed, and this went unnoticed when we left. We got clear of the harbour and were in the process of clewing up the forecastle head for sea, when the anchor was observed to be hanging in the water! On hearing this the mate said 'For f....-sake get the bloody thing in!' When heaving up the anchor on the windlass, back into the hawsepipe, a length of what appeared to be old rope was seen to be draped across the anchor flukes. A bosun's chair was rigged and I was sent over-side to clear the obstruction off the anchor. Only to find it was not a length of rope but a torn section of electricity cable with a copper core some two inches in diameter. A hacksaw was sent for and I cut through the cable, dropping it to the sea floor. What the consequences were on the *Athenic's* bridge and in the local Shaw Savill office at Curacao, I can well imagine!'

In port, seamen earned extra pay by being rostered for the duration of a port stay as night watchmen. The job involved patrolling the ship to ensure her moorings and gangway were all secure as she moved with the tides or with changes in the weather during the night. There was only the one crew gangway to attend to; passenger gangways were looked after separately by the ship's quartermasters. Warwick Thomson: 'We ABs all took turns at the job from 6 p.m. to 6 a.m. earning us two hours overtime at 2/6d an hour. Unofficially if one was on good terms with the watch-keeper fireman (with a boiler to tend, he couldn't afford to sleep!) he would alert us if needed so that it was possible to get a bit of shut-eye after all the important people were on board for the night, and if the tides were not too severe. I remember one occasion in the *Runic* on the Queensland coast when the spur on the bottom of the gangway got hooked into the eye of the backspring. I was roused just in time and with the fireman's help, managed to prevent it doing serious damage to itself and to my reputation. That was the last time I ever slept on duty! I remember being told by someone that the trick was to tie one's shoelaces so tight that after a time, pins and needles would wake the sleeper. It never worked for me!'

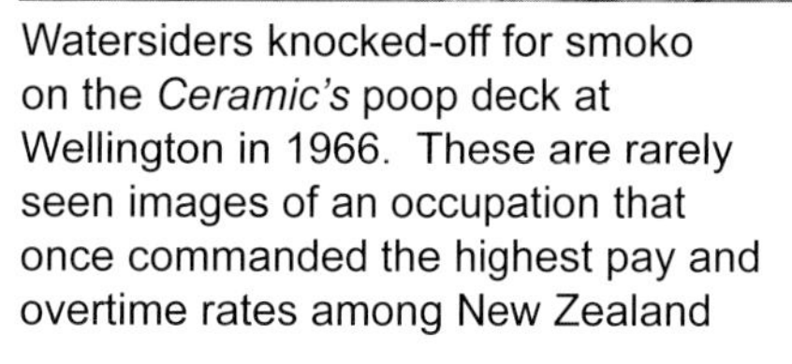

Watersiders knocked-off for smoko on the *Ceramic's* poop deck at Wellington in 1966. These are rarely seen images of an occupation that once commanded the highest pay and overtime rates among New Zealand workers. So fierce were the hostilities between the waterside workers' union and the institutions of employers and government that the wharfies, ever suspicious, did not allow themselves to be photographed lest the results be used against them. A youthful Vic Young has won acquiescence on this occasion but the stony looks on the men's faces convey their disdain for cameras. *[V.H. Young and L.A. Sawyer]*

Cadets

All the Big Ics carried deck officer cadets, also known as apprentices. These were young men getting the necessary sea time while studying for their Second Mate's Certificate of Competency. Pay for a cadet in the early 1950s was around £7 10s a month when an able seaman earned £20 to £24. Captain Ian Condie made two voyages aboard the *Gothic* as a cadet from September 1954 to July 1955. He recalls: 'Apprentices kept watch on the bridge with one or other of the deck officers when the ship was approaching land or coasting. They were obliged to take sights as often as possible and to keep a lookout while the officer on watch worked out the ship's position and distances run, from his sight. In general they paralleled the officer's work while also making tea, running errands, doing rounds of the ship at four bells and calling the reliefs for the next watch. When not standing watch they worked very much as sailors but usually apart from the ratings except when assigned to the carpenter or lamptrimmer for training. Cadets were required to complete a correspondence course to prepare them for sitting their second mate's ticket.

In port, apprentices kept cargo watches with an officer. Once again, they did the rough work, keeping a cargo log book, tallying mail bags and acting as watchmen and security guards against cargo pilfering. Curiously, they were responsible for the keys to the hatches and for making sure the accesses to the cargo were locked and unlocked. As the cargo was often valuable and portable, this was quite a responsibility. They also rigged lights and guard wires in the 'tween decks, lockers and other spaces. In otherwise deserted parts of the holds this could be a hazardous job. A friend of mine was killed when he fell down a hold doing just such a task.' Captain Condie later sailed as the *Corinthic's* Fourth Officer from November 1956 to February 1957, and as her Second Officer between January 1961 and February 1962. He commanded the *Corinthic* for a coastal voyage in British waters in mid-1969, and was also Third Officer on the *Ceramic* from September to December 1957.

Captain Graham Pepper remembers: 'I joined Shaw Savill as a cadet on 16th April 1964 when I boarded the *Cedric* (11,232/1952; Captain C.L. 'Bubbles' Carroll) in the Royal Albert Dock, London, as she was loading for Apia, Suva, Lautoka, Bluff and Timaru. Two years later I left her after five voyages and joined the *Ceramic*, again in the Royal Albert Dock, where she was loading for New Zealand. This was different as the *Ceramic* had accommodation for 85 first class passengers and a rather more genteel atmosphere to that I had been accustomed to in the *Cedric*. The Master was Captain N.S. ('Bay Boat Ben') Milne, Chief Officer was E. (Ted) Buckle, Second Officer I.P. (Peter) Carr, Third Officer D.R. (Robin) Mallam and Junior Third Officer N. (Norman) Cook. There were three cadets, Senior P.C.S. (Pat) Vance, me and Junior G. (Geoff) Robins.

Other notables on board were Chief Engineer J.W. (Daddy) Brew, Second Engineer D. (David) Jory, Purser E. (Eric) Scales and Catering Officer E.J. (John) Bayer. Both the Chief Engineer and the Catering Officer were on their last voyages prior to retirement.

We sailed from London on the evening of 29th April 1966 with a full complement of 84 passengers of whom two were Sir Walter Nash (retired Prime Minister of New Zealand) and his sister as well as a number of 'Ten Pound Poms'. Daybreak found us anchored off Gravesend (for a reason which now escapes me) and thus convincing certain of the passengers that we stopped overnight - a theory which we cadets certainly did nothing to discourage.

The voyage was via Curacao (for bunkers), through the Panama Canal, Pitcairn Island to discharge stores and then to Wellington where the passengers disembarked on 31st May 1966. Our New Zealand coastal voyage took in discharging at Wellington and Port Chalmers where we began to load before moving on to Timaru, New Plymouth and Wellington from where we sailed on 15th July via Pitcairn Island, the Panama Canal and Trinidad for Avonmouth, arriving on 15th August.

Life aboard the *Ceramic* was different, particularly for a young cadet. I shared a cabin with Geoff Robins and all the officers had shared shower and toilet facilities along the alleyway. We three cadets were on watches in coastal waters and on departure from London I was with the second officer on the 12 to 4. One of my duties was to take the position chits around the ship to all departments after the noon sights had ascertained where we were – no GPS in those days. I also had to call in to the passenger smoking room and pin a chit on the notice board so that the winner of the sweep to predict the day's run could claim his or her prize. Sir Walter Nash always made a point of coming to the board and asking about the distance. After we had been at sea for a few days, I was instructed to report to Captain Milne who told me that 'if Sir Walter invites you to have a drink with him when you visit the smoking room, you may accept half a pint of beer'. Thus I had a drink with Sir Walter every day until we reached Wellington!

At mealtimes the cadets dined in the passenger dining room which meant that we ate extremely well. A glance at a dinner menu from the 1960s in these ships shows up to six courses with a choice of turkey, venison or fillet steak for a main – and that was after an equally substantial lunch which was preceded by a breakfast that would put many hotels to shame. Hungry young cadets were, of course, renowned for attempting to empty the storerooms so the fare did add much to the voyage.

Once the ship was clear of the land and on a trans-ocean passage, the cadets went on to daywork under the watchful eye of the chief officer. This could involve any deck maintenance task ranging through washing down paintwork, chipping paint and rust from steelwork, painting, holystoning the wooden decks, helping the bosun with overhauling cargo gear and working with the carpenter. We also had time set aside for working on our correspondence course (usually Sunday afternoon) and appearing on the bridge to do morse signalling with the aldis lamp or to recite the 'Rules of the Road'.

While the ship was in New Zealand ports working cargo, the cadets worked with the deck officers in overseeing the discharge and loading of cargo, noting the times of any work stoppages, damage to cargo and, when we started loading, contributing to the very detailed cargo plan. Cargo working hours were from 8 a.m. to 5 or 6 p.m. so there was no evening or night work nor any work on a Saturday afternoon or Sunday. One of us was always duty cadet with the duty officer but other than that we could usually go ashore although any thoughts of a beer were not often quenched as we were under-age (and local publicans seemed good at picking us out) and, anyway, the pubs still closed at 6 p.m.

Parties ashore were popular and usually easy to arrange so overall life was very pleasant. I left the ship at Avonmouth in August 1966, never to return, at least, not while she was carrying passengers. I have to admit to being something of a naughty young man and, even worse, getting caught being a naughty young man! Pat Vance and I got on extremely well and we got up to all kinds of tricks but I got caught - I did not hold it against him - it was just bad luck on my part. Ted Buckle was quite rightly mortified by my conduct and was all for me being sacked when we arrived home - a very heavy penalty for a young cadet. However, Captain Milne detected some good in me and did not back the Chief Officer's view and I was not sacked but called into the London Dock Office for a major dressing down, identified as USPS (unsuitable for passenger ships) and sent to the *Romanic* (9,785/1944) a dreadful war-built ship that Shaw Savill had been forced to take over from Royal Mail.'

'Ginger' Smith

Just prior to sitting the examination for his Second Mate's Certificate of Competency, Philip Griffin made his final trip as a cadet on the *Ceramic* between 24th November 1954 and 7th April 1955: 'The Master was Captain F. (Francis) A. Smith, a Scot and a bear of a man with a reputation of having taken recalcitrant bosuns and ABs ashore behind dockside sheds, and taught them their manners. As he was in his sixties and had hands like hams, I presume the teaching was in the nature of fisticuffs. His nature was quite unpleasant. The *Ceramic's* Second Officer, winding the chronometer one day as Captain Smith came on the bridge, wished

Underway at sea, 25th June 1958. In this view the *Ceramic* has the additional posts and derricks that were fitted ahead of her funnel to improve the working of cargo from Number 3 hatch. *[J. and M. Clarkson]*

him 'good morning' to which the master replied 'I didn't ask you for a weather report!' Strangely, when officers requested the marine superintendent for a transfer, the reply was usually 'Why? his reports about you are extremely complimentary'. A strange man; he put the fear of God in me and I tried to avoid him in all situations which was a bit difficult, my being 6 feet 2 inches in height and eleven stone soaking wet.

I was one of two deck officer cadets aboard the *Ceramic* that trip, and we stood watches on the bridge with the second and third officers; I was with the third officer on the 8-12 watch. This included taking morning sights, taking noon sights and working out the day's distance run, the total distance run and ship's speed up to the current day. We had to submit our positions and day's run chits to the master, independently of either the other cadet or officers. The master also took morning sights and did the run ups, and he took a noon sight with us. Normally the officers takings sights calculate a mean of their respective positions and, using this, their day's run figures are thus the same. These are what is usually given to the master. Not with Frank! Everyone submitted a chit independently but only the second officer's position went in the log book.

On Christmas Day 1954 we were sailing a composite Great Circle course from Cape Town to Fremantle along the 40°parallel. This put us fairly close to the St. Paul-Amsterdam Islands and we were all standing around waiting for noon which was at about 11.45 a.m. ship's time. Out came Frank (no one called him Frank within his hearing) and roars 'Well, which of you figured out that we are in the middle of a total eclipse?' Sure enough the sun was in eclipse; not quite total, but none of us had realised it. Could it be that being Christmas Day our celebrations had interfered with our professional undertakings? I don't know, but we had all missed the total eclipse. As I said, not quite total but what an embarrassment! This episode governed my future time as Second Officer; I never ever set out on a voyage without looking at the eclipse pages in the Nautical Almanac first.

Another memory of fearsome Frank Smith: In Melbourne we were busy discharging a general cargo. Frank liked to walk up and down outside his cabin on the port side of the Boat Deck where he could also see what was happening at Number 3 hatch, which lay between the bridge house and the funnel. This particular day the hatchman had placed two of the freezer beams directly onto the wooden deck, instead of placing them on dunnage. Frank was well known on the Melbourne waterfront. He called the hatchman over and told him to get some dunnage to place under the beams. The hatchman said he would get the winches to lift the beams but Frank told him just to get the dunnage. Frank then lifted each end of each bean and the hatchman slipped the dunnage under the lifted beam. I walked around the corner of the accommodation as he was doing it. My Captain was in his white tropical uniform and he didn't turn a hair. I later tried to lift one of those beams; the hatchman told me not to bother, he only knew of three people who could do it: two of his wharfie mates and Frank'.

Captain Francis Alexander Smith was born on 28th January 1895 at Leith in Scotland. Known variously as 'Ginger Smith', 'the Smiling Bastard' and other unprintable names, it seems he is not remembered with any affection by those who sailed under him. Officers were required by Captain Smith to wear their caps at all times when outside their cabins, which resulted in officers proceeding to bathrooms clad only in a towel but still with the mandatory hat on head. Shaw Savill maintained strict dress codes for officers, these being promulgated in a book entitled 'Standard Types of Uniform'. There were five different types of officer uniform worn on the *Ceramic* and her sister passenger liners. Standard uniform comprised a double-breasted, navy-blue reefer jacket with eight brass buttons, four each side, with gold lace insignia on the cuffs according to the wearer's rank. Accompanying this were blue cloth trousers, black shoes and socks, a white shirt and collar with a black tie. Campaign ribbons were worn on the left breast for veterans of the world wars, along with ribbons for decorations awarded.

In hot weather, on the master's orders, officers changed into tropical kit, known as whites and comprising white shorts of naval pattern, white shoes and white knee-length stockings together with a white, open-necked, short-sleeved shirt with epaulettes displaying rank on each shoulder. This uniform could only be worn up until 6 p.m. after which officers changed into Number 10s. Also white, this consisted of starched long white trousers and a starched, single breasted patrol jacket that fastened right up to the neck. It featured five brass buttons, epaulettes and campaign medals.

There were two types of mess kit for officers' attire in the first class dining saloon and when mingling with passengers of an evening. They were known as mess uniform and tropical mess kit. Both involved stiff white shirts with wing collars, cummerbunds, black bow ties and either a navy-blue or a white jacket. Officers had to pay for all this gear out of their wages. Uniforms bought

There was a time when seafarers and ship lovers would take their boats along rivers and across harbours so they could admire the fine lines and proportions of a vessel like the *Ceramic*, seen here in an unknown port with engines just keeping way on her. Or maybe this is romanticising the boatmen in this photo, who are probably out for a day's fishing with nothing but glancing interest in the big ship whose stern they've just passed. *[Ships in Focus]*

'off the peg' were considered inferior; officers always had their uniforms made-to-measure by tailors who would despatch agents known as runners to measure up an officer in his cabin. S.W. Silver and Co., Miller, Raynor and Haysom Ltd. and Harveys were the firms Shaw Savill officers mostly dealt with, and the quality of their workmanship was exemplary. Uniforms lasted for decades against all the rigours of life and bad weather at sea.

Bay Boat Bennie

When Captain Smith retired, Captain N.S. Milne became the *Ceramic's* Master, his date of appointment being 1st July 1961. Born at Leith on 25th April 1904, Captain Milne continued the tradition of very long service aboard the Big Ics by senior company masters. Peter Carr remembers him:"Our Master under God was Nicol Stanley Milne a fine captain and strict disciplinarian known affectionately as 'Bay Boat Bennie' or 'Bay Boat Ben' because of the many years he spent on the *Moreton Bay* and the *Largs Bay*. Bennie was short in stature but large on professionalism and we all very much respected his command. The Old Man liked to have a game of deck tennis about three times a week with the purser, chief officer and second officer. And Bennie always won! That was until we had aboard the former New Zealand Prime Minister, Sir Walter Nash. We were taking him and his sister home to New Zealand and he elected one day to stand at the net and watch the game. As the Old Man called out the (usually) erroneous score in his own favour, the Right Honourable Sir Walter Nash GCMG CH, 27th Prime Minister of New Zealand, would correct the call. Eventually the true winners were revealed! Which meant Bennie 'packed a sad' and we did not play any more all the way across the Pacific.'

Captain Adrian (Pat) Chandler sailed on the *Ceramic* as a cadet under Captain Milne: 'He used to get up early each day at sea and wander through to the wheelhouse around 6.30 a.m. to see what had happened during the night. This was the hour when our junior cadet would be getting his steering practice, and as the Captain had to pass the electronic course recorder on his way to the wheelhouse, he could see how good a course the cadet had been steering. I gather his favourite comment was 'a bloody fireman could steer a better course with his shovel over the stern!'

Warwick Thomson recalls another story of 'Bennie Milne' when he was Master of the *Largs Bay* and Thomson was her Fourth Officer in 1957: 'It was he who dragooned me into acting as church hymn accompanist on our first Sunday at sea. He said there weren't any piano-playing passengers so I had to do it. Protestations from me about an inability to sight-read music were loftily swept aside; Bennie told me I had all of two hours in which to practice as he handed me the sheet music! Alas my performance lived up to the warnings I'd tried to give him. The following Sunday, a passenger volunteered to do the job, realising they couldn't be worse than me, and I was not bothered again.

Bennie later accused me of cowardice. We were working cargo at night in Melbourne; the *Largs Bay* had no cadets so I as her Fourth was duty officer keeping an eye on things around the hatches. I missed the return of some drunken firemen who chose to fight with each other in the vicinity of the gangway (so I learned later) just as Bennie himself was coming back aboard. As I'd not intervened to stop the fight, Bennie decided I'd run off to hide! Perhaps he might have remembered that, a couple of weeks earlier, I'd been kicked in the groin by a cook while interceding in another dispute. Fortunately our captain must have forgotten about his craven Fourth Officer by the end of the voyage as he gave me a good report!'

1968 was a crowning year in Captain Milne's long career at sea; he was appointed OBE, this being gazetted in London on 8th June, and he became Commodore of Shaw Savill in September. Captain Milne lived to the age of 90, dying on 2nd January 1995.

Like her sisters, the *Ceramic* was used as a venue for diverse social occasions. If the event happened to be in a different New Zealand port from where she was at the time, cargo work would be halted, hatches closed and the ship made ready for sea. She would then proceed round the coast to where she was needed, then afterwards steam back to resume loading or discharge.

Pitcairn Island

The *Ceramic* was a regular caller at Bounty Bay. Unlike Captain 'Pitcairn' Jones of the *Corinthic*, Captain Milne did not have a friendly disposition toward the islanders. Peter Carr: 'Each voyage, outward and homeward, all four Big Ics called for two hours at

Pitcairn. With four liners making three return trips per year between New Zealand and London, the islanders had a very good service. The star of the Pitcairn callers was Captain Jones and the islanders adored him. Captain Milne meanwhile was far from their most popular ship's master, and two hours at Pitcairn meant just that. We were instructed to sound the ship's whistle five minutes prior to departure and, regardless of whether there were still islanders aboard, push the engine telegraph handles to slow ahead as the two hour limit was reached. This resulted in a mad scramble for their long boats and an immediate halt to the pillaging of our old dunnage.'

(Top) Cargo for Pitcairn Island being readied on deck for loading into the islanders' whaleboats (bottom). *[Peter Carr]*

Maritime photographer Vic Young is a descendant of one of the *Bounty* mutineers and grew up on Pitcairn. He writes: 'The passenger and cargo vessels of Shaw Savill and the New Zealand Shipping Company were the lifeblood of Pitcairn Island. That is, until mass air travel moved both the ships and the service they offered into history. The long sea passage across the Pacific between Panama and New Zealand, taking around sixteen days, was broken only by a stop off Pitcairn and perhaps passing close to Rapa if the island was abeam in daylight hours.

In those now-distant times a ship stopped off Pitcairn, on average, every seven days. The rugged island, one of the most isolated spots in the world, is without a landing point suited to anything larger than a whale boat. Two miles in length, one mile wide and rising to one thousand feet, Pitcairn is ringed mostly with cliffs, sheer to the sea. In the mid 1950s the descendants of the *Bounty* mutineers, who had settled Pitcairn in 1790, numbered around 170. The visiting ships were their only connection to the outside world. While there were the one-off visitors, with ships of the Port Line, Blue Star, Ellerman, U.S. Lines and other British and foreign tramps being well known, the *Corinthic*, *Athenic*, *Ceramic* and *Gothic* were special. There were many friendships between their crews and the islanders.

Operating from the radio station established atop the island at Taro Ground, operator Tom Christian would usually raise each ship and confirm her estimated time of arrival 24 to 30 hours beforehand. There was always competition amongst the young boys to be the first to sight the incoming vessel from the island's peak. The whale boats would soon be away from Bounty Bay to meet the ship, usually in the lee of the island. For the *Ceramic* and her sisters, the use of two boats would be the norm. Using a painter from the ship, they would make fast, usually in line with the well decks, and sometimes both boats would raft up forward. If the visit was outside of school hours, boys aged around 11 and upwards would go with their parents. For a young lad on Pitcairn, it could be said that there was as much to be learnt boarding the *Ceramic* in a seaway, as there was ashore in the classroom. Once onboard, the islanders mingled with both passengers and crew. There was the usual sale of fruit, stamps and island curios to the passengers. Depending on their needs, families often preferred to barter with the crew. Used seaman's clothing, magazines and books were popular. Many of the ships' carpenters, lamp trimmers and bosuns were good friends to the Pitcairn community. There were often old sails, tarpaulins, vent covers, paint of any colour, nails, turpentine and brushes waiting under the forecastle. These items were most often exchanged for fruit. In the galley, the chief steward was usually very willing to offer milk powder, sugar, flour and the like, for the chance to top up his fridges with fresh produce. Some island families developed a close relationship with the chief steward and would grow and deliver produce to order, albeit on a small scale.

For the island's young boys, the excitement of these visits never waned. The youngster followed his father in carrying, lifting, watching, listening and learning. Towards the end of the visit, if things had gone well, a lad would perhaps be allowed a shilling and a few minutes to gaze in wonder at the stock in the *Ceramic's* barbershop. A little help from the shopkeeper could stretch the shilling sometimes to cover a Kit-Kat, Crunchie and a postcard of the ship, for there were no shops on Pitcairn. While hove-to off the island, depending on weather and sea conditions, the ship was kicked ahead at regular intervals to maintain a lee side. The length of the visit depended on the master. Ninety minutes to two hours would be the norm. A long blast on the whistle would tell the islanders to make their way to the boats into which they would lower their island kitbags, full of supplies. Apart from the usual sacks of mail, often there was official cargo for the island: radio spares, building materials, drums of diesel and other heavy items. This would often require a longer than usual stay, with one of the ship's derricks being used for the transfer to the whaleboats. Except at times when the weather would not allow, the letting go of the painter was accompanied by a hymn, sung from the boats by the islanders. 'In the Sweet Bye and Bye' was a favourite: '…in the sweet bye and bye we shall meet on that beautiful shore…' or perhaps 'Brightly Beams': '... brightly beams our Father's mercy from his lighthouse evermore, but to us he gives the keeping of the lights along the shore…' As the ship slowly got underway and the boats drifted towards the wake, hymns such as these, sung over water, left memories with many. Passing astern after an early morning visit, it was often possible for those in the whaleboats to smell freshly baked bread from the ship's galley! If the vessel was homeward-bound from New Zealand, the master would sometimes allow the chippie (carpenter) and bosun to retain spare dunnage. This would be set up in a tarp in the aft well deck. At the end of the visit, after letting go of the whaleboats, the ship would pass close inshore to windward, putting the dunnage over the side to drift ashore. Timber was valuable on the island.

When thinking of Pitcairn, the *Ceramic* and her sisters, it would be difficult not to recall Captain A.C. Jones of the *Corinthic*. His magnificent assistance to the community is still remembered on the island many decades after the *Corinthic* was scrapped. He delivered trees and plants and took a special interest in projects to assist Pitcairn. His visits in the *Corinthic* were usually considerably longer than those of her sisters. Shaw Savill's directors in Leadenhall Street, London would have perhaps been surprised at just how close inshore Captain Jones took the *Corinthic*, with those on the cliffs ashore looking down on her decks. Captain Jones was a most superb ship handler. On at least one occasion his assistance extended to lifting two of the Pitcairn whaleboats onto the *Corinthic* for a 112 mile passage up to Henderson Island, before making for Panama. The islanders then stayed on Henderson for a week, collecting wood, before sailing home on their boats. Captain Smith of the *Ceramic* was also willing to assist on his visits. However, there were times when it appeared the master would perhaps rather not have made the scheduled visit to Pitcairn. The *Athenic's* calls with Captain Heywood in command, sometimes left this impression. His visits often were brief, giving little consideration for small boats and the need for a good lee side.

The Shaw Savill ships were of a size that made their regular calls something of a personal experience. It was a time before mass communication and entertainment, Pitcairners were welcome in crew cabins where seamen still put ships in bottles, made decorative shell boxes and produced traditional rope work. *Corinthic*, *Athenic*, *Ceramic* and *Gothic* served Pitcairn well and their visits are part of the island's history.'

The Ark of the Governor

The differing schedules of voyages run by the *Gothic* and the *Ceramic* in 1953 meant that it was the *Gothic*, not the *Ceramic*, that would be available when the time came to convert one of them into Queen Elizabeth II's royal yacht. But 15 years later it was the *Ceramic's* turn to participate in similar distinction, although to a lesser scale. In 1967 The Right Honourable Sir Arthur Espie Porritt Bt GCMG GCVO CBE was appointed by the Queen to be her representative in New Zealand as the country's eleventh Governor-General (representing the Queen as Head of State). His term of office began on 1st December 1967 and concluded on 7th September 1972. On Sunday 29th October 1967 Sir Arthur, Lady Porritt, their son Jonathon and daughter Joanna embarked on the *Ceramic* at London for their journey to take up residence at Government House, Wellington. The *Ceramic* had been in service for not quite 18 years; there were plenty of newer, bigger, faster British liners on the New Zealand route but fittingly it was she that was chosen for this role. The honour was all the greater as most New Zealand governors-general had previously come and gone aboard liners belonging to the New Zealand Shipping Company.

Also joining the *Ceramic* in October 1967, finishing his sea time before sitting the examination for his second mate's certificate, was Captain Adrian (Pat) Chandler. He writes: 'I was the senior cadet and one of only two appointed to the ship. The Master was Captain N.S. Milne, a fairly short, neat man who rarely seemed to smile, but he had a very dry sense of humour which came to the fore later in the voyage. My immediate boss was the *Ceramic's* Chief Officer, Edward (Ted) Buckle, a large man in every sense of the word, but genial and very efficient. He also had a rather wicked sense of humour which provided much entertainment on the trip ahead.

It quickly became clear that something out of the ordinary was going to occur during this trip, as teams of French-polishers, decorators and furnishers came aboard. All the wood panelling was polished, new carpets were laid and new covers for the lounge suites appeared. The passenger accommodation really gleamed and we had strict instructions not to enter that part of the ship unless required by our duties. Two days before we sailed, all the officers were instructed to meet in the forward lounge where the reason for all this mysterious work was made clear. We would be embarking the following day the New Zealand Governor-General Designate, his family and staff, and taking them to New Zealand. As well as this sizeable contingent, the ship was fully booked, virtually unheard of by then, as only the *Ceramic* and *Gothic* of the four passenger Big Ics were still carrying passengers and they rarely sailed fully booked. It proved to be the swansong of these ships as passenger liners as, very soon after, both the *Gothic* and *Ceramic* ceased passenger operations.

The following day, 30th October 1967, passengers boarded and that evening we sailed. The voyage out to New Zealand followed a very familiar route, across the Atlantic to the Caribbean, but on this occasion we sailed to Port of Spain in Trinidad, where we anchored for a few hours while Sir Arthur Porritt and his aides went ashore on an official visit to his colonial counterpart. This set the scene for the rest of the voyage and was vaguely reminiscent of her sister ship's duties as royal yacht, only on this occasion we were very much the vice-regal yacht. We were met at Colon by a US Coast Guard cutter and escorted in to berth in the city, where the vice-regal party made official visits to the US Governor of the Panama Canal Zone. After passing through the canal we headed out into the Pacific, where our next stop was to be Pitcairn Island. This would be the first time that a governor-general would have set foot on the island. Especial care had to be taken while we drifted off the island, and the ship manoeuvred for some time to give a suitable lee in the swell to allow Sir Arthur and his party to disembark safely.

Life as a junior officer on the *Ceramic* was rather different from my earlier time on her sister ship the *Gothic*. Now I was training hard to take the responsibilities as a watch keeping officer, and honing my skills as a navigator. I kept the 12-4 watch with the second officer, a keen young New Zealander who was a very competent navigator and taught me a great deal of practical navigation that stood me well in my years at sea. The junior deck officers and the radio officers shared a table in the dining saloon with the *Ceramic's* nursing sister. Close by the doors to the main galley, it was rather noisy and we had a lot of traffic past our table, but at least the food was piping hot, and we ate from the same menu as the passengers. For dinner, we had to wear mess kit, and the girls wore evening gowns. Things were a bit more informal during the day, when off watch we could play deck games with the passengers and had many mighty tournaments of both deck golf and deck tennis. The vice-regal party mixed well with everybody, and we became good friends with Sir Arthur's aides (a Royal New Zealand Navy Lieutenant and a Royal New Zealand Air Force officer) and his private secretary. Sir Arthur's children who were both young adults we had less contact with; Jonathon, his son, went on to become quite a famous environmentalist. We only spoke to Sir Arthur or Lady Porritt to answer questions. Not that he was unapproachable or stuffy, as I remember some lively conversation emanating from the captain's table in the dining saloon, with plenty of laughter.

The Chief Officer, Ted Buckle, also had a table in the dining saloon, not that he had any of the vice-regal party at it, but he did have one lady passenger who felt she should always try and outshine Lady Porritt. Her gowns were always a little more glitzy, and she always had a few more jewels sparkling and rather put on airs and graces. Ted found this highly amusing, and one evening on being served a fish starter, had a quiet word with his waiter who, looking slightly dumbfounded, went off then returned a few minutes later with a very large silver fish slice. Without batting an eyelid Ted then used this outrageous implement to fillet his fish and to delicately remove the bones. He then politely offered it to the lady on his right, who manfully tried to repeat the exercise with her fish. By this time the dining saloon had become rather hushed and there were fits of hastily suppressed giggles. I understand the lady asked later to be moved to another table. Ted later brought the house down by appearing at the final dinner before our arrival in New Zealand, wearing a Beatles wig. I understand that Captain Milne was not quite so amused by that.

On our passage from Pitcairn Island to New Zealand, Captain Milne exhibited his own wry sense of humour as we approached the French island of Rapa. The small township on the island is located at the head of a large bay, well sheltered from the prevailing westerly winds. Captain Milne's favourite party trick was to invite passengers up to the bridge as we approached the island, where he would stand with his back to the wheelhouse windows casually talking to his guests. All the while the ship would appear to be heading straight for the beach at full sea speed of 17 knots. He would enjoy the look of increasing anxiety on his guests' faces as he appeared to be unconcerned at the ship heading for its doom. He knew that the moment he saw the headland out of the corner of his eye he could nod to the helmsman, who would casually swing the ship in a gentle arc around to port and out of the bay, with plenty of room to spare. I often wondered what would have been the result if the steering had suddenly jammed!

The *Ceramic* was an old ship by then; she had been in service for nearly 20 years and had proved herself to be a very steady and reliable ship with a large cargo-carrying capacity. Though very out-of-date compared with modern ships from a passenger's point of view, she still had quite a few clients who regularly travelled on her, and she had a good reputation. She was probably quite an expensive ship to run as her boilers consumed fuel oil at a rate that was typical of the immediate post-war period, but becoming increasingly expensive as the price of oil escalated.

It was our approach to New Zealand that made it clear that our arrival was going to be out of the ordinary. About 200 miles off the coast we were met by two Royal New Zealand Navy frigates that took station on us ahead and astern for the final run into Wellington. On the morning of 30th November, as the ship entered the harbour, a 21-gun salute was fired from the Royal New Zealand Artillery's saluting battery of 25-pounder guns at Point Jerningham, and there was a fly-past by the Royal New Zealand Air Force. We were escorted to the Overseas Passenger Terminal where we berthed. Nobody was allowed ashore until the official welcoming ceremony was completed.

As we finished tying up, a large honour guard of army and air force personnel marched onto the wharf, accompanied by a military band, and formed up opposite the *Ceramic's* main gangway. At 10 a.m. Sir Arthur in his full colonial governor's uniform, complete with cocked hat decorated with white plumes, stepped down the gangway to the strains of 'God Save the Queen' from the band. 'Royal Salute, Present Arms' was ordered by the officer commanding the honour guard. Prime Minister Keith Holyoake, his cabinet ministers and other dignitaries then officially welcomed their new vice-regal liege, after which Sir Arthur inspected the guard. He was next driven away to his new official residence at Government House with his wife, son and daughter. The rest of the party followed shortly afterwards.

That was our last bit of glory. The same evening the ship sailed for Auckland to start her discharge of cargo and returned some weeks later to Wellington, where we completed discharge. It was when we were sailing that the ship really showed what she was made of. As we moved out into the harbour heading for the entrance the pilot commented that we would have some company on our passage to New Plymouth as there was a new Blue Star ship sailing at the same time also for New Plymouth. Sadly I cannot recall her name.

Now Captain Milne was aware that there was only one berth available in New Plymouth so he had a quiet word with the chief engineer, saying he wanted her to really fly, as otherwise we could be swinging around the anchor for a week or more. We bundled the pilot off at the entrance and worked up to full speed. At times on that passage we recorded speeds of over 22 knots, probably the fastest she had ever been. We were lucky it was calm and there was little wind, but the smoke from the funnel had to be seen to be believed. Well, we got there first, and got the berth, and when we sailed five days later for Lyttelton the Blue Star ship was picking up her anchor to take our berth. I heard later that the company head office was not amused at the amount of fuel consumed on this short passage.

The passage home was uneventful, and on our return to the UK in February 1968 I signed off and went to the School of Navigation at Warsash near Southampton to study for my Certificate of Competency, passing this some months later. It was not to be the last time I saw the *Ceramic*, though.'

Feathered hats and falling bridges

Captain Edward Buckle, the *Ceramic's* Chief Officer, wrote his memories of this same voyage for an article that was published in Ships In Focus 'Record' 24 in June 2003. After having been delayed leaving London by a dock workers' strike, the *Ceramic* went to Rotterdam to complete loading, then sailed from there for Curacao on 1st November 1967. 'The vessel had to be dressed overall for the arrival at Willemstad, where a guard of honour would be waiting on the quayside. Sir Arthur Porritt was a very tall man and therefore he was unable to wear his plumed ceremonial hat until he stepped onto the gangway platform, having made his way down from the observation platform on top of the bridge house. He was not used to walking up and down ships' gangways, especially with a sword dangling at his side. So this had to be practised going up and down the baggage room stairs, which were of a similar size.

In Wellington harbour with pilot aboard, 7th October 1970. Note the absence of fins at the sides of the *Ceramic's* Thornycroft funnel top. These had been removed because, over the years, the funnel flue gases had caused extensive corrosion. Novel and possibly effective with a head wind, the Thornycroft funnel tops were never widely accepted or used by ship owners in the 1950s. *[V.H. Young and L.A. Sawyer]*

We had had a bad start to the voyage due to the strike in London, but here at Willemstad another big surprise was awaiting us. As we entered the port, we saw that the pontoon bridge across the harbour entrance had been removed to allow our passage. An official who had come aboard with the pilot was up on the monkey island observation platform, explaining to the Governor that a new fixed bridge was under construction. Half of this new bridge had been completed, and they were just commencing the other section. Then, without warning, the anchorages holding the completed half suddenly collapsed and the bridge fell into the harbour right ahead of us! Full astern was very quickly ordered on the *Ceramic's* engines, and we had to then go through the tricky operation of backing out of the harbour again. This was made difficult by the strong current which runs across the harbour entrance. We now had to proceed just up the coast to Caracas Bay where there were just refuelling pontoons and no place for a guard of honour.

So all the hours of practice had now to wait until Balboa. It was to be Cristobal initially, but due to the delay on arrival at the Panama Canal we immediately joined the convoy which was just starting to transit to the Pacific Ocean. Everything went smoothly for the Balboa arrival and the Governor's ADC was full of praise regarding the ship's crew. Our next stop was Pitcairn Island and special permission had to be obtained for the vice-regal party to land. There was no Rolls Royce for him here; photos I saw later show Sir Arthur, his wife and daughter on the back of scramble bikes on the road up the steep incline from Bounty Bay to Adamstown.

Next stop was Wellington where we arrived on 1st December 1967. What always stood out in my mind was that the evening before, unannounced, Sir Arthur visited all the messrooms to say thank you to the ratings. This was very much appreciated and the men mentioned it many trips later, even when they had left the ship.

She was an excellent sea ship, well built and very comfortable in all sea states. Very seldom was she delayed due to heavy weather and rarely did she receive heavy weather damage. The *Ceramic* was always a happy ship and the crew were just like one big family, and that is perhaps why she was so well-liked by passengers and so successful as a cargo carrier. Going from the *Ceramic* to the *Northern Star* or *Southern Cross* was like going from Harrods to Woolworths.'

Last of the four Big Ic liners

As with the *Corinthic* and *Athenic*, the *Ceramic's* career was free of major incident, triumph and tragedy being reserved exclusively for the *Gothic*. A total of 56 voyages were made during her 23½ years in service, 43 of these between Great Britain, New Zealand and then back to Great Britain. A further 12 were between Australia and Great Britain, with the *Ceramic* going on to load in New Zealand ports on seven of these voyages. Near the very end of her life she made one return voyage between Great Britain and South Africa. The *Ceramic* had her share of engine troubles, minor groundings and occasional diversions to other ports and trade routes to pick up or unload cargoes. She made her only transit of the Suez Canal on 5th and 6th September 1950, while coming home laden with Australian wool. During one of her annual refits in the 1950s an extra set of samson posts with derricks and winches was fitted to the *Ceramic* forward of the funnel, serving Number 3 hatch. The same modification was made to each of her three sisters in an endeavour to speed up the working of cargo. In 1952 at the end of Voyage Number 9 the *Ceramic* called at Plymouth for the first time, where her passengers were disembarked using tenders. From there it was to Hull and then Hamburg to discharge her New Zealand cargo. Between 16th October and 9th November 1954, during Voyage 13, the *Ceramic* had to be dry-docked and repaired at Hamburg after touching bottom when arriving there from New Zealand. Boiler trouble forced her to put back to Southampton between 21st and 23rd January 1962, after having departed London on 18th January at the commencement of Voyage 34. Ten voyages later she was delayed at Cristobal on the eastern (Atlantic) side of the Panama Canal, with turbine problems. By late 1967 the fins and louvres at the sides of her Thornycroft funnel top had been cut away, the result of advancing corrosion. She continued taking passengers until 1968 when she arrived in London from New Zealand on 3rd July, with 37 aboard. These were the last fare-paying passengers to travel 'Big Ic.'

Unlike the *Corinthic* and *Athenic*, the *Ceramic* did not have her superstructure cut down to facilitate easier cargo handling at Number 3 and 4 hatches. Her two after-most lifeboats were, however, removed and landed with their davits left in place. Now that her passenger-carrying was over, the *Ceramic* followed a much more varied schedule of port calls. She was at Southampton discharging cargo between 8th and 20th February 1969, then went to Hamburg, Sheerness, Liverpool and Cardiff then back to Liverpool where she loaded for Australia. From 4th to 15th February 1970 the *Ceramic* loaded at Southampton for New Zealand then came home for discharge firstly at Avonmouth then to Southampton again, where she arrived on 20th June at the end of Voyage 52. She was in Wellington during October 1970. Next year the *Ceramic* made a round voyage to Australia before being laid up at London from 30th July to 17th September 1971. She then went to New Zealand for Voyage Number 54, discharging at Picton between 3rd and 8th December 1971 after which she crossed Cook Strait for a month at Wellington loading her final refrigerated cargo from New Zealand.

The *Ceramic* departed Wellington for the very last time on Sunday 9th January 1972, fully laden and on passage for Liverpool. Six months later she was sold for scrap, having outlasted the *Corinthic*, *Athenic* and *Gothic* by almost three years. Each had gone to Kaohsiung for scrapping in 1969, beginning with the *Gothic* which arrived there on 13th August having been condemned to be first to go because of the cost of permanent repairs following her 1968 fire. *Corinthic* and *Athenic* followed in the third week of October 1969. After 1969 the *Ceramic* and the *Suevic* were the only survivors of the original seven Big Ics.

Reaching Liverpool from Wellington on 6th February 1972, the *Ceramic* discharged her cargo then set out for Cape Town, arriving on 28th April 1972 to load a cargo of fruit which took until 8th May. This was her very last cargo-carrying voyage - Number 54 - and she was back alongside at Southampton on 23rd May. Captain Adrian (Pat) Chandler takes up her story: 'In May 1972 I was waiting for a new appointment, having sailed as Third Officer on the last liner voyage of the *Southern Cross*, which was then being laid up in Southampton prior to moving to the River Fal to wait for a buyer. I had been appointed Second Officer (navigator) of the latest Shaw Savill acquisition, the *Ocean Monarch* (25,971/1957) which was returning on a liner voyage from Australia. In the meantime I was asked to stand-by the *Ceramic* in Southampton. Her Master was Captain F. Yearney. A few days into my time on board we heard the ship had been sold to Jos Boel et Fils at Tamise in Belgium for breaking.

All the *Ceramic's* passenger cabins remained fully furnished, though they did not have linen. The forward passenger lounge was used as the deck officers' lounge, their original wardroom having been a poky little space in the centre of the bridge house, lit only by a skylight. I certainly remember sitting in the forward lounge watching TV during our time in Southampton. So far as I remember, the only item removed was the grand piano, which went to the *Ocean Monarch*. The old smoking room on the Promenade Deck was used as the engineers' lounge, though we were often found there in the evenings as it had a fully functioning bar. Most of the original furnishings were still there. All the deck officers' (and I think engineers') original cabins were closed up. The chief officer's original cabin was used as a pilot's cabin; when she was de-rated to cargo only, the chief officer took over the passenger suite with its own private sitting room on the starboard forward corner of the Promenade Deck. Most of the other deck officers used passenger cabins on the same deck that had their own bathrooms. The height of luxury, though the baths were saltwater only!

We all fully expected the ship to be destored before she went to Belgium, but were told by the marine superintendent that the company had no use for any of the furnishings or stores, so they would go with the ship. I remember thinking that some of the

Last of the *Corinthic* class, the *Ceramic* at Cape Town where she took aboard her last cargo. The date is 8th May 1972 and she is departing this, her last foreign port, to return to Great Britain for the last time. At the end of May she will leave Southampton for Belgium and demolition. *[V.H. Young and L.A. Sawyer]*

lounge furniture would have been very welcome on some of the older cargo ships that I had sailed on, but it was not to be.

On Tuesday 30th May we left Southampton for the last time and steamed up the English Channel, arriving off the River Scheldt a couple of days later. It was at anchor there that we received a visit from the new owner who apparently was delighted with his purchase. He had thought he was getting a cargo ship, I do not think he had realised that he was getting a fully equipped passenger-cargo liner instead.

At lunch that day, the Chief Steward asked me whether there was anything I would like to take back to the UK with me and, bearing in mind I was getting married in a few months, I said I would quite like some of the large fluffy bath towels and maybe some table cutlery. An hour later, a steward arrived at my cabin with six brand-new bath towels, still wrapped in cloth and bound with tape, and a complete eight-person dinner service of silver plate and stainless steel cutlery, including tea and coffee pots, sugar bowl and jugs. They were still wrapped in tissue paper as supplied by Mappin and Webb to the ship in 1948, and never taken out of the stores. Even today, some 40 years later, these items are still in regular use and show how high the original quality was.

We left the ship tied up to an old wooden wharf, still in excellent condition, clean and fully equipped. After a short coach trip to Zeebrugge, we flew home to Southend - my first commercial flight and the forerunner of many subsequent flights to and from ships in my career at sea that lasted until the mid-1980s.'

Following the ignominy of three months lying deserted, scrapping of the *Ceramic* got underway on 25th September 1972. She was gone by the end of that year, but she is not forgotten. *Ceramic* belongs forever in the roll-call of magnificent British passenger liners that once sailed the great trade routes between Great Britain, Australia and New Zealand. She was not the fastest or the biggest or the most glamorous, but for exclusive and exquisite first class travel at sea there was none better.

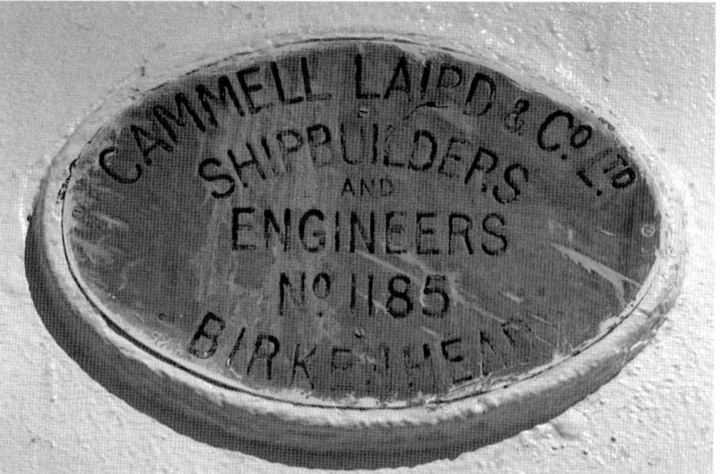

The *Ceramic's* bell (left) was mounted on a davit up on her forecastle, in front of the windlass. The *Ceramic's* builder's plate (right) was fixed centrally to the front of her superstructure on the Bridge Deck, just below the teak rail. *[Bruce S. Nicol/Russell Priest collection]*

Lifeboat drill and the *Ceramic's* chief officer has ordered sails rigged at Hobart in March, 1954. A pleasant, breezy, sky-blue day for a spot of tacking and close-hauling (though not for the boat crews on the *Ceramic's* port side nearest the wharf). *[David Kirby/ Russell Priest]*

Above: Steaming into head seas, October 1957. *[V.H. Young and L.A. Sawyer]*
Right: At Avonmouth in the early 1970s, probably discharging her last foreign cargo. Spiralling costs have destroyed the long-standing ethic where no major shipping company would ever allow a vessel's paintwork to fall into neglect like this, no matter how near she is to scrapping. *[R.M. Parsons/Malcolm Cranfield]*

The view from one of the *Ceramic's* bridge windows, looking past her foremast with its heavy-lift derrick to her impeccably-kept forecastle. *[Peter Carr]*
Evening on the *Ceramic* somewhere at

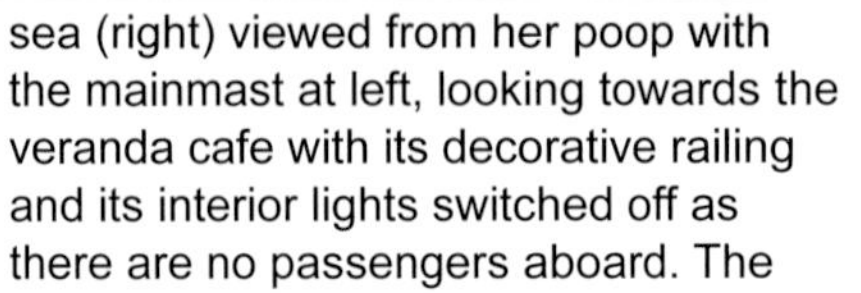

sea (right) viewed from her poop with the mainmast at left, looking towards the veranda cafe with its decorative railing and its interior lights switched off as there are no passengers aboard. The derricks are topped, which means she is most likely on a coastal trip between New Zealand ports while working cargo. *[Peter Carr]*

Above: *Ceramic* in the Thames at London and as fine-looking as ever. *[V.H. Young and L.A. Sawyer]*

Below left: *Ceramic's* tripe 'organ pipe' steam whistles high on the front of her funnel, photographed on 13th September 1970. Each had a different tone, but they could only be sounded as one. The whistles were made either of brass, gunmetal or some other copper-based alloy. Polishing them was a regular task for the ship's seamen. When activated, there was always a delay accompanied by a slight spluttering noise, as the steam had to reach the whistles and then vent any condensate. After that, you held your ears. *[V.H. Young and L.A. Sawyer]*

Below right: Before its fins were removed, the *Ceramic's* funnel with its Thornycroft top. The photographer is looking aft from the roof of the bridge house with one of its four electric cargo winches at right. *[Captain Ian Condie]*

The Queen's ship; *Gothic* in the English Channel passing Dover on a cold Friday, 14th May 1954. In this photo she is 'coasting' in home waters, her royal odyssey over. Part of her cargo loaded during the royal visits to New Zealand and Australia has been discharged at KGV Dock London and now she is going round to Liverpool to complete discharge. Very shortly after her arrival there, the *Gothic* will be taken in hand by Cammell Laird for conversion back to Shaw Savill's passenger operations. Her hull will be repainted black, making this the last time the *Gothic*, most photographed merchant ship in the world during the 1953-54 Royal Tour, will be at sea in her royal yacht livery. Note the enlargement made to the Boat Deck house forward of her funnel for the additional wireless gear. The royal barge and the admiral's barge are no longer to be seen on her aft well deck, having been landed at London. *[FotoFlite incorporating Skyfotos, 11963]*

GOTHIC THE GREAT

History maker

No other ship before or since can equal the *Gothic's* unique place in maritime history. She is the only merchant vessel ever to have been used as a royal yacht by a reigning British sovereign. To her belongs the honour of first ship ever to take a reigning British sovereign around the world. From her decks the Head of State for Australia and for New Zealand came ashore and set foot in those lands for the very first time. During the *Gothic's* service in this role she became the world's most photographed ship, carrying as she did the newly crowned Queen Elizabeth II and her husband Prince Philip, Duke of Edinburgh. On the evening of 26th April 1954 the *Gothic's* Master was invested by the Queen as Knight Commander of the Royal Victorian Order. Captain Sir David Aitchison KCVO is the only modern-day British Merchant Navy seafarer to have been so honoured aboard his own ship.

Entering service in December 1948 the 15,911 grt *Gothic*, Official Number 182351, call sign MAUQ, became the last of the *Corinthic* class quartet to be completed, putting to sea some 20 months after the *Corinthic*. Today she is by far the best remembered of all four ships not only by virtue of the magnificent service she gave in 1953-54 as a royal yacht, but also because of the tragic fire that befell her in 1968. Regardless of this, her sisters deserve history's acknowledgement in their own right for the *Corinthic*, *Athenic* and *Ceramic* were, in their fittings and appointments, every bit the equal of the *Gothic*. Indeed it can be argued that, while a ship of imposing visual proportions, she was the least good-looking of all of them. The differing widths of stanchions used on the *Gothic's* Promenade and Bridge Decks, and their uneven styles and spacing, were very much a throwback to the 1930s. But this is not to detract from the illustrious role for which the *Gothic* was chosen in 1953, and the sterling manner in which she and every member of her crew performed that role.

The building of Ship 1759

When tracing the beginnings of a ship, one of the most fascinating sources to explore is the files of long-archived letters, memoranda and notes exchanged between the owner of the vessel and the shipyards tendering to build her. Where accessible, they can reveal a tale of troubles and bickering alongside great achievement. Such is the case with the *Gothic* and the papers concerning her building that are held by the Tyne and Wear Archives and Museums at Newcastle-upon-Tyne.

When Basil Sanderson arrived in Perth aboard an RAF service flight on or about 21st November 1945, he had been away from Australia and New Zealand for ten years. Having been appointed Managing Director of Shaw Savill and Albion in April that year, his trip to the Antipodes was a fact-finding mission to assess the shipping needs of both countries following the resumption of peacetime international trade. Sanderson quickly realised, as he talked to the company's local managers, that the new-building programme Shaw Savill already had underway was not large enough to meet the demands of this trade between Britain, Australia and New Zealand. He cabled his head office in London, instructing them to try and add two more vessels to the two already on order.

In the records of Swan, Hunter and Wigham Richardson Ltd. there is an internal memo dated 17th November 1945 about a meeting at Shaw Savill's London Head Office the previous day, concerning the second of these two extra ships. The memo describes this ship to be an exact repeat of another vessel, first of the two and in due course to be launched as the *Ceramic,* ordered from Cammell Laird on 18th January 1946. On 10th December 1945 Swan Hunter wrote to Shaw Savill offering to build one ship, with an option for a second ship, for one of two prices: £827,373 for a 14,000 SHP steam ship or £883,910 for a 14,000 BHP diesel-engined ship. Shaw Savill was told there would be an additional cost 'if you decided to fit passenger accommodation at a later date'. In a further letter, dated 28th December 1945, Swan Hunter refers to accommodation in the proposed vessel for 12 passengers only. Delivery was offered for September 1947 if steam propulsion was specified, or November 1947 if the ship was to be diesel-engined. To produce a 19-knot service speed, three main engines coupled to three propeller shafts would be necessary.

Shaw Savill's directors lost no time in accepting Swan Hunter's offer on 18th January 1946 and, as instructed by Basil Sanderson who was then in New Zealand, further accepting the option of passenger accommodation for an extra £70,840. This would provide 85 berths. Shaw Savill was very familiar with the firm of Swan, Hunter and Wigham Richardson of Wallsend, for it was here that the company's flagship *Dominion Monarch* had been built between July 1937, when her keel was laid, and late January 1939 when she was completed. In its acceptance letter Shaw Savill stipulated the new vessel, referred to as Ship 1759, be 'exactly similar to the ship being built by Cammell Laird', this vessel being the *Ceramic*. There is also mention of tank testing for both vessels being done jointly in the facility at Teddington, Middlesex. With basic hull form having been established as long ago as the second *Waiwera* (10,800/1934), these tests centred on the increase by one foot in the breadth of the two new ships compared to the *Corinthic* and *Athenic*. Engine power was also significantly more than the earlier two ships, rising from 14,000 to 18,400 SHP. They were to be at least a knot faster and, at this stage, have an intended service speed of 19 knots.

Almost as an afterthought in this polite exchange of letters, Swan Hunter was given responsibility for applying to the British Admiralty for a licence to build a refrigerated cargo ship. The relevant document, Form M.S.1 was duly filled in, dated 5th February 1946 and sent to the Whitehall bureaucracy. On a scruffy sheet of paper still there in the archived file, the Admiralty issued a licence date-stamped 12th February 1946 with two caveats. One was that the keel must be laid by 31st May 1946 and, harking back to the war years, the new vessel was to be subject to 'any alterations which the Admiralty may require'. There was a later echo to this for, in the settlement of the final costs for Ship 1759 dated 10th February 1949, the Admiralty were debited by Swan Hunter for £957 this being 'the cost of gun stiffening'. Just where precisely this stiffening had been incorporated into the ship is a detail lost to history.

The hull specification for Ship 1759 ran to 103 pages. Its contents betray a meeting of traditional ways for building a ship, alongside new technology introduced during the war years. The hull was to be 'built to the approved half block model'. This went back to a method devised nearly a century before, at the time of the first hulls built of iron, when the shape and size of individual steel plates were measured-off using a scale model. Juxtaposing this was 'the scheme of welding' in an addendum to the hull specification dated 25th May 1946. Electric arc welding had come to British shipyards from the USA during the Second World War. Some of the standard clauses still included in 1946 were clearly pleading for deletion: 'vessel not to be rigged with sails'. In other areas the detail, by contrast, was exhaustive: sound insulation was to be fitted under the cargo winches, eight of which were sited over the accommodation at Boat Deck level. A portable swimming pool on the fore deck was to measure exactly 20 feet by 15 feet by 6 feet. Thirty three pages were devoted to fitting out and furnishing all of the accommodation. Probably because the new ship was to be the last of four near-identical sisters, the requirement for 'the builders to provide a full-scale model' was dispensed with.

A subsidiary of Swan Hunter, the Wallsend Slipway and Engineering Co. Ltd. of Point Pleasant, near Wallsend, was to supply the turbines and boilers for the new ship under a contract numbered 1003. A first hint of discord surfaces in the exchange of letters that accompanied this contract, R. John of Wallsend Slipway and Engineering telling John W. Elliot, Vice Chairman of Swan Hunter, that 19 knots at 18,400 SHP and the propellers turning at 125 revs per minute 'could not be achieved' and 'under no circumstances would we give them [Shaw Savill] the right to reject the ship' if these desires were not met when the vessel undertook her sea trials. After further correspondence Elliot backed down and told Shaw Savill that Swan Hunter could not guarantee 19 knots but they could a performance of 17 knots for the first five years of the ship's life.

While this was going on, the link between Swan Hunter and the *Dominion Monarch* had been reasserted with Shaw Savill's mighty quadruple-screw flagship, amongst the most powerful motor ships in the world thanks to her four 8,000 BHP Doxfords all in one engine room, about to be fully reconditioned by her builders after a hard war. Captain R.J. Noal, Shaw Savill's long-serving Marine Superintendent, is recorded as hoping that 'Simpson, a first class foreman joiner would be involved' both with the fitting out of Ship 1759 as well as the *Dominion Monarch*. As often happened in those times, the owners were giving the ship the personality that goes with a name whilst the builders were still using a yard number.

No time was lost in senior managers from Swan Hunter going to Birkenhead to meet with their counterparts at Cammell Laird, as directed by Shaw Savill. The first meeting took place on 11th February 1946 and all subsequent meetings were likewise held at Birkenhead. From reading Swan Hunter's file there is the impression that, though usually accompanied by three colleagues, Swan Hunter's Vice Chairman Elliot was no match for Sir Robert Johnson, Chairman of Cammell Laird. What came out of the two yards consulting each other is not recorded; it can be assumed not a lot. Cammell Laird, about to launch the *Corinthic*, now had the design of the *Ceramic* well advanced. Although Sir Robert would, of course, never hint at any such disinclination towards a good customer like Shaw Savill, there was no commercial reason why he should help a rival yard in building a ship that his company might just as easily have taken on itself. Perhaps a more redoubtable emissary from Swan Hunter should have been chosen to do the fact-finding job; that one was not sent may reveal the pressure Swan Hunter was under at the time with so much post-war building and refit work on its books. One difference between the two yards that emerges from the files was how they were being paid. Cammell Laird followed the traditional way of five equal stage payments. Swan Hunter, by contrast, took in 10% instalments.

The keel of Ship 1759 was laid on 30th May 1946, just within the Admiralty's deadline. Erection of the frames started on 9th July 1946 but from then everything seems to have proceeded at a less than earnest pace, for it was not until over a year later that the framing was completed on 14th August 1947 and the plating started. Things then got a move on. By 8th November the hull was completed and the launch of Ship 1759 took place on Friday 12th December 1947. She was named *Gothic* by Lady May Murrant, wife of the chairman of the Furness Withy Group, and sent down into the Tyne. Photos show a particularly dark and dreary winter's day. She had taken 18½ months from keel laying to launch, compared to 12½ months for the *Corinthic* and 17½ for the *Athenic*.

The cause of this less-than-creditable performance by Swan Hunter was probably a combination of things. Steel shortages became extreme in post-war Britain with shipyards often receiving less than 50% of their needs. It is probable that priority was given to some of the other ships that Swan Hunter was building at the same time, for anything that was to earn foreign currency would be designated as more important. Ships under construction in neighbouring berths included a passenger cargo ship for Scindia, at that time the Indian national shipping line; two ships of that same type for Chargeurs Reunis and two ferries for trans-Mediterranean services, also for French owners. Then of course there was the severe winter weather in 1946 that lasted into March 1947, a length that was unprecedented and made worse by dire shortages of fuel.

Completely missing from the Swan Hunter files are letters of complaint about why the *Gothic* was taking so long to build.

Lady May Murrant, the *Gothic's* sponsor, at Wallsend on launch day, 12th December 1947. The expression on her face suggests less than joyousness at the occasion, caused perhaps by the cold weather or some irksome delay in the proceedings. Or maybe the explanations from shipyard managers about launching weight, declivity of keel and height of water on the way-ends have become just a little tedious. Shaw Savill's Chairman Basil Sanderson stands at right with head bowed, his thoughts not far from the many hold ups and huge jumps in cost to build the *Gothic*. *[Captain Graham Pepper, Shaw Savill Society]*

This could have been because the *Dominion Monarch* had arrived in the yard in July 1947 for a process of reconditioning that was to last 15 months. Shaw Savill was keener to get her back into service, with her capability for 517 first class passengers and 590,000 cubic feet of refrigerated cargo, than to take early delivery of the fourth of their passenger-cargo quartet. But there survive letters a-plenty about how the cost of the *Gothic* was rising. By 1st July 1946, five and half months after the contract with Swan Hunter was signed, this had increased by 4% to £934,722 of which £55,000 was declared as the yard's profit and £83,000 for 'establishment charges'. By 19th November 1946 John Elliot was writing to Basil Sanderson's deputy Errington Keville, stating that steel prices had doubled since the contract was placed, wages were up by 8%, national insurance by 2% and timber, a large amount of which would be going into the refrigerated holds and the accommodation, by 50%. All this resulted in the *Gothic's* delivered price now reaching £1,004,722, 12% above the contract price at a point in her building when she still had not even been fully framed. At this rate she would be £2 million before her trials at some indeterminate time in the future, more than twice the *Corinthic's* final cost. Rampant price escalation for new ships was becoming a favourite post-launch speech topic for Basil Sanderson. Doubtless very troubled by this and by so little progress with the *Gothic*, he paid Swan Hunter a personal visit on 9th June 1947. The delivered price was discussed and one day later Sanderson was told by Elliot that this would be £1,062,075.

Once afloat, the *Gothic's* fitting out seems to have been no faster than the plating had been for it was nearly a year later, and after the *Dominion Monarch* had departed, that she was ready for trials held on 4th and 5th December 1948. With these successfully completed, the *Gothic* sailed from the Tyne for the Clyde on 7th December where two days later, after the entire refrigerated cargo system had been tested to everyone's satisfaction, she was handed over. The itemised cost of the *Gothic's* construction runs to many pages of detail: 24 different types of timber had been used, £743 had been spent on teak decking, £4,955 on plywood; 16,000 dowels had been used by carpenters when laying the timber decks, with each one costed. On 10th February 1949 Swan Hunter sent an invoice to Shaw Savill for £1,306,825, considerably in excess – by

Afloat in the Tyne, Friday 12th December 1947. *[Captain Graham Pepper, Shaw Savill Society]*

QSMV *Dominion Monarch.* Diesel-powered and one of the most remarkable British liners of the Twentieth Century, she was Shaw Savill's flagship from her introduction in February 1939 until the arrival of the *Southern Cross* at the end of March 1955. Flying her paying-off pennant, the *Dominion Monarch* is seen here in April 1962 at the finish of her Shaw Savill career. *[J. and M. Clarkson]*

A very early photograph of the *Gothic*, dated January 1949 at Cape Town during her maiden voyage. *[J. and M. Clarkson]*

nearly a quarter-million pounds – of Vice Chairman Elliot's June 1947 pledge and a horrendous 45% above the contract price of not quite three years before. (John W. Elliot succeeded to the chairmanship of Swan, Hunter and Wigham Richardson on 31st December 1949, and was awarded a CBE in the King's Birthday Honours of 1951.)

At the end of the file is to be found the biggest surprise of all. On 10th December 1949 Shaw Savill mortgaged the *Gothic* to Swan Hunter for six years, repaying the amount in six monthly instalments. What was the company's motivation for this? Enhancing Furness Withy's liquidity? The arrangement was a repeat of that used for the *Dominion Monarch* in 1939. Perhaps the answer lies in Basil Sanderson's annoyance, to put it mildly, at Swan Hunter having taken 31 months to build the *Gothic* while the near-identical *Corinthic* had required just 22 months, despite a near-ruinous fire, and for a cost 30% lower. Sanderson was a widely connected and widely respected figure in the British and Empire shipping industry; Swan Hunter might well have felt it prudent to offer this mortgage facility by way of keeping a lid on the Chairman of Shaw Savill's disfavour. The last item in the file is dated 30th May 1950 in which Swan Hunter reimbursed Shaw Savill for £676 1s 7d, this being for work done in London on the *Gothic,* between voyages, under the guarantee provisions in her building contract. The necessary work was carried out, not by Swan Hunter, but by Harland and Wolff's ship repair division. It was perhaps no coincidence that not until 1962-1963 did Shaw Savill return to Swan Hunter with orders for building the *Megantic* (12,226/1962) and *Medic* (12,220/1963). The *Gothic* had taken too long and cost too much.

Her first Master was Captain R.G. James who joined the *Gothic* on 7th December 1948, the day of her departure from the Tyne prior to sailing on her maiden voyage from Liverpool to Sydney on 23rd December. Nine months later on 13th August 1949 the *Gothic* called at Falmouth for the first time, where she disembarked her passengers. Normally these calls were made at Plymouth whenever the *Gothic* or her sisters were not finishing a voyage at London but were, instead, going elsewhere to discharge their refrigerated cargoes. At Plymouth in 1949 British Railways operated a passenger landing service using two large tenders based at a jetty with a rail head in Millbay Docks. We do not know for certain, but the *Gothic* most probably anchored at Falmouth Bay (at the entrance to Carrick Roads) because Plymouth was busy that day with other scheduled liners calling. The passengers would have been taken ashore to Falmouth Docks in 'quay punts' - large open launches operated by local boatmen. As August in 1949 was the middle of the holiday season, pleasure launches must have been busy. From the docks the *Gothic's* passengers were moved by coach to Truro Railway Station, their baggage following in a truck, probably to connect with the 11 a.m. Cornish Riviera Express. This would have got them into London's Paddington Station just before 5 p.m. after changing at Plymouth where, for those wanting it, there would have been a connection on The Cornishman at 1 p.m. to the Midlands and the north of England.

Royal selection

To Shaw Savill had gone the honour of providing a merchant ship for the long-planned royal tour of the British Commonwealth. This followed the realisation that HMS *Vanguard*, Britain's newest battleship that had been used for the 1947 royal visit to South Africa, was too deep draughted for entry into some Antipodean ports. HMRY *Britannia* was then at an early stage of construction; her keel was laid on 16th June 1952 at the Clydebank shipyard of John Brown and Co. Ltd. and she would be launched on Thursday 16th April 1953. Of the four *Corinthic* class ships, the *Gothic* and the *Ceramic* were the anointed candidates because they had a two knot reserve of speed in the event of delays to the Queen's timetable. The *Athenic* and the *Corinthic,* with their different, less powerful steam turbines, could not offer this. Unlike various Royal Navy warships that were considered for the task, the *Gothic* and *Ceramic* also had all the space needed for the royal retinue plus a Royal Navy party made up of royal yachtsmen, radio communicators and technicians, a Royal Marine band as well as a small group of press and BBC people.

The schedules of the *Ceramic* and *Gothic* dictated it would be the *Gothic* that was chartered by the British Admiralty when the time came to prepare one or the other for royal use. She had arrived at Liverpool on 23rd June 1951 whereas the *Ceramic* was away on the New Zealand coast loading cargo, having reached Auckland from Liverpool on 14th May. *Ceramic* became the stand-by royal yacht. Having discharged all her cargo, on 15th July 1951 the *Gothic* moved across the river to Birkenhead where, over the next five months, she was converted by Cammell Laird to become royal yacht for King George VI and Queen Elizabeth. Accompanied by their younger daughter Princess Margaret, the King and Queen were to embark on a tour of the Commonwealth planned for early 1952. The *Gothic's* hull was repainted white with buff hull riband. Topgallant masts each 30 feet in length were fitted, air conditioning gear multiplied on her upper decks and substantial alterations were made to her passenger interiors. Four two-bedded staterooms comprising the aft end of the deckhouse on the Boat and Games Deck, two of which had private bathrooms, were extensively modified to become two single royal bedrooms each with its own bathroom. Forward on this deck, a nest of single-berth cabins became wardrobes for clothes and accommodation for dressers, equerries, pages, valets and ladies-in-waiting. Immediately below on the Promenade Deck, the smoking room was cleverly divided lengthwise to give two royal day rooms. A central ante-room provided entrance to both rooms while the veranda cafe, directly aft, was turned into a private outdoor sitting area and renamed the sun room. A small pantry was installed just off the ante-room.

The passenger lounge and dining saloon at the forward end of the Bridge Deck were each similarly partitioned. A royal reception room was created, occupying two thirds of the lounge on its starboard side with a private dining room opening off its aft end for the King, Queen and Princess Margaret. This took up one third of the dining saloon's area. To port was a lounge and dining mess for staff from the royal household, the *Gothic's* officers, and Royal Navy officers. Preparatory to dining, the royal family would come down the main stairs at the forward end of the Promenade Deck, into the drawing room which could be screened off from the stairs by heavy curtains.

Furniture for these royal apartments was transferred to the *Gothic* from the *Victoria and Albert*, the old royal yacht launched in 1899 for Queen Victoria and shortly to be scrapped. All of it would later be transferred again, from the *Gothic* to HMRY *Britannia* at Malta on 4th May 1954 following *Britannia's* commissioning (which took place on 11th January 1954). Remodelling of the *Gothic's* interiors was done under the direction of the British Admiralty in conjunction with Shaw Savill, using plans approved by George VI. She was to retain her full Merchant Navy crew including Shaw Savill's Commodore, Captain A.V. Richardson, who was appointed to the *Gothic* as her Master on 9th October 1951. A full general cargo would be loaded for the voyage out to New Zealand and Australia with the King and Queen aboard.

Royal Navy staff officers and members of the royal household were accommodated in the Boat and Promenade Deck passenger cabins, with the Flag Officer Royal Yacht, Vice-Admiral C.E. Lambe RN, occupying the *Gothic's* suite with private sitting room in the Promenade Deck's forward starboard corner. Temporary accommodation was built into the *Gothic's* Shelter Deck, one level below her Bridge Deck in what had formerly been part of Number 3 upper 'tween decks, for use by Royal Navy petty officers and ratings. New port holes appeared in the *Gothic's* hull outboard of these mess decks. Cradles were erected over Number 5 hatch in the *Gothic's* aft well deck, to take the 40-foot long royal barge and the smaller admiral's barge. Above the wheelhouse, the monkey island was modified to become a viewing platform and saluting bridge for the King, Queen and Princess Margaret. Meanwhile the children's play room on the Boat and Games Deck was equipped as a work room for the King and Queen's personal staff.

The fore end of the deck house where the children's room was located, was itself extended forward almost to the after edge of Number 3 hatch. This was done to provide space for the S.W.B. Eleven long-range, short-wave broadcast transmitter-receiver that the Admiralty fitted to the *Gothic*. Having a continuous rating of 10 kW output it was by all accounts a massive radio apparatus so powerful that, despite prominent insulators fitted to the mainmast rigging, it electrified much of the after part of the ship when transmitting. Flashing red warning lights and hazard signs were fitted around the base of the mainmast to alert the crew about shocks and sparks. Cloaked in Cold War secrecy, the S.W.B. Eleven was state-of-the art for its time; it could even send photographs by wireless. It also permitted the Queen during the 1953-54 tour to speak with her government ministers in Britain from the opposite side of the world, and with her two children: Prince Charles, born on 14th November 1948 and Princess Anne, born on 15th August 1950.

On 10th October 1951 it was announced that, because of the King's declining health, the royal tour would be made by his heir and daughter Princess Elizabeth accompanied by her husband Prince Philip, Duke of Edinburgh. The *Gothic's* refit was completed on 15th December 1951 and she departed Liverpool for Southampton on the 19th of that month. On 5th January 1952 after 16 days alongside at Southampton, the *Gothic* sailed for Mombasa in Kenya, going via Las Palmas and Cape Town, there

The snowy volcanic peak of Mount Egmont-Taranaki, 2,518 metres (8,261 feet) high, hovers above the *Gothic's* bridge in this 1952 view at New Plymouth, New Zealand. She is working cargo after cancellation in February that year of the tour by Princess Elizabeth and Philip, Duke of Edinburgh. *[Barrie Davis]*

A relic of the cancelled tour. *[Captain Graham Pepper, Shaw Savill Society]*

The *Gothic's* master and senior officers for the cancelled royal tour. From left: Dr P. Brownlees, Chief Engineer O. S. Walker, Captain A.V. Richardson, Chief Officer H.O.V. Andersen, First Radio Officer J.C. Smith and Purser E Cordery. Photographed on the *Gothic's* Boat Deck aft of the bridge house, 7th January 1952. Chief Officer Andersen, Purser Cordery and Dr Brownlees were aboard for the 1953-54 tour. *[Reuters. Alexander Turnbull Library, Wellington New Zealand, EP-Transport-Ships-Gothic-01]*

to await the royal couple who were to depart by plane for Kenya on 31st January. Their tour schedule had them boarding the *Gothic* at Mombasa on 7th February for passage to Australia. It was, however, not to be. King George VI died on 6th February 1952 in the 17th year of his reign, aged 56. Princess Elizabeth and Prince Philip returned immediately to London, their Commonwealth tour abandoned. All staff for the tour were disembarked and the *Gothic* left Mombasa on 9th February for Australia without passengers, to unload her cargo. Then she went to New Zealand from Sydney to load refrigerated goods.

Arriving back in Liverpool on 18th May 1952, the *Gothic* was sent to Cammell Laird again where all the furniture in the royal apartments was landed into storage. These spaces were then closed off. The *Gothic* resumed her normal commercial trade but with passenger numbers reduced to 52 because of the royal tour alterations. Still painted white, she was now a royal yacht-in-waiting for Buckingham Palace had announced that the new queen was to proceed with the tour at a later date. The Prime Ministers of Australia and New Zealand wanted it done by April 1954 so that they could, on the back of a triumphant royal progress, then call general elections. To achieve this, the tour would need to begin in December but HMRY *Britannia* would not have completed her fitting out and working up by then. So the *Gothic*, already converted for the role, remained the favoured option. Shaw Savill was paid a holding fee of £125,000 by the British Government to keep her at the Queen's disposal. In the meantime there were plenty of paying passengers eager to travel on the ship intended for their new sovereign. Doubtless some of them, having exercised the right amount of charm towards their officer hosts, were shown past locked doors into the royal bedrooms and sitting rooms, emptied of their contents but filled with mystique nonetheless.

Master of the royal yacht

Captain Arthur Richardson retired from the *Gothic*, and from the sea, on 30th April 1953 one day after he turned 65. Force of circumstances meant he was never to be master of the Queen's royal yacht. That eminence instead fell to Shaw Savill's next senior master, Captain David Aitchison, who at the beginning of 1953 was in command of the flagship *Dominion Monarch*. On 26th March 1953 he was appointed to command the *Gothic*, then discharging refrigerated cargo at Liverpool. Captain B. Forbes Moffat took Aitchison's place as the *Dominion Monarch's* master. Born in Sunderland, County Durham on 26th September 1892, David Aitchison first went to sea in 1909 as an apprentice with the Sunderland firm of V.T. Thompson and Company, owners of tramp ships.

Following cancellation of the 1951 tour the *Gothic* made four voyages to Australia and New Zealand. Captain Aitchison was her master for the fourth and last of these, a round trip that proceeded outwards to Auckland to discharge, then loading homeward at Bluff and Wellington. Sensibly Shaw Savill had already chosen senior members of their sea staff for the *Gothic* and on this trip they all got to know each other. Her Merchant Navy officers for the royal tour comprised:

H.O.V. Andersen	Chief Officer
H. Riding	Second Officer
I.K. McIntosh	Third Officer
M.W. Robinson	Fourth Officer
R.L. Reid	Fifth Officer
J. Glyde	Sixth Officer
C.H. Roberts	First Radio Officer
A. J. Cade	Second Radio Officer
M.D.J. Pilgrim	Third Radio Officer
D.C. Clayton	Fourth Radio Officer
O. Charters	Chief Engineer
D.M.V. Parkinson	Senior Second Engineer
R.J. Drennan	Intermediate Second Engineer
W.H. Frost	Junior Second Engineer
D.Taylor	Senior Third Engineer
T. Adams	Junior Third Engineer
W.N. Blake	Fourth Engineer
E. Bledge	Fifth Engineer
D.R. Porter	Sixth Engineer
R. Parker	Seventh Engineer
J. Reaich	Eighth Engineer
S. Newton	Ninth Engineer
D.A. Ransome	Assistant Engineer
M. Galbraith	First Refrigerating Engineer
T.M. Coulter	Second Refrigerating Engineer
W.A. Lewis	First Electrical Engineer
T.J. Williams	Second Electrical Engineer
J.A. Parker	Third Electrical Engineer
E.M. Robertson	Supernumerary Engineer
E. Cordery	Purser
Dr P.A.K. Brownlees	Surgeon
Miss M.O. Davies	Nursing Officer
W.A. Ray	Chief Steward
C.P. Foulstone	Second Steward
T. Taylor	Chef (Chief Cook)

Born in Glasgow on 23rd November 1908 Harold O.V. Andersen, who was known throughout Shaw Savill as 'Hov', had been the *Gothic's* Chief Officer under Captain Richardson for the cancelled 1952 royal tour as had Ted Cordery, Shaw Savill's most senior purser, and Dr Brownlees. Harry Riding, lieutenant-commander RNR, served as the *Gothic's* Third Officer during that voyage. Chief Engineer Oliver Charters was born on 20th May 1898 and originally joined Shaw Savill as Third Engineer of the *Tairoa* (7,983/1920) on 22th August 1927. He replaced O.S. Walker as the *Gothic's* Chief, staying with the *Gothic* until February 1961.

In 61-year-old David Aitchison the royal tour of 1953-54 found the ideal man. Although he was Master of the *Gothic* and in command of the ship, overall command lay with Vice-Admiral E.M.C. Abel Smith CB CVO RN, who had been formally appointed Flag Officer Royal Yacht (FORY) on 2nd February 1953. British Merchant Navy masters in those times were, by very definition, autocrats. Few would have happily tolerated the presence on their bridge of a Royal Navy admiral watching over their shoulder and commenting freely. Diplomacy and courtesy on the part of the *Gothic's* Master were essential to make the relationship work, and Captain Aitchison proved himself to have these skills in as great a quota as he did navigation and seamanship. Aitchison gives a prime example in his 1958 book 'Royal Standard Red Ensign' when on the afternoon of 27th October 1953 the *Gothic*, flying the White Ensign and with Vice-Admiral Abel Smith on the bridge, came into the Royal Navy base on the Isle of Portland and was moored to a buoy in the harbour. A tug was used by Captain Aitchison to hold the ship's port bow up into the wind while cables were secured. The Admiral expressed his displeasure at the ship being seen to need a tug in this way, while picking up her moorings. Royal Navy commanding officers were expected to show dash and agility when manoeuvring their vessels in harbour; tugs were an admission of feeble ship-handling. Big, sluggish and heavily laden, the *Gothic* was no destroyer and in the Merchant Navy tugs were, of course, always used to assist. But from then on Captain Aitchison deferred to Royal Navy sensitivities and made as infrequent use of tugs as he safely could.

It was on the pre-royal tour voyage that at the suggestion of a friend, Milford Sound in Fiordland, New Zealand was included in the royal voyage to come. Mentioned by Captain Aitchison to the harbour master and his board at Bluff they, with enthusiasm, put the idea to Ralph Hanan the local Member of Parliament with a swiftly successful result. It had already been announced that, 1953 being the Coronation Year, the newly crowned Elizabeth II would tour her Commonwealth from November during the Southern Hemisphere summer. On 18th August 1953 the *Gothic* departed London for the Mersey and Cammell Laird once again, to have her royal accoutrements reinstated.

The décor for the royal apartments was altered considerably from that provided for the late King. Everything was done with meticulous care, officials coming from Buckingham

The royal apartments. Top left, the reception room. Top right, the dining room. Bottom left, the Queen's day room. Bottom right, the Duke of Edinburgh's day room. *[Captain Graham Pepper, Shaw Savill Society]*

Palace to supervise the new colours, plasterwork and paint schemes chosen by the Queen and the Duke of Edinburgh. The Queen's day room aft on the Promenade Deck's starboard side was given ivory walls, carpeting in clove grey and light turquoise curtains. A maple writing desk was fitted for her use; placed on it were two cream-coloured telephones, one for 'secret' and the other for 'normal" conversations. Queen Victoria's mahogany writing table from HMRY *Victoria and Albert* was installed in the Duke of Edinburgh's day cabin. He was also provided with a record player. In the ante-room linking both day cabins hung an illuminated map showing the *Gothic's* position with the route of the royal tour traced in lights. Down in the royal dining room was an extending table with 22 seats along with polished silver candelabra, all brought to the ship from Buckingham Palace. Two sideboards from HMRY *Victoria and Albert* complemented the table setting. Amidships at Bridge Deck level a pair of navy boat booms were secured to the hull, one to port and the other to starboard.

On Tuesday 6th October 1953 the *Gothic's* crew signed on. Among them was 20-year-old Able Seaman Warwick Thomson of Auckland, New Zealand, who had arrived at Cammell Laird to work-by the *Gothic* four days earlier. Pay for working-by was £9.00 a week with a daily 9 a.m. start. He remembers: 'Deep down, those of us who had been selected were chuffed but that didn't stop us joining in disrespectful banter. The company had selected crewmen for the *Gothic* about whom they knew something – I would have been a prime candidate having sailed with them continuously for the previous three and a half years, but they finished up trawling the pools - taking anybody to make up the numbers for there were 40 of us on deck alone, without counting the greasers and stewards.' Warwick Thomson later went on to become a Shaw Savill navigating officer, surmounting the challenge of achieving a second mate's ticket and then his master's ticket.

Captain Aitchison joined the *Gothic* at Birkenhead on Sunday 11th October, at the conclusion of her refit. She had by then received the same Thornycroft funnel top added to the *Ceramic*, giving her a mightiness of bearing that had not been there when she was prepared for the 1952 tour. Two barges and two accommodation gangways, each of these in three sections, were hoisted on to the *Gothic's* aft well deck: the royal barge weighing 12 tons was the same craft used by King George VI

Gothic's seamen in their tropical white uniforms. Able seaman Warwick Thomson is at right. At all times the deck crowd had to wear this rig, including hats, while carrying out maintenance work on the royal yacht's upper decks. Difficulties in getting paint, varnish and grease out of these uniforms can be imagined. *[Warwick Thomson]*

during his visit to South Africa in 1947. It was powered by two Gardner marine diesels each of 100 HP. The smaller 35 feet long admiral's barge, also known as the staff barge, weighed seven tons. Resplendent in her white, green and buff livery the *Gothic* left the Mersey in drizzle, getting underway at 11.30 a.m. on Tuesday 13th October and steaming north to the Firth of Clyde where, early on the morning of 14th October in fine weather, she anchored off Roseneath on the western shore of the Gareloch, opposite Greenock.

Wintry rain soon set in over the *Gothic's* anchorage. Warwick Thomson, whose marvellous diary from 1953-54 gives us a young seaman's perspective of that entire royal tour, records how he and his mates listened clandestinely on a forbidden radio to the *Gothic's* officers speaking by radio telephone to their bosses in London. Having tested all her equipment including the boat booms, gangways, barges and the S.W.B. Eleven installation, the *Gothic* left Roseneath a week later on 20th October in a wind and rain storm to return to Liverpool. When she arrived, the Mersey was blanketed in fog and the *Gothic* was almost run down by a big Japanese tanker laden with some 16,000 tons of crude, adrift on the tide with a fleet of tugs in attendance. While manoeuvring to her berth in the Canada Dock, the *Gothic* struck the stern of a Greek freighter, bending the latter's poop rails. Some 6,000 tons of general goods were loaded for New Zealand with the heaviest items going into the bottom of her holds: motor cars and farm tractors, salt, chemicals, paper and corrugated iron sheets. Also at Liverpool the ship's Royal Navy contingent embarked: 15 naval ratings for communications duties, 16 yachtsmen from the Royal Yacht Service who were to man the royal and admiral's barges, and thirty members of the Royal Marines Band.

Vice-Admiral Abel Smith, Flag Officer Royal Yacht, came aboard with his staff. A former RAF and Fleet Air Arm pilot, Edward Michael Conolly Abel Smith of Longhills, Lincolnshire (later Sir Conolly Abel Smith GCVO CB) was 53 years of age having been born on 3rd December 1899. Accompanying the Admiral were his Operations Officer, Commander C.D. Madden DSC RN; his Communications Officer, Commander R.R.B. Mackenzie MBE RN; Major F.V. Dunn, MVO RM, Director of Music and the Cipher Officer, Lieutenant Commander N.E.F. Dalrymple-Hamilton DSC RN. Commander Dalrymple-Hamilton had with him a team of three WRNS (Women's Royal Naval Service) officers. The *Gothic* sailed from Liverpool at 11.30 a.m. on Monday 26th October for a two-day coastal passage to London. The opportunity was taken to rehearse the procedures for a full ceremonial departure with the Queen on board. Up on the Boat and Games Deck the Royal Marines Band played 'Oh what a beautiful morning' despite the cold and lack of sun. The ship's crew paraded in their uniforms. Out at sea, she was soon pitching into a full autumnal gale; Warwick Thomson remembers waking that night to find items being thrown about his cabin.

Next the *Gothic* called at Portland, arriving there at 3 p.m. on Tuesday 27th October for a cursory Royal Navy work-up. The ship cruised the degaussing range, to eliminate unwanted magnetic fields in her steel hull, then at 4.30 p.m. a ceremonial arrival was rehearsed. More rehearsals took place with the gangways, hoisting the barges in and out, and with dressing ship with flags and with night-time festoon lights. These comprised some 280 electric bulbs suspended from the forestay, between the mast tops and down the mainmast's backstay to her stern. Removable gooseneck davits were fitted to either side of the aft well deck for handling the royal gangways. While at Portland, and for the only time ever, the *Gothic* flew the White Ensign which was hoisted from her stern at 2 p.m. on 27th October. This was probably done to remind her Merchant Navy crew that the forthcoming voyage was going to be different. At 1.30 p.m. on Wednesday 28th November the *Gothic* departed Portland for London. That afternoon, in company with a Royal Navy destroyer, exercises were held in ship-to-ship transfers while underway at sea, a midshipman and sub-lieutenant being sent over to the *Gothic* from the destroyer by breeches buoy.

Vice-Admiral Abel Smith meanwhile took over the royal dining room as his admiral's mess. Impressive though his decorations and those of his officers were, there was at that same dining table a former army man who had been given equally high recognition. During the First World War Basil Sanderson, Chairman and Managing Director of Shaw Savill, served as an officer in the Duke of Lancaster's Own Yeomanry and saw action in the trenches of Western France. On 12th October 1916 he was awarded the Military Cross for gallantry. Thirty seven years later Sanderson boarded the *Gothic* at Liverpool and spent the two-day voyage to London inspecting the ship and assuring himself that she was ready for her forthcoming task.

The *Gothic* came up-river to the King George V Dock on the evening of Thursday 29th October. Warwick Thomson recalls police and secret service men 'swarming aboard' as soon as the ship was alongside. Next day the holds were opened and all the cargo was checked. All the crew had their cabins searched for stowaways and contraband; crew members now had to carry special passes and they were also issued with tropical white uniforms. Despite the miserable rain and chill London fog Warwick and his fellow seamen were put to work washing the funnel, holystoning the timber decks and sugiing paintwork.

Royal baggage was loaded for the voyage ahead, including the Coronation dress and jewellery that was to be worn at three state openings of parliament. By law no state crowns are allowed to leave British shores but three tiaras, five necklaces and numerous brooches from the royal collection were in the baggage. On Monday 9th November, one day prior to sailing, trucks and vans came and went from the wharf bringing the last food stores to be taken aboard, then next afternoon their place was taken by Rolls Royce limousines conveying to the ship the first of her passengers from the royal household who were not flying to Bermuda and Jamaica with the Queen. There were five of them: Captain Viscount Althorpe (later to be father to Diana, Princess of Wales) Commander (S) Richard Colville CVO DSC RN, who was the Queen's Press Secretary, the New Zealand Equerry, Lieutenant Jeremy P.D. Hall RNZN, and the Australian Equerry, Wing-Commander Michael Cowan DSO RAAF. The star of the quintet in Captain Aitchison's eyes was Earl Mountbatten of Burma's daughter Lady Pamela Mountbatten: 'She was one of the most agreeable persons I have ever met, simple, natural and very easy to talk to'. Also making up the passenger list, as far as Jamaica, were the Errington Keville couple, he the Chief Executive of Shaw Savill (and Basil Sanderson's deputy), she having been sponsor at the *Ceramic's* launch in December 1947. By all accounts this diverse group of people got on with remarkable accord, so much so that when the Queen and the Duke embarked at Jamaica they found themselves welcomed into the pleasant atmosphere of an established house party.

The tour commences

Representatives from the British and Australian news media also joined the ship. She sailed at 11.30 p.m. from King George V Dock for Jamaica on the night of 10th November 1953. The departure of the *Gothic* being towed stern-first out into a mist-shrouded Thames was in total contrast to the great spectacle and ceremony soon to come. Steaming out into the Atlantic, the *Gothic* encountered a heavy swell, Warwick Thomson and his seamen companions finding the decks deserted as they sugied paintwork and holystoned the timber planking. Temperatures and sea conditions improved as the ship neared Jamaica, the seaman often having the pleasure of sugiing to music as the band of the Royal Marines worked on its repertoire.

Between 19th and 21st November awnings were erected over Numbers 3 and 4 hatch and on the poop deck. Jamaica was reached on 21st November, all hands being called at 5.15 a.m. next day as the *Gothic* entered harbour at Kingston and came alongside the oil wharf at 7 a.m. to take on bunkers. Another early start came next morning, 23rd November at 6 o'clock, when she moved out to anchor in the harbour. Here the ship's hull was repainted by shore labour while, onboard, her seamen were harried into touching up all paintwork particularly on her starboard side which would be visible to the royal gaze when the Queen and Duke embarked at the end of that week. Special quick-drying paint was used. The ship was dressed overall with flags on Wednesday 25th November, the men working overtime until 10 p.m. Navy launches patrolled the ship's flanks while divers checked her hull for limpet mines. Her interiors, decorated with fresh flowers, received their final spruce up. When shown off to the press at London there had been some criticism that the style of furnishings was too traditionally floral and comfortable; why not reflect on what had been seen at the recent Festival of Britain? The answer was scarce resources in austerity Britain; the décor had accordingly been kept conservative with as much use as possible made of existing furniture from Buckingham Palace and from the *Victoria and Albert*.

On 26th November the Queen and Duke of Edinburgh arrived at Montego Bay by plane from Bermuda, then on Friday 27th November the *Gothic* weighed anchor at 7 a.m. and steamed down to Fort Royal, anchoring off Garrison Pier at 7.45 a.m. Members of the royal household, who had travelled on the same flight as the Queen, joined the ship along with the last of the royal baggage. The day was fine with a light breeze, becoming very hot during the afternoon. At 3 p.m. the seamen were knocked off from a last-minute flurry of cleaning and painting. As Warwick Thomson recounts in his diary, they were 'told to reappear in white uniform. This done, we lined up on the poop as the Queen drew alongside'.

The royal barge with the Queen, the Duke of Edinburgh and Vice-Admiral Abel Smith came alongside the *Gothic* at 3.55 p.m., ten minutes ahead of schedule. As the Queen climbed the gangway to the aft well deck, the royal standard was unfurled from the truck of the *Gothic's* mainmast and the lord high admiral's flag from her foremast. Simultaneously the Royal Marines Band played the British national anthem. Aboard the escorting cruiser HMS *Sheffield*, at anchor nearby, a 21-gun salute thundered out. The

The royal barge bringing the Queen and the Duke of Edinburgh out to the *Gothic* for the first time, at Fort Royal, Jamaica on 27th November 1953. *[Warwick Thomson]*

Queen and the Duke were introduced to Captain Aitchison and then to the *Gothic's* senior officers lined up in their best white uniforms. Next the royal couple were shown to their air-conditioned quarters. An hour later, with the royal barge hoisted in and the gangway unrigged and stowed, Her Majesty's Royal Yacht *Gothic* got under way, escorted ahead by the cruiser HMS *Sheffield* (11,350/1937). Dressed in a yellow frock, Queen Elizabeth came out into the sun room to watch while the Duke set off to explore. Warwick Thomson records: 'The Duke....hadn't been aboard more than a quarter of an hour when he was found up on the funnel deck, the dirtiest and most untidy deck on the ship'.

Next landfall was Panama. With HMS *Sheffield* stationed one quarter of a mile ahead, the *Gothic* entered the port of Cristobal and berthed there at 8.55 a.m. on 29th November. As in all ports she entered from now on, aircraft and boats accompanied her, ranks of soldiers and brass bands were drawn up on the wharves, cannon salutes were fired and gentry of all manner came aboard to wait on the Queen's presence while crowds jammed the shoreline. The Queen and the Duke disembarked for engagements on shore while the *Gothic's* seamen went back to mooring stations, the ship leaving to transit the Panama Canal. The royal party reboarded at the Miraflores Locks. There were more engagements on shore at Balboa, which was reached at sunset, then at 6 a.m. on 30th November 1953 she was underway into the Pacific.

Her Majesty's first order of business for the Pacific crossing was to visit HMS *Sheffield*. On Captain Aitchison's advice this needed to be done before the vessels got out into the mid-ocean swell. That same afternoon, 30th November, a gangway was rigged, HMS *Sheffield* closed with the *Gothic* and both vessels stopped engines. The cruiser sent over her admiral's launch and the Queen and Duke were gone for two hours. After returning, the royal couple could be seen through the windows of the seamen's poop deck messroom, strolling in the sun room and playing deck tennis under the awning at the aft end of the Boat Deck (which had been renamed the Royal Deck. The deck house in which the Queen and Duke's cabins were located, was similarly renamed the Queen's House). Warwick Thomson notes in his diary that, from then on, rules and restrictions with which the seamen had been cajoled only a week before, were slowly lightened. 'As an AB I spent most of the time on the voyage as a day worker doing normal maintenance duties often in full view of the royals. Ventures onto the royal decks were strictly on a needs-only basis and uniform was worn at all times on deck. When we were mucking about greasing and overhauling cargo gear we were allowed some latitude but bare torsos were out. The biggest burden was having to wear caps all the time. Keeping our tropical whites clean was a challenge.'

Steaming for Fiji, the *Gothic* crossed the Equator on Friday 4th December. Watched by the Queen, the Crossing the Line ceremony was held at 5 p.m. on the fore well deck, where a swimming pool had been erected beside Number 2 hatch. On 8th December HMS *Sheffield's* anaesthetist was transferred by breeches buoy to the *Gothic* for an urgent appendectomy performed on the stewards' night watchman. Just after 9 a.m. the following morning, HMS *Sheffield* was relieved as royal guard ship by the Royal New Zealand Navy's cruiser *Black Prince* (7,410/1943). 'Tonight while I was up working on the Promenade Deck alone', records Warwick Thomson, 'the Queen and Duke passed within a foot of me. I saw them coming and did some fast thinking on modes of address, but thought discretion the better part of valour and said nothing....the Queen was wearing a grey evening dress.'

Fiji was reached on 17th December 1953 for a two day call, next was Tonga on 20th December. Then on a rainy, drab morning, Wednesday 23rd December 1953 the *Gothic* arrived off Waitemata harbour at Auckland, New Zealand and the royal tour started in earnest.

Turbine troubles and tragedy

Between rain squalls Little Barrier Island was visible at 5.30 a.m. when the *Gothic's* seamen on day work were called from their bunks. At 6.30 a.m. they started dressing the ship overall with

HMRY *Gothic* was moored at Suva, Fiji between 17th and 19th December 1953. Here on the royal yacht's Boat Deck above Number 3 hatch, the Queen with the Duke of Edinburgh seated beside her is receiving a ceremonial whale tooth, or Tabua, from a Fijian chief. Tabua are considered by Fijians as a kavakaturanga or 'chiefly object.' *[Warwick Thomson]*

flags. Despite poor weather an armada of small boats was on the water to greet the royal yacht as, steaming at 10 knots, she came past Rangitoto Island. On her bridge the Auckland Harbour Master, Captain W.G. Kelsey, was piloting the ship. Turning under starboard helm to enter Waitemata harbour, artillery fire boomed out across the sea as the battery high on North Head commenced firing a 21-gun royal salute. With HMNZS *Black Prince* astern, the *Gothic* was manoeuvred alongside Berth B at Central Wharf to a cacophony of car horns, military bands, locomotive steam whistles and ships' sirens, among them the *Runic* (Warwick Thomson's previous ship) and the passenger liner *Orcades* (28,164/1947) berthed nearby. Assisting her were the Auckland Harbour Board tugs *William C. Daldy* (346/1936) and *Te Awhina* (220/1908). A westerly wind was gusting to 30 knots as the rain came and went in drizzly showers. But she was right on time: 10 a.m., and immediately once all mooring lines were secured Lieutenant-General Sir Willoughby Norrie, Governor-General of New Zealand, hastened aboard followed by the Prime Minister of New Zealand, the Right Honourable S.G. Holland. Their visit, paying first homage to the royal arrivals, was brief; 20 minutes later they were back on the wharf waiting for the Queen and the Duke of Edinburgh to step ashore. They did so shortly before 11 a.m.

The 38-day royal tour of New Zealand that commenced that morning was a stupendous event. It is estimated that three quarters of the country's population, which at the time numbered just 2.075 million, went to see the Queen and the Duke at one or more of their numerous public appearances. Elizabeth II had been proclaimed New Zealand's Head of State from 6th February 1952, on the death of her father, and she was the first ever to visit in person. New Zealand in 1953 regarded itself most fervently as British. The local economy was completely dominated by farming and forestry; what limited manufacturing there was served only to support the production of agricultural goods for export. Sixty seven per cent of those exports went to Great Britain in 1953-54, and 56% of the country's imports came from there as did 65% of immigrants who arrived to settle in New Zealand during 1953-54. Across the land, towns and cities rivalled each other as to how enthusiastically they could display 'loyal greetings and affection' for the Queen. She in return made a hugely favourable impression especially when, the day after the tour began, the joyful celebration of her coming was interrupted by a national disaster.

Above: HMRY *Gothic* seen from the New Zealand light cruiser *Black Prince*. *[Ian J. Farquhar collection]*
Right: The arrival at Auckland, New Zealand, on 23rd December 1953. Soldiers of the 9 Coast Regiment Memorial Saluting Battery, Royal New Zealand Artillery, fire a 21-gun royal salute from the South Battery emplacement on North Head, Devonport, at the eastern end of Waitemata harbour. The pieces they are firing comprise four 18-pounder field guns used by the New Zealand Division in France during the First World War. Behind them is a preserved breech-loading, eight-inch Mark VII Armstrong Disappearing Gun, one of ten purchased by the New Zealand government in 1885 during a Russian invasion scare. It was so named because when fired the gun recoiled downwards out of sight into a loading room below ground, where the gun's crew was protected from incoming fire. *[Murray Robinson]*

Around 10.21 p.m. on Christmas Eve, 24th December 1953, the overnight express train running between Wellington and Auckland plunged off a rail bridge into the Whangaehu River near the settlement of Tangiwai, in the centre of the North Island. The Ka Class steam locomotive pulling the train, along with the first six of its 11 carriages, went into the flooded river killing 151 of 285 passengers and crew. Moments before, the bridge's pillars had been undermined by a six-metre-high wall of water escaping down the Whangaehu River from the crater lake atop the nearby 2,797 metre (9,177 feet) high Mount Ruapehu, an active volcano. Known as the Tangiwai Disaster, it stands as New Zealand's worst-ever railway accident. Because the country's population was so small, almost everyone knew someone who had either died aboard the train or got out alive. On a comparable population basis for 1953, it equates to some 4,000 people in Great Britain losing their lives in a single event. When the following evening she made her first-ever Christmas Day broadcast to the Commonwealth, the Queen ended by expressing sympathy for the families of the dead. Next day she and the Duke visited one of the survivor families at their home in Epsom, Auckland. Accompanied by the New Zealand Prime Minister, Prince Philip was present at the funeral service held at Karori Lawn Cemetery on 31st December 1953 for 21 victims of the disaster whose remains could not be identified.

The Queen did not use the *Gothic* during her five-week tour of the Dominion. At Auckland the royal entourage, the royal baggage and Royal Navy personnel including Vice-Admiral Abel Smith left the ship in entirety. Her status reverted to that of just another cargo vessel, with discharge to take place in Wellington. Much of the homeward cargo was also to be loaded at Wellington, the balance coming aboard at Sydney. This meant that wherever the ship was photographed on the tour from her arrival at Auckland to her departure from Fremantle on 1st April 1954, she appeared fully loaded. With nothing of the spectacle from the preceding week, at noon on Wednesday 30th December the *Gothic* backed away from Central Wharf. Assisted at her stern by the steam tug *William C. Daldy* she turned for the open sea and the two-day run down to Wellington. Full ahead was ordered on the bridge telegraphs. The engine manoeuvring platform answered with full ahead but then the starboard indicator unaccountably went back to stop. Captain Aitchison waited until Chief Engineer Charters arrived on the bridge. He informed the Master that the rotor of the starboard high-pressure turbine had bent out of its true alignment while being started, and was now unusable. The news came as a hefty shock. Captain Aitchison had the Auckland Harbour Board pilot promise not to divulge what he had just heard; any revelation that the royal yacht had suffered a major engine breakdown would be a catastrophic embarrassment for the tour and for Shaw Savill.

Without delay she proceeded to sea on her port engine only. Out beyond Cuvier Island, having rounded the northern tip of Coromandel Peninsula, the *Gothic* hove-to for 16 hours until 6.30 the following morning while the starboard high-pressure turbine was uncoupled from the starboard intermediate- and low-pressure turbines. Compounded in this way, these would now turn the starboard propeller on their own with the high-pressure turbine disengaged. Astonishingly, and to Captain Aitchison's very great relief, the *Gothic* worked up to 17 knots. She berthed without trouble at Wellington's Glasgow Wharf Number 2 right on time at 8 a.m., 1st January 1954. On shore, nobody knew of the problem with her turbine or suspected anything was amiss.

The royal and admiral's barges were hoisted off Number 5 hatch by the Wellington Harbour Board's floating crane *Hikitea* and placed at the seaward end of Glasgow Wharf. The hatches were opened and working of cargo got underway. Not long into January, Chief Steward W.A. Ray suffered a cerebral haemorrhage. He was taken from the ship on a stretcher then by ambulance to hospital. Second Steward C.P. Foulstone took over as the *Gothic's* acting Chief Steward. Three and half weeks were spent alongside, then on 26th January the *Gothic* departed Wellington at 10.30 p.m. for Bluff at the southern extremity of the South Island. She was once more deeply laden. Numbers 3, 5 and 6 holds had been filled with refrigerated and general cargo; the remaining three holds were to be topped up at ports on the Australian coast. Her white hull had again been painted, as had all the masts, posts and derricks. Warwick Thomson records in his diary that the *Gothic's* lamp trimmer had issued 145 gallons of 'over-side white' and 45 gallons of gloss white paint. Three tons of sandstone had been expended on regular cleaning of the *Gothic's* timber decks.

Vice-Admiral Abel Smith and his staff were back aboard for the journey south. Mid-passage as she steamed across the Canterbury Bight, the ship was informed by radio that Chief Steward Ray had died in a Dunedin hospital. He was buried at Dunedin on 29th January, leaving a widow in Great Britain. Public acclaim for the *Gothic* was not dampened by this sad news. Irreverently her seamen had by now re-named her 'the white elephant'. At the request of the local harbour board the *Gothic* stood in towards the port of Timaru, passing the breakwater at slow speed where she was mobbed by small craft packed with spectators. She was alongside at Bluff, a sea port of a few thousand residents, by 7.15 a.m. on 28th January. HMNZS *Black Prince* berthed just prior to the *Gothic*.

After inspecting one last royal guard of honour, and after shaking hands with the Governor-General, the Prime Minister and their wives one last time, Queen Elizabeth boarded her royal yacht at 10.10 a.m. on Saturday 30th January 1954. Five minutes later on the high tide the *Gothic* let go all mooring lines, her departure watched by a tumultuous crowd of 21,000 people massed anywhere that offered a glimpse of the Queen and the Duke. Included in these vantage points were the cargo ships *Haparangi* (11,281/1947) lying ahead of the *Gothic* at the same wharf in Bluff harbour, and the elderly *Tweedbank* (5,626/1930) at the wharf opposite her. Able Seaman Warwick Thomson wrote in his diary that the *Tweedbank* even had spectators clambering up around her radar scanner to get a better view. Carpenters had built temporary grandstands for the occasion, and everywhere were prodigious displays of cut flowers in wooden planter boxes. Pipe bands and military brass bands competed to see which could generate the most sound against a bedlam of cheering from thousands of loyal throats. Her Majesty stood on the saluting platform above the *Gothic's* wheelhouse to acknowledge the farewell. A Maori choir sang *Haere ra* – goodbye. Then steam was applied to the tug *Awarua's* triple-expansion engines as she began towing the *Gothic's* bow round towards Foveaux Strait and the open sea. Black smoke poured from the tug's funnel top, smothering the *Gothic's* bridge and forcing the royal couple to hasten aft to the Royal Deck.

She had gone from her people but perhaps the finest part of that first royal visit to New Zealand by Queen Elizabeth II was now to come. Leaving Bluff, the *Gothic* rounded the bottom of the South Island then during the early hours of Sunday 31st January steered north east along the coast of Fiordland keeping three miles to seaward. From the bridge Captain Aitchison watched as the sun's warmth dispersed the early morning fog to reveal the splendour that awaited them. When the Queen had finished her breakfast and appeared on the saluting platform above the wheelhouse, he turned the *Gothic* in through the entrance to Milford Sound. HMNZS *Black Prince* remained out at sea.

The labyrinth of waterways, sounds and inlets that make up Fiordland National Park in south-western New Zealand is the product of immense glaciers carving the mountain rock as they descended to the sea during the great ice ages. When the climate

The *Gothic* underway in Wellington harbour in January 1954 during the royal visit. *[V.H. Young and L.A. Sawyer]*

Left: Bluff harbour on Saturday morning 30th January 1954. Top: Across the wharf from HMRY *Gothic* is the 346 grt *Wairua*, a steamer built at Auckland in 1913 then converted to diesel power at Port Chalmers in 1948. From December 1944 until June 1959 she operated the New Zealand government's passenger and cargo service between Bluff and Stewart Island. Ahead of the *Gothic*, dressed with flags, is the New Zealand Shipping Company's 11,281 grt *Haparangi*. The cameraman is aboard Bank Line's *Tweedbank*. *[Bluff Maritime Museum/Chris Howell]*

Bottom: Queen Elizabeth II exchanges final pleasantries with Prime Minister S.G. Holland (at right) a few minutes before embarking for Australia. Behind them, the Duke of Edinburgh is accompanied along the wharf by Mrs Florence Holland. Remembered for his crushing of the maritime unions during the great 1951 waterfront dispute, Sidney George Holland was the first of 15 prime ministers of New Zealand who have spanned Elizabeth II's reign during the 60 years since her accession in 1952. *[Bluff Maritime Museum/Chris Howell]*

warmed at the end of the last ice age, the glaciers retreated leaving awesomely deep valleys that were flooded by rising sea levels. For a young crowned head of state the panorama that now opened before the *Gothic* must surely have been inspirational, for here indeed was the true definition of sublime earthly majesty. She steamed slowly up the sound to Harrison Cove, a distance of seven miles inland from the sea, and between Mitre Peak (5,551 feet, 1,692 metres) and the Lady Bowen Falls (plunging 531 feet, 162 metres) Captain Aitchison turned the *Gothic* and stopped engines. The weather was perfect. Beneath the *Gothic's* keel her echo sounder found no bottom at 330 fathoms (600 metres). Covered in lush rain forests, the near-vertical flanks of the mountains rose up from the sea's edge to tower above the dwarfed *Gothic* in a great kingdom of snow-clad peaks. The royal yacht lay stopped until the Queen indicated she had seen enough. Captain Aitchison took her back out to open water for the three day crossing to Australia.

Advance Australia

Into the Tasman Sea the weather became rough with gales and rain. At 11 p.m. Warwick Thomson and his fellow seamen were roused from their bunks to take in the awning on the Royal Deck over Number 4 hatch, before it carried away. 10.30 a.m. next day, 1st February, and the cruiser HMNZS *Black Prince* bade farewell to the royal yacht, her ship's company manning the sides and cheered ship as she fired a last 21-gun salute. Units of the Royal Australian Navy (RAN) had been sighted ahead, steaming in single column. Under the command of Rear-Admiral R.R. Dowling RAN in his flagship, the heavy cruiser HMAS *Australia* (13,630/1928), the Australians now took up royal guard stations. The destroyers HMAS *Anzac* (3,400/1951) and HMAS *Quadrant* (2,700/1942) moved on to either beam of the royal yacht, the aircraft carrier HMAS *Vengeance* (18,040/1945) followed astern and the flagship was positioned close ahead. From mid-morning on 2nd February the RAN performed

HMRY *Gothic* is escorted out of Bluff on 30th January 1954 with the Queen and Duke of Edinburgh watching from beneath the awning aft on the Boat Deck. Ahead is the steam tug *Awarua* (412/1932). She had supposedly been bunkered with non-smoking coal for the occasion but smoke belching from her funnel can be seen trailing aft of the royal yacht. The *Awarua's* master will be keeping an unwavering lookout right ahead so that he avoids the reaction from the *Gothic's* bridge. *[Bluff Maritime Museum/Chris Howell]*

Visiting the grandeur of Milford Sound, Sunday 31st January 1954. *[Ian J. Farquhar collection]*

exercises with their ships and planes, flying past the *Gothic* to dive-bomb targets laid in the sea. It was a prelude to the enormous choreographed welcome awaiting the royal yacht and her passengers when, her naval escort now in line astern of her, she came through Sydney Heads at 8 a.m. on Wednesday 3rd February 1954.

No matter how exuberant the demonstrations of loyal greeting in New Zealand, it was outdone by the momentous spectacle now confronting the *Gothic* as she came up Sydney harbour in bright morning sunshine. 'What a welcome!' Warwick Thomson wrote in his diary later that day. The royal couple were in full view from the saluting platform above the *Gothic's* bridge. Hundreds of small boats besieged them while on shore, tens upon tens of thousands of Sydney-ites watched and waved. Amid a tumult of noise and frenzied boat wakes the *Gothic* dropped anchor in Athol Bight, for the Queen was to land from her royal barge after receiving her first official visitors on board. From 9.15 a.m. they began climbing her gangway: Field Marshall Sir William Slim, Governor-General of Australia, Lieutenant General Sir John Northcott, State Governor of New South Wales, Prime Minister Robert Menzies and New South Wales State Premier Joseph Cahill. Each received a full ceremonial welcome from the *Gothic's* officers, all other crew members having been banished from sight.

At 10.20 a.m. the royal couple disembarked and went ashore in the royal barge, manoeuvring through a great press of clamouring spectator boats massed around the *Gothic's* stern. Down came the royal standard from her mainmast. At midday the *Gothic* weighed anchor and moved to a berth at Circular Quay in Sydney's inner harbour. That evening, watched by still more thousands of people, she was lit up by search lights and huge displays of fireworks. Mooring stations for her seamen were ordered for next

HMRY *Gothic* departing Sydney on 18th February 1954 for Hobart, with the Queen and Duke of Edinburgh embarked. This photo will have been taken from the top floor of an apartment block on the southern shore of Kirribilli, using a telephoto lens. The westerly breeze denotes a hot summer's evening. Lying at Number 1 Circular Quay, with the sun reflecting off her hull, is either the *Taiyuan* (7,472/1949) or the *Changsha* (7,412/1949) of the China Navigation Co. Ltd. This wharf was later demolished to make way for the Sydney Opera House, located just to the east. *[Ian J. Farquhar collection]*

morning at 6 when the *Gothic* shifted berth to Pyrmont to begin loading frozen meat into her forward holds. Her crew were given free passes for use of Sydney's public transport. She remained there until a few days before the Queen and the Duke re-embarked on Thursday 18th February at the end of their New South Wales visit. By then the *Gothic* had a replacement starboard high-pressure turbine discreetly fitted and successfully trialled, the work having been carried out by engineers from Cockatoo Dockyard at Sydney. In 'Royal Standard Red Ensign' Captain Aitchison states that this turbine was taken from the *Gothic's* sister ship *Ceramic* at London. But examination of voyage cards for the *Ceramic* held in London's Guildhall Library casts doubt on this, as the *Ceramic* was about to leave for Cape Town at the time of the *Gothic's* engine breakdown in Auckland. Exactly where that turbine came from is thus uncertain; it might have been a spare held by Shaw Savill at London for eventualities such as this. What is known is that it was air-freighted in a chartered aircraft from London to Sydney.

Whatever the case, the *Gothic* experienced no further turbine problems during the tour. To have her engines performing flawlessly was of huge importance for she was expected to depart from her wharf and arrive at the next one exactly on time, not a minute too early or late. Captain Aitchison writes that Vice-Admiral Abel Smith 'never liked being late for anything'. Exact punctuality had to be achieved regardless of the strength of tides, winds and currents, and despite the hazards from small boats jostling close to the ship. Tens of thousands of people watched the *Gothic* leave Sydney at 6.30 p.m. on 18th February, in record high summer temperatures and with all normal harbour ferry sailings stopped. Her next destination was Hobart. Bass Strait, notorious for its very rough weather, proved kind to the royal stomachs: Warwick Thomson describes the sea conditions for the *Gothic's* crossing to Tasmania as 'a bit choppy'. Arriving at Hobart mid-morning on Saturday 20th February, escorted by HMAS *Australia* and HMAS *Anzac* in line astern, she was given the now familiar rapturous welcome. Departure, this time without the Queen and Duke, was taken three days later, the *Gothic* going up to Melbourne where she was alongside Station Pier by 2.30 p.m. on 24th February. Even without her royal passengers a huge crowd had gathered for the *Gothic's* arrival. Eleven days were spent in Melbourne, the last of her homeward cargo being loaded while royal baggage was taken ashore as the Queen continued her Australian tour. With one exception the *Gothic* would not have the royal couple onboard again until the tour's final port of Fremantle.

At Melbourne, as at Sydney, the *Gothic's* officers and crew were treated to dances, receptions, parties, sports tournaments and sight-seeing trips out into the countryside. Australian hospitality did not, however, interrupt the demands of shipboard maintenance; on Saturday 27th February the seamen began painting the *Gothic's* white hull for a third time since leaving Britain. Working of cargo was completed on Tuesday 2nd March, with all hatches secured, and at 5 p.m. on 7th March the *Gothic* left for the 1,800-mile sea voyage up the Australian coast to Townsville. With a pilot taken aboard at Caloundra Head she entered the inner Barrier Reef passage on the afternoon of 11th March, anchoring close to Magnetic Island off Townsville at 11 a.m. the following day. Derricks at Numbers 2 and 3 hatches were topped off and the ship's 'catamaran' floating fenders hoisted out. Once in the sea, this platform was dragged aft and made fast to the gangway in time for the royal couple with their entourage, who came out to the ship from Townsville aboard HMAS *Anzac*. In a choppy sea inside Cleveland Bay the destroyer was placed alongside the floating fenders at 5 p.m. for the royal embarkation. Captain Aitchison relates in his book how, whenever the Queen and her household came back to the ship, as on this occasion, the shipboard atmosphere livened up immediately. Royal baggage was transferred from HMAS *Anzac*, then the floating fenders were lifted back inboard. Queen's yacht once again, the *Gothic* got underway for the run to Cairns with HMAS *Australia* and HMAS *Anzac* in company.

Next morning at 8 a.m. she dropped anchor off Fitzroy Island, some 20 miles to seaward of Cairns, and the Queen and Duke went ashore in HMAS *Anzac* returning later that day. By 10 a.m. next morning, Sunday 14th March, she was off the entrance to the Whitsunday Passage in perfect sun and sea conditions. Steaming south through the passage, the *Gothic* came to anchor off Seaforth Island. At 1 p.m. after lunch the royal couple went ashore on the east side of the island for an afternoon's leisure. The story goes that the Queen and Lady Pamela Mountbatten, her lady-in-waiting, were sitting on a deserted beach with the men having gone to climb to the island's summit, when a boat full of locals looking for the royals drew up close to the beach. They enquired if the two women had seen the Queen? 'Yes' the pair replied, 'around on the other side of the island'. The boatload headed off accordingly.

Arriving at Hobart, Tasmania on 20th February 1954. *[Archives Office of Tasmania AB713-1-2621]*

The royal yacht weighed anchor at 3 a.m. next day and steamed for Mackay, anchoring at 8 a.m. near Flat Top Island. In a rain squall the Queen and Duke boarded HMAS *Anzac* and were taken into Mackay, the *Gothic's* draft of 29 feet seven inches preventing her from entering there. All the royal household and baggage accompanied them, swung over to the warship by the *Gothic's* derricks. Emptied of monarch, admiral, press, royal and navy staff and no longer under escort, the *Gothic* set out alone for Adelaide. A leaking tube in the starboard boiler and then very bad weather off Adelaide meant she berthed there at 8 on the morning of Sunday 21st March 1954, two days late. Here the *Gothic* was immediately quarantined because of an outbreak of polio in Western Australia, where she was headed next.

After loading stores all day, the *Gothic* undocked at 6 p.m. on 22nd March for transit of the Great Australian Bight. Initially she met head seas bad enough to make staunch seafarers like Warwick Thomson feel 'a little off-colour'. But then the weather flattened to total calm and she was alongside at Fremantle at 8.10 a.m. on Friday 26th March. Soldiers with fixed bayonets barricaded the wharf entrances. Her arrival there was three days ahead of the tour timetable, which had now been drastically altered because of the polio situation. In those times, before the Salk vaccine,

Left: Looking up at the *Gothic's* bridge as she steams into the port of Hobart. The Queen is on the saluting platform under the canopy, the Duke of Edinburgh is behind her with Vice-Admiral E.M.C. Abel Smith, Flag Officer Royal Yacht, standing just aft of the Duke. Below the three sailors standing together on the bridge house roof is the door and window to Captain Aitchison's day cabin. *[Archives Office of Tasmania AB713-1-2622].*
Right: Disembarking at Hobart. *[Archives Office of Tasmania AB713-1-2623]*

poliomyelitis was a recurring threat in Australia and New Zealand. No chance could be taken with exposure to it. Throughout their visit to Western Australia the royal couple were to live and eat aboard the *Gothic*, which would be strictly quarantined from all contact with the local population. The Queen and Duke would continue with shore engagements but would not shake hands and neither eat nor drink anything from outside the ship. None of the *Gothic's* officers and crew were permitted to go ashore.

The morning after arrival at Fremantle, with the Queen onboard, both the *Gothic's* diesel-powered electricity generators stopped. Exactly what caused their sudden and simultaneous breakdown is not known but it resulted in the failure of all lighting and ventilation. Steam had to be raised in the main boilers to get into operation the steam turbines that drove the ship's other two electricity generators. This took three hours. Unflustered, the *Gothic's* cooks served breakfast on time in the royal apartments but the quarantine had to be broken to allow shore engineers aboard to help with repairs.

The church mutiny

Later that same day tensions came to a head between the *Gothic's* Chief Officer and his seamen. Keen to impress, H.O.V. Andersen had performed his role with very great diligence throughout the tour but the seamen had grown weary of his endless carping. Favourite had been his persistent admonition that the seamen must do their job without ever being heard or seen by the royals, as if they were somehow beneath the monarchical gaze. Now he wanted their co-operation for the following morning, Sunday 28th March 1953, when a church service was to be held under the awning at Number 3 hatch. Officiating would be the Archbishop of Western Australia, with the Queen and Duke in attendance. The service was to be broadcast on Australian and BBC radio. With no visitors permitted aboard, the seamen were asked to attend so as to provide the necessary volume for hymn singing. Because of the generator emergency, no one could be spared from the engine room crew. 'At 1 p.m. on Saturday the Mate came down and asked how many would be attending the church service tomorrow', Warwick Thomson wrote in his diary. 'Not one of us volunteered. This riled him and he started cajoling, but he got no further.' Only when Captain Aitchison himself spoke to the seamen next morning did some of them relent.

Three years later Warwick Thomson, by then holder of a brand new second mate's ticket, joined Shaw Savill's *Arabic* (6,497/1956) as Third Officer. She was under the command of H.O.V. Andersen, the *Arabic* being his second ship as Master since his time as Chief Officer of the *Gothic*. Thomson writes: 'My relationship with Hov was a bit out of the ordinary. When I joined the *Arabic* he didn't appear to know me at the time but as we headed for the Suez Canal during the first week of the voyage on the ship, I'd noticed him studying me with what I imagined to be a 'where-have-I-seen-him-before?' expression when he came on the bridge during the 8 to 12 watch to write up his night orders. It was several days before he brought himself to ask the question I'd been expecting.

'Have we sailed before? Was it the *Gothic*?' 'Yes sir,' I replied. 'I was an AB.' He nodded and turned his gaze to the horizon. I braced myself for his next question but he merely grunted, and said goodnight. I breathed a sigh, but knew it was only a matter of time before he dug deeper. It came next night.

'I've been wanting to ask this question for a long time. Why did the crowd respond like that – to my request to attend church that day?' There was no need for him to say what day or which church. His had hardly been a request though; that was the day we 'mutinied'. On the *Gothic* we seamen had no time for our bullying and humourless Chief Officer so when he breezed into our messroom that day after we had knocked off for the weekend we were in no mood to co-operate, whatever the task. But now, with a three-month voyage ahead of us, I didn't want to offend Captain Andersen by telling him the absolute truth. 'I suppose we were all pretty jaded at that stage of the voyage, sir,' I said. 'We'd been away for nearly six months by then, and you'll remember that none of us had had any shore leave for about three weeks.'

'Mmmm'. He stared at me and grunted. 'It just all got on top of us I guess', I added. He nodded, left the bridge and never mentioned it again. H.O.V. Andersen's first command was as temporary Master of the *Taranaki* (8,696/1928) from 6th February 1955. He was later confirmed in this appointment, with seniority backdated to 28th July 1955. Captain Andersen went on to command the *Corinthic* and the *Gothic*, the latter fittingly being his very last ship. He died on 23rd March 1985 at the age of 76.

Royal adieu

On Thursday 1st April 1954 the *Gothic* prepared for sea, being ready in all respects by 1 p.m. The hour of departure from Australia at the end of Her Majesty's visit was at hand, and a huge assemblage of people had gathered in Fremantle to watch the pageantry of her leaving. Brass bands played, troops marched, cameras rolled, school choirs sang and all the notables of the land made their farewells. Aboard HMAS *Anzac*, waiting ahead of the *Gothic* to escort her out of harbour, oily black smuts poured from her funnel bathing the royal yacht in filth. Greasy fumes blew in through the open windows of Vice-Admiral Abel Smith's day cabin; immediately he sent a bollocking by signal to HMAS *Anzac's* Commanding Officer. Then the radio office had to be told to stop transmitting via the S.W.B. Eleven set, which as usual was electrifying the after part of the ship including the winches which were needed to take in her mooring ropes.

She sailed at 5.20 p.m. bound across the Indian Ocean for the Cocos Island, then Colombo and finally Aden where she berthed at 8 a.m. on 27th April 1954. The royal escort was led by HMS *Ceylon* and then by HMS *Newfoundland*, both of them Royal Navy cruisers from the East India Station. It must have been with relief that the royal couple and their household snatched these days of informal peace onboard after the hectic visits to the Australian states. Captain Aitchison: 'The royal pair had travelled an average of 230 miles every day; 10,000 miles by air, 2,500 by road, 900 by train, and of course there was our little voyage up the Queensland coast. Thousands of people had been presented, and goodness knows how many hands had been shaken. There were almost 500 replies to addresses of welcome and many more speeches each word of which had to be most carefully weighed. It was most comforting to know that, at the end of this strenuous living, they were still the same charming, unaffected, young couple.' 'Royal Standard Red Ensign' also chronicles many hidden stories, some serious, some humorous, coming from the voyage as told by the *Gothic's* Master.

Having left Sydney Heads behind, Captain Aitchison went on the bridge just before going down to dinner with the royal party, to find the *Gothic* heading north instead of south to Hobart. He was told this was because the royal standard, which was flying from the mainmast, was fouling the truck of the mast above the active main radio aerial. With a rendezvous to keep with the frigate HMAS *Shoalhaven* (2,106/1946) next morning, Aitchison, ordering the ship to be put back on her southerly course, then stalked off the bridge in high dudgeon, indifferent to the fate of the royal standard. Eventually, when the short wave radio could be stopped, a seaman was sent aloft to bring down the torn remnants.

Sailing from Hobart without the royal party on board but shadowing them to Melbourne, there was a problem unberthing. Sailing time had been put back to 8.15 a.m. to allow colours to be hoisted with so many warships being in port. Arriving on the *Gothic*'s bridge, the pilot announced that there were no watersiders available to let go the moorings until an incoming cargo ship had berthed. Having heaved in all the moorings except a head rope and a stern rope, the master and Vice-Admiral Abel Smith sighted two of the Queen's household, Lieutenant Colonel Charteris and Richard Colville, disembarking. They were asked to deputise for the absent mooring gang which, with some banter, they willingly did. As Captain Aitchison recalled in his book: 'Thus it came about that two important members of the household let go our remaining ropes and as we backed away from the wharf, they politely raised their bowler hats'.

Departure from Fremantle and Australia, 1st April 1954. The royal standard flies from the *Gothic's* mainmast, the Lord High Admiral's flag from her foremast. *[Ian J. Farquhar collection]*

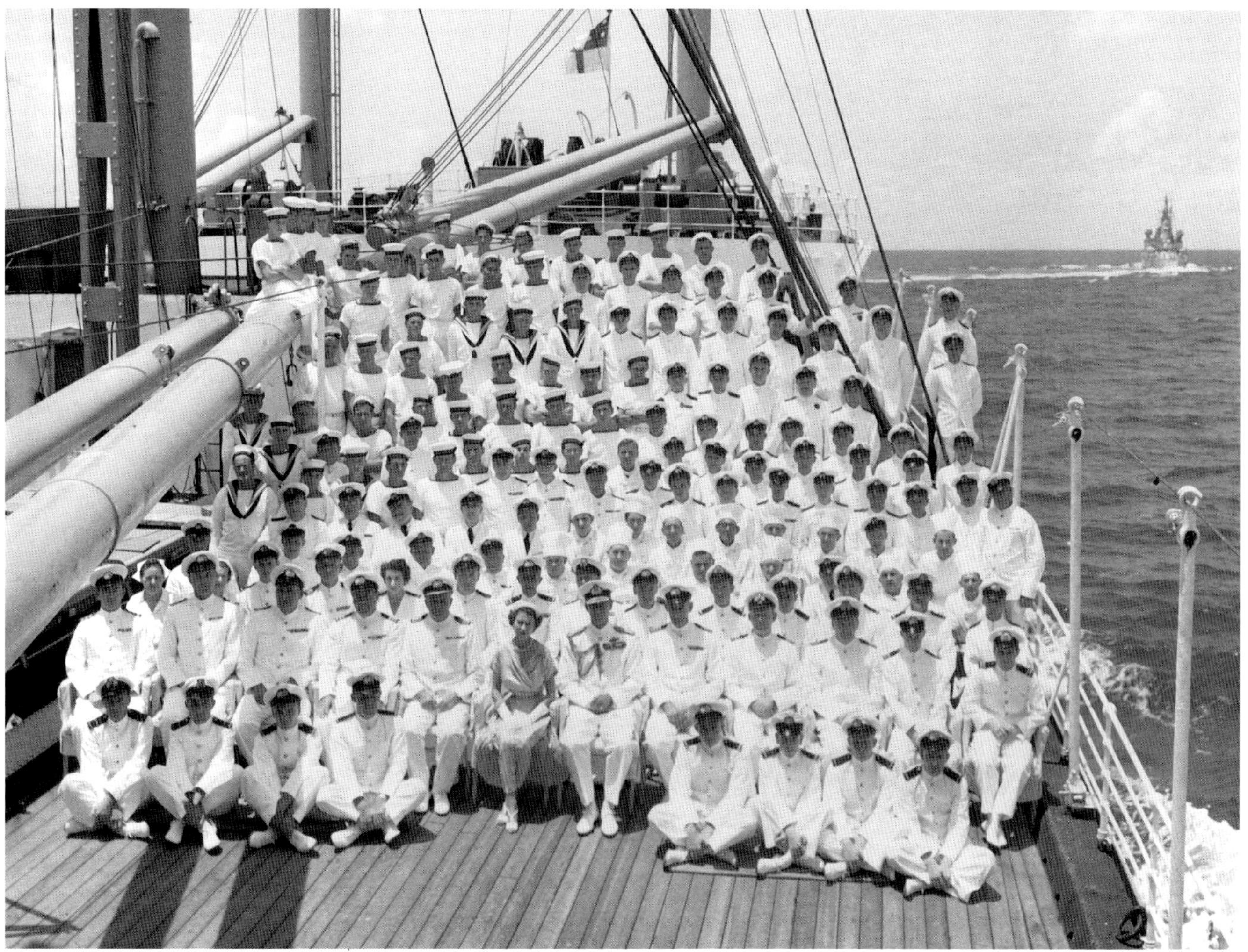

The master, officers and crew of HMRY *Gothic* with the Queen and Duke, photographed on the fore well deck while on passage from Colombo to Aden, 11 a.m. Saturday 24th April 1954. Presumably there is someone on the bridge and in the engine room. HMS *Newfoundland* can be glimpsed to starboard. *[Warwick Thomson]*

At New Queen Elizabeth Wharf, Colombo, April 1954. *[Warwick Thomson]*

Between Cocos and Colombo a rendezvous was arranged with Orient Line's then brand-new *Orsova* (28,790/1954). Given permission to pass one mile off late at night, the royal passengers viewed the spectacular sight of a 29,000 ton liner, ablaze with lights, firing off flares, flashing signals and sounding her siren.

Leaving Colombo after ten days in what was then Ceylon, on the last sector of the voyage with the royals onboard, a birthday party was held for the Queen at which she was given a bedside clock. It had been carefully chosen and engraved at a Melbourne jeweller's shop as a gift from all the *Gothic's* crew. On Saturday 24th April at 11 a.m. they assembled in the forward well deck to have their photo taken with the Queen and Duke. That evening the Queen gave a thank you party to which the senior and junior officers were invited (but not the ratings). Next day at 10 a.m., at the Queen's request, a parade and inspection of all hands was held on the Royal Deck. Dressed in their white uniforms, the seamen, engine room crew and stewards marched on and formed up for the Queen. As she walked along the ranks the Royal Marines Band played 'Early One Morning'. The Sunday church service followed.

On the *Gothic's* last night at sea before reaching Aden, Monday 26th April, the Queen held a private investiture in her day cabin. She bestowed a knighthood upon Captain Aitchison; he became a Knight Commander of the Royal Victorian Order. Everyone acknowledged that this was a KCVO thoroughly deserved, delivered personally by the Master of the Merchant Navy to Sir David on his own ship. The Chief Engineer, Chief Officer, Purser, Acting Chief Steward and the Senior Second Engineer each became Members of the Royal Victorian Order (MVO). Selected crew members were awarded the Royal Victorian Medal, others received autographed photos and presents. The engineers and ratings responsible for keeping the *Gothic*'s air-conditioning working were singled out for particular thanks.

All the rest including Able Seaman Warwick Thomson were given mass-produced bronze medallions, although not by the Queen. To the humble seamen must go the fullest accolade for making the *Gothic* such a visual triumph in her role as royal yacht. Men like Thomson spent the entire voyage sugiing paintwork, holystoning decks, re-painting her sides and superstructure, hoisting barges and gangways, rigging awnings and constantly keeping the *Gothic* looking immaculate. Their labours meant the Queen's majesty was never in doubt each time the *Gothic*, flawless, sumptuous and gleaming in her white and buff livery, arrived in the many Commonwealth and foreign ports she visited during the tour.

The *Gothic* berthed at Aden next morning day at 8 a.m., Tuesday 27th April and commenced bunkering. Vice-Admiral Abel Smith and his staff left the ship that morning, bound for Malta to join the newly commissioned royal yacht *Britannia*. Now for their final day with the *Gothic*, the Queen and Duke were directly in the care of Captain Sir David, his officers, crew and Shaw Savill. Very early next day at 3.30 a.m. they left the ship on the royal barge for a long flight to Entebbe in Uganda. All officers and men were on hand as the Queen disembarked. Stewards locked the royal apartments and readied the *Gothic* to take on fare-paying passengers for the balance of her journey home to Great Britain. She sailed from Aden at 8.30 a.m. as soon as they were aboard, and on 1st May passed through the Suez Canal, clearing Port Said at 10 p.m.

One final royal duty remained. Crossing the eastern Mediterranean, on 4th May the *Gothic* came into the Grand harbour of Malta at 8.30 on a fine clear morning with the Royal Marines Band playing one last time. She moored near the brand new royal yacht *Britannia*, of which Vice-Admiral Abel Smith had just assumed command. Everything from the royal tour was now transferred to this vessel. The band and the RN ratings disembarked, the royal baggage and all the royal furniture was hoisted over-side into landing barges and taken to the *Britannia*. From the new royal yacht came Prince Charles and Princess Anne, aged five and three, for a two-hour visit to the *Gothic* beginning at 11.30 a.m. Ship-to-ship furniture removal was all done by noon; also leaving the *Gothic* was a small yacht given to Prince Charles by the people of New Zealand. It had been stowed in Number 4 hold amongst stacked cases of canned apricots. More passengers embarked for the trip to London, most of them people from the British armed forces.

Departure was taken at 3 p.m. Sir David finishes his description of their stay: 'We had started moving and were barely beginning to gain speed when I saw a naval launch rounding the stern of the *Britannia*. It was flying the royal standard. I looked and saw a slim young figure stepping out of the launch. It was the Queen. I saw her run swiftly up the gangway steps, vanish inside for a moment and then re-appear on the upper deck with the two children, all of them waving hard. What could we do to acknowledge? Would three long blasts be a suitable greeting for the Queen? I took off my cap and waved like mad. All the other officers on the bridge followed suit, and we waved till we were out of range. It was an inadequate acknowledgement but we could think of nothing else and we hoped that Her Majesty would know that our hearts went out to her with that farewell greeting. All too soon we were out and full away. A wonderful chapter in our lives was over. We still had the voyage to finish but there would be no more contact with royalty. For us the magic was over. The glory was indeed departed.'

Normal day-to-day routine at sea now came back to the *Gothic*. Although almost all of her refrigerated cargo was for Liverpool, the first port of call was London to land the two barges and the two gangways plus accumulated gifts presented to the Queen during the tour. The commercial passengers from Malta and Aden were disembarked at Tilbury mid-afternoon on Monday 10th May, and she was alongside in the Royal Docks by 10 p.m. On the evening of Thursday 13th May she got underway for the coastal voyage to Liverpool. The crew including Warwick Thomson were paid off the ship on 17th May. 'Woopee! No more bosun!' wrote Warwick Thomson in his diary's last entry. *Gothic's* charter to the British Admiralty was at an end.

Even before her cargo was discharged, workers from Cammell Laird were back aboard, this time to strip the royal apartments. Every vestige of her royal duties was removed completely. The Queen's and the Duke's day rooms were converted back into the first class passenger smoking room, the sun room became the veranda cafe again, and the forward lounge and dining saloon were restored to exactly as they had previously been. The long-range radio equipment was landed and the radio office reduced to its earlier proportions. Naval ratings' accommodation in the 'tween decks was demolished in entirety (but the portholes remained). And the royal bedrooms on the Boat and Games Deck again became ordinary passenger cabins. At Cammell Laird she was docked and her hull repainted black. Down came the topgallant masts. Her master and senior officers had all been decorated but curiously and sadly it seems no memorial or memento was left

Empress of the seas; the *Gothic* arriving at Grand Harbour, Malta on 4th May 1954. Her Red Ensign on the poop is being dipped to a Royal Navy warship on her port hand. Note the royal and admiral's barges under tarpaulins on the aft well deck. Although the royal apartments have been locked, the veranda cafe appears to be in use by passengers embarked at Aden. Its glazed Essavian screens have been slid open. *[World Ship Society Limited]*

Retired Shaw Savill fleet commodores, from left: Captain G. Campbell, Captain L.J. Hopkins, Captain J.W. Hart, Mr W.R. Russell (managing director of Shaw Savill), Captain A.C. Jones, Captain Sir David Aitchison. *[Captain Graham Pepper, Shaw Savill Society]*

Farewell in the *Gothic's* officers' lounge for Charles Simpson, her Chief Engineer, who retired from this ship and from the sea at the end of November 1967. Back row, from left: G. Butler, Catering Officer; Bernard (Jim) McGovern, First Radio Officer; Ernie M. (Robbie) Robertson, First Electrician; Michael A. Clark, Chief Officer; Michael (Noddy) G. R. Moore, Ninth Engineer; David M. Jones, Second Radio Officer; J.R. Oakley, Seventh Engineer; Peter Stockings, Junior Third Officer; Leslie Bell, Fourth Engineer; Kenneth Strachan, Second Refrigerating Engineer; Wayne D. Coldicut, Sixth Engineer; Dr Michael Buchanan, Surgeon; T. (Tony) Williams, Third Engineer. Middle row, from left: R. Prince, Second Steward; Michael Gochin, Third Mate; Mrs Helen Simpson; James E. Buist, Third Refrigerating. Engineer; James Christie, Second Electrician; Charles Simpson, Chief Engineer; George B. Unwin, Third Electrician; R.R. (Bob) Mullen, Second Engineer, Mrs Cooke, Nursing Sister; E. Mervyn (Merlin) Price, Junior Second Engineer; Adrian Cope, Second Officer. Front row, from left: Fred Harrison, Purser; Terry Woodhouse, Eighth Engineer; C. Lewis, Deck Cadet; James (Jimmy) L. Hogg, Fifth Engineer; Reynold Rogers, Assistant Purser; Ian Hindemarsh, Deck Cadet. Not present: Captain H.O.V. Anderson, Master, R.J. Baird, First Refrigerating Engineer; M. Hodges, Purser's Writer. *[George Wood]*

aboard the *Gothic* in recognition of her royal service. A plaque or a signed photographic portrait of the Queen and the Duke hung in the lounge or dining saloon would have been fitting, but all trace of the royal voyage was expunged.

Back among the commoners

Cammell Laird also carried out some modifications to the *Gothic's* cargo gear. She sailed out of the Mersey on 4th September 1954 to rejoin Shaw Savill's fleet and resume her normal passenger and cargo sailings. Captain K.D.G. Fisher took command on the first day of that month, succeeding Captain Sir David Aitchison who transferred to the emigrant liner *New Australia* as her Master. Between 1950 and 1957 this quadruple screw, 20,256 ton vessel, owned by the British Ministry of Transport, was chartered to the Australian government as an immigrant liner and sailed under the management of Shaw Savill. The two men exchanged ships, Captain Fisher having previously been Master of the *New Australia*. For Sir David the *New Australia* was a temporary berth until he was appointed Master of the newly completed *Southern Cross* on 3rd January 1955. He retired from the sea on 1st December 1957 and died on 15th January 1975 at the age of 82.

Born on 13th December 1896, Kenneth Desmond Gronow Fisher is remembered as a quiet, reserved man, a 'very fine officer and a thorough gentleman' as Captain Ian Condie describes him. Former *Gothic* Assistant Purser Dick Ashford, who sailed in the *Gothic* for her two voyages immediately following the royal tour, confirms this memory of Captain Fisher: 'a perfect gentleman' who had been decorated for gallantry during the Second World War. In January 1943 when Chief Officer of the liner *Akaroa* (15,182/1914, formerly *Euripides*) Fisher climbed down a two-feet square air chute

One of the great men of the Big Ics; a smiling Charles Simpson, chief engineer of the *Gothic* and of the *Ceramic* for ten years before that, in the master's day cabin with his wife Helen and an unknown guest at the time of his retirement in September 1967. Chief Simpson died less than two years later. *[George Simpson]*

Gothic in the King George V Dock, London, after she ceased carrying passengers. Perhaps her crew has been disposed of, too, as both the port-side lifeboats are missing. More probably they have been landed for maintenance and survey, and will be returned to their davits in time for the ship's next sailing. *[Ambrose Greenway]*

to rescue the *Akaroa's* Chief Refrigerating Engineer and a shore carpenter, after both men collapsed having been overcome by lack of breathable air. Discarding his gas mask because it impeded his freedom of movement, Fisher got one of the two back to the open deck, then returned down the air chute for the second man. Both survived. In December 1943 Chief Officer Fisher was awarded the George Medal, which at the time was Britain's second-highest civilian award for bravery. Such was his manner that Captain Fisher always refused any attention being drawn to his George Medal's red ribbon with its five equally spaced thin blue stripes, worn on his uniform jacket.

Unlike her three sister liners the *Gothic* never had a master who remained with the ship for a period of many years and became identified with her. Because of her royal association the *Gothic* was consistently popular with the travelling public. The only interruptions to 14 mishap-free years between 1954 and 1968 were engine trouble at Bremen in June 1955 and the accidental flooding of her engine room while she was being prepared for dry-docking at London on 1st May 1959. In addition to being chartered for two royal tours, the *Gothic* made 39 commercial voyages during her life of 20 years and eight months from December 1948 until August 1969. Thirty one of these were return voyages on the Great Britain - New Zealand route, via Panama. The remaining eight were between Great Britain and Australia, the *Gothic* going on to load in New Zealand ports during two of these eight voyages. In 1948 during her Voyage Number 2, the *Gothic* sailed home from Australia via the Suez Canal. Along with her sister ship *Ceramic*, the *Gothic* customarily spent at least six weeks and often more than eight weeks in New Zealand ports between the outward and homeward legs of each voyage, discharging and then loading cargo. She experienced a fire in a store room while on the New Zealand coast during Voyage 16, and on 20th July 1965 another fire occurred while she was berthed at Wellington, this one in her engine room. Putting to sea shortly afterwards, the *Gothic* was then forced back to Wellington with boiler trouble and was held there for repairs from 27th July until 5th August 1965. It seems she may have had recurring engine and boiler problems the following year, for the *Gothic* was laid up at London for over two months, from 9th May until 12th July 1966

Ship on fire

The *Gothic's* last fare-paying passengers disembarked at London in June 1968, at the conclusion of voyage Number 37. Her passenger accommodation was left as-is, the forward lounge becoming the officers' bar, and all her lifeboats remained in place (unlike her three sisters). Officers and engineers moved into the Promenade Deck, most of them occupying two adjoining passenger cabins with connecting door and a private bathroom. What formerly had been the passenger suite with private sitting room, now became the chief engineer's quarters. The chief officer converted the ladies' hair-dressing salon for use as his office. Cargo-only, the *Gothic* resumed her sailings to New Zealand, her first destination Nelson now that she had no passengers for either Auckland or Wellington. But trouble with her starboard propeller shaft forced the ship into Wellington, where repairs took ten days. In late July 1968 the *Gothic* was berthed at Bluff, topping off her homeward cargo. Loaded down to her marks with 6,038 tons of refrigerated foodstuffs and 2,500 tons of general cargo, she departed Bluff on the high tide at 2 a.m. on Sunday 28th July, bound for Liverpool via the Panama Canal.

Her Master was 35 year-old Captain B.H. Agnew of Watcombe in Dorset. The *Gothic's* senior officers were:

J. McKinnon	Chief Engineer
G.R. Griffin	Chief Officer
J.H.B. Heffernan	Supernumerary Chief Engineer
C.P. Wickham	Second Engineer
R.M. Newall	Chief Steward

Aboard were 80 men and women. They included the wife of the Chief Officer, two deserters on conveyance orders to Great Britain, and two distressed British seamen, one each from the *Romanic* and *Doric* who because of illness were also being returned to Great Britain. Seven of the crew had deserted from the *Gothic* while she was on the New Zealand coast and they had been replaced by four new men. An eighth crew member had signed off to join the *Amalric*.

Also aboard, travelling to England for two months' vacation, was the Halliday family. John and Eileen Halliday had settled in New Zealand in 1963, coming from London where Mr Halliday was an employee of Shaw Savill. In Wellington he had worked for the New Zealand Stevedoring and Wharfingering Co. Ltd. Accompanying them were their two children, both young boys. The family lived at Plimmerton, just north of Wellington.

The *Gothic* was seaworthy in all respects. Her last Board of Trade survey had taken place at London on 24th April 1968 and the certificate of survey issued to her was valid until 22nd April 1970. The vessel had four lifeboats with a total capacity for 302 persons plus three 20 person liferafts. There were eight lifebuoys and 100 new lifejackets aboard.

For the first four days the voyage was entirely normal, the *Gothic* steering east across the South Pacific and passing south of the Chatham Islands. Initially sea conditions were fair but there had been a gradual deterioration throughout the last 24 hours of July. By evening that day, Wednesday 31st July, she was steaming into a north-easterly gale with freshening winds of approximately 48-52 knots (88.5-96.5 kilometres per hour, 55-60 miles per hour). Speed was 15 knots, the engines turning the propellers at 98 r.p.m. At 12 midnight the watches changed and a fire patrol, as required in ship's standing orders, was carried out. All was well. Day workers had turned in for the night while the third officer, the second steward and a number of engineers who had just come off watch, gathered in the cabin of the *Gothic's* fourth engineer for a drink and to talk and relax. The master had gone to bed shortly after making a final visit to the bridge at 11 p.m.

Generally while at sea the forward lounge was seldom used after dinner. Tonight it was empty but the lights remained on. In the fore port corner of the lounge was an Electrolux refrigerator with a waist-high bar counter standing in front of it. We will never know for certain but, hidden behind that counter and not noticed by anyone glancing into the lounge, a cigarette very probably lay smouldering where it had been discarded. Whether or not it was in fact a cigarette, something right next to the refrigerator started burning very slowly in the evening hours after the lounge was vacated by its last occupants. This was around 8 p.m. and they were most probably the Halliday family, all of whom were to die that night. Junior Third Officer Frank Quick passed them on the main stairs at about 7 p.m. as they walked down to the lounge. The counter was made of painted wood. Or maybe the slow build-up of heat reached the varnished timber panelling on the lounge walls. Or perhaps it was the long, heavy curtains that covered the lounge windows. Whatever their source, sometime just after 2 a.m. ship's time on Thursday 1st August 1968 flames broke out in the front, port corner of the lounge on the *Gothic's* Bridge Deck.

The Second Officer, Peter Garlick, had the watch on the bridge from 12 midnight. With him was Cadet Timothy Latcham and seaman Peter Hales, who was rated an Efficient Deck Hand (EDH) and whose job was lookout. The *Gothic* was on automatic pilot, steering a course of 075 degrees true. A moderate to heavy swell was running, with the gale on the ship's port bow. Visibility extended some seven to eight miles despite frequent rain showers. Cadet Latcham was keeping watch in the darkened wheelhouse and Second Officer Garlick had gone to the chartroom, immediately abaft the wheelhouse. Around 2 a.m., halfway through the watch, seaman Hales went to the small pantry located behind the chart room, inside what had been the officers' wardroom during the *Gothic's* passenger-carrying days. Here he made coffee for himself and the other two men on the bridge. Everything was normal and quiet. Then, around 2.25 a.m., a warning bell rang in the smoke detection cabinet on the rear bulkhead of the wheelhouse, next to the chart room door.

Leaving the chartroom, Second Officer Garlick saw that the Number 13 indicator had sounded, having detected smoke in the area of the galley, officers' dining saloon and forward lounge. Immediately he smelled a change in the air he was breathing inside the wheelhouse. Cadet Latcham was ordered to run below and investigate. Seaman Hales had, meanwhile, exited the pantry with cups and coffee-pot in hand, heading for the chart room. On his right as he left the officers' wardroom he saw thick smoke coming up the internal stairwell that led down to the Promenade Deck from the bridge house. Abandoning the coffee, he hurried down the stairwell and into the main entrance area at the forward end of the Promenade Deck, in front of the purser's bureau. Next he went down the wide stairs that came out into the forward lounge on the Bridge Deck. It was filled with smoke. He saw the running figure of Cadet Latcham. Immediately Hales set off back up to the bridge where he told the second officer that smoke was overflowing from the lounge and coming up the main stairs leading from the Bridge Deck to the Promenade Deck.

Timothy Latcham had run down those same stairs into the lounge where right away he saw that the area behind the bar counter was on fire. He could not see what exactly was burning but the flames were no more than five feet in height. At the bottom of the stairs on its starboard side was a wall locker containing a big 2½ gallon portable fire extinguisher. Wrestling with the doors of the locker, he found he could not open them. So he headed up the stairs to the Promenade Deck to find another extinguisher, shouting 'fire! fire!' as he went. All the cabins on this deck had sleeping occupants. Pulling a fire extinguisher from a locker in the Promenade Deck's starboard alleyway, Latcham returned to the lounge to confront the flames. But uselessly the jet from the fire extinguisher gave out after a few seconds. He turned to strike the knob of the extinguisher against a nearby bulkhead, trying to get it to activate properly. Now a large window in the port forward corner of the lounge, where the bar was, suddenly cracked under the fire's heat. In came the 50-knot wind straight off the *Gothic's* port bow. Instantly the fire erupted into a giant blast furnace. In what fire fighters call a flash-over the flames roared out across the deckhead of the lounge, propelled and gluttoned by the wind. They were over Cadet Latcham's head, charging towards the wide stairs leading up to the Promenade Deck. There was a metal fire curtain in the stairwell; as he was driven up the stairs by the suffocating heat and fumes Latcham tried to pull this curtain down. But he could not breathe. Semi-conscious and on his hands and knees he made his way back up to the bridge chased by the smoke and flames.

Meanwhile Second Officer Garlick had pushed the button that sounded the *Gothic's* alarm bells. They began ringing all over the ship. Turning to Hales he ordered him to go and wake all the officers in their cabins. The entrance to the master's day cabin was immediately on the right of the door at the back of the chart room. It was open; Garlick went in and knocked on the wall beside the inner door to the master's sleeping cabin, shouting 'fire!' as he did so. Next he telephoned the *Gothic's* Chief Officer, Raymond Griffin. He and his wife Judith were asleep in the chief officer's cabin just abaft the wheelhouse on the starboard side of the bridge house. Because the *Gothic* carried three watch-keeping officers in addition to himself the chief officer was a day worker, standing no regular watch on the bridge. He had turned in around 9 p.m. after doing his final rounds of the ship for the night.

Wearing his uniform jacket and trousers over his pyjamas, Captain Brian Agnew came on to the bridge immediately. He noticed smoke as he passed through his dayroom, which was located on the port side of the bridge house; the forward lounge was right below his feet, two decks down. In the wheelhouse Second Officer Garlick was clambering into a self-contained breathing apparatus which he had taken from its stowage in the chart room. Captain Agnew telephoned the engine manoeuvring platform, telling the engineers on watch to be ready. The master then moved the engine telegraph handles to stand-by. Cadet Latcham now came into the wheelhouse, half-asphyxiated by smoke from the main stairway. He told Captain Agnew that the forward lounge on the Bridge Deck was severely on fire. Ordered to take over the steering wheel, Latcham switched off the auto pilot. On the master's command he turned the wheel to starboard to get the wind off the front of the *Gothic's* superstructure. The helm did not answer. Now the wheelhouse was filling with smoke as the fire, seated directly beneath, moved outwards and upwards at tremendous speed, fed by the gale. There were no sprinklers or automated fire screens aboard the *Gothic*.

Next Cadet Latcham was sent aft by the master to clear away the lifeboats ready for lowering. Captain Agnew meanwhile pushed the telegraph handles to stop. Then he used the engines to turn the *Gothic* to starboard so as to get her head off the wind. The liner swung obediently. Perhaps no more than five minutes had elapsed since the fire was discovered, but already it had risen through two decks and was consuming the bridge house. Leaving the engine telegraph handles at stop, Captain Agnew hastened aft to the *Gothic's* radio office. On the way he passed Third Officer David Buck who was pulling the chief officer's wife through a port hole from her husband's smoke-filled cabin.

David Buck had turned in at approximately 1.30 a.m. after coming off watch on the bridge at midnight. This was his first trip aboard the *Gothic*. About an hour later he was woken by the smell of smoke. On leaving his cabin he found the interior of the Promenade Deck filled with a thick, choking haze. The fourth engineer was crawling past on his stomach with a fire extinguisher, trying to reach the purser's bureau. But the fumes and flame were too much and they were forced back, climbing out onto the open deck through the window in Buck's cabin. The third officer made for the bridge. Captain Agnew ordered him to ascertain the ship's position but this was impossible with the chart room now dense with smoke and the lights having failed. It was later determined to be 44.24 south 149.04 west, with the *Gothic* some 1,802 miles (2,900 kilometres) east of Bluff. The wheel had gone dead then suddenly the bridge itself burst into flames. Along with Cadet Latcham, Second Officer Buck began preparing the lifeboats. Boats Number 1, 2 and 4 were lowered to their embarkation gates on the Bridge Deck and secured there. Covered in smoke, the davit winch for Lifeboat 4 could not be reached.

Arriving on the bridge from his cabin, Chief Officer Griffin was told by the second officer that the forward lounge was on fire. Immediately he hastened below to take charge of fire fighting. Gorged and accelerated by the wind, the flames had dramatically taken hold, within minutes engulfing the *Gothic's* entire forward superstructure. When he got down to the Bridge Deck, the chief officer saw the lounge and dining saloon had become an orange inferno; windows were shattering and smoke was boiling out of them. Having come to starboard off the wind the *Gothic* lay beam-on to the seas, rolling heavily and assaulted by 50- to 60-knot wind gusts. In these conditions her crew turned-to and began rigging hoses to save their ship; two hoses were already in operation by the time Chief Officer Griffin arrived. Under his direction parties manning 12 hoses went to work against the flames, advancing along both sides of the Promenade and Bridge Decks. Full and continuous water pressure was maintained on all hoses. Though her hull and engines were not affected, she was in mortal danger. At the aft end of the dining saloon, lined with timber panelling, was the steel trunk for Number 3 cargo hatch. The 'tween decks of Number 3 hold were filled with bales of wool, highly inflammable. If the fire got into this cargo, containing it would be near-impossible. And just aft again from Number 3 hatch were the ship's lifeboats and the ventilators supplying fresh air upon which the *Gothic's* boilers and diesel generators relied.

In the engine room Second Engineer Colin Wickham, the *Gothic's* senior watch-keeping engineer, was in charge. Having escaped with very great difficulty from the burning Promenade Deck, where he had been off-watch asleep, the second engineer arrived on the engine room plates dressed only in a towel. He ordered the *Gothic's* general services pump activated as backup to the main water supply pump. Both were delivering a water pressure of 100 pounds per square inch on the ship's fire main. Meanwhile the emergency diesel generator, located on the Shelter Deck between the boiler and engine casings, was manned by Junior Second Engineer Philip Stanton. He had been on watch in the engine room when the master had first telephoned, telling Stanton to prepare to stop and then manoeuvre the ship. Now Wickham waited on the engine manoeuvring platform for further orders from the bridge. But all telephone contact had failed and, as the fire reached the engine telegraph communication cables, the telegraph bells began ringing continuously. Their pointers moved erratically to 'finished with engines' and then off their display dials.

Having satisfied himself that all was under control in the engine room, John McKinnon, the *Gothic's* Chief Engineer took charge of fire fighting on the port side of the Promenade Deck. He then went aft to confer with the master at the emergency steering wheel on the roof of the deckhouse up on the *Gothic's* poop. Captain Agnew had found the *Gothic's* Radio Officer, Roger B. Cliffe, on the Boat Deck near Number 3 hatch, and had ordered him to transmit an SOS. Noticing that the ship was still moving ahead and finding he was unable to return to the bridge house which was now completely alight, Captain Agnew next went down to the engine manoeuvring platform. Here he told Second Engineer Wickham that the bridge was evacuated and on fire. Standing beside Wickham on the manoeuvring platform, the master ordered stop engines. Back on deck, Captain Agnew proceeded aft to the emergency steering wheel. He had sent Frank Quick, the Junior Third Officer, ahead of him to put the ship on emergency steering and set up a relay of messengers to convey orders to the engine room.

The *Gothic's* radio office was on the Boat Deck at the forward end of the funnel house. A timber-lined staircase led down from it to the Promenade Deck, one level below. There was no door at the foot of the stairs, where a blanket store room located next to it was in flames. When Radio Officer Cliffe hastened into the radio office to broadcast the SOS, as ordered by the master, he found the room thick with smoke coming up the stairs. The main power supply had failed, so he switched on the Reliance emergency transmitter and the Alert emergency receiver. Both were battery-powered. Going out on deck to breathe while the sets warmed up, Cliffe came back to find the battery electrical supply was also cut. All he could do now was grope his way through the smoke for the two lifeboat emergency transmitters and receivers that were stowed inside the radio office. By the time he got both of them out on deck, the room was fully ablaze.

In the port forward corner of the Promenade Deck, directly above the bar in the lounge where the fire had started, were two small double berth cabins each off a narrow entrance corridor, opposite the purser's bureau. Occupying the after-most of these cabins was passenger John Hubert Halliday, aged 41. His two sons John David Miles Halliday and Alan John Halliday were in the forward cabin. All were asleep for the night. Such was the speed and violence of the fire that, tragically, neither Mr Halliday or the two children were able to leave their cabins or be rescued.

Their mother, 37-year-old Mrs Eileen Joan Halliday, was occupying a double cabin with private bathroom on the starboard side of the Promenade Deck, just aft of the chief engineer's suite. Second Engineer Colin Wickham had succeeded in getting Mrs Halliday out of her cabin and had ordered her to move aft, away from the smoke which had forced both to crawl on their stomachs. She had complied, despite wanting to search for her boys. Seamen tried to get her into one of the port-side lifeboats that had been cleared away and lowered to the Bridge Deck rails. Around her, personnel not needed for fire-fighting or the engine room were boarding the boats. But she refused, screaming for her children, and disappeared through a door back into the accommodation. No one saw Mrs Halliday alive again.

The fire was spreading so fast that Captain Agnew believed they must evacuate the ship before it consumed the lifeboats. His officers urged him to manoeuvre the *Gothic* so as to bring the wind over her stern. Using engine and helm movements from the emergency steering position, Captain Agnew turned the *Gothic* to get her steaming downwind with the gale on her stern and the smoke blowing forward across the starboard bow. Having successfully done this, he ordered half ahead on the engines. On the engine manoeuvring platform, Second Engineer Wickham and his colleagues answered every engine order despite thick, acrid smoke coming in through the ventilators. At no time did the *Gothic's* boilers, turbines, pumps or generators falter. Leaving Junior Third Officer Quick on the wheel, Captain Agnew returned to the fire fighting. By around 6 a.m. some three and a half hours after it was discovered, the fire was under control and Captain Agnew began ordering hoses shut off to limit the quantities of water accumulating in the ship. Roughly at around 7.30 a.m. the fire was out. The bridge house, radio room, forward lounge, dining saloon, purser's bureau and main staircase plus all cabins at the forward end of the Promenade Deck, were completely destroyed. Such was the fire's intensity that these areas were reduced to charred, buckled steel shells filled with wreckage and collapsed fittings. Water from the hoses dripped and sloshed everywhere. The main galley, aft of the dining saloon, was severely damaged. But the flames had been kept from penetrating the hatch trunking to Number 3 hold and its wool cargo. Likewise the inferno did not reach the vital engine and boiler casings.

The *Gothic* had been saved but soon it became clear the fire had exacted a terrible price. No less than seven of her complement were dead. In the port forward corner of the Promenade Deck the remains of the two Halliday boys and their father were found by the master and the chief engineer. All three were so badly burned as to no longer be recognisable. Even more tragically, the body of Eileen Halliday was discovered lying nearby; she had returned to the fire in an endeavour to save her family, only to be asphyxiated by smoke.

Mrs Halliday was in the port alleyway on the Promenade Deck outside the cabin of Paul Raymond Richard Goldfinch, the *Gothic's* Ninth Engineer. Twenty-one years old, he was found dead from suffocation in his cabin. Also killed in his cabin by entry of smoke was the *Gothic's* Fifth Engineer, 26-year-old Peter Daniel Mulcahy of Hartlepool. At the height of the emergency Brian Jordan, a greaser on the *Gothic*, had climbed through the window of Mulcahy's cabin in a desperate effort to rescue him. Mr Mulcahy was lifted out through the window but, on being examined by Chief Engineer McKinnon, was found to be dead. Chief Cook Alfred Phillips tried mouth-to-mouth resuscitation but without success.

Lastly and perhaps most sorrowful of all, Edward Skelly, the *Gothic's* Third Electrician, had disappeared entirely. It was later established that he had been outside the lounge on the port side of the Bridge Deck, helping direct a hose at the fire. Breathing had become almost impossible because of toxic smoke; the fire fighters were relieving each other, each taking short spells on the hose. Skelly was seen to run forward and pick up the hose as others were driven back. He must have drowned after falling overboard from the ship as she rolled in the heavy seas, or as a result of having been overcome or blinded by smoke. Just 21 years old and a first tripper, Edward Skelly was from Liverpool. No one saw him fall to his death in the sea. The body of this courageous young seafarer was never recovered.

Judith Griffin had been married to the *Gothic's* chief officer for 50 days. Having been unable to escape from the bridge house because of smoke and failure of the lights, she had been pulled through a 12-inch diameter porthole from the bathroom of the chief officer's cabin. The porthole faced forward on the starboard wing of the bridge. Her rescuer was David Buck, the *Gothic's* Third Officer, who gave her shoes, a coat and lifejacket then directed her to the lifeboats. Here she waited for the next three hours, seated in a partially lowered lifeboat lashed against the rails amidships on the Bridge Deck. Below her the storm-driven waves leapt and tumbled against the hull of the *Gothic*; in those conditions there was little if any prospect of their getting clear and staying afloat if the boats had to be used to evacuate the ship. Meanwhile Robert Maxwell, the *Gothic's* Chief Steward, had turned his cabin into a medical centre. Here Judith Griffin, a registered nurse by profession, began treating a number of crew members suffering eye and breathing difficulties from the smoke.

'Fire now out, assistance required'

At 10.05 p.m. New Zealand time late on the evening of Sunday 4th August 1968 the duty operators at ZLW Wellington Radio, located up on the Tinakori Hills above Wellington City, received a telephone call from their colleagues at ZLB Awarua Radio in

Her bridge eviscerated by fire, the *Gothic* ploughs into giant head seas as she makes for New Zealand. She is being navigated from the docking bridge and emergency steering position right aft. A Wellington newspaper hired a plane and sent a cameraman out to find the *Gothic* and 'scoop' this dramatic headline picture. *[Evening Post collection, Alexander Turnbull Library, Wellington New Zealand]*

Bluff, New Zealand. A garbled, weak Morse transmission had been intercepted from a ship by name of *Gothic*: 'POSN 0300Z 40S, 168 West crs easterly speed 16 kts sre .... re .... damaged .... radio.' Efforts were made to re-contact the sender, but it was not until some ten hours later, at 8.15 a.m. on Monday 5th August that the full message was heard: 'Gothic 03002 40°S, 168W severe ship fire – now out, assistance required, using lifeboat radio, stop. Any ship in area please indicate.' At 9 a.m. the New Zealand Oceanic Search and Rescue authorities in Auckland requested the Royal New Zealand Air Force (RNZAF) to despatch one of its Lockheed-Martin P-3B Orion maritime surveillance aircraft to find the *Gothic*. The aircraft, NZ4205 of 5 Squadron RNZAF, took off from Whenuapai Air Base at 1.30 p.m. Its commanding officer was Group Captain D.B. Flintoff; also aboard was Squadron Leader L.J. Thompson of the RNZAF's Para-Medic Unit. Forty minutes earlier, at 12.50 p.m., the *Gothic* revealed more fully her plight as she came within closer signal range to New Zealand: 'Severe fire now out, speed 16 knots, navigation and charts destroyed, require assistance, making landfall North Island 42°S 169° 30"W.'

The fire in the *Gothic's* radio room had soon been extinguished but not before consuming everything within. Radio Officer Roger Cliffe had placed both emergency transmitters near the lifeboats. Once the fire was out, he had set up the Salvita set on the Boat Deck just forward of the gutted radio room, rigged an aerial and begun sending on the 8MHz distress frequency. The set had an internal generator that needed to be cranked by hand; this gave it a power output of about two watts. Its companion set, known by the product name Survivor, had been damaged by water from the fire fighting and could no longer be used. The Salvita set was manned continuously together with a receiver down in the stewards' accommodation on the Bridge Deck. This receiver would not function when placed any closer to the transmitter.

It would be four days until the transmissions from Radio Officer Cliffe found a listener, for the *Gothic* was totally alone in the great ocean wilderness of the southern Pacific. Under the leadership of her master, chief engineer, chief officer and chief steward the crew got organised. All the charts, navigating instruments, the gyro compass, radar, cargo stowage plans, crew discharge books, survey certificates, all the ship's administrative records in the purser's bureau along with her register of cargo gear and the bridge log book, were totally gone. Using only the magnetic compass at the after steering position plus a small chart and tables found in the lifeboats, a course was laid off to get her to the nearest port of Wellington, passing a safe distance north of the Chatham Islands. Seamen patrolled the burnt-out area and watched Number 3 hold in case of any new outbreak of fire. The bodies of the six dead were prepared for burial at sea. The small crew galley in the poop deckhouse, under the emergency steering position, became the ship's main galley; three cooked meals were served to all crew members every day. From the wings of the aft docking bridge Captain Agnew maintained vigil over his ship, using a cabin at the aft end of the Bridge Deck for brief periods of sleep. The *Gothic's* turbines, worked up to full power, drove her through the storm-laden seas at 16 knots. 'Stop engines' was ordered at 9 p.m. ship's time on Friday 2nd August when the bodies of engineers Paul Goldfinch and Peter Mulcahy were committed to the sea. At 9 p.m. on the following evening, Saturday 3rd August, the ship paused again and hove-to for the burial at sea of the Halliday family.

HMS *Blackpool*

The *Gothic* was found by the RNZAF Orion aircraft at 3.30 p.m. New Zealand time on 5th August 1968. Descending to low altitude, the big four-engine turboprop passed along the sides of the *Gothic* and in front of her. Roger Cliffe could hear the Orion's radio traffic but the aircraft could not hear him broadcasting on his Salvita set. His Morse was relayed to the Orion by Wellington Radio. Messages were also exchanged by Aldis lamp. A number of spectacular photographs were taken from the aircraft's flight deck and also from a private plane hired by Wellington's 'Evening Post' newspaper. When published on 7th August those photos caused an immediate sensation in New Zealand where the *Gothic* had become so well known from her royal yacht duties. They showed the burnt-

HMNZS *Blackpool* in Otago harbour. Built at Belfast by Harland and Wolff Ltd., she was launched on 14th February 1957 and commissioned into the Royal Navy on 14th August 1958. The Royal New Zealand Navy, to which *Blackpool* was loaned from June 1966 to June 1971, had two very similar frigates in commission at the time: the Rothesay class Type 12 HMNZS *Otago* (F111) and HMNZS *Taranaki* (F148). After her New Zealand service HMS *Blackpool* went into reserve at Portsmouth and was then used as a trials and target ship until her sale for demolition at St Davids, Firth of Forth in May 1978. *[V.H. Young and L.A. Sawyer]*

out forward superstructure, huge white seas exploding over the *Gothic's* bow, and the ship regardless of her plight looking as big, awesome and majestic as ever. NZ4205 landed back at Whenuapai at 8.10 pm that evening.

1968 was only seven months old but already that year there had been two major shipping calamities in New Zealand. This was the third. The *Wahine* disaster, an event of foremost significance in the country's history, took place in Wellington harbour on Wednesday 10th April 1968, just three and a half months earlier. The Union Steam Ship Company's passenger and drive-on vehicle ship *Wahine* (8,944/1966) had been carried onto Barrett's Reef when overwhelmed by sudden hurricane-force winds. She later had to be abandoned, 51 of her 734 complement dying in the sea. Then on 13th June 1968 the 739-ton coaster *Maranui* was lost with nine of her 15 crew in extreme weather off the Coromandel Peninsula when her cargo of wheat shifted.

Aboard the *Gothic* tremendous relief was felt at the ship having been located. But there was no ship in the *Gothic's* vicinity to come to her assistance; nearest was the Union Steam Ship Company's *Navua* (1,952/1955) berthed at Wellington. She headed to sea and was the first to make visual contact, sighting the *Gothic* off the south-eastern coast of the North Island at 2.30 p.m. on 6th August. HMS *Blackpool*, alongside at the naval base at Devonport, Auckland, was ordered to proceed to sea at once and rendezvous with the *Gothic*. A Royal Navy Whitby Class Type 12 anti-submarine frigate, *HMS Blackpool* (F77, 2,560/1958) had been loaned to the RNZN for five years from June 1966 while HMNZS *Canterbury* was built. She had a top speed exceeding 30 knots. Historian and writer Gerry Wright takes up her story:

'The week following Exercise Longex had been planned to be the first full week alongside in three months. A lot of maintenance and defect repairing was planned. But this was not to be. At 1800 hours on Monday 5th August, the ship was ordered immediately to prepare for sea. The Shaw Savill vessel *Gothic* had experienced a major fire east of New Zealand. The Chief of Naval Staff ordered *Blackpool* to proceed with all dispatch to intercept the crippled liner.

A general recall was ordered for the *Blackpool* crew at 1720 and four hours later the frigate was ready for sea. The ship's officers and senior ratings returned onboard, many from their leave, very quickly indeed and those junior ratings that missed the ship were most disappointed that the recall of the crew had not been broadcast on television. Fortunately many of the senior ratings were still in the naval base at the Senior Rates Mess. The staff of the dockyard store depot and Fleet Maintenance Unit returned to work promptly to provide stores and reassemble stripped equipment. There was no shortage of volunteers to back up the ship's company.

HMS *Blackpool* slipped at 2130 steaming on one boiler. Her commanding officer was Commander Derek Cheney RNZN. With an enhanced crew, a strong medical team made up of Surgeon Lieutenant Commander Albie Green RNZN and six medical assistants, plus additional firefighting equipment and stores, the ship proceeded at her best speed to meet the *Gothic*. On clearing Auckland harbour a course was set for Colville Channel and, with the second boiler then ready, speed was worked up to 28 knots. The radio office tuned into all likely radio frequencies in the hope of hearing any signal from the liner. Off the east coast a rising westerly wind and seas caused the commanding officer to keep close to the sheltered coastal waters as the frigate raced towards the estimated position of the *Gothic* off the Wairarapa Coast. The following morning an updated position for the *Gothic* was received from an RNZAF P-3 Orion aircraft and following another update from the Union Steam Ship Company's freighter *Navua*, she was detected by radar at a range of 23 miles.

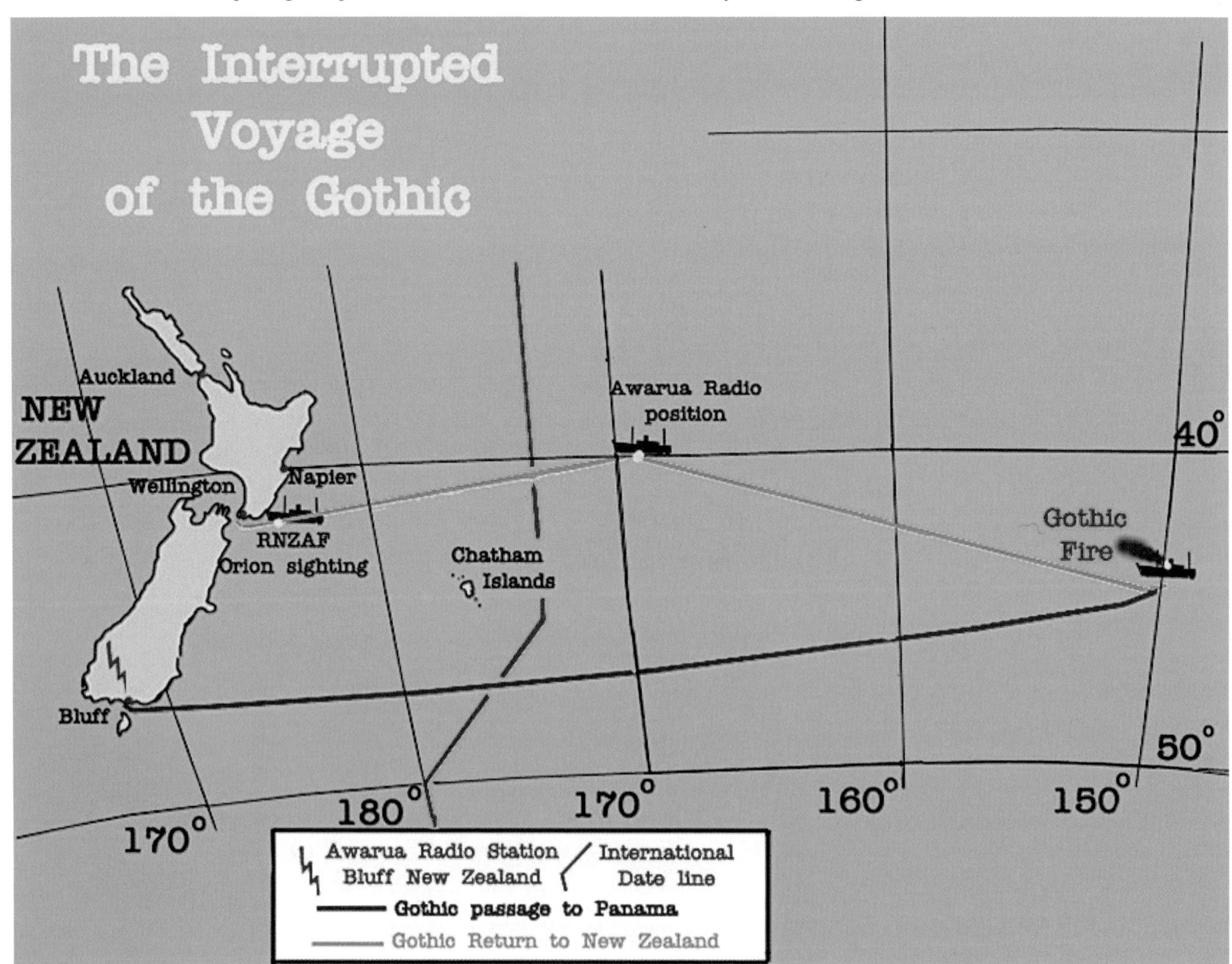

[Martin Cahill]

At 1725 (5.25 p.m.) on 6th August 1968, 20 hours after leaving Auckland, *Blackpool* had the *Gothic* in sight and managed to establish communications with a flashing light. The liner was following an erratic course for Wellington under emergency steering, and making 16 knots. Assistance in the form of providing a chart of Wellington was offered and declined by her master. HMS *Blackpool* then took up a position on the *Gothic's* port quarter at half a mile to oversee the vessel's navigation towards Wellington. At Palliser Bay, a Wellington Harbour Board pilot boarded the *Gothic* and two harbour tugs joined to help her into port and berth at Aotea Quay. Once *Gothic* was secured *Blackpool* also berthed to refuel. Two and a half hours later, at 0215 (2.15 a.m.) *Blackpool* slipped and sailed for Auckland at a more sedate speed of 15 knots.'

NZ4205 of 5 Squadron RNZAF landed back at Whenuapai Air Base at 8.10 pm on the evening of 5th August after having found the *Gothic*. Eight and a half hours later this same aircraft made a second sortie out to the ship, taking off at 6.20 a.m. under the command of Flight Lieutenant J.B. Irvine. It circled the *Gothic* until HMS *Blackpool* arrived, then returned to Whenuapai Air Base at 11 p.m. At that point 5 Squadron stood down.

The bureaucratic blow-torch

The *Gothic* was made fast alongside Number 3 Berth at Aotea Quay at 11.35 p.m. late on Tuesday evening 6th August 1968. Watchmen were sent aboard to relieve the crew, who gratefully turned in for the night. Next morning a procession of visitors from the halls of local officialdom began climbing her gangway. One by one they toured the wrecked and burnt-out forward lounge, the dining saloon, the cabins and alleyways on the Promenade Deck where the Hallidays had perished and where the two engineers had suffocated to death. They peered inside the *Gothic's* bridge house, its stark interior completely incinerated. They picked their way through the main galley on the Bridge Deck where, testifying to the performance of the ships' crew, the fire had got no further than the galley's after bulkhead. Damage here was limited only to smoke and superficial charring. And, even more miraculously, they saw the steel trunk of Number 3 hatch positioned between the dining saloon and galley. Although the wood panelling on the outer faces of the trunk was destroyed, its steel walls were little affected. All the experts in their various fields agreed: the fire on the *Gothic* had been of immense and devastating power and the achievement of her master, officers, engineers and crew in confining and controlling it had been nothing short of 'fantastic' and 'almost superhuman', to quote Wellington's Chief Fire Officer. Had they not done so, the *Gothic* would have been gutted right to her stern. The Wellington Fire Chief, W.J. Henderson, went on to assert that even with the full resources of his fire brigade and with the *Gothic* alongside a wharf, the fire would have posed an enormous task to quell.

In his report dated 9th August 1968 a surveyor of ships from the District Office of the Marine Department noted the 'severe sagging and buckling of the entire deckhead' over the lounge and dining saloon. 'Front plating is extensively warped and buckled also window frames, side plating and bulwarks....The main staircase and supports is completely collapsed.' On the Promenade Deck he further noted 'severe structural damage....the port fore and aft girder is fractured, all deck beams, girders and plating (are) sagging to varying degrees (and) supporting plate pillars either side of the purser's office are buckled and distorted...' He went on to describe the total ruination of the wheelhouse, chart room, monkey island, master and deck officers' cabins and the radio office. The ventilation supply fans and the four sets of cargo winches on the roof of the bridge house at its after end, similarly were fried and useless.

A police sergeant had boarded the *Gothic* from the pilot launch *Tiakina* in Cook Strait. He had been accompanied onto the ship by Captain D.W. Galloway, Wellington Harbour Master, and by Wellington's Chief Fire Officer. At 8 next morning, Wednesday 7th August, detectives from the New Zealand Police's Criminal Investigation Branch began their enquiries into the fire and the seven fatalities. All crew members were questioned and their written statements taken. Two inspectors from the Wellington Municipal Electricity Department were brought in to assist. They examined the two three-pin electrical sockets located behind curtains next to the refrigerator in the lounge's port forward corner. The fire was believed to have originated within 12 inches of these sockets. Although heavily damaged by the fire, no evidence was found that either had caused it, nor had the refrigerator or its plug and electrical cord. The electrical switchboard in the forward lounge was also ruled out as culprit.

On 8th August a detective superintendent took over the investigation. Analysts from the Department of Scientific and Industrial Research arrived aboard the *Gothic* along with electrical engineers from the New Zealand Electricity Department. T.W. Watson, Shaw Savill's General Manager for New Zealand and Captain A.E. Smith, Shaw Savill's Marine Superintendent in New Zealand, were both on the ship together with a Board of Trade surveyor who had flown out from Great Britain. The Chief Fire Officer and his deputies were still there. Doubtless the *Gothic's* only functioning galley, aft in the poop deck house, turned out the obligatory morning teas for all while getting on with preparation of the crew's midday meal. In tandem with this regiment of functionaries and experts, B.F. Scully, Superintendent of Mercantile Marine in Wellington, was conducting his own preliminary inquiry. He did so under authority vested in him by the New Zealand Shipping and Seamen Act 1952. Superintendent Scully's job was to recommend to the Minister of Marine, W.J. Scott, whether a full court of inquiry into the fire and loss of life aboard the *Gothic* was warranted. His recommendation was that it was not.

Later that same morning, 8th August 1968, the detective superintendent convened a conference in his office at the Wellington Central Police Station of all involved, to try and pinpoint the cause of the fire. Second Officer Peter Garlick was present on behalf of the *Gothic's* Master. The police had been unable to establish who had last been in the forward lounge, and they could reach no definite conclusion as to how and why the fire had started. It was resolved that the most likely source was a smouldering cigarette left in the forward lounge, or an electrical fault. The latter was considered to be a much more remote possibility.

The police inquiry focused in particular on the defective fire extinguisher which Cadet Timothy Latcham had been unable to operate successfully. It was a new extinguisher of the soda-acid type that fired a jet of water under pressure, and it had been fully approved and certified by the Board of Trade. However, on close examination by Department of Scientific and Industrial Research analysts, its manufacture was found to be defective. A strainer was provided at the intake end of the tube through which water was discharged when the extinguisher was operated. Hitting the knob at the top of the extinguisher caused an acid bottle to break, and the purpose of the strainer was to catch pieces of glass from this bottle. But the strainer had not been securely fixed to the discharge tube when the extinguisher was manufactured. Two slivers of glass had escaped the strainer and blocked the discharge tube.

A coroner's inquest was held on 30th August 1968. He found the deaths of John Hubert Halliday and his two boys to have been caused by 'either suffocation from smoke arising from the fire...or severe burns received in that fire. Alan Halliday was aged 11 and his brother David was seven. Their mother Eileen Joan Halliday, who had tried so courageously to rescue them, was found to have died of suffocation from smoke.

Survive to die

Of all the many visitors who came to the fire-scarred *Gothic* as she lay at Aotea Quay during that second week in August 1968, the most significant was Captain H. Rome, Shaw Savill's Chief Marine Superintendent. He flew to New Zealand to assess the fire damage, then a few days later went back to London to make his report to the company's senior managers at their Leadenhall Street Head Office. The *Gothic's* hull, engines and her cargo under refrigeration had all been untouched by the fire. Wellington had the facilities to carry out full repairs to the *Gothic* but it was decided by Shaw Savill to do only what was necessary to get her and her cargo home to Great Britain. Once there, the vessel's future would be decided. A repair

The forward lounge, where the fire started. *[Evening Post collection, Alexander Turnbull Library, Wellington New Zealand]*

Inside the burnt-out wheelhouse, looking across to the port wing. *[Evening Post collection, Alexander Turnbull Library, Wellington New Zealand]*

Top left: Tradesmen erecting partitions to create cabins inside the bridge house. Apart from being painted white, the buckled deckhead was left as it was.
Top right: Inside the repaired wheelhouse, showing the temporary fit-out that was to remain in place for the 15 months left to the *Gothic*.
Above left: Concrete being laid on the steel of the *Gothic's* Boat Deck outboard of the bridge house, to replace scorched and charred deck timber that has been pulled up.
Above right: The *Gothic's* fire-blackened wheelhouse and fore superstructure, showing windows that were either blanked-off or left unglazed during repairs at Wellington. *[Evening Post collection, Alexander Turnbull Library, Wellington New Zealand]*
Below: The *Gothic* alongside Aotea Quay, Wellington showing her fire damage with repairs having started, August 1968. Note the collapsed accommodation ladder. *[V.H. Young and L.A. Sawyer]*

contract was awarded to William Cable Ltd., mechanical, structural and electrical engineers based at Kaiwharawhara in Wellington.

The first task was to remove 95 tons of wreckage and debris left by the fire. Charred deck planking was also ripped up. Three dozen tradesmen then started reconstructing the bridge house. Heat from the flames had severely twisted the steel deck while the deckhead had sagged to such an extent that it was not possible to stand up in what had been the wheelhouse. Carpenters built a false floor made of plywood sheets laid over heavy timber bearers. Using mechanical jacks the deckhead was pushed up by some 16 inches to give sufficient head room, with approximately half the depth of sag left. Five forward-facing bridge windows received glass taken from passenger cabin windows elsewhere in the *Gothic's* superstructure. The rest had steel patches fitted across them. Fire-blackened surfaces were cleaned and painted. Nothing was done to straighten or replace heat-distorted steel. Nor was any of the bridge woodwork reinstated. On the bridge wings and Boat Deck concrete was laid where the deck planking had been.

A complete new outfit of navigation, steering, engine telegraphs, radar, communications, gyro compass, ventilation and smoke detection gear was provided for the wheelhouse. Some of it was obtained locally, other components were air-freighted from Great Britain by Shaw Savill. Included was a new Marconi Oceanspan radio transmitter and Atalanta receiver. Behind the wheelhouse, timber partitions were erected to form a chart room and accommodation for the master. The remainder of the bridge house was made weather-tight and left empty, its windows sheathed over. All deck officers and engineers were now accommodated in former passenger cabins in the deck house under the funnel on the Boat Deck, immediately abaft the radio room. Fire and smoke damage here was repaired and the radio room fully re-equipped. Materials taken from other parts of the old passenger accommodation were used as much as possible. The officers and engineers set up a bar and lounge for themselves in what had been the children's play room in the fore starboard corner of the deck house. The blackened Promenade Deck interior was left closed off and uninhabited.

On the Bridge Deck the main galley was fully repaired and put back into service. All plumbing lines and electrical wiring was renewed. Forward of the galley an officers' dining area was created by partitioning off part of the burnt-out dining saloon. What had been the forward lounge was walled-off and left empty, its windows sheathed over. Some 100 gallons of white paint were applied, but many internal areas not essential for operation of the ship were left without paint or repair.

A memorial service for the Halliday family was held at St Andrew's Anglican Church, Plimmerton, north of Wellington, at 11 a.m. on Saturday 10th August. Captain Agnew and 30 members of the *Gothic's* crew attended the service, held in the church where the Hallidays had been worshippers.

On the morning of Thursday 5th September 1968, 29 days after she arrived, the *Gothic* left her berth at Aotea Quay to undergo engine and steering trials in Wellington harbour. Apart from a faulty boiler tube, the trials were successful. So on Saturday 7th September, under the command of Captain Agnew, she sailed from Wellington to resume her voyage home to Liverpool. Although Shaw Savill had offered to fly to Great Britain any crew member wishing to leave the ship, no one from her crew had asked to pay off. The *Gothic* transited the Panama Canal on 25th September and reached Liverpool 10th October 1968, the voyage having been without further mishap. Her crew were paid a bonus by Shaw Savill, reportedly £100 each, at Liverpool. A condition of the bonus was that none of them were permitted to sign on the *Gothic* again. She arrived in Avonmouth for discharge of cargo on 18th October.

Looking up at her from the wharf, only the plated-over windows on the *Gothic's* bridge and superstructure front seemed different. But once on board there was evidence a-plenty of the fire's voracity. The interior of the Promenade Deck at its fore end, where passenger cabins, the main stairway and the purser's bureau had been, was now a blackened open space with twisted steel and empty window squares. Plonked amidst the emptiness was a solitary table on which the ship-to-shore telephone sat. The bridge house interior was just as desolate except for what looked like plywood boxes fixed against the rear bulkhead of the wheelhouse, containing the chart room and master's cabin. On the Bridge Deck the forward lounge was completely sealed off, such was the destruction there. For those who saw the fire's results it must

At the King George V Dock, London on 24th November 1968, loading cargo for the *Gothic's* final trip to New Zealand. Note the many windows absent from her bridge front. Nine months from this photo and she will be gone. *[V.H. Young and L.A. Sawyer]*

have come as no surprise when it was learned that no permanent repairs were to be made to the *Gothic*. Estimated to cost £250,000 to £300,000 in 1968, the price was too much for a ship in her 21st year with her boilers no longer in the prime of efficiency. Moreover, now that the *Gothic* did not carry passengers there was no economic gain from refurbishing the burnt-out Promenade Deck cabins and the forward lounge. No further repair work was done on the ship. Cargo already booked for the *Gothic* was loaded for her next voyage – Number 38. With Captain B.H. Agnew as Master she was back in Wellington, New Zealand on 7th January 1969. Seven thousand tons of general cargo was discharged, after which the *Gothic* steamed to Lyttelton to complete her unloading. She then loaded refrigerated cargo at Wellington and in northern New Zealand ports before sailing for the United Kingdom.

On her arrival in London it was announced that the *Gothic* was to be withdrawn and sold for breaking after one final trip. She went out to Australia with general cargo and left Sydney on 1st August 1969, her holds empty. This was her first visit to Sydney since the time of the royal tour. On 13th August the *Gothic* arrived at Kaohsiung and was handed over to the Hwa Zon Iron and Steel Company. Her demolition commenced 12 weeks later on 5th November 1969.

When the cutters reached the *Gothic's* propellers part of one of them was brought back to England and given by Shaw Savill for use as a memorial plaque to the Halliday family. It was mounted in St Andrew's Anglican Church at Plimmerton, New Zealand. Their grave is the Pacific Ocean but their names are forever linked with the merchant ship given the honour of bringing the very first reigning British sovereign to visit her dominions of Australia and New Zealand.

Magnificent misfits

The story of the *Corinthic*, *Athenic*, *Ceramic* and *Gothic* would not be complete without mention of the three passenger and refrigerated cargo liners that all too briefly succeeded them. Originally built for Royal Mail Lines' UK to South America trade, the *Amazon* (20,368/1959) *Aragon* (20,362/1960) and *Arlanza* (20,362/1960) were vessels also deserving of the title magnificent. Twin screw, 17.5-knot motor ships, they were known with much fondness as the 'Three Graces'. Their comeliness did not, however, extend to sustainable profit-making and after less than a decade they were withdrawn. Everywhere at that time the viability of passenger-cargo ships was being destroyed by airliner competition, soaring operational costs, labour troubles and by the coming of containerisation. Furness Withy, owner of Royal Mail and Shaw Savill, believed these big ships with accommodation for 464 passengers in three classes might do better on a round-the-world service between Great Britain, Australia and New Zealand. The *Amazon* was transferred to Shaw Savill in February 1968, being renamed *Akaroa*. *Aragon*, renamed *Aranda* and *Arlanza*, renamed *Arawa*, followed in 1969.

Fully air-conditioned, beautifully furnished, white-hulled and fitted with escalators, anti-roll stabilisers and three upper deck swimming pools, they were repainted with Shaw Savill's funnel colours, reconfigured to take 470 passengers in one class and marketed as the 'White Heron Fleet'. It might have worked had it been 1950 and not 1970. Huge running costs and lack of profitability saw their demise in early 1971 when, for little more than their scrap value, all three went to Norwegian interests for rebuilding as car carriers.

Above left: An interesting view of the *Gothic* in one of the graving docks at London on a quiet weekend day. Note the timber frames hanging against the veranda cafe windows to protect them while cargo is swung on the derricks. *[Ambrose Greenway]*

Above: An early morning view of the *Gothic* laid up at the Shops' Berth, Royal Albert Dock. London. *[Chris Howell]*

Above: The *Gothic* at Liverpool probably during the interval between the tour that was cancelled following the death of King George VI, and the tour made by Queen Elizabeth II. *[Newall Dunn collection]*

Left: HMRY *Gothic* photographed as if from a circling plane on 11th January 1953, but in fact she is about to steam under the Hobart bridge on her way to Risdon to load zinc. During her service as royal yacht hundreds of aircraft flew over and around the *Gothic* in a manner that would never be tolerated in today's security-fixated age. With photographers and admirers crowding the aircraft windows, they were rewarded with spectacular views not unlike this one. *[David Kirby/Russell Priest collection]*

Opposite page, top: The royal yacht *Gothic* in all her splendour, with the Queen and Duke of Edinburgh aboard, arriving at Hobart. This was the only arrival during the entire tour when the *Gothic's* complement was in 'blues' (dark winter uniforms). *[Roger Martin/Russell Priest collection]*

In the lower view she is alongside on the 23rd February with the royal standard and Lord High Admiral's flag off her mast tops, the royal visitors having disembarked for their shore engagements. *[Reg Wilson/Russell Priest collection]*

GOTHIC

GOTHIC

At anchor off Bluff, waiting to load. *[Ian J. Farquhar collection]*

A handsome stern view of the *Gothic*, taken in April 1967. She is still carrying passengers but not for much longer; the ship's last passenger voyage will conclude at London just 14 months from the time of this photo. [*George Gould collection, World Ship Society Ltd. 11645*]

The *Gothic* at sea (above), after the royal tour. *[FotoFlite incorporating Skyfotos, 354212]*

Raised out of the sea and revealed in all her stateliness, the *Gothic* in Wellington's Jubilee Floating Dock where she seems to be having her boot topping or anti-fouling paint either inspected or renewed (right). The date is 7th February 1965, high summer in New Zealand with the *Gothic's* flags asserting themselves in the stiff north-westerly breeze. *[V.H. Young and L.A. Sawyer]*

Three years and seven months later in early September 1968, the *Gothic* berthed at Aotea Quay in Wellington harbour (below right). Her fire damage has been repaired just enough to make her seaworthy. Not even a seagull can be seen on the deserted wharf or on the ship; the date is probably the Sunday prior to her sailing for Liverpool. She is no longer a first class passenger liner and her paintwork, when compared to its gleaming, faultless standard in the floating dock view, testifies to this. Behind the plated-over windows are burnt-out interiors, cleared of debris but never to be reinstated. *[V.H. Young and L.A. Sawyer]*

The *Persic* leaving Cape Town at the end of her first visit, January 1950. Oily smoke belches from her funnel; the wind is carrying most of it over-side but the chief officer will be watching with dismay as greasy effluent falls upon his freshly-painted upper decks. A telephone from the bridge will soon be ringing on the engine manoeuvring platform where the senior engineer on watch, or maybe the chief engineer himself, if he's on the plates, will want to know who the culprit is. Note the animal pens on her fore and after well decks. *[Ships in Focus]*

PERSIC: NOBLE PRINCE WITH NO PASSENGERS

First of the cargo-only Big Ics

In addition to its *Corinthic* class, Shaw Savill soon began ordering cargo-only refrigerator ships to replace the company's war losses. The first and second of these new vessels were the *Doric* (10,674/1949) and *Delphic* (10,691/1949). At 509 feet in length, each was a twin-screw, 17-knot motor ship and they came respectively from the yards of the Fairfield Shipbuilding and Engineering Co. Ltd. at Govan on the River Clyde, and from R. and W. Hawthorn, Leslie and Co. Ltd. of Hebburn-on-Tyne. For its third new ship Shaw Savill returned to the successful design of the *Corinthic* and her sisters. She was ordered on 21st January 1948, the 14-page contract for her building being signed on 10th December that same year. It provided for a twin-screw steam ship 530 feet in length between perpendiculars, 72 feet moulded breadth, with engines producing 15,400 SHP on a loaded draft of 'about 29 feet 6 inches...with propellers running at about 123 r.p.m.' Clause 12 of the contract set out the 'provisional contract sum for the vessel' - £1,054,000. This was to be paid in five equal instalments of £210,800 'when the keel plates are laid on the blocks', 'when the vessel is framed', 'when the vessel is fully plated', 'when the vessel is launched', and 'when the vessel has been delivered'. The figure of £1,054,000 excluded the supply and fitting of refrigerating plant and the insulation of the ship's holds; Shaw Savill arranged separate contractors to do this work.

She would carry no passengers and so the centre superstructure was reduced in length at its aft end, allowing Number 4 hatch to be on the same deck (the Shelter Deck) as Numbers 5 and 6. The Promenade Deck was eliminated, leaving only the Boat Deck and Bridge Deck, but she was given the same-sized oval funnel (which seemed much larger on her) while the two masts were in the same position as aboard the *Corinthic*. Visually she was a ship of remarkably handsome proportions on a hull that matched the *Corinthic* but with breadth increased by one foot. Length overall was 561 feet or 535 feet 5 inches between perpendiculars fore and aft. Moulded breadth was 72 feet and she had a draught of 31 feet 11 5/8 inches. Her draught when light was 14 feet 10¼ inches.

Gross register tonnage at 13,594 was, of course, considerably smaller with the deletion of passenger accommodation. The new vessel was built as Hull Number 1202 by Cammell Laird and Co. Ltd. at Birkenhead, the same shipyard that had produced the *Corinthic* and *Ceramic*. Her keel was laid on the South Slipway Number 2 on 11th May 1948. Thirteen months later on Friday morning 10th June 1949 she was named *Persic* and launched into the Mersey by her sponsor, 20-year-old Miss Pauline Sanderson, daughter of Shaw Savill's Chairman of Directors, Basil Sanderson MC. After the ceremony Miss Sanderson, who was studying French at Oxford University, was presented by Sir Robert Johnson, Chairman of Cammell Laird, with a Twelfth Century copy of 'Le Chanson de Roland', the oldest surviving major work of French literature. Miss Sanderson's father was not quite so generous in the speech he gave at the luncheon once the new vessel was afloat. He reflected on the *Persic* having cost four times what she would have had she been built in 1930, and two-and-a-half times more than the equivalent cost in 1939. 'If everyone', he said, 'from the top of the scale to the bottom, would give a day's full work for a day's full pay, we would find our costs of production coming down enormously in this country'. Mr Sanderson went on to comment that, because of the soaring cost for replacing old ships with new building, a number of obsolete coal-burning vessels would have to be kept in service. Interestingly his views did not long deflect the company from its programme of renewal. After the *Suevic*, last of the Big Ics, in 1950 just two years elapsed until the *Cedric* (11,232/1952), first of the company's excellent C class of four motor ships, entered service.

After five and a half months fitting out, acceptance trials took place in the Firth of Clyde on 24th November 1949. *Persic,* Official Number 183578, was completed and handed over

Shaw Savill's 10,691 grt refrigerated motor ship *Delphic* of 1949. She and the *Doric* were the first motor ships built for Shaw Savill following the end of the Second World War. The *Doric* could be distinguished from her sister by the samson posts on her forecastle. Such was the inferior quality of steel from which they were built that extensive renewal of their hull plating was needed when they were only ten years old. The *Doric* was broken up in 1969, the *Delphic* in 1971. *[J. and M. Clarkson]*

Top left: The bottle bursts instantaneously as the camera shutter opens. His arms folded, Shaw Savill Chairman Basil Sanderson watches his daughter Pauline send the *Persic* down to the Mersey on 10th June 1949. On her left, facing the camera, is Sir Robert Johnson, Chairman of Cammell Laird. Top right: The *Persic* dropping off the way-ends, with her stern about to lift. Note the fore-poppets to port and starboard of her bow. Their function was to support the *Persic's* hull at this crucial moment when its fore end is still on land but her stern is suddenly afloat and lifting to its own buoyancy.
Bottom: *Persic* is successfully launched and is moved into Cammell Laird's fitting out basin. *[Captain Graham Pepper, Shaw Savill Society]*

to Shaw Savill two days later, after final adjustments, and sailed from Liverpool on 29th November to begin her working life. Ship spotters, a plentiful breed in those days, would have found little to complain about in the new vessel's sturdy good looks. She went first to Antwerp to load general cargo from 1st to 4th December, then crossed to London to complete loading. Under the command of Captain E.T. Baker the *Persic* departed London to commence her maiden voyage on Wednesday 21st December 1949 with a crew of 74. First port of call was Cape Town, then to Fremantle in Western Australia for first discharge of cargo. After further calls at Australian ports the *Persic* sailed for New Plymouth and Wellington, New Zealand to load frozen and general merchandise for return to the UK. Over the next 20 years she served this trade, voyaging back and forth from London or Liverpool to Australia and New Zealand, discharging and then loading for home. In total she made 14 visits to Port Chalmers, New Zealand to work cargo, the first of which was on 11st October 1950, the last on 17th November 1965. In 1966 the *Persic* made a voyage for the Montreal Australia New Zealand Line Ltd. (MANZ Line) with New Zealand Meat and Dairy Board produce which she unloaded at Charleston, Hampton Roads, Philadelphia, New York and Boston in the USA, then at St. Johns, New Brunswick, Canada, before crossing the Atlantic to London.

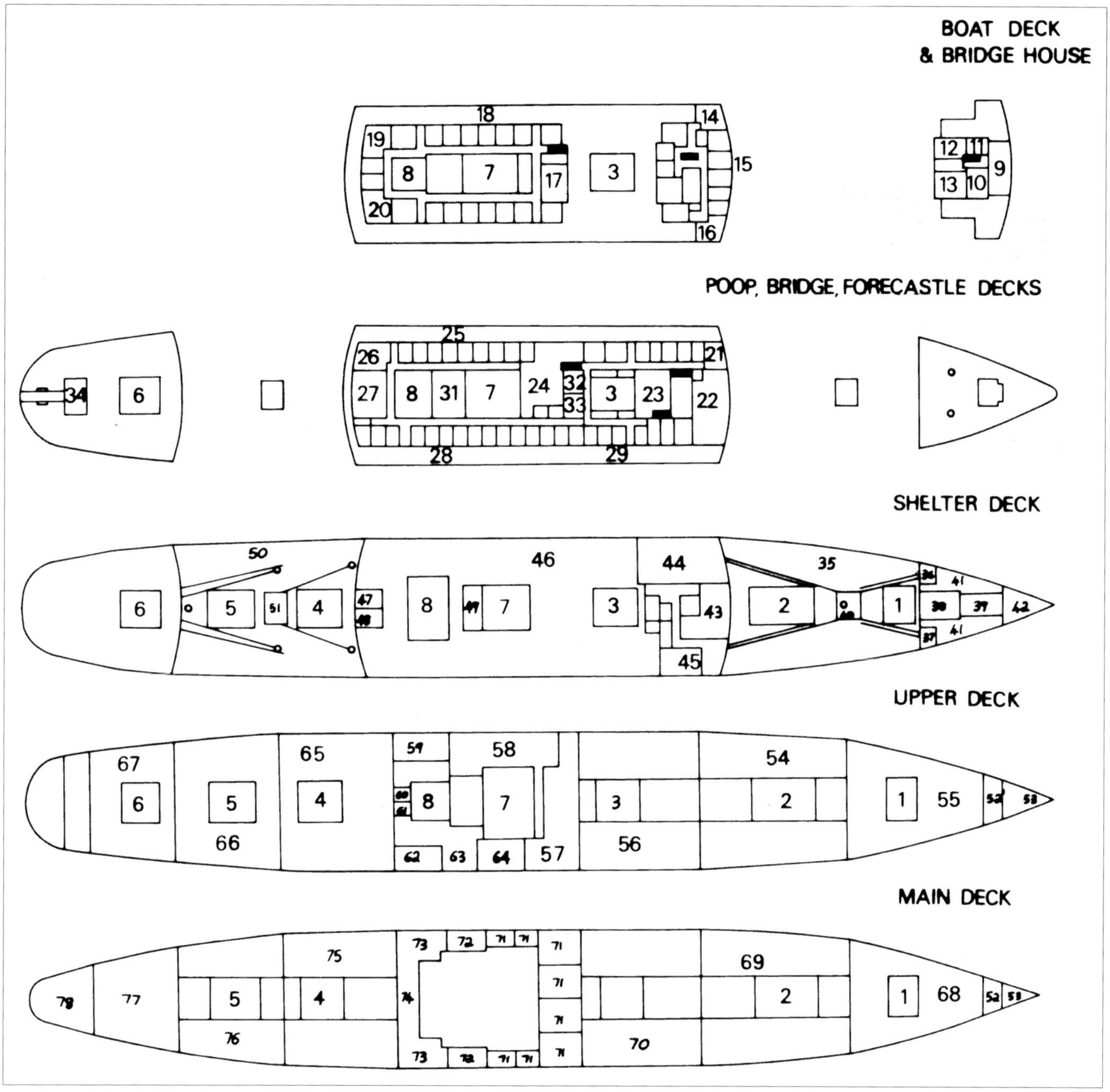

BOAT DECK & BRIDGE HOUSE

POOP, BRIDGE, FORECASTLE DECKS

SHELTER DECK

UPPER DECK

MAIN DECK

Deck plans for the *Persic*, as built, drawn from general arrangement plans held by the Wirral Archives Service:
1. No. 1 cargo hatch.
2. No. 2 cargo hatch.
3. No. 3 cargo hatch.
4. No. 4 cargo hatch.
5. No. 5 cargo hatch.
6. No. 6 cargo hatch.
7. boiler casing.
8. engine casing.
9. wheelhouse.
10. chart room.
11. radio office.
12. master's sleeping cabin.
13. master's day room.
14. chief officer's cabin.
15. deck officers' single-berth cabins and smoking room.
16. second officer's cabin.
17. engineers' smoking room.
18. engineers' single berth cabins.
19. chief engineer's suite.
20. second engineer's suite.
21. chief steward's cabin.
22. officers' dining saloon.
23. galley.
24. crew's mess room.
25. seamen's two-berth cabins.
26. hospital.
27. crew's recreation room.
28. firemen, greasers and stewards two-berth cabins.
29. petty officers' single berth cabins.
30. crew bathrooms.
31. crew bathrooms.
32. petty officers' mess.
33. petty officers' bathroom.
34. poop deck store.
35. fore well deck.
36. paint store.
37. lamp trimmer's store.
38. mail room.
39. windlass machinery.
40. winch contactor house.
41. forecastle 'tween deck general cargo.
42. store.
43. winch contactors.
44. insulated food stores
45. grocery stores.
46. general cargo.
47. carpenter's workshop.
48. fan control room.
49. fan flat.
50. after well deck.
51. winch contactor house.
52. chain locker.
53. store.
54. No. 2 upper 'tween deck – insulated.
55. No. 1 upper 'tween deck – insulated.
56. No. 3 upper 'tween deck – insulated.
57. brine room.
58. refrigerating compressor room.
59. CO_2 bottles.
60. electricians' store.
61. electricians' workshop.
62. engineers' store.
63. engineers' workshop.
64. evaporators.
65. No. 4 upper 'tween deck – partially insulated.
66. No. 5 upper 'tween deck– general cargo.
67. No. 6 upper 'tween deck – general cargo.
68. No.1 main 'tween deck – insulated.
69. No.2 main 'tween deck – insulated.
70. No.3 main 'tween deck – insulated.
71. fuel tank.
72. distilled water tank.
73. turbo generator.
74. main switchboard.
75. No.4 main 'tween deck – insulated.
76. No.5 main 'tween deck – insulated.
77. No. 6 main 'tween deck – general cargo.
78. steering gear.

[Murray Robinson]

Only two incidents seem to have interrupted the regularity of her life, both of them occurring in 1958. On 9th February the *Persic* cleared Port Chalmers for the long voyage home to London after loading on the New Zealand coast. Her first destination was to be Callao across the Pacific in Peru, where she was to off-load a deck cargo of Corriedale sheep valued at £30,000. Three days out and 1,700 miles east of Wellington, a fire took hold in the area of the bridge and master's quarters early on the morning of 12th February 1958. The *Persic's* crew toiled for many hours with the ship on emergency steering from the poop, before they succeeded in getting the fire out. Initially she turned back for Wellington but it was then decided to continue the voyage to Peru where temporary repairs were made.

Less than two months later, while on passage from Hobart, Tasmania via the Suez Canal to the port of Avonmouth, the *Persic* diverted to rescue 31 crew members from the steamer *Pan Ocean* (5,155/1923) after she sprang a leak and began sinking 160 miles north-west of Alexandria, Egypt. The date was 6th April 1958 and the *Pan Ocean*, belonging to the Pan Ocean Navigation Company of Liberia, had been carrying iron ore from Mormugao in India for Genoa.

The Navy commander

The *Persic's* Master when this Mediterranean rescue took place was Captain G.W. Houchen OBE RD RNR. Born in Wayland, Norfolk in December 1906, George William Houchen had a distinguished war record and was appointed Master of the *Persic* on 24th March 1958. Warwick Thomson remembers him from the 16½ months he spent aboard the *Persic* as second officer, joining the ship at Liverpool on 7th April 1959 after having been promoted from third officer on the *Dominion Monarch*: 'George Houchen was great to sail with. He liked his pink gins and was an RNR man through and through. He wore his Blue Ensign with pride wherever he could hoist it aloft either with or without the mandatory number of RNR personnel under him.

Late on the night of 23rd May 1960 we'd arrived at the pilot station off Lyttelton, intending to anchor. This was during one of the three voyages out to Australia and New Zealand that I did on the *Persic* (with three home trade loading voyages to the Continent between them). As a dutiful second officer I'd left the tidal information pinned up in the chart room for Captain Houchen, but he was convinced I couldn't read tide tables. At least that's the opinion with which he greeted me with some vigour when I arrived on the bridge at midnight to begin my watch. George (as he was affectionately known to us) had had a drink or three that evening and that always made him a bit tetchy when he was on duty. The ship had not behaved as she ought and was surging around the anchor as I rechecked the tide tables.

Just then, the port's signal station called us up on the lamp (this was before general use of V.H.F.) instructing us to get out because something unusual was happening with the tide. We picked up the anchor and since we were then head-in, George began to turn the ship short around on the engines. While doing so, there was a tremendous vibration and we looked at each other: had we touched bottom? I'd often seen George mildly pixilated in the time I spent with him aboard the *Persic* but I'd never seen him sober up as quickly as he did that night. We discussed the situation briefly, then rang the engine room to see if they'd noticed anything unusual. They hadn't, so it was put down to cavitation of the screws – or some sort of shallow water effect. Anyway, it didn't go in the log book. It transpired that our arrival had coincided with a tsunami caused by an earthquake in Chile. It had surged into Lyttelton 2.7 metres above the normal tide level, causing havoc in the port during the night of 23rd-24th May 1960 and keeping us out at anchor for about three days watching flotsam surging in and out of the harbour. One of the Crusader ships was the first to enter after things calmed down. When she berthed without incident, we followed. The experience didn't put George off his tipple!'

Captain George Houchen was found dead in his cabin on the morning of Wednesday 16th March 1966 while the *Persic* was on passage from Panama to New Zealand. He had died in his sleep during the night, aged just 59, with the cause of death reported as heart failure. Captain Houchen was buried at sea. John Sayers, the *Persic's* Chief Officer, took over as Acting Master and was

Northbound in the Suez Canal during what must have been a winter transit as no awnings are rigged: these were vital in summer. The derrick raised at Number 5 hatch is for lowering and then recovering the boat that canal boatmen will use for getting ropes ashore, should the *Persic* need to moor alongside the canal banks to allow a southbound convoy past. *[Ambrose Greenway]*

later confirmed in this position with his seniority backdated to 17th March. He continued as the *Persic's* Master until he resigned from Shaw Savill while in New Zealand on 30th September 1966. Other well-known Shaw Savill masters who commanded the *Persic* were Captain Roger Frisby and Captain J.A. Williams.

Space, suppliers and specifications

The *Persic* had six holds and 'tween decks. In addition there was space in her forecastle, in the centre island below the Bridge Deck and in the poop, all of which was used for general cargo. The latter was also carried in Number 6 hold, Number 5 upper 'tween decks and part of Number 4 upper 'tween decks. All other cargo spaces, including all the three forward holds, were fully insulated. The centre compartments in the 'tween decks of Numbers 2 and 3 holds were reserved for chilled produce while all other insulated space was for frozen goods.

All of the *Persic's* equipment was British-made for in 1949 Great Britain led the world in shipbuilding and marine heavy engineering. Her refrigeration machinery, electrically driven, had been supplied by the Dartford firm of J. and E. Hall Ltd. The windlass on the forecastle was also electric; its manufacturer was Clarke, Chapman and Co. Ltd. of Gateshead. Brown Brothers and Co. Ltd. were responsible for supplying the electro-hydraulic steering gear, which came from their factory in Edinburgh. The Winsor Engineering Co. Ltd. of Glasgow provided the mechanical ventilation system for the accommodation areas. Smoke detectors and carbon dioxide fire-extinguishing plant for the ship was supplied and installed by the Walter Kiddle Co. Ltd. of Northolt, Middlesex. Gravity davits, on which were cradled the *Persic's* three 40-person lifeboats and one motor lifeboat, were by Welin-Maclachlan. The three non-motorised boats had Fleming hand-propelling gear, by which occupants moved vertical hand-levers back and forth to activate the propeller. The levers were known to seamen as barmaids.

There was a different layout of samson posts aboard the *Persic* compared to her Belfast-built sisters *Runic* and *Suevic*, neither of which carried a mainmast. Derricks with five and twelve ton lifting capacities were mounted on five sets of twin samson posts and on both the *Persic's* masts, along with a 50-ton heavy lift derrick on the foremast at Number 2 hatchway. Powering the gear on these derricks were 22 electric winches made by Laurence, Scott and Electromotors Ltd. of Norwich.

Engines

Shaw Savill had built 10 diesel-engined ships before the Second World War, culminating in the 27,155 ton *Dominion Monarch* with her four massive Doxford oil engines. During the war years huge advances had been made in both high-pressure water-tube boilers and in reduction gearing for steam turbines. The success of the *Corinthic* class fully demonstrated the merits of this improved technology for passenger vessels: as well as being economical, steam turbines were trouble-free, reliable and quiet, and their speed could be decreased by small amounts of propeller revolutions to suit sea conditions, thus aiding steering, sea keeping and passenger comfort. Although they carried no passengers, steam was an obvious choice for the *Persic* and her sisters. Their hulls had the same internal layout of decks and compartments as the *Corinthic* ships such that, if they were to be fitted as motor ships, this would necessitate a full redesign of their engine spaces. After the oil shock of October 1973, when prices rose 70%, the economic virtues of steam turbines were quickly destroyed. But that was not an issue in the immediate post-war years.

From the July 1949 edition of 'The Shipbuilder and Marine Engine-Builder' the following is quoted: 'The [*Persic's*] propelling machinery consists of two sets of single-reduction geared turbines developing 14,000 shaft horse power at 119 revolutions per minute in service. Each set comprises a high-pressure, intermediate-pressure and low-pressure turbine of equal power driving a separate pinion. High-pressure and low-pressure astern turbines are incorporated in the intermediate-pressure exhaust casings of both sets. Superheated steam is supplied by two Foster Wheeler oil-fired, controlled-superheat boilers, the pressure at the turbines being 385 pounds per square inch and a temperature of 740 degrees Fahrenheit. The installation operates on the Weir closed-feed system. Two turbo-driven pumps, each capable of meeting the full-power requirements of the boilers, are installed together with the necessary auxiliaries. A steam generator provides steam for the auxiliaries at sea, and produces 4,000 pounds of steam per hour at 125 pounds pressure when supplied with saturated steam from the main boilers. The steam from this generator is used for make-up feed water [fresh water that has been purified for adding to the boiler feed water] fuel-oil heating [the fuel-oil in the double bottom and side tanks had to be warmed to make it flow] and domestic purposes [ship's galley, drying rooms].

For harbour use [when the main boilers and steam generator were shut down] there is a Cochran oil-fired boiler capable of generating 2,800 pounds of steam per hour at a pressure of 125 p.s.i. The engine room auxiliaries [pumps, condensers, air ejectors] generally are electrically driven, the necessary power at sea being supplied by two BTH [British Thomson-Houston] 600 kW turbo generators each with condenser, extraction pump, circulating pump and air ejector. These generators take steam at the full pressure and temperature of the main boilers, and supply direct current at 220 volts. For harbour use [with the main boilers shut down] there are two Allen two-stroke 400 kW diesel generators.'

Too good to get out of bed?

Shaw Savill's *Delphic*, launched two months before the *Persic* and commanded by Captain R.G. Ireland, was berthed at Auckland when the *Persic* was there after returning to New Zealand waters in August-September 1950. Both were due to sail for South Island ports on 23rd September to continue loading but, while in Auckland, their particularly high standard of crew facilities caught the interest of a local newspaper man: 'Who said sailors don't care? The Shaw Savill and Albion Company thinks they do. And in two of their new ships, the *Persic* and *Delphic*, which are making their first visit to Auckland, they have given the crew accommodation in which the men can take a genuine pride.'

Gushingly the reporter went on: 'No dipping forecastle or noisy stern for these seamen. Their quarters are amidships; single- and two-berth cabins which are comfortably furnished and get plenty of fresh air. As well as bunks and well-sprung mattresses each cabin has a settee, a panelled wardrobe and the nautical equivalent of a dressing table. The men have a messroom [there were separate messrooms for the seamen and the engine room crew] and a spacious recreation room with table tennis, dart boards, a radio and easy chairs. Then there is an electric washing machine, drying rooms, oilskin lockers and an all-electric galley which would grace most big passenger ships. A movie projector, with a good supply of recent films, operates three nights per week.'

The photo accompanying this newspaper article shows a man in dungarees washing his hands in the basin (with hot and cold running water) of his single berth cabin. The porthole has curtains, there is a bookshelf and mirror, an armchair, a monogrammed counterpane with fresh bathing towel adorning the bed, plus sets of drawers for packing enough clothes to give that washing machine as leisurely a voyage as the seamen - if only the reporter's word picture was correct. Warwick Thomson puts matters straight: 'You could have fooled me! I believe the reporter selected a petty officer's cabin [bosun, carpenter, lamptrimmer or engine room storekeeper] for his misleading article. The cabin is too small to be an officer's cabin, and anyway, no Shaw Savill officer of that period would have dreamed of posing in dungarees presumably washing his hands or doing anything else [officers wore boilersuits over uniform to do any dirty job]. And seamen definitely had two-berth cabins and no hand basin. The washing machine was for the use of officers and maybe also the petty officers; no self-respecting seaman in those days would ever have contemplated putting his clothes into such a device.'

Top: Robbed temporarily of her white hull band, the *Persic* in 1966. The decision to paint out the hull band was the cost-saving inspiration of zealous head office book-keepers. Its absence detracted greatly from the appearance of ships like the *Persic*, and the hull band was soon reinstated. Welded studs marked its correct position on the ship's hull. *[J. and M. Clarkson]*

Right: Rafted up outboard of the *Ceramic* at London's Royal Docks, 1st February 1969. Ahead lies one of Glen Line's *Glenlyon* quartet on that company's outward loading berth. *[V.H. Young and L.A. Sawyer]*

Cargo gear stowed, down to her marks and pilot on the bridge: the *Persic* underway at Cape Town on 1st February 1969 after leaving Duncan Dock. Note the containers on her fore well deck, portent of the cargo-handling revolution that would shortly banish the *Persic* and fleets of ships like her to the breakers' yards. *[V.H. Young and L.A. Sawyer]*

For the *Persic's* officers and engineers there were two separate smoking rooms each with its own pantry, and each decorated with polished veneered panelling in maple, eucalyptus and other woods. The furniture was made of mahogany. Warwick Thomson again, from his time aboard the *Persic* as her second officer from 7th April 1959 to 27th August 1960: 'The second officer's cabin was on the starboard side with windows facing forward and to the side. It was somewhat triangular, resulting from the curve of the bridge front. My bunk above a chest of drawers was on the inboard bulkhead with feet facing the door. On the bridge front was a decent-sized desk with more drawers and at the rear of the cabin was an L-shaped settee with one leg along the inboard bulkhead around from the door, and a shorter leg on the after bulkhead. For the life of me I can't remember where my hand basin fitted into the scheme of things! It was probably somewhere on that same after bulkhead.

The other officers' cabins, rectangular in shape, were across the bridge front each with a window forward. The fourth officer's was next door to me and the third officer about amidships. The chief officer's larger cabin was to port. He had a separate sleeping cabin as well as a day cabin with an electric fire, and his own private bathroom.

The dining saloon on the deck below was central and flanked on the port side by cabin accommodation for the chief steward and the second steward. Immediately aft of the saloon was the ship's galley. As I also recall, there were three long tables in the saloon. Senior officers (master, chief engineer, chief officer and second engineer) sat at the centre one, deck officers at the one on the starboard side and engineers to port. Many engineers chose to eat in their own separate duty messroom to avoid having to get into uniform. They had that option. And that's brought to mind another little annoyance (as a seaman). Engineers sometimes used to come out on deck for a cup and a fag in their dirty overalls and lean their greasy backs against our nice white paintwork! We didn't approve but could do nothing about it'.

Demise

The *Persic* was the only one of the seven Big Ics to be renamed and to bear the livery of another shipping company. At the end of July 1969 she was transferred to the Royal Mail Line, becoming its *Derwent*. Her last master under Shaw Savill is believed to have been Captain M.J.A. Clark and the *Persic* was at London at the time, having discharged cargo from Australia there and at Belfast. Royal Mail put her to work on its South American trades, her funnel repainted buff-yellow. She replaced Royal Mail's 20-year-old steamer *Duquesa* (9,762/1949) formerly of Furness-Houlder Argentine Lines, which was sold for scrap 1970. As the *Derwent* she lasted just two more years. Warwick Thomson recalls seeing her on one final occasion: 'I was sailing on Auckland Harbour about this time when I saw a ship with a familiar profile arriving. It was my grand old *Persic*, now called *Derwent*. She was but a shadow of her former self and looked decidedly dowdy in her new livery, an impression underscored by the elimination of the white band around her hull. In later Shaw Savill years the white band had been removed for a while as an economy measure but it must have been generally agreed that the ships looked better with it and so it was restored.'

Older ships like the *Derwent* and *Duquesa*, heavy on maintenance, high on wages with their big crews and hungry for fuel oil, were rapidly outmoded by the arrival of containerisation. The *Derwent* ex-*Persic* was sold for demolition by Hierros Ardes S.A. at Bilbao, where she arrived at the end of her last voyage on 25th November 1971 after being in service not quite 22 years. Demolition began in March 1972

Purists might disagree but the *Derwent* ex-*Persic,* seen here on 25th February 1970, looks most handsome in the funnel colours of Royal Mail. External maintenance was soon let go, however, as the time of her final voyage drew near. *[FotoFlite incorporating Skyfotos, 70-608]*

Top left and right: *Persic* in the Royal Docks, London. *[V.H. Young and L.A. Sawyer]*
Right: Arriving at Lyttelton, with the harbour board tug *Lyttelton II* (303/1939) alongside. *[Neil Hamilton]*
Bottom: In the stream at Wellington, the harbour's eastern hills behind her, on 18th October 1965. *[V.H. Young and L.A. Sawyer]*

Top: Just as pleasing to the eye in Royal Mail colours, the *Derwent* ex-*Persic* at Rotterdam in June 1970. *[V.H. Young and L.A. Sawyer]*

Bottom: Unaccountably back in Shaw Savill funnel colours, the *Derwent* in this photo dated May 1971 is berthed in the Royal Docks at London. She is at the very end of her life, as the unkempt state of her hull testifies. *[Malcolm Cranfield collection]*

Brand new and steaming her trials, the *Runic* in Belfast Lough on 23rd March 1950. *[Ulster Folk and Transport Museum 12579]*

RUNIC AND THE REEF

A fine ship

The twin-screw refrigerated and general-cargo vessel *Runic,* Official Number 183591, was the second and middle ship of the trio introduced to Shaw Savill's fleet by the *Persic*. She and her sister ship *Suevic* were built at Belfast by Harland and Wolff Ltd., the *Runic* as Hull Number 1414, the *Suevic* as Hull Number 1415. Identical in tonnage and design, the absence of a mainmast in each made them easily recognisable from the two-masted *Persic*. On Wednesday 30th June 1948 the keel of the *Runic* was laid on Number One Slip at Harland and Wolff's Queen's Shipyard - the same slipway beneath the Arrol gantry where the *Athenic* was built. Framing was completed on 14th January 1949 and the hull was fully plated by 7th July, one year and one week after the keel laying. Mrs H.E. Davis, wife of the London director of the New Zealand Dairy Products Marketing Commission, launched the *Runic* into the River Lagan at 10.15 a.m. on Saturday 21st October 1949. After fitting out, she departed for her sea trials at 11 a.m. on 23rd March 1950. These were successfully completed the following day and at 4 p.m. on Friday 24th March 1950, with the *Runic* underway in Bangor Bay, the new vessel was handed over to Shaw Savill. She was some three and a half months ahead of the *Suevic* which was still fitting out, and had cost nearly £1,500,000 to build. Her port of registry was Southampton and the *Runic's* call sign was GGCS.

Following her acceptance the *Runic* left Belfast on 24th March 1950 and crossed to Liverpool where she was berthed from 25th March to 3rd April, loading a general cargo for Australia. On 4th April she arrived at Glasgow where the new ship remained until the 22nd of that month, completing her loading and presumably also undergoing final adjustments by her builders. Under the command of Captain W.G. West, who had been appointed to the *Runic* on 22nd March 1950, she departed Glasgow on Saturday 22nd April for her maiden voyage. Travelling via Suez and bunkering at Aden, the *Runic's* first port of call for cargo unloading was Fremantle in

Going down the ways to the River Lagan on the morning of 21st October 1949, beneath the Arrol gantry erected for the White Star liners *Olympic* and *Titanic*. *[Ulster Folk and Transport Museum 12424]*

The *Runic* afloat and picked up by tugs that will move her to a fitting out jetty in Harland and Wolff's Abercorn Basin. *[Ulster Folk and Transport Museum 12428]*

The *Runic*, her boilers in steam, leaving the Musgrave Channel with the tug *Meadow* (242/1942) in the foreground. She is passing the Union-Castle Line's *Carnarvon Castle* (20,063/1926) undergoing her post-Second World War refit at Belfast. *[Ulster Folk and Transport Museum 12580]*

Western Australia. She then proceeded around the Australian south coast to Adelaide, Melbourne, Sydney and Brisbane, where final discharge of her cargo was made. From Brisbane the *Runic* sailed for Bluff in Southland, New Zealand to commence loading frozen lamb and dairy produce. Calls were made at Timaru and then Lyttelton to complete loading preparatory to beginning the return voyage to London via Panama across the Pacific. The *Runic* at that time was the largest vessel ever to load cargo at Timaru.

This first trip set the pattern for the remainder of the *Runic's* career. Captain West remained in command until May 1951, when he transferred to the liner *Arawa* (14,462/1922, ex *Esperance Bay*) as her master. Captain R.G. Ireland succeeded him as the *Runic's* second master. At 13,587 grt and 9,440 nrt, the *Runic* had an overall length of 561 feet 0 inches, or 530 feet 0 inches between fore and aft perpendiculars. Breadth at its widest was 72 feet and her normal working draught was 32 feet. Powerful and beautiful in her looks, her high oval funnel and single mast carried only a slight rake and she was given a soft-nosed bow and cruiser stern. There were seven sets of twin samson posts and four tall engine room ventilators aft of the funnel. A crossbar was fitted at the top of the foremost set of samson posts and centrally on this was mounted the fore navigation light and the anchor light.

The hull of the *Runic* was subdivided by seven bulkheads giving her eight watertight compartments. These were the forepeak, the Number 1 hold, the Number 2 hold, the Number 3 hold, the engine and boiler compartment, Number 4 hold, Number 5 hold, and the Number 6 hold and after peak. There were seven double bottoms and each of these was subdivided longitudinally into port and starboard tanks. The port and starboard Number 1 tanks, right forward, and the port and starboard Number 2 tanks were used for water ballast or oil fuel. Fresh water was held in the port and starboard Number 3 tanks. Numbers 4 and 5 tanks were used for storing oil fuel, reserve feed water for the boilers and lubricating oil. The port and starboard Number 7 tanks and Number 8 tanks held either water ballast or oil fuel. Deep fuel tanks were also located at the sides and across the fore end of the engine and boiler compartment, and at the sides and between the shaft tunnels below Numbers 4 and 5 holds. Total oil fuel capacity was 4,000 tons with a further 240 tons for the ship's diesel auxiliaries.

She was an enormous freezer ship. Within five of her six holds 508,080 cubic feet was insulated for the transport of refrigerated foodstuffs. In addition the *Runic* had 225,180 cubic feet of space for general cargo, comprising all of Number 6 hold, the upper 'tween decks in Number 5 hold and part of the upper 'tween decks of Number 4 hold. There was additional space for general cargo in the forecastle and poop. All six hatchways aboard the *Runic* were 18 feet wide; largest of them was Number 2, measuring 34 feet by 18 feet, and the smallest was Number 6 at 17 by 18 feet. Numbers 4 and 5 hatchways were the same in length at 26 feet six inches, while Number 1 hatch at the break of the forecastle was 18 feet in length. Number 3 hatchway was located aft of the bridge house at Boat Deck level, and was 25 feet six inches long. Serving these six hatchways were 14 derricks each with a seven ton capacity, and eight derricks able to lift a maximum of 10 tons. The latter were situated on the after-most set of samson posts, plumbing Numbers 5 and 6 holds, and on the set of samson posts outboard of the mast, plumbing Number 1 and 2 holds. Raised over Number 2 hatch and slung from the mast was a 50-ton heavy-lift derrick. Four of the *Runic's* 22 electric winches were rigged for operating this derrick, while the two after-most winches were modified so they could also be used for warping the ship alongside the berth. Her decks over the insulated holds were all wood-sheathed while the poop deck and the deck over Number 6 hold, which was used for general cargo - wool, hides, tallow - were only partially wood-sheathed.

A twin-screw vessel, the *Runic* was powered by two sets of Parsons single-reduction geared steam turbines manufactured by Harland and Wolff at their Queen's Island engine works. Each set comprised a high-, intermediate- and low- pressure reaction turbine and in total they produced 14,000 shaft horse power at 120 revolutions per minute, giving a maximum speed of 17.5 knots. Normal service speed was 16 to 16.5 knots. Superheated steam at 425 pounds per square inch pressure and 750 degrees Fahrenheit was provided for the turbines by two Foster Wheeler D type marine

The *Runic* arriving at Wellington in a stiff north-westerly breeze, 14th January 1954. *[V.H. Young and L.A. Sawyer]*

water-tube boilers constructed by Harland and Wolff under licence from Foster Wheeler Ltd. The boilers were fitted with superheaters, air heaters and fuel economisers. Fuel oil consumption at normal service speed averaged at about 35 tons per day.

Supplementing the boilers was a Cochran vertical auxiliary boiler, which provided steam for the ship when she was in harbour with the main boilers shut down. There was also a steam generator for heating the fuel oil and for making feed water for the main boilers. The air ejectors, feed pumps and one of the air compressors were all steam-powered; the remainder of the auxiliary machinery along with the refrigeration plant and the windlass on the forecastle were electrically driven. Electricity for the ship was supplied by two 500kW, 220-volt steam-driven generators, plus two 400 kW 220 volt diesel generators. All of this machinery was manufactured by Harland and Wolff. Throughout the ship there were some 1,000 electric lights.

Accommodation for the *Runic's* officers and crew of 72 was proclaimed by Shaw Savill to be the best of any merchant ship at the time. Unlike the *Corinthic* class, all of it was located in the centre superstructure. No passengers were carried, and thus she did not have a purser. Cabins were larger and better furnished, the deck officers having theirs on the boat deck under the bridge while the engineers were aft of Number 3 hatch in the deck house below the funnel and lifeboats. There were smoking rooms for both groups of officers. Jeremy Theakston, who was the *Runic's* chief officer from 9th October 1956 to 6th March 1957 recalls:

'In the *Runic* the chief officer had a large dayroom, a bedroom and a bathroom leading aft from the bedroom. The dayroom was on the port forward corner of the superstructure and so had windows facing forward and to port. There was a large desk at the fore end of the room and, if my memory is correct, a very comfortable settee and a couple of armchairs as well as an upright chair for the desk. And I think there was a coffee table in the middle of the room but I can't remember if this was secured or not. The bathroom had a large bath which I'm sure must have had a shower attachment. I think the bath must have used freshwater because, looking through my diary, I wrote that when second officer of the *Persic* in 1955 I had a bath in London to try and warm up (it was freezing and so was I!). I wouldn't have done that if it used dock water! That means the officers' bathroom must also have had a bath.'

On the deck above, the master's quarters comprised a day room, bedroom and private bathroom all located aft of the wheelhouse. The chartroom and ship's radio office were also on this deck. One deck below the officers, on what was called the Bridge Deck, the seamen had their cabins on the port side with the greasers and firemen to starboard. Older hands signing on the *Runic* who had once lived in freezing bare-steel forecastles, or in accommodation located directly over propellers, could ease back in quiet and comfortable two-berth cabins fitted with bunks, chests of drawers, reading lights, air ventilation and, best of all, linoleum flooring. Separate messes for seamen and for the firemen and greasers were provided, as well as a combined recreation room at the after end of the accommodation. Fitted with upholstered seats this room was, in 1950, a quite remarkable change from long-held attitudes by ship owners where the discomfort of seamen, firemen and greasers was generally ignored. Traditions at sea are, however, very hard to break and the recreation room was seldom used by the deck and engine ratings who preferred keeping to themselves in their respective messes. There were no laundry facilities; clothes and dungarees were scrubbed on the tile floors of the bathrooms then rinsed in buckets and hung in drying rooms. No self-respecting seaman ever wore a pair of new dungarees without scrubbing the blue dye out of them until they looked worn and well-used.

Right forward on the Bridge Deck was the officers' dining saloon. This deck, further aft, also contained the ship's galley, bakery and scullery, the ship's office and the petty officers', cooks' and stewards' accommodation. The ship's petty officers: bosun, carpenter, lamp trimmer, donkeyman and engine room storekeeper (the title petty officer was not used by Shaw Savill) all had single berth cabins each fitted with a wardrobe, chest of drawers, armchair, mirror, bookshelf, curtains over the porthole and hand-basin with hot and cold running water. Aft again of this was the seamen's, greasers' and firemen's accommodation. Air was circulated

Three photographs taken during *Runic's* 11 years afloat.

Top: With derricks topped off and pilot aboard. *[Russell Priest collection]*

Middle: In the Royal Docks, London. *[World Ship Society Ltd.]*

Bottom: Loading at New Plymouth. *[Captain Ian Condie]*

throughout these living spaces by a mechanical ventilation system, with the officers' cabins also having electric radiators. Small electric heaters were later provided for the crew cabins.

Four lifeboats each 24-feet long were carried on Welin-Maclachlan gravity davits on the *Runic's* boat deck. One of them had a diesel motor, the others were fitted with Fleming hand-propelling gear.

Beachings, bashings and boilers

The *Runic* made her first visit to Port Chalmers, New Zealand on 8th June 1951 and berthed there on five subsequent occasions, the last of which was 18th December 1956. Several mishaps punctuated the *Runic's* career during the 1950s. The first of these occurred on 23rd April 1951 when she stranded in Gallions Reach on the Thames while coming up-river in fog. She had to be towed off.

Then in October 1953 the *Runic* struck a concrete wall while berthing at Hamburg. Captain Ian Condie, who was a cadet aboard the *Runic* and on her bridge at the time, recalls: 'Arriving in Hamburg was an eye-opener, much of the war damage that RAF Bomber Command had done still being very apparent. Our Chief Engineer was Charlie Simpson, a ferocious little man from Aberdeen who would tolerate fools not at all but who ran a highly efficient engine room. The German pilot had, of course, been told we were a twin-screw turbine ship but, owing to the ability of the engineers on the manoeuvring platform, he refused to believe this. No steam turbine, insisted the pilot, could be manoeuvred as quickly as that. Alas, he had to back and fill to turn us into the berth, and he forgot he wasn't on a diesel ship. The pilot became impatient and ordered a double ring astern on the engine telegraphs. The Captain questioned this but the order was repeated by the pilot, who then got exactly what he'd asked for. The *Runic* began going astern like a speed-boat and, in spite of double rings for full ahead, she continued running stern-first towards a solid concrete wall. I remember the master and the pilot standing on the bridge wing, looking aft and saying in a sort of duet (in English): 'she'll hit...she won't hit....she'll hit...' And she did. The *Runic's* cruiser stern was knocked in and the deck inside the steering gear flat was buckled to within a foot of the steering motor.' She had to be repaired in Hamburg; doubtless the costs for this were met by the unfortunate pilot's employer.

Three days out from Wellington in July 1955, on passage for London with a full cargo, the *Runic* experiencd boiler trouble and was forced to turn back to Wellington. Repairs delayed her by six weeks. More engine repairs were needed at Fremantle between 22nd and 24th April 1958. A strike by British seamen kept her in Wellington for six days from 17th to 23rd August 1960. In the light of all these incidents it has been written that the *Runic* was a troubled ship, unhappy and unpopular with crews. Warwick Thomson remembers differently:

'I joined the *Runic* in September 1952 as an EDH - efficient deck hand - a rating between senior ordinary seaman and able seaman but to all intents and purposes an able seaman (AB) on the ship's statutory complement of the day. I was the only seaman who hadn't been in the ship the previous voyage - and only got the job because the fellow I replaced failed to get back in time to sign on. That 100% return was most unusual and speaks well of the ship. As an EDH I did one short loading voyage to the Continent and one deep-sea voyage to Australia before sitting for my AB's certificate. I then did another Continental and deep-sea voyage to Australia as an AB. Had I not been recruited for the *Gothic* in September 1953 when she returned to London, I would have stayed with the *Runic*. We had a great crew including old Jack the Bosun and a lamp trimmer who I can picture in my mind but can't remember his name. So from the deck seamen's point of view she was a happy ship. And I was getting on well with the cadets in preparation for sitting for my second mate's ticket in 1955. They being a source of gossip never as far as I can remember said she was an unhappy ship.'

When Jeremy Theakston joined the *Runic* in October 1956, his very first appointment as chief officer, all the ship's deck officers from the previous voyage had been changed. The previous

Runic firemen take a break while cleaning the *Runic's* funnel uptakes. *[Bill Aston]*

Seamen aboard the *Runic* in 1954 sugiing paintwork and scrubbing deck planking. *[Captain Ian Condie]*

Noon sights on the *Runic's* starboard bridge wing. From left: Third Officer Charlie Wood, Second Officer Barry Creese, Chief Officer Arthur Borthwick. *[Author's collection]*

Runic officers with mess kit and libations. *I must go down to the smoke room again, where a gin bottle waits for me, and all I ask is that some other bloke, doesn't squeeze on this seat meant for three. [Author's collection]*

chief officer apparently had not enjoyed a good relationship with Captain C.W. Sendall, the *Runic's* master. Jeremy Theakston, however, found no difficulty with him.

Forecastle fumings

Captain L.H. Edmeads, who went on to command the liners *Southern Cross* and *Northern Star*, was Master of the *Runic* during the 12 months Warwick Thomson was aboard her. She was still a new ship when, aged 18, Warwick shipped out from London when the *Runic* departed there on 20th September 1952 for Hamburg to load cargo. Further loading took place at Rotterdam and Antwerp before she commenced the long voyage to Australia. Fremantle was, once again, the first port of call after which the *Runic* worked her way east and then north along the Australian coast as far as Cairns, discharging her cargo. At each port Thomson was assigned the cushy job of cleaning and painting the *Runic's* hull from a punt moored alongside the ship. He and another seaman spent all their working hours on this task, happily out of sight of the bosun. As the discharge of cargo proceeded and she rose higher in the water, they scrubbed along the boot-topping in preparation for repainting. Then, as the ship began loading with refrigerated and general cargo for the homeward voyage, Thomson and his mate applied deep red boot-topping paint starting from the waterline up as she went lower with the filling of her holds. 'In one of the Queensland ports we were about to sail when my mate and I noticed bunker oil seeping from a rivet amidships, maybe from a settling tank or a deep tank. Joyously we reported the problem, thinking we were all going to get the weekend off with sailing delayed until the leak was fixed. No such luck! Chippy got over the side with a hammer and cold chisel and sealed off the leak in a few minutes.'

Hutchison, the *Runic's* chief officer, proved to be a querulous man of less than rock-steady disposition. 1952 was just seven years since the finish of the Second World War and the chief officer's easily rattled temperament no doubt was a legacy from his service on merchant ships throughout the war years. Relations between Captain Edmeads and Hutchison had been tetchy throughout the voyage. Warwick Thomson was at the wheel on the *Runic's* bridge when, still on the Australian coast, she arrived at the port of Gladstone in Queensland to load cases of canned corned beef from the local Borthwicks meatworks. There was just one wharf in the port, and it was too short to accommodate the *Runic's* full length. Her bow was accordingly to be moored to a dolphin pile located ahead of the wharf's outer end. Captain Edmeads was on the bridge while, on the forecastle, Chief Officer Hutchison had ordered lines secured round the dolphin so that she could be heaved alongside it, using the windlass. But, regardless of the power applied by the windlass, the *Runic's* bow would not shift from its position 20 feet out from the dolphin. It was most probably caught in the mud of the seabed.

As futile efforts to move her continued, Captain Edmeads, himself a veteran of the Merchant Navy's war at sea, grew impatient. Orders from the master, telling Hutchison what to do and to hurry up about it, began flowing in ever more strident volume from the telephone on the forecastle. The day was hot and tempers rapidly shortened. Assailed by the hectoring voice from the bridge, the chief officer was seen to leave his position by the windlass and stride aft to the break of the *Runic's* forecastle. Gripping the rail in white-knuckled fury, he yelled a four word obscenity relating to sex and travel in the direction of the bridge wing where the master stood. Warwick Thomson, privately delighted at this spectacle of open revolt, watched as the chief officer turned and retraced his steps along the forecastle. Absolute silence prevailed on the bridge and Captain Edmeads, turning purple, ceased his goading. The chief officer, having decided she could not be hauled any closer to the dolphin, had her tied up where she lay. What was discussed afterwards in the master's day room can well be imagined, but Hutchison stayed as chief officer for the remainder of the voyage.

Master on the bridge

Born on 6th January 1905 at Gravesend, Kent, Leslie Henry Edmeads the *Runic's* third master lived to the age of 84, dying at Stratford-upon-Avon on 11th March 1989. His last command was the Shaw Savill liner *Northern Star* (24,731/1962). A shy, reserved man, Captain Edmeads seemed to Warwick Thomson to be almost

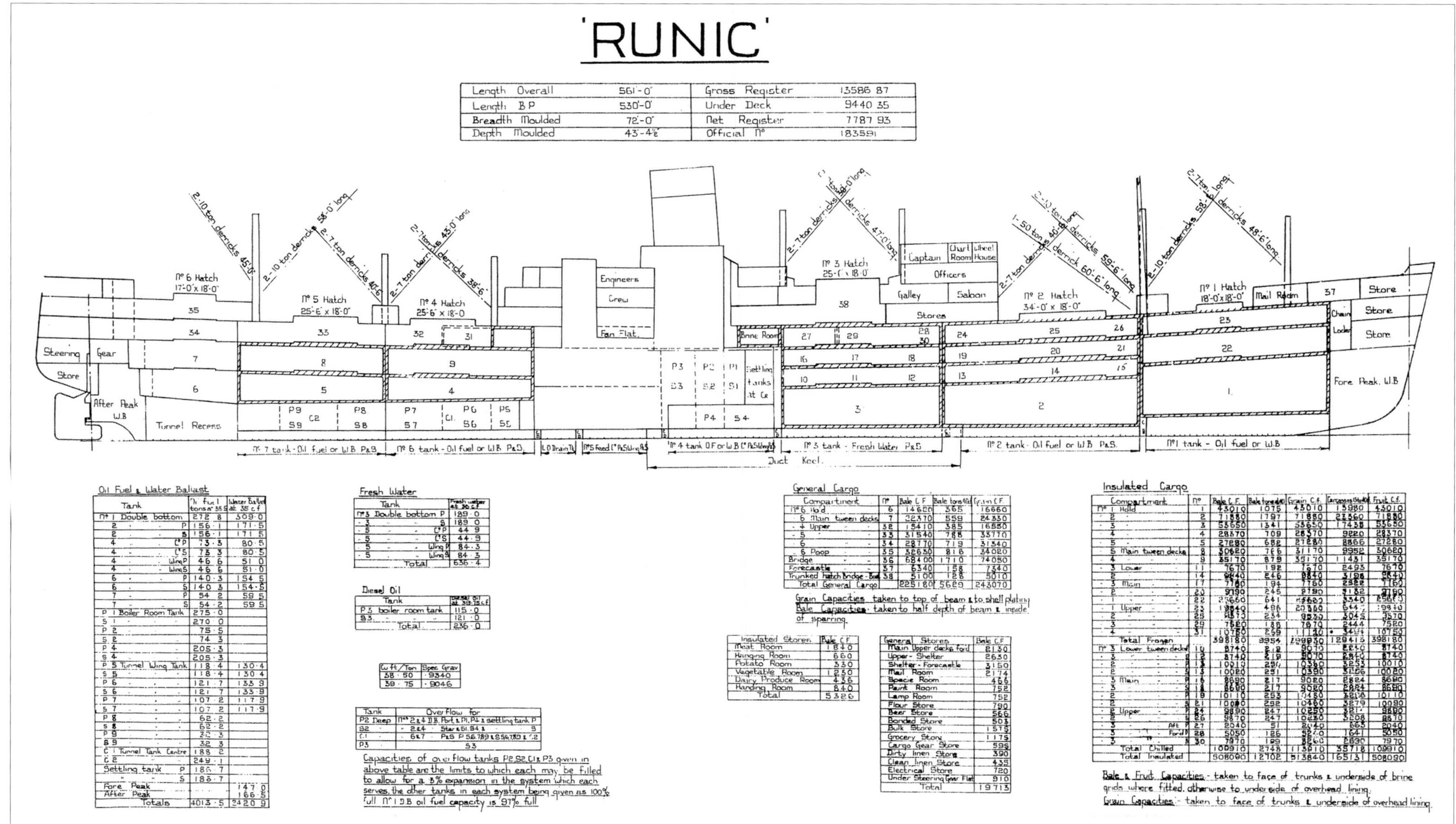

A capacity plan for the *Runic*. [*Ian J. Farquhar collection*]

permanently dour and displeased of mood. Edmeads had a habit of constantly sniffing. Thomson recalls an occasion when he was on the wheel during the 4 to 8 a.m. watch as the ship was being piloted up the Queensland coast along the Great Barrier Reef. The master, dressed only in his underwear, scratching himself indiscreetly and sniffing loudly, would emerge from his sleeping cabin aft of the bridge to check the ship's progress during the night. Having done so with an absolute minimum of words, Captain Edmeads would return to his cabin. Officers and the three cadets by comparison would be sternly rebuked by the master if he caught them on the bridge in dirty or incorrect uniforms. (Officers wore uniforms at all times when on duty, when moving about the ship and when in the dining saloon. Boiler suits were worn over their uniforms when they were doing work likely to get their clothing dirty.) Thomson also remembers hearing Edmeads chastising the Australian-born second officer in front of seaman on watch on the bridge, for foolishly pandering to the engineers' request to have the clocks advanced or retarded in smaller tranches than the customary half hours as the *Runic* crossed the Pacific.

The *Runic's* bridge, identical to that of her sister ship *Suevic*, was equipped with the latest and best technology available in 1950. This included radar, a radio direction finder, an echo sounding device, an electric log, a rotating clear-view screen on the wheelhouse windows, a Sperry gyro compass, loud-speaking and internal communications telephones, loud hailer and whistle control (including an automatically operated fog signal). In front of the helmsman's position was a magnetic steering compass housed in its teak and brass binnacle. There was another binnacle with a standard compass on the monkey island above the wheelhouse. Immediately at left of the steering wheel, mounted on its pedestal, was the gyro compass repeater. This plus the gyro repeater on each of the bridge wings was controlled by a master gyro situated on a lower deck in the ship. Further to the left of the wheel was the radar console. In front of the wheel was the mechanism for the hydraulic telemotor steering assist, while just to its right was the twin-handled engine room telegraph on its pedestal. Beside and just forward of this telegraph was a docking telegraph, seldom used as orders to mooring parties on the forecastle and stern were nearly always conveyed by telephone. Both telegraphs were electrically operated. There was no seating; officers and seamen on watch were strictly forbidden to sit down on the bridge but a wooden pilot's stool, without any padding, was kept in the wheelhouse for the master's use if he chose.

Warwick Thomson: 'All ships of that class were a delight to steer even at slow speed. I once managed to keep within one degree of the course for a whole two hours in the Red Sea. Suspicious of what I was up to, having not heard the usual ticking of the course recorder in the chart room as the wheel was adjusted to bring her back on course, the watch officer kept eyeing me in disbelief that such a feat could be managed.'

Middleton Reef

The *Runic* was not quite halfway through her expected lifespan when, shortly after 1 a.m. on Sunday 19th February 1961, she went aground on the western side of Middleton Reef in the Tasman Sea while on passage in ballast from Brisbane to Auckland. Commanded by Captain C.W. Sendall, she was on the outward leg of Voyage Number 22 having discharged her cargo in Australian ports and then been ordered to Auckland to load for the United Kingdom.

Voyage Number 22 had begun at Liverpool from where the *Runic* sailed on Friday 16th December 1960. She had earlier loaded cargo at Glasgow before leaving there on 4th December, then was alongside at Liverpool for final loading from 5th to 16th December. Transit of the Suez Canal took place between 24th and 25th December. After taking on bunkers at Aden from 29th to 30th December the *Runic* steamed for Fremantle, which was reached on 11th January 1961 and where for two days she discharged cargo. On to Adelaide, where she called for a further two days between 17th and 19th January, then to Melbourne from 21st January to 3rd February. Further cargo discharge most probably took place at Sydney, where she would have gone after Melbourne though this is not recorded on her voyage cards. Next to Brisbane, where the *Runic* arrived on Thursday 16th February for what would prove to be her last-ever port of call.

Middleton Reef and its companion Elizabeth Reef lie in the northern Tasman Sea some 555 kilometres due east from the Australian coastal city of Coffs Harbour. Each is a coral habitat and together they form the Elizabeth and Middleton Reefs Marine National Nature Reserve, administered by the Government of Australia. Part of the Lord Howe Rise, both reefs are the tops of long-extinct volcanoes separated by 45 km of deep water. Described as platform reefs, each is like a great level table, covered by the sea at high tide with just a few small outcrops of sand visible. Low water exposes the reefs as vast, flat, pot-holed expanses of coral. For the unwary seafarer making his approach by night, no rock pinnacle or white water can be discerned to warn of the great hazard they represent.

Larger of the two, Middleton Reef is an immense low-lying obstacle in the shape of a kidney, measuring 8.9 km by 6.3 km and with a central lagoon of blue water. In 1961 its position had long been fully charted and the need to give both it and Elizabeth Reef a wide berth, because of the fickle East Australian current, was fully known.

The *Runic* sailed from Newstead Wharf at Brisbane, having discharged the last of her cargo from Great Britain, at 2.30 a.m. on Saturday 18th February 1961 for what was expected to be a routine passage across the Tasman Sea. Light ship, her draught was 18 feet 10 inches forward and 21 feet aft. She was carrying a crew of 72 plus the wives of the master and the chief engineer, along with two supernumeraries. Overcast skies throughout that day meant no sun sights could be taken to verify the ship's position. Dead reckoning instead was used, the noon position being calculated at 27.32 south, 155.04 east. Nothing in this was out of the ordinary.

Prior to departure from Brisbane Second Officer A.N. (Neil) Hamilton, who was the *Runic's* navigating officer, had laid out the course for their passage across the Tasman Sea. From Brisbane the *Runic* would steer up the Queensland coast to Caloundra where the pilot would be dropped. From Caloundra she would head out into the Tasman on a course of 114 degrees, bound for North Cape at the top of New Zealand's North Island. But Captain Sendall, seeing the course drawn up on the chart in the chart room, ordered Hamilton to change the *Runic's* point of departure from Caloundra to Cape Moreton at the north-eastern tip of Moreton Island. This meant the *Runic* would now proceed from Caloundra to Cape Moreton, before heading into the Tasman on a course for North Cape slightly to the south of the second officer's proposed track. Captain Sendall's decision in this regard was entirely in keeping with the practice followed by most masters when crossing the Tasman Sea from Brisbane. The new course would take the ship 15 to 20 miles north of Middleton Reef, whereas Hamilton's course would have allowed them to pass the reef's northern flank by 20 to 30 miles. Sendall told the second officer, who had only recently joined the *Runic* after 13 months aboard the Crusader Shipping Company's *Crusader* (3,461/1957), that on the *Runic's* previous Tasman crossing she had been set too far to the north. The new course would avoid this, so the master believed, while still providing an adequate margin of clearance from Middleton Reef.

Captain Sendall retired to his cabin on the evening of 18th February leaving nothing specific in his night orders concerning the reef, nor asking to be called to the bridge as his ship neared it very early next morning. Aged 54 at the time, Cyril William Sendall had been the *Runic's* master for just over seven years since 12th November 1953. Born on 20th September 1906 at Horsham in West Sussex, he was a highly experienced navigator well familiar with the Tasman Sea and all its moods and hazards. The rocks and shoals of Captain 'Sandy' Sendall's temper had become equally well known; harassed subordinates invented another first name for him by reversing his C.W. initials. Taking this lavatory association further, he also became known as 'Shithouse' Sendall. He was disliked in many quarters of Shaw Savill; one correspondent refers to him as 'not the brightest light in the Shaw Savill firmament', and this was perhaps the reason why Captain Sendall was left in command of the *Runic* for so long and not advanced to newer ships within the company's fleet.

At midnight on Saturday 18th February 1961 Second Officer Hamilton relieved Third Officer Paul Revell as usual and took over as officer of the watch (OOW) on the *Runic's* bridge. Seas were moderate and all was quiet aboard the ship, with most of her complement asleep. Third Officer Revell stayed on the bridge talking with Hamilton for about 20 minutes before leaving to carry out his rounds of the ship's outer decks. At about 12.20 a.m. the seaman lookout on the *Runic's* forecastle came on the bridge and requested that he stand his lookout from the bridge wing because of sea spray coming over the ship's bow. Hamilton agreed to this and posted the seaman on the starboard wing with a cadet keeping lookout on the port wing. The ship was on manual steering with a qualified able seaman at the wheel. Speed was 16.5 knots.

Just after 1 a.m., anticipating the *Runic's* passing Middleton Reef in an hour's time, Hamilton switched the radar on. In those days radar for merchant ships was not the precise, all-weather aid to navigation on which today's bridge teams rely. Vessels like the *Runic* generally used it only for navigating in and out of harbour and when on coastal passages. As well as taking a considerable time to warm up, the *Runic's* radar was unlikely in the prevailing sea conditions to detect the reef's edge that night, it being hidden in sea clutter on the radar screen. Despite this, Hamilton decided to have it running just in case the radar might be of assistance. Meanwhile Third Officer Revell, having completed his rounds, arrived back on the bridge to report all was well. The two men had gone into the chart room when at 1.13 a.m. they felt a sudden, sharp thud. Immediately the ship's pitching motion ceased. Hamilton described her as feeling 'absolutely dead'.

In the engine room, Fourth Engineer Jimmy Andrew was engineer of the watch (EOW) in charge of the 12 midnight to 4 a.m. watch in place of the *Runic's* third engineer who, having only recently joined the ship, was still familiarizing himself with her steam-powered machinery. Andrew had been checking the auxiliary boiler feed pump and one of the two steam turbine-driven main feed pumps. Both were located on the floor of the engine room formed by the tank tops - the upper level of the ship's double bottom - just four or five feet above the *Runic's* keel. Suddenly he felt a massive bump. He recalls how it 'threw me off my balance, and then this was followed by a lesser bump'. Realising something very serious had gone wrong, Fourth Engineer Andrew picked himself up and headed for the alarm button on the engine manoeuvring platform.

Rushing into the darkened wheelhouse from the chart room, Second Officer Hamilton pulled the engine telegraph handles to stop. When lights inside the wheelhouse were switched on, he saw that he had mistakenly rung 'finished with engines' on the telegraphs instead of stop. Immediately he moved the handles to stop. But the pointers on the telegraphs, which would indicate whether his orders had been received and carried out in the engine room, did not shift from full ahead. Believing the engineers on watch may have been confused by his mistake, Hamilton quickly telephoned the engine manoeuvring platform. He states that his call was not answered.

Neither lookout on the bridge wings had reported any sighting so, with Aldis lamp in hand, Hamilton peered over the wings to try and discover what they had hit. It took only a moment to realise the ship was aground. Middleton Reef was the only possible culprit; below him in the lamp's piercing light the sea was washing noiselessly over the reef's edge. There were no breakers, no crashing surf, nothing at all above the ordinary background sounds of wind and sea to mark the reef's presence.

Eight decks below, Fourth Engineer Andrew on the manoeuvring platform noticed the floor of the engine room had taken on a distinct upwards slant towards the bow. The noise from the turbines had also changed to a lower pitch as the propellers went deeper into the sea. He ordered the engineers in the boiler room to watch carefully the boilers' steam and water levels. Now the electric gongs for the telegraphs sounded as the pointers swung from full ahead to finished with engines. Three or four minutes later, the gongs rang again and the pointers moved to stop.

Summoned by the alarm bells, the first of the off-watch engineers reached the engine room. Among them was A.F. Lesley, the *Runic's* Chief Engineer for the past 11 of her 22 voyages. He took command immediately, ordering the engines to be kept turning but at lower revolutions and for his engineers to stand-by to stop or reverse them. Because of the ship's bow-up position, attention focused very closely on water levels in the boilers.

Woken by the impact, Captain Sendall arrived on the bridge almost immediately. His reaction can be imagined: the *Runic* had been steering 114 degrees in compliance with his orders; the two bridge lookouts, having seen or heard nothing, had been able to give no warning. Now, through none other than faulty navigation, she was hard aground on a well-charted hazard surrounded by hundreds of miles of deep water. Alarm bells sounded throughout the ship, bringing all crew to muster stations. On the bridge there was understandable shock, crisis and disbelief as other officers quickly arrived. The carpenter was sent for and ordered to sound her holds and double bottom tanks then report if they were making water.

The *Runic's* draught at the moment she took the ground was later calculated as 18 feet 10 inches forward and 21 feet 10 inches aft. She was carrying 2,502 tons of oil fuel, 598 tons of fresh water, 147 tons of water ballast and 300 tons of ship's stores. There was no cargo in any of her six holds. (A report to the Salvage Association of London by Captain J.P. Williams, dated 11th March 1961, states that the *Runic* had 'some 5,000 tons of water ballast and fuel on board' at the time of stranding.)

The telegraph pointers had now moved to slow ahead on the engine manoeuvring platform. Chief Engineer Lesley meanwhile ordered a junior engineer to phone the bridge and find out what had happened. Fourth Engineer Andrew recalls that after a delay of about four minutes or so, a voice on the other end of the phone told them 'we think we've hit a reef!' Half the engineers now stayed to maintain watch in the engine room while the remainder were sent back to their cabins.

At 3.40 a.m. New Zealand time on Sunday 19th February 1961, approximately 27 minutes after the stranding (Middleton Reef was two hours behind New Zealand time), the auto alarm went off in the Receiving Office at Wellington Radio ZLW, situated on the Tinakori hills above Wellington city. Two minutes later the duty operator logged an SOS transmitted from GGCS, the *Runic's* call-sign: '*Runic* struck reef possibly Middleton Reef holed forward extent of damage unknown. Master.'

An early morning cablegram from the *Runic* also had lights coming on in the windows at Shaw Savill's Australian Head Office in Sydney: 'Regret RUNIC on route Brisbane to Auckland aground on Middleton Reef. Vessel attempting refloat at high water. Will keep you advised.' The news was immediately cabled to Lord Sanderson, Chairman of Shaw Savill's directors, who was travelling aboard the company's flagship *Dominion Monarch* at the time.

A number of ships heard and responded to the SOS. The closest was Chapman and Willan's motor vessel *Brighton* (8,497/1960) on passage across the Tasman Sea with a deck cargo of timber and about 90 miles away. At 5.13 a.m. New Zealand time (3.13 a.m. aboard the *Runic*) she radioed: 'Proceeding to *Runic* arriving noon approx. Master.' With the *Brighton* designated as the ship going to the *Runic's* assistance, all other vessels that had answered the *Runic's* call were, at 5.26 a.m., advised to 'proceed on your normal voyage'.

Perhaps during those frantic hours Captain Sendall may have paused to contemplate the career-destroying enormity of what had just happened. At around 2 a.m. he was interrupted by the arrival on the bridge of the *Runic's* Chief Engineer. Sixty years of age and having joined Shaw Savill in 1927, Albert Frederick Lesley had been Chief Engineer aboard the *Runic* since October 1955. He is remembered by Bill Aston as 'a very nice person and a good boss'. Bill Aston sailed on the *Runic* from 9th April 1954 to 3rd October 1960, working as a fireman and greaser then becoming her Engine Room Storekeeper for 14 of the *Runic's* 22 voyages. He left the ship at the end of Voyage Number 21, just before this final one. 'On most Saturday evenings Chief Engineer Lesley would invite the carpenter, the donkeyman and myself up to his day cabin for drinks. He always addressed me as 'Stores' and I always called him 'Chief'.' From commencement of the voyage two months earlier, Sendall's working relationship with Lesley had become increasingly fractious. 'I don't think there was much love lost between the Chief Engineer and Captain Sendall', recalls Bill Aston. 'It never showed when I saw them together, but I don't recall seeing or hearing them speak to each other.'

When Lesley entered the wheelhouse looking for the master, the tension broke into a furious argument between the two. Captain Sendall had been told by Second Officer Hamilton that the time of impact was 1.13 a.m. but the Chief Engineer strongly disputed this, insisting that no engine telegraph orders had been received on the manoeuvring platform at this time. Captain Sendall chose to agree with Lesley and wanted Hamilton to change the time of the stranding. But Hamilton, backed up by Third Officer Revell, refused and stood his ground. A simmering feud quickly developed with the senior engineers teaming up against Second Officer Hamilton, who steadfastly rejected their version of events.

Long-serving *Runic* fireman, greaser and engine room storekeeper Bill Aston in his cabin. *[Bill Aston]*

The chief officer accompanied by the bosun and Carpenter soon ascertained that the ship was holed forward and taking water in Numbers 1, 2 and 3 double bottoms. A moderate sea was running and her hull started grinding and pounding on the rocks beneath her. It was feared the seas might swing the vessel broadside against the reef so that her hull would strike all along its length. But conditions eased after daybreak, which revealed the *Runic* had driven up onto Middleton Reef for more than a third of her 561 foot length, her bow high out of the water. She had grounded on the north-western flank of the reef at an area called the North-West Horn. Not far away on the port hand was a wide break in the reef's edge, known as the Sound, that gave entry to Middleton Reef Lagoon. The *Runic's* position was some 2.4 miles from what had been the three-masted sailing vessel *Annasona* (1,436/1892). This wreck, conspicuous with bowsprit pointing eerily skyward, was located on the south side of the reef and had been there since January 1907. At low tide it was possible to walk round the *Runic's* forefoot where it sat high on the coral.

A member of the crew, trained in the Royal Navy as a skin-diver, climbed down the *Runic's* side to examine her underwater hull. Only the starboard side of the vessel was accessible. The diver found a six-inch diameter hole in the plating of Number 1 double bottom, together with heavy indentations approximately five feet long and two feet deep abreast Numbers 2, 3 and 4 double bottoms. Rivets were missing, bottom plates had corrugated and sprung, and gaps could be seen between the edges of plates. Fuel oil was observed to be leaking from the ship. Under Number 3 double bottom the vessel was sitting on a hump of rock that stretched to the turn of the bilge on both sides. This had pushed up the tank tops by some 15 inches on their port side and 10 inches on the starboard side. She was being held on the reef at this point, like a pivot. Sharks were circling in the sea around the ship.

Despite all this, the prognosis for refloating her was entirely favourable. The engine compartment was intact and fully operational, and flooding in the double bottoms could be managed fully by the ship's pumps. The *Runic's* propellers and rudder were in deep water, clear of the reef. When the diver reported them to be undamaged Captain Sendall ordered water ballast pumped aft from forward. Eight hundred of the 2,502 tons of fuel oil aboard the ship was jettisoned into the sea. Then, having waited for the next high tide, he ran the engines full astern. The time was around 10 a.m. on 19th February, nine hours after the stranding. But Sendall could

Ashore on Middleton Reef. The *Runic* on a calm day during the effort to save her with the tug *Fearless* standing by. *[Ian J. Farquhar collection]*

Chapman and Willan's 8,497 grt *Brighton* in May 1964. *[J. and M. Clarkson]*

not dislodge his ship. Her astern turbines generated only about 60% of the power for ahead steaming, and thus were not sufficient to reverse her from Middleton's clutches. With the propellers turning, her stern instead fell away to starboard so that she now lay side-on to the edge of the reef, making her predicament considerably worse. After having settled earlier, the seas were becoming very rough again and once more the *Runic's* hull was pounding against her captor.

Salvage epic

Shaw Savill quickly contracted United Salvage Pty. Ltd. of Melbourne, headed by Captain J.P. Williams, to go to the *Runic's* assistance and get her back to the nearest port. Captain Williams (later Captain Sir John Williams CMG OBE) was the very best in the business and famous for his role in successfully recovering 555 gold bars from the sunken liner *Niagara* (13,415/1913) off Bream Head, New Zealand in 1941. The tug *Woona* (294/1953) left Sydney on Monday afternoon 20th February for the *Runic* at her top speed of eight knots with towing hawsers, diving gear and a deep-sea diver aboard along with Captain M.J. Anderson from United Salvage. From Brisbane the Queensland Tug Company's *Fearless* (249/1945) put to sea on the afternoon of 19th February, and was expected to reach the *Runic* early on the evening of the 21st. Meanwhile Captain Williams began negotiations with the Royal Australian Navy about chartering the boom defence vessel *Karangi* (971/1941) laid up and out of commission at Garden Island, Sydney. His plan was to load her with all the salvage gear he would require. In addition to the tugs *Woona* and *Fearless*, all of them steam, Captain Williams had the Waratah Tug and Salvage Company's diesel-powered *Wooree* (210/1957) available. He also made initial inquiries about utilising the US Navy's fleet salvage ship *Conserver* (2,048/1945) based at Honolulu.

Fresh water in the punctured Number 3 double bottoms had been contaminated by the sea as soon as she grounded, causing a water shortage aboard the ship. Much greater peril struck the *Runic* on the night of 19th-20th February when the edge of a tropical cyclone passed Middleton Reef, bringing gale force winds and more heavy seas. At midnight a cablegram was despatched from the ship to Shaw Savill's Sydney Head Office: 'Owing to very rough seas and excessive pounding unable to refloat on p.m. tide and now preparing to abandon ship'. Two hours later at 2.06 a.m. New Zealand time on Monday 20th February, Wellington Radio ZLW heard the stricken vessel calling: 'SOS RUNIC aground Middleton Reef position 29.28S 159.04E pounding heavily position precarious and may have to abandon ship any time. Master.' Winds were at near-gale force and the *Brighton,* having neared the *Runic's* position, was trying to locate her both visually and by radar. For the next six hours Wellington Radio logged transmissions between both ships, each firing rockets to guide the *Brighton* as she sought to close with the *Runic. Brighton*: 'Please send up a rocket and put on lights we think we have you......are your rockets up?' *Runic*: 'Have you seen our rocket?' *Brighton*: 'No rockets seen'. *Runic*: 'Now flashing aldis lamp can you see us?......could you flash yours?..... please could you send up one rocket?' *Brighton*: 'Stand-by first rocket. See it?' *Runic*: 'Not yet could you send another?' *Brighton*: 'Second rocket up'. *Runic*: 'Can you see the reef on the radar?' *Brighton*: 'No radar; how our rocket?; *Runic*: No rocket yet. Reef clear on our radar'.

And so it continued, the *Brighton's* master proceeding with utmost caution in the bad visibility and raging seas in case he, too, ended up on Middleton Reef. With an area of some 56 square kilometres the low-lying reef was a most horrendous obstacle for a ship caught anywhere near it in adverse weather. At Wellington Radio the operator noted in his log that signals from the *Runic* and the *Brighton* were weakening from around 4 a.m. New Zealand time but, from fragments received, both were still trying to locate each other. Nothing further was heard after 6 a.m.

Brighton finally hove-to near the *Runic* on the afternoon of that same day, Monday 20th February, in very poor weather. She stood by the *Runic* for the next three days. The storm continued throughout 21st February, but at last the tug *Fearless* reached Middleton Reef that afternoon. Next day the destroyer HMAS *Vendetta* (3,600/1958) arrived, relieving the *Brighton* whose cargo had shifted as she lay hove-to. HMAS *Vendetta*, commanded by Captain J.M. Ramsay RAN, had been exercising in Jarvis Bay off the southern coast of New South Wales. Despite the big ocean swell one of her officers immediately boarded the *Runic* to confer with Captain Sendall. Later on 22nd February the storm departed as fast as it had come, leaving a slight sea with the wind from the west at Force 3: seven to 10 knots. At 9 p.m. that evening the tug *Woona* hove in sight, joining the *Fearless*. Captain Sendall radioed that his ship was now lying quietly heading 068 degrees. Her heading at the time when she grounded had been 114 degrees, so 068 degrees meant the *Runic's* stern had slewed some 46 degrees round to

The Australian tugs *Woona* (top) *Wooree* (middle) and *Fearless* (bottom) that stood by the *Runic* at Middleton Reef. It was believed the *Woona* and *Wooree's* combined pulling power, together with the *Runic's* cargo winches, would be sufficient to dislodge her from the reef's grip. Despite their maximum efforts, in the final analysis it was the failure to obtain larger, deep-draft salvage tugs with much greater pulling power that, in turn, led to the failure to save the *Runic*. *[Top and middle: J. and M. Clarkson collection, bottom; Ian J. Farquhar collection]*

On Middleton Reef at low tide. *[Left: Neil Hamilton, right: Captain Graham Pepper, Shaw Savill Society]*

starboard - towards the reef - under the force of the weather and because of the earlier refloating attempt. She had assumed a slight list of 3½ degrees to port.

The *Runic's* bow was tilted up, clear and dry, for some 40 feet aft of her forefoot at low water. But from that point on, the ship's bottom, lying with its starboard side to the reef, was touching the ground for its entire length right back to her rudder post. In March 1961 the tidal range on Middleton Reef was five feet six inches (1.67 metres) with spring tides adding another six inches to this height. At low tide, the depths of water in which she was sitting varied from two to eight feet along her starboard side with just 14 feet under the *Runic's* stern. Depths taken along her port side were just as ominous; no more than three feet forward to 13 feet at the stern. One report from the ship, dated 24th February, stated there was just two feet of water below her rudder.

Resulting from this storm, the situation with the forward double bottom tanks, particularly Number 3, was also now much worse. Timber sheathing in Number 3 was found to be covered with fuel oil, indicating that the bulkhead separating Number 2 and Number 3 double bottoms had ruptured. Traces of fuel oil were also detected in water ballast pumped from the *Runic's* forepeak. Up-thrusting had occurred inside Number 3 hold, transmitted from the double bottoms via the hold pillars into the lower 'tween deck, which had been forced up by approximately three inches. Fresh water in the Number 5 double bottom tanks had become contaminated and unfit for drinking.

With sea conditions now favourable Captain Sendall's priority was to evacuate all crew members not required for salvage work. Early on Thursday morning 23rd February HMAS V*endetta* took aboard the wives of the master and the chief engineer, together with three deck boys and four stewards. Also transferred to the destroyer by naval cutter were two people referred to in cablegrams as 'Gray and wife from Perth'. With two tugs now standing by the *Runic*, HMAS *Vendetta* did not delay, leaving at 8.19 a.m. for Sydney where her passengers were safely landed 24 hours later. *Brighton* was also making for Sydney to reload her deck cargo. It had first been intended to take off the majority of the *Runic's* crew, leaving a small party of deck officers, engineers and seamen on the ship. While steaming for the *Runic,* HMAS *Vendetta* had intercepted the tug *Woona* so that Captain Anderson plus the diver could transfer to the

Salvage equipment being lifted on board *Runic* and the steam tugs *Woona* and *Fearless*, viewed from the stern of the *Runic*. *[Ian J. Farquhar collection]*

HMAS *Vendetta*. Built at Williamstown Dockyard in Victoria, Australia and commissioned on 26th November 1958, she was the second of four Daring class destroyers that served with the Royal Australian Navy, each having a top speed of 30.5 knots and armed with six 4.5 guns. She was later fitted with an enclosed bridge. *Vendetta's* sister was HMAS *Voyager*, tragically cut in half by the aircraft carrier HMAS *Melbourne* during night-time exercises south-east of Jervis Bay on 10th February 1964. Eighty two of her complement were lost. *[Russell Priest collection]*
Upper middle, left and right: Looking across the *Runic's* perch on Middleton Reef's edge from aboard the ship during salvage work. *[Neil Hamilton]*

Four views of salvage preparations aboard the *Runic*: Lower middle, left: heavy cables in position along her Bridge Deck alleyways ready for heaving on the anchors spread astern. Lower middle right: Looking across the aft well deck and the poop deck with the big cables running to the *Runic's* stern and salvage gear everywhere. Bottom left: One of the anchors being lifted ready to be dropped astern of the ship. Bottom right: Dumping hatch beams overboard. *[Neil Hamilton]*

much faster destroyer. Both went aboard the *Runic* at 8.45 p.m. on 22nd February from HMAS *Vendetta*. It was then decided not to remove any of the crew other than the stewards and ship's boys. Full manpower would be essential for the task ahead.

From 23rd February normal watches were broken as, under Captain Anderson's direction, the *Runic's* officers and crew set to work preparing to haul her from the reef. The salvage men were fully confident she could be freed, but much would first need to be done. Negotiations were still unresolved with the Australian Navy concerning the *Karangi*, which had to be brought out of lay-up, refitted and then loaded with gear before she could make for the *Runic*. In the meantime pumps, generators and compressors, anchors, heavy towing wire plus a host of other gear along with food, fuel supplies and water were all taken out to the *Runic* aboard Shaw Savill's motor vessel *Alaric* (6,500/1957, Captain G.S. Sheldon). She arrived on 27th February after sailing from Newcastle at 2 a.m. on the 25th. Also aboard the *Alaric* was Captain Williams, who immediately took command of operations as Salvage Master. *Alaric's* cargo of salvage gear and stores was transferred to the *Runic* by lifeboat and hoisted aboard using her derricks. No time was wasted. A spread of five anchors was laid off the *Runic's* stern using lifeboats from the ship under the command of Third Officer Revell. Each seven-ton anchor with 30 fathoms (55 metres) of cable was lowered by derrick from the *Runic* and suspended between two boats. They were then taken out to the tugs, standing off in deep water. Once the boats were alongside the tugs and the weight had been transferred to them, lashings securing the anchors were cut and the tugs then moved each anchor to where it was to be dropped. This task took until 13th March to complete.

Meanwhile, aboard the ship Second Officer Hamilton worked with the *Runic's* seamen rigging and making fast the heavy wire purchases and backers that were secured to the anchor cables. Considerable work was involved as the purchases had to be laid right round the Bridge Deck of the *Runic's* centre superstructure so as to obtain the necessary grip. Obstructions were cleared from the decks and bridges built where this was not possible, so that the purchases and moving blocks could run freely. Serving the derricks at the three holds aft of the main superstructure were ten big electric winches. The purchases were bent on to these and each was tested to its full 75 tons safe capacity to ensure that everything held. The combined pulling power of the winches, amounting to approximately 100 bollard tons, was to be the main source of exertion in hauling her from the reef. The tugs *Woona* and *Wooree* by comparison had a pulling power of about 25 tons each. Six-inch towing wires from each tug were made fast to mooring bollards at the *Runic's* stern.

The plan was to turn the *Runic* on the spring tides due around 17th-18th March, so that her stern lay in deeper water at a 90 degree angle to the reef. The spring tides would increase high water by a further six inches to six feet (1.8 metres). Moving her stern without causing renewed entry of water into the forward double bottoms was the most critical part of the whole operation. Once this was successfully done, the *Runic's* after holds would be flooded so that she trimmed by the stern. This would lift her bow so that she could be pulled off the rock hump that had penetrated the ship's double bottom below Number 3 hold. She was being held on the reef by this rock. If this tactic was not successful in freeing the ship, it was proposed to use explosives to blow the rock apart. Work was also concentrated on Number 1, 2 and 3 holds, where hatch boards were rigged as platforms suspended inside each hold on wires run from the ship's derricks above. Pumps were then lowered and set up on these platforms. By suspending them in this manner, the pumps could be raised or lowered as the water level in the hold changed when she came off the reef. Discharge hoses from the pumps were led out through holes cut in the ship's hull plating. Their suction hoses ran down through the inspection covers into the flooded double bottom tanks. Out on deck, big compressors were set up ready to drive air into the double bottom tanks via their sounding pipes. This would assist the pumps when the refloating attempts were made, by forcing water and oil out of the double bottoms.

The *Runic's* men and the salvage party laboured from dawn to dusk. In her engine room boiler pressure was maintained with the turbines kept operational and the steam and diesel-powered generators supplying full electricity to the ship. All her officers and crew, including the master, were paid large bonuses; Neil Hamilton remembers his as a substantial sum compared to his second officer's monthly salary of around £80.00. Seamen by comparison were being paid £8.00 per week on top of their normal wages, plus a further £8.00 for 'loss of clothes'. Meals were served just as usual, although without the waiter services of stewards and ship's boys who were no longer aboard. After work, films were shown out on deck during the warm, late-summer evenings. Crew members also caught sharks, as many as 18 on one day with some of them more than seven feet long. At low tides they explored the reef, collecting shells and coral. These wanderings were soon terminated, however, when the crew learned that the reef's deeper holes and crevices were inhabited by poisonous stonefish. These, the most venomous species of fish in the world's oceans, are so-named because of their ability to camouflage and transform themselves to look like the surrounding rock.

Captain Williams and his deputies Captain Anderson and Captain Taylor toiled alongside everybody else but Captain Sendall and the *Runic's* Chief Officer J.M. Estill took no part in the salvage effort. Captain Williams, himself a hard-nosed, straight-talking Australian who had learned his trade in sailing ships, strongly disapproved of this; he expected Sendall would, temporarily at least, put aside his status as master, roll up his sleeves and work with the rest of them for the preservation of his ship. A rift soon flared between Captain Sendall and the salvage men; only Hamilton and Revell were given any credit in the progress reports Captain Williams was sending every day to Shaw Savill and to Lloyd's of London. The master's attitude is perhaps understandable. After having ploughed headlong into a well-charted reef surrounded by hundreds of miles of open ocean, Captain Sendall knew the verdict awaiting him from the *Runic's* owners. Captain Williams was now, for all intents and purposes, in command of the *Runic* and had transformed the ship's once pristine outer decks into a grimy clutter of machinery, cables and towing gear. Captain Sendall found it all completely overwhelming.

On 27th February Captain Williams cabled the Salvage Association in London from the *Runic* with his estimate that repairing her hull damage and refitting her after the salvage work, would cost AUST£600,000. On top of this was the cost of the refloating operation, which he put at AUST£85,000. Meanwhile preparations continued and the weather stayed fine and calm. More salvage equipment was required but the *Karangi* was still not available; haggling with the Royal Australian Navy over the price for chartering and refitting her would, astonishingly, go on until agreement was reached on 7th March. She would then have to be dry-docked and made seaworthy. At Sydney, discharge of cargo from Shaw Savill's motor vessel *Illyric* (11,256/1960, Captain N.S. Milne) was hastened so that she could be used to transport additional gear out to the *Runic*.

Winds and seas rose briefly on 2nd March and again on 6th March; all the *Runic's* double bottom tanks were filled with seawater to hold her quiet and stop any renewed pounding. The *Illyric* had got away from Sydney on Friday 3rd March at 1 p.m. and arrived the following day. Transfer of stores from her to the *Runic* and the tugs began immediately, using the *Runic's* boats. One of these, powered by a temperamental diesel motor, was kept continuously in operation by John House who had been Junior Second Engineer on the *Runic* until he was transferred to the *Alaric* as her Acting Chief Engineer while the *Runic* was at Sydney. Returning to the *Runic* aboard the *Alaric*, House's motor boat provided essential transport to and from the *Runic* and the other vessels attending her. When not in use this boat was kept moored alongside the *Runic* at her companionway ladder, where a floating platform had been built.

On 6th March, her task completed, the *Illyric* left to return to Sydney with Captain Williams aboard. Captain Anderson remained in charge on the *Runic* as preparation work continued without letup. Presumably Captain Williams' journey to the mainland was with the intention of lighting a fire under those responsible for the desultory progress with the *Karangi*. In retrospect, Captain Williams would have been much better advised, as soon as the problems with chartering the *Karangi* became apparent, in simply dispensing with her and instead utilising the USS *Conserver*, equipped as she was with the most comprehensive maritime salvage plant anywhere in the Pacific Ocean.

The costs of hiring the *Conserver* had deterred him from doing this, but by 7th March the total price for the salvage operation had, in Captain Williams' revised estimate, increased to AUST£132,000 from the earlier £85,000. If the refloating attempt planned for the 17th-18th was not successful and the USS *Conserver* had to be brought south to assist, another AUST£85,000 to £100,000 would be added to the bill. It would take USS *Conserver* 15 days to reach Middleton Reef. On top of this was the projected AUST£600,000 cost to repair the *Runic*. Senior management brows were becoming increasingly furrowed in the accounts department at Shaw Savill's Sydney office.

The weather at Middleton reef continued fine and calm during the second week of March and into the third week. On 10th March the tug *Fearless* returned to Brisbane, her contract terminated. This left the *Woona* and *Wooree* on station with the *Runic*. Other news was all good: at Sydney the *Karangi* was expected to be ready for departure on 14th March. All preparations for the refloating attempt had been completed the day before, ending three weeks of intensive work. A radio message from Captain Williams summarised the position: '...five sets [of] heavy ground tackle laid and ready. Salvage pumps rigged [at] Numbers 1, 2 and 3 double bottoms and hope [these will] control inflow. Other compartments fitted [for] compressed air. Tugs with combined horse-power 4,500 engaged. Intend attempt turn stern seaward around March 18. Weather fine, all well.'

On Tuesday 14th March the pumps and compressors were started on all double bottom tanks under the forward three holds. Fourth Engineer Jimmy Andrew had responsibility for overseeing this. From Sydney the *Karangi* radioed that she was at last at sea, having departed 8.30 a.m. on 15th March. She was expected at Middleton Reef on the morning of the 17th at her best speed of 11½ knots. A total of AUST£13,637 had been spent on dry-docking, refitting, fuelling, storing, crewing and equipping the *Karangi*.

With Captain Williams now back from Sydney, a preliminary trial of all salvage gear deployed was made on Thursday 16th March. The *Runic's* stern moved slightly in response. Then on the spring tide the following day, 17th March, the tugs took the strain on their hawsers and the *Runic's* winches were started as the long-awaited full-scale attempt to move her stern began. It resulted in complete disappointment. The sea had been flat and her stern would not budge. Three further pulling attempts were made, one on Friday morning 18th March and two the following day. In total the *Runic's* stern was shifted by no more than 20 feet. It was now realised that any large-scale movement was not going to occur until there was a southerly swell running, to assist the tugs and winches by lifting the ship. Captain Williams had believed the combined effort of the two tugs and the *Runic's* winches would be sufficient to haul her stern to seaward, and that this could be done without the *Karangi's* additional engine power.

Cablegrams now began flowing as far afield as Furness Withy's New York office, asking that the USS *Conserver* be 'engaged soonest possible'. She would cost US$2,500 per day, rising to US$3,500 per day on 15th April which was considered the earliest date she could arrive at Middleton Reef from Honolulu at 15 knots. Meanwhile it was proposed to lay additional ground tackle which the *Karangi* had brought with her, while reducing the *Runic's* crew to 40 men and doing everything further to lighten the ship.

It was all too late. Salvage operations such as this require a modicum of luck as well as great expertise; the Australian liner *Wanganella* (9,576/1931) had enjoyed both when she stranded on Barrett Reef at the entrance to Wellington harbour, New Zealand in January 1947. Pinned at the bow like the *Runic*, the *Wanganella* was successfully hauled free after 18 days aground. Whatever luck remained with the *Runic* probably deserted her around the end of February 1961, when the opportunity to get the *Conserver* on station at Middleton Reef by the 17th March spring tide was not taken. Neither the *Woona* or the *Wooree* were deep-draught, ocean-going salvage tugs and the absence of a vessel or vessels of this nature was the deciding factor as to why the *Runic's* stern could not be moved any further than it was.

Catastrophe

The annual tropical cyclone season was meant to have ended by mid-March but the biggest weather disturbance for that season was yet to come. Known as the New Caledonia-Lord Howe Cyclone of 15th to 23th March 1961, it began west of the islands of Vanuatu and passed the northern tip of New Caledonia on 19th March. From there it came rapidly south into the Tasman Sea, deepening and intensifying. Middleton Reef lay directly in its path. Radio warnings sent the tugs and *Karangi* hurrying out to sea at maximum speed, away from the reef, leaving the *Runic,* her crew together with Captain Williams and his salvage party to face the rapidly deteriorating winds and seas. As the cyclone approached, Numbers 6, 7 and 8 double bottom tanks were ballasted to keep her still. Then, hoping the rising seas might give the necessary leverage to her hull, a last attempt at refloating was made next morning, Monday 20th March. Pumping overboard of ballast commenced at 5.30 a.m. and five hours later the cargo winches recommenced hauling on the ground tackle, with the *Runic's* engines going full astern. Once again it was futile. Around 11.30 a.m. the turbines

Exploring Middleton Reef at low tide (left) and recovering one of the *Runic's* lifeboats that had been in use as a work boat, after it was swept away during the 20th-21st March tropical cyclone. *[Neil Hamilton]*

Left: sunbathing at Cronulla, Sydney prior to flying home to England after the *Runic's* abandonment. From left: one of the ship's cadets, Second Officer Neil Hamilton, First Electrician Derek Ward, Fifth Engineer Jimmy McShane. Right: outside the Hotel Cecil, Cronulla. From left. Fourth Engineer Bruce (Jimmy) Andrew, Second Officer Neil Hamilton, Fifth Engineer Jimmy McShane, First Electrician Derek Ward, Extra Second Engineer Alex Simpson, a cadet and one of the *Runic's* radio officers. *[Bruce Andrew]*

and winches were stopped, never to be powered-up again. The priority now was re-ballasting her double bottoms; this continuing all day from 11.30 a.m. with the ship taking on some 6,000 to 8,000 tons of water to try and immobilise her against the growing force of the storm.

Throughout the night of 20th-21th March huge waves burst against the *Runic's* port side as Middleton Reef was lashed by the cyclone. Fourth Engineer Jimmy Andrew remembers green water clearing the top of the *Runic's* funnel from the waves' impact. Repeatedly and violently her hull was lifted and dropped onto the reef's edge. The men could do nothing but wait in their lifejackets for the storm to pass. Then at 1 a.m. the alarm sounded in the engineers' accommodation: the seas had broken through the port main circulating sea-inlet boxes. The port condenser now had to be stopped. The engineers changed over to the starboard condenser but soon there was no circulation of water for this. Both turbo generators and the main boilers had to be shut down, leaving only the port diesel generator running in the engine room for supplying electrical power to the ship. The starboard diesel generator had earlier been stripped for repair. There was nothing more the engineers could do.

At 4 a.m. the lights failed. The seas were flooding into the *Runic's* engine room through the refrigeration high suction inlet, which had been forced back on its stud mountings by the waves. At 8 a.m. on Tuesday 21st March the *Runic* radioed: 'Using emergency batteries and transmitter ….Cyclonic storm. Anchors parted, ship driving on reef. Engine room filling. Further damage yet unknown probably serious. Crew safe and well. Williams.' By 11 a.m. water in the engine room was level with the armature on the starboard diesel generator. Although fully ballasted she was grinding heavily on the reef, bending up the tank tops that formed the floor of the engine room. The stern had been pushed further round to starboard and she had gone up onto the reef by what was later reckoned to be an additional 115 feet. On the Boat Deck, one of the starboard lifeboats was missing from its davits, swept away, while the other starboard boat was still there but badly damaged. The motor boat on the port side was filled with water; Engineer John House set to work to get it running again.

At 4 p.m. came another radio call: 'Further internal examination reveals whole of port side engine room set in and water level [rising and falling] according to tide. Both engines set up [lifted from their foundations] and generators under water. Vessel [has] moved approximately 40 feet further on reef aft and still pounding heavily.'

All electric power aboard the ship was gone with the *Runic's* engine and boiler rooms now opened to the sea, the storm's pounding having wrenched her boilers, main turbines and generators from their beds. All the double bottoms had been crushed and destroyed. The after holds had water in them with the tank tops pushed up and the bulkheads cracked and buckled. She was in imminent danger of breaking her back.

With this extensive damage to her hull there was no prospect of her salvagers ever refloating the *Runic*. 'RUNIC position now hopeless and underwriters working on basis of total loss' stated a cablegram from Shaw Savill's London Head Office on 22nd March. The mood on the ship, highly optimistic until then, now turned despondent. So much hard work, all for nothing. On 22nd March 1961 the *Runic* was declared a constructive total loss. Work commenced on removing all salvage gear from the ship and loading it aboard the *Karangi*, while the following day negotiations

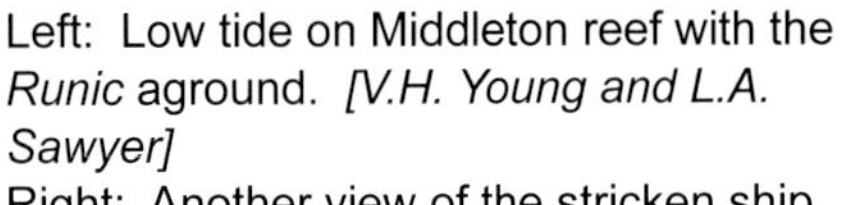

Left: Low tide on Middleton reef with the *Runic* aground. *[V.H. Young and L.A. Sawyer]*
Right: Another view of the stricken ship

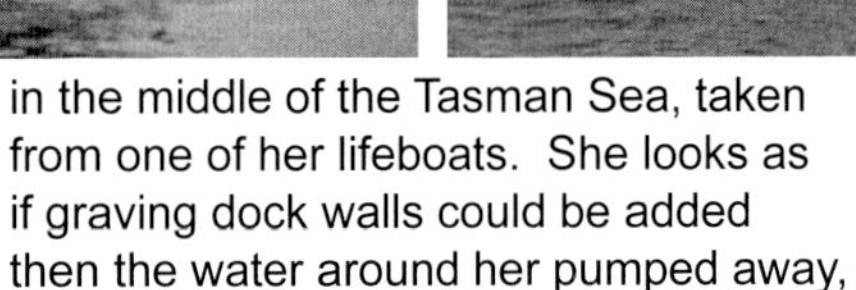

in the middle of the Tasman Sea, taken from one of her lifeboats. She looks as if graving dock walls could be added then the water around her pumped away, and she will be all ready for routine hull cleaning and painting. But the *Runic* is impaled forever and she will not make port again. *[Neil Hamilton]*

began with other parties interested in buying the *Runic* for salvage or scrap 'as she lies'. Very little in the way of stores and gear belonging to the *Runic* was taken off: a cablegram dated 29th March set out part of the huge inventory that remained aboard: 'refrigerated pumps and motors, various pump motors for main engine and auxiliaries, boiler room pumps and motors, motor starters and boxes of starter spares, steering motors and pumps complete with spares, winch motor controllers and contactors, induced and forced draft fan motors with starters and contactors, windlass motors and contactors, diesel and turbo generators with mechanical spares, boiler mounting spares, refrigeration plant spares...'

On Friday 24th March the *Karangi* was forced to break off loading work and return to Sydney. Her boilers were giving trouble with excessive consumption of oil fuel and water, and would need five to six days of repairs at a projected cost AUST£3,000. Rightly exasperated with her, Captain Williams began looking for another ship. He found one in a 660 grt vessel called the *Basspoint* and began negotiations with her owners. As well as reliable engines the *Basspoint* had three derricks for lifting aboard his salvage equipment from the *Runic*. Back at Middleton Reef it was now simply a case of preparing to leave. 'Lawyers request you ensure all ship's records to be brought ashore by master are kept in safe custody as required for enquiry here', read a cablegram to Australia from Shaw Savill's London Head Office. With no electrical power, officers and crew resorted to burning dunnage in 44 gallon drums, over which they cooked and heated water in a makeshift kitchen.

At 8 a.m. on Sunday 26th March Shaw Savill's cargo vessel *Arabic* (6,497/1956, Captain D.T. Mouldey) arrived and at 3 p.m. the *Wooree*, last of the tugs, departed for Sydney. Seas were slight and the day fine and clear at Middleton Reef as final salvage stores and equipment along with bonded goods were transferred to the *Arabic*. Occasional rain showers set in on the afternoon of the following day, Monday 27th March 1961 as the very last entries were made in the *Runic's* bridge log: '1700 SS *Runic* abandoned, all hands transferred to MV *Arabic* in *Arabic's* motor boat'. The entry was signed by Captain Sendall, who was the last to leave. At her stern and from her mast the Red Ensign and the house flag of Shaw Savill and Albion were left hoisted and flying. The *Arabic* berthed at Sydney late on the evening of 28th March. Just eleven years old, the *Runic's* value at the time was £2,750,000.00.

The crew were accommodated in navy barracks at Sydney's Garden Island while the master, officers and engineers were put up at the Hotel Cecil at Cronulla Beach. Some of the *Runic's* engineers were given supernumerary positions on other Shaw Savill ships in Australian waters; Jimmy Andrew was appointed Fourth Engineer and John House Extra Second Engineer aboard the *Runic's* sister ship *Suevic*. Before leaving Shaw Savill in 1965 Andrew went on to become Second Engineer of the *Southern Cross*, the *Suevic* and the *Gothic*. Nine days after disembarking from the *Arabic* all the others, 65 in number including the two wives, were flown back to London on a BOAC flight which left Sydney at 9.10 a.m. on 5 April 1961.

As soon as they reached London an inquiry was held by company executives at Shaw Savill's Head Office. The findings of this inquiry were never publicly disclosed and any written report appears no longer to exist. Captain Sendall was interviewed personally by Lord Sanderson on or about 25th April. In a letter dated 15th June 1961 Shaw Savill was advised by the British Ministry of Transport that 'after careful consideration, the Minister does not intend, on the evidence available at the present time, to order a formal inquiry, though, of course, he reserves his right to do so should new evidence come to light'.

So, what was the outcome of that head office inquiry? There are clues that can be gleaned from reading the letters, memos and other documents concerning the *Runic's* loss held by the National Maritime Museum at Greenwich. It would seem that both Captain Sendall and Chief Officer Estill told the inquiry they were very experienced at navigating the Tasman Sea and, on this particular trip, they had done nothing different from usual. The course set on leaving Brisbane had been used before, without any problem. Both were at a complete loss to explain how, on this occasion, the *Runic* had been set approximately 20 miles to the south of her course during the first hours of her trans-Tasman voyage so that she collided with Middleton Reef. Nothing could lawfully be established to say that the master and chief officer were in default. Until evidence of any breach was found, the Ministry of Transport could not be provided with grounds on which to base a formal inquiry. And there the matter ended.

Second Officer Neil Hamilton was cleared of any blame and returned to sea immediately, having been appointed to the passenger-carrying *Athenic* as her Second Officer and navigator. This was a promotion for him. He never saw Captain Sendall again. The *Runic's* last master retired from the company's service without further command. Leaving Great Britain, he went to New Zealand and took a job as Oamaru's Harbour Master. Cyril William Sendall died in New Zealand on 27 May 1965, aged just 58. The cargo that the *Runic* had been scheduled to load in Auckland and other New Zealand ports was transferred to Shaw Savill's *Taranaki* (8,696/1928).

Chief Engineer A.F. Lesley joined the *Persic* in August 1961 and stayed with her for two voyages - Numbers 24 and 25 - until January 1962 when he went on sick leave. He retired from the sea on 31st August 1962.

A year after the stranding, with the *Runic* still sitting fully intact on the reef, New Zealand newspapers reported that insurance underwriters had sold her for an undisclosed price to a Sydney businessman who intended to cut her up for scrap. Nothing came of this nor various other projects from salvage interests who had hoped to remove her from her mid-ocean lair. Their intentions had all been defeated by cyclones, the remoteness of Middleton Reef and by falls in the value of scrap metal.

During 1970 divers recovered the *Runic's* two propellers, bringing them back to Sydney along with other saleable metals taken from the wreck. The propellers, comprising some 30 tons of manganese-bronze, were worth AUST$20,000 as scrap. By the end of the 1970s her stern had broken away but the rest of the ship lay massively on the invisible reef like some great, defiant sentinel with the Tasman Sea's vast horizon all around. Derricks were topped off on the samson posts just as they had been left, the funnel and foremast still stood and her lifeboat falls hung down to her waterline where huge gashes had opened in her hull. As such she became one of the world's most spectacular shipwrecks, proud and upright. Cyclones and tides have, however, ensured her slow, relentless destruction. By the stranding's 40th anniversary the *Runic* had collapsed into a near-featureless wreck, her rusted steel bright orange and brown against the blues and greens of Middleton Reef and its lagoon. Another 40 years and she will be gone.

At Queens Wharf, Wellington; the *Runic* bow-on and dressed with flags. *[Captain Ian Condie]*

The *Runic's* funnel with her steam whistles. *[Jeremy Theakston]*

The wreck of the *Runic* on 25th September 1997. *[Captain Gerry Wright]*

Runic in January 2005 with a stranded fishing boat. *[Peter McManaway]*

Seventh and last of a great lineage, the *Suevic* underway in the open sea for the very first time. She is steaming her builder's trials in Belfast Lough with Shaw Savill's chief superintendents and their minions aboard. The date is 4th July 1950. *[Ulster Folk and Transport Museum 12968]*

SUEVIC, GOOD AND FAITHFUL SERVANT

Last of the Big Ics

The *Suevic*, Official Number 183613, is remembered by those who sailed on her as a fine ship, well-maintained, well-run and a pleasure to live and work aboard. To her goes the distinction as last of the Big Ics to be completed and last to be withdrawn from service. She was also the longest-lived. During her 24 years there was always a degree of confusion over the correct pronunciation of her name. Some spoke it as *SOOVIC*, others thought it should be *SWEEVIC*. The name is that of the barbarian kingdom of the Suebi, which ruled lands that now comprise Galacia and northern Portugal on the Iberian Peninsula. The Suebic, or Suevic Kingdom was established in 410 and lasted until 585 AD when it was overrun and conquered by the Visigoths.

Tonnage, dimensions and machinery were the same as that for the *Runic*. Built on their Number 3 Slip, Queen's Shipyard, as Harland and Wolff's Hull Number 1415, her keel was laid on 21st October 1948 with erection of frames 85% complete by 3rd May 1949 and then fully complete 17 days later. Launching took place at 12.45 p.m. on Tuesday 7th March 1950 with the ceremony performed by Mrs S. Thompson, wife of Shaw Savill's Assistant General Manager. Four months later on 4th July 1950 *Suevic* proceeded to sea for trials in Belfast Lough. She was handed over to Shaw Savill at 1 p.m. next day, Wednesday 5th July, her trials successfully completed. Port of registry, as with all the Big Ics, was Southampton. Sailing from Belfast, the *Suevic* berthed at Liverpool the following day and commenced loading for her maiden voyage. On 25th July, under the command of Captain B.J. Tillott, the *Suevic* departed Liverpool with a full general cargo. Following the same track as the *Runic* had done on her first voyage three months earlier, the new ship went via Suez to Fremantle, which she reached on 17th September. Calls at Adelaide and Sydney followed. Loading for home began at Newcastle from 5th to 14th October with most probably a wool cargo. The *Suevic* was at Sydney between 14th and 26th October, then to Melbourne from 28th October to 16th November when loading was finished. That day she sailed for Liverpool and then Antwerp with calls at Colombo and Aden.

Looking up the building slip on 3rd May 1949, with side framing of Hull Number 1415 being set up. Note the rows of triangle-shaped brackets at three heights on the frames. Transverse beams will be fixed to these to form the decks. The tank tops have yet to be plated but one of the after bulkheads has been erected. Work is in progress on the aft-end structure, where the circular openings for the propeller tail shafts can be seen. An overhead crane is holding in position the cast-steel stern-frame, on which the rudder will later be mounted. Workmen on the floor of the berth, at bottom of the picture, and on staging either side of the stern frame are engaged in a process called lining-off, whereby the stern frame is moved and adjusted until it is exactly in position. *[Captain Graham Pepper, Shaw Savill Society]*

Top: Mrs S. Thompson about to perform the naming and launch ceremony for Hull Number 1415. The man at right is believed to be W. Errington Keville, Shaw Savill's General Manager and Deputy Chairman. *[Ulster Folk and Transport Museum 12531]*

Bottom: The *Suevic*, 2nd March 1950, on Number 3 Slip of Harland and Wolff's Queen's Shipyard. She will be launched in five days time. *[Ulster Folk and Transport Museum 12424]*

Top: the *Suevic* going down her slipway and entering the River Lagan On her port hand is Victoria Wharf and the roof of the Victoria Shipyard plating shed. Number 3 Slip, from which the *Suevic* was launched, was next to the great Arrol gantry in Queen's Shipyard. Its mammoth size dwarfing the *Athenic*, the gantry was built between 1907 and 1909 for the liners *Olympic* and *Titanic*. Its vast, elaborate steel lattice-work was supplied by Sir William Arrol and Co. Ltd. of Glasgow. When completed the Arrol gantry was, literally, a towering feat of engineering but by the 1960s it had fallen into disuse, its maximum ten-ton lifting capacity no longer sufficient. After the Queen's Shipyard was closed in late 1965 the gantry was cut up for scrap. *[Ulster Folk and Transport Museum 12537]*

Right: the *Suevic's* funnel being lifted aboard during her fitting out, 3rd May 1950. *[Ulster Folk and Transport Museum 12832]*

Taking on oil fuel from the tanker *Peter M* (970/1937, built as *Algol* by Deutsche Werft, Hamburg) in the Musgrave Channel on 12th June 1950. Steam will next be raised in the *Suevic's* boilers for the first time, and the turbines will be run. Almost complete, the *Suevic* will sail for her builder's trials in three weeks from the date of this photo. *[Ulster Folk and Transport Museum 12948]*

Top: At Tenerife in the Canary Islands. *[Ambrose Greenway]*.
Bottom: The *Suevic* on the move in a British port while discharging cargo. Unloading of Numbers 1 and 2 holds appears to have been completed as their gear is down. Hull paintwork, tarnished by contact with wharves and lighters, will be put right by the time she departs on her next foreign-going voyage. *[J. and M. Clarkson]*

Suevic light ship in July 1962. *[J. and M. Clarkson]*

The *Suevic's* hold capacity is recorded as differing slightly from that of the *Runic*: 512,780 cubic feet of insulated space, plus 225,180 cubic feet for general cargo. For *Runic* the equivalent figures were 508,080 cubic feet and 225,180 cubic feet. In addition to her regular New Zealand-Australia-UK trade, the *Suevic* made at least one call at Philadelphia or New York with refrigerated meat and dairy produce for the MANZ Line. With three exceptions her career was incident-free. While underway in the Scheldt Estuary on passage to Antwerp, the *Suevic* collided with another vessel whose name is not recorded. The date was 9th January 1963. She then went aground and was not refloated until 1st February, after which the *Suevic* was dry-docked at Antwerp.

A much more serious event took place on 23rd November 1968 while the *Suevic* was at Sydney discharging a cargo of whisky from the UK. Fire broke out in Number 5 hold and became so intense that fire-fighters could not get near it. Eventually, after a four-hour battle, they succeeded in putting the fire out by flooding the hold with 1,600 tons of water. Extensive damage was found to have been done to the hold's interior and its steel hull plating. All the hold's refrigeration plant was destroyed. Cleaning up and repairs took two weeks, with the hold then being reloaded with general cargo. The *Suevic* sailed for New Zealand on 8th December to continue loading.

She was in the Caribbean on passage to New Zealand three years later when, on the night of 21st December 1971, the *Suevic* was radioed by a US Coast Guard C-130 Hercules aircraft from Elizabeth Air Station, North Carolina, and asked to go to the assistance of a vessel in distress 740 miles south east of Bermuda. At 5 p.m. a ship's lights followed by red flares were sighted from the bridge. On turning to investigate, the *Suevic* came across a lifeboat with 13 occupants, which she stopped to pick up. They identified themselves as having come from the Norwegian motor cargo ship *Jark* (1,246/1968), which was lying nearby and on the point of foundering. Watched from the *Suevic*, the Hungarian-built *Jark*, which had been on passage from Rotterdam to Aguadilla on the island of Puerto Rico, was seen to suddenly capsize and disappear. The *Suevic* landed the vessel's crew at Curacao four days later on 25th December 1971.

She is recorded as having visited Port Chalmers, New Zealand 15 times over a 20-year period from 22th August 1952 to 24th August 1972. The *Suevic* was also a regular caller at Wellington. In August 1967 the *Suevic* was moored on the River Fal in Cornwall alongside and inboard of the *Corinthic*, while maintenance work was carried out on her boilers by her engineers. A similar period of lay-up took place two years later between 7th August and mid-Sept 1969, this time on the River Blackwater in Essex. During her last years, with the first container ships entering service, maintenance was cut to the essentials and she fell into poor condition. Leaking stern glands became a recurring problem. On 9th October 1972 the *Suevic* departed Lyttelton, New Zealand for a voyage that took her to Genoa, Piraeus, Thessalonika, Limassol and then Malta from 1st to 8th January 1973. She was forced to put back to Malta with boiler trouble and did not leave again until 17th January. Reaching London, she commenced loading for her final voyage to New Zealand. Her Master was Captain J.G. Street. The *Suevic* was Shaw Savill's very last steam cargo ship and by now her old boilers increasingly were having to be nursed. A call was made at Rotterdam on 23rd February before the *Suevic* crossed the Atlantic for one last transit of the Panama Canal. Discharge of cargo took place at Auckland, New Plymouth and finally Lyttelton. Departure with all holds empty was taken from Lyttelton on Saturday 18th May 1974. In Cook Strait next morning, the *Suevic* circled the approaches to Wellington Harbour where a number of boats had come out to bid her farewell. Turning east, she then set out on the long voyage to Kaohsuing and demolition, arriving there on 6th June. When her Red Ensign was lowered that day, never to be hoisted again, the last of the illustrious Big Ics passed into history.

Passing the White Cliffs of Dover outward bound in Spring 1972. *[FotoFlite incorporating Skyfotos BW72-2336]*

The *Suevic* off Queen's Wharf (at right) in Wellington harbour, manoeuvring with the aid of the Union Steam Ship Company's tug *Taioma.* (232/1944, ex *Empire Jane)* *[V.H. Young and L.A. Sawyer]*

Top: *Suevic* alongside at Timaru, New Zealand in 1964. *[V.H. Young and L.A. Sawyer]*

Middle: At Nelson in April 1967. *[Ian J. Farquhar collection]*

Bottom: The *Suevic* at Adelaide in January 1968, taken with a telephoto lens which has fore-shortened her appearance. *[Chris Finney/Malcolm Cranfield collection]*

Suevic, light ship, arriving at Hobart on 22nd August 1973. *[David Kirby/ Russell Priest collection]*

In Wellington harbour, 16th January 1972 with part of Somes Island at left. *[V.H. Young and L.A. Sawyer]*

A broadside view while underway. *[Ambrose Greenway]*

SUMMARY OF DIMENSIONS AND CAREERS

All ships were owned by Shaw Savill and Albion Ltd., registered in Southampton and classed 100A1 by Lloyd's Register of Shipping.

Name:	***Corinthic***	***Athenic***	***Ceramic***	***Gothic***	***Persic***	***Runic***	***Suevic***
Official number:	167909	167927	182344	182351	183578	183591	183613
Yard number:	1175	1326	1185	1759	1202	1414	1415
Builder:	Cammell Laird and Co. Ltd., Birkenhead	Harland and Wolff Ltd., Belfast	Cammell Laird and Co. Ltd., Birkenhead	Swan, Hunter and Wigham Richardson Ltd., Wallsend	Cammell Laird and Co. Ltd., Birkenhead	Harland and Wolff Ltd., Belfast	Harland and Wolff Ltd., Belfast
Keel laid down:	14th May 1945	12th June 1945	12th November 1946	30th May 1946	11th May 1948	30th June 1948	21st October 1948
Launch:	30th May 1946	26th November 1946	30th December 1947	12th December 1947	10th June 1949	21st October 1949	7th March 1950
Sponsor:	Mrs Gwen Douglas	Mrs J.A. Beasley	Mrs Isobel Keville	Lady May Murrant	Miss Pauline Sanderson	Mrs H.E. Davis	Mrs S. Thompson
Sea trials:	25th March 1947	15th July 1947	27-28th October 1948	4th and 5th December 1948	24th November 1949	23rd and 24th March 1950	4th July 1950
Handed over:	Late March 1947	16th July 1947	28th October 1948	9th December 1948	26th November 1949	24th March 1950	5th July 1950
First master:	Captain T.V. Roberts	Captain D. Aitchison	Captain A.V. Richardson	Captain R.G. James	Captain E.T. Baker	Captain W.G. West	Captain B.J. Tillott
Maiden voyage commenced:	12th April 1947	1st August 1947	16th November 1948	23rd December 1948	21st December 1949	22nd April 1950	25th July 1950
Radio call-sign:	GZYL	GBLS	GFLM	MAUQ	GDRZ	GGCS	GKJV
GRT:	15264	15187	15896	15911	13594	13587	13587
Length:	561 feet overall, 530 feet between perpendiculars (171/161.5 metres)	561 feet overall, 530 feet between perpendiculars (171/161.5 metres)	561 feet overall, 530 feet between perpendiculars (171/161.5 metres)	561 feet overall, 530 feet between perpendiculars (171/161.5 metres)	561 feet overall, 535 feet between perpendiculars (171/163 metres)	561 feet overall, 530 feet between perpendiculars (171/161.5 metres)	561 feet overall, 530 feet between perpendiculars (171/161.5 metres)
Moulded breadth:	71 feet (21.6 metres)	71 feet (21.6 metres)	72 feet (21.9 metres)	72 feet (21.9 metres)	72 feet (21.9 metres)	72 feet (21.9 metres)	72 feet (21.9 metres)
Draught fully loaded:	29 feet 7 7/8 inches (9.1 metres)	29 feet 7 7/8 inches (9.1 metres)	29 feet seven inches (9.017 metres)	29 feet seven inches (9.017 metres)	31 feet 11 5/8 inches (9.8 metres)	32 feet (9.75 metres)	32 feet (9.75 metres)
Number of watertight transverse bulkheads:	seven	seven	seven	seven	seven	seven	seven
Number of watertight compartments:	eight	eight	eight	eight	eight	eight	eight
Number of holds:	six	six	six	six	six	six	six
Insulated hold space:	524,703 cubic feet	517,903 cubic feet	514,386 cubic feet	512,078 cubic feet	513,756 cubic feet	508,080 cubic feet	512,780 cubic feet
Non-insulated hold space:	170,250 cubic feet	172,004 cubic feet	147,656 cubic feet	145,642 cubic feet	224,388 cubic feet	225,180 cubic feet	225,180 square feet
Number of passengers:	85, first class	85, first class	85, first class	85, first class	None	None	None
Crew (when new):	124	124	124	124	72	72	72

Longest or best-known master :	Captain A.C. Jones	Captain G.H. Heywood	Captain F.A. Smith	Captain Sir David Aitchison	Captain G.W. Houchen	Captain C.W. Sendall	Captain G.M. Robertson
Chief engineer with longest service aboard:	F.H. Papworth	F.W. White	C. Simpson	O. Charters		A.F. Lesley	
Propulsion:	Twin-screw, single-reduction-geared steam turbines	Twin-screw, single-reduction-geared steam turbines	Twin-screw, single-reduction-geared steam turbines	Twin-screw, single-reduction-geared steam turbines	Twin-screw, single-reduction-geared steam turbines	Twin-screw, single-reduction-geared steam turbines	Twin-screw, single-reduction-geared steam turbines
Service speed:	17 knots	17 knots	17 knots, maximum 19.5 knots	17 knots, maximum 19.5 knots	17 knots	17.5 knots	17.5 knots
Turbine output:	14,000 SHP	14,000 SHP	18,400 SHP	18,400 SHP	14,000 SHP	14,000 SHP	14,000 SHP
Boilers:	Two oil-fired Yarrow type, five-drum water-tube	Two oil-fired Yarrow type, five-drum water-tube	Two oil-fired Foster Wheeler water-tube	Two oil-fired Foster Wheeler water-tube	Two oil-fired Foster Wheeler water-tube	Two oil-fired Foster Wheeler D Type water-tube	Two oil-fired Foster Wheeler D Type water-tube
Boiler steam pressure:	375 p.s.i.	375 p.s.i.	500 p.s.i.	500 p.s.i.	385 p.s.i.	425 p.s.i.	425 p.s.i.
Boiler temperature:	750 deg F	750 deg F	800 deg F	800 deg F	740 deg F	750 deg F	750 deg F
Electricity supply:	Four 350 kW diesel generators; DC current.	Four 350 kW diesel generators; DC current.	Two 500 kW steam-driven turbo generators; two 480 kW diesel generators; DC current.	Two 500 kW steam-driven turbo generators, two 480 kW diesel generators; DC current.	Two 600 kW steam-driven turbo generators, two 400 kW diesel generators; DC current.	Two 500kW, steam-driven turbo-generators, two 400 kW diesel generators; DC current.	Two 500kW, steam-driven turbo-generators, two 400 kW diesel generators; DC current.
Number of voyages completed:	42	42	56	39 plus 2 royal tour charters.		22	
Major career events:	1. Severe fire at shipyard while fitting out, 4th January 1947. 2. Visit by King George VI, Queen Elizabeth and Princess Margaret, 30th October 1950. 3. Downgraded to cargo-only, 5th July 1965-13th February 1966.	Downgraded to cargo-only, 23rd May-14th August 1965.	1. Stand-by royal yacht, 1951-52 and 1953-54. 2. Brought Sir Arthur Porritt, Governor-General of New Zealand and family to Wellington, November 1967.	1. Service as royal yacht for Queen Elizabeth II, 1953-54. 2. Severe fire at sea, 1st August 1968, seven deaths.	1. Fire at sea, 12th February 1958. 2. Rescued 31 crew from sinking *Pan Ocean*, western Mediterranean, 6th April 1958. 3. Transferred to Royal Mail Line as *Derwent,* July 1969.	Aground Middleton reef, Tasman Sea, 19th February 1961. Declared constructive total loss and abandoned, 26th March 1961.	1. Collided with another ship and went aground in Scheldt Estuary on passage to Antwerp, 29th January 1963. Refloated 1st February. 2. Fire at Sydney, 23rd November 1968. 3. Rescued crew of Norwegian *Jark*, Caribbean Sea, 21st December 1971.
Broken up:	At Kaohsiung, Taiwan from November 1969.	At Kaohsiung, Taiwan from November 1969.	At Tamise, Belgium, from September 1972.	At Kaohsiung, Taiwan from November 1969.	At Bilbao, Spain, from November 1971.	Wreck still in situ, Middleton Reef (2011)	At Kaohsuing, Taiwan, from June 1974

THE DEMISE OF FURNESS WITHY

And with it, the end of Shaw Savill

Shaw Savill's acquisition by the Furness Withy Group was a result of the Kylsant crash of 1930-1931. The company had been drawn into the web of Owen Philipps, first and only Viscount Kylsant, and his empire of financial mirage in 1926 as part of White Star Line's purchase from a US conglomerate which had owned the latter since 1902. White Star was to have been the pearl-without-price in the Viscount's corporate coronet. What might have been an historic, world-dominating shipping group associated with technologically pioneering ships was killed by a false prospectus that had attempted to expand the Royal Mail Group, Kylsant's holding company.

The corporate wreckage was extensive and initially handled by a set of voting trustees who had to unravel what had been described as 'a business of national importance'. Furness Withy's first offer for Shaw Savill, made in May 1931 in competition with P. Henderson of Glasgow, was for £1.04 million. Neither this nor the Henderson offer was accepted but in March 1933 a link with the receivers was established when the joint purchase with P&O of the Aberdeen and Commonwealth Line was accomplished. Through this, Furness Withy got its hands on the five passenger/cargo 'Bay Boats' which Shaw Savill was staffing and managing. Furness Withy's next attempt was made by Frederick Lewis, Viscount Essendon, to buy the whole Royal Mail Group but, correctly suspecting that a monopoly would be created, HM Treasury said no. From this position Furness Withy offered £1.5 million in December 1935 which the Trustees accepted and Shaw Savill at last became a wholly-owned subsidiary. As Basil Sanderson was to record in his memoirs: 'This greatly increased profit potential but with little capital base'. His boss John Macmillan lost no time in following the Vesteys to Belfast and ordering three refrigerator ships for £1 million each and so it was that the *Waiwera* (10,800/1934; lost 1942) *Waipawa* (10,727/1934) and *Wairangi* (10,801/ 1935; lost 1942) became 'the biggest money earners we ever had built'. This trio were the direct ancestors of the seven Big Ic ships a decade later.

Voluminous though they are, the annual reports of the Furness Withy Group mention Shaw Savill in successive years but do not list the line's financial contribution. Just once in 1955, a weekly shipping magazine reported a consolidated trading profit by Shaw Savill of £1,043,803 for the financial year 1954-1955, which was down from £1,278,115 the previous year. Accompanying details listed £700,451 as being 'attributable to [the] parent company'. Furness Withy's subsequent history over the next 40 years is a study of a company rich in assets that lost the imagination to build upon them. In spite of the Second World War here was a company with a composite fleet of ships from passenger liners to short-haul coasters, resort hotels and an established cruise shipping venture as well as a long-established shipping agency network. Furness Withy's trade routes had been honed to profitable, self-sustaining sectors. It also had a dominance of Bermuda's shipping lifeline and its tourism, while its abilities at political strategy even got the better of the Perons in Argentina.

There were sparks of inspiration, business planning and leadership within the Furness Withy Group but it never became contagious. Manchester Liners became the first British container shipping company, running from the centre of Manchester to Montreal. As Robert Stoker, the pioneer of this successful venture wrote in 1985: 'We had to start from scratch, train the staff and write our own textbooks'. The *Manchester Challenge* (11,898; 500 TEU/1968) built on Teeside was followed into service by three 20-knot sister ships. The biggest 'what if' and lost opportunity in Furness Withy's closing chapter was in 1965 when W.R (Bob) Russell, a Shaw Savill director, saw what the Australian consortia Associated Steamships Pty. Ltd were doing on the Australian states' inter-coastal trades. Having built the *Kooringa* (5,825/1964) they were bravely getting Australia into door-to-door container transportation. Bob Russell in league with Swedish Transatlantic, at that time major operators with a fleet of modern ships, proposed to form with Shaw Savill a jointly-owned company that used Associated Steamships in Australian terminal ports, serving Europe-Australia-New Zealand and North America. Concurrently with this scheme, Furness Withy's Chairman Sir W. Errington Keville was acceding to P&O, Ocean, and British & Commonwealth's blandishments to join in forming Overseas Container Line. This was all happening with Shaw Savill's John Maconochie not being

Wairangi, ship-shape and Bristol fashion, sailing from Liverpool. *[B. and A. Feilden/J. and M. Clarkson collection]*

made aware of developments. If this was a glimpse of how Furness Withy operated at the top, it was neatly summed up by a confidential memo circulating in OCL that Furness Withy was 'the weakest of the four, financially, technically and in terms of senior management'. Yet this belied the fact that Furness Withy controlled, in 1965, 96 ships, trades to both coasts of North and South America and Shaw Savill's main business which was carrying New Zealand's refrigerated exports. They had also built the *Southern Cross* (20,204/1955) in a shape that passenger ships were to follow for years to come.

At the same time as becoming an OCL partner Furness Withy took the decision, in 1965, 'not to replace any Royal Mail Line and Pacific Navigation Company ships'. 1966 saw the abdication and withdrawal from Bermuda of that famous stalwart the *Queen of Bermuda* (22,575/1933) which had only been expensively modernised in 1963, and the younger *Ocean Monarch* (25,971/1950) specifically built for the link to the USA. In 1968 the trio of passenger/cargo ships built in 1959-1960 for Royal Mail's River Plate route were transferred to Shaw Savill for use in a round-the-world service that only lasted three years, after which they were sold in 1971. The climactic point came on 13th November 1970 when Furness Withy stated that they would dispose of 23 ships, which included Shaw Savill's commitment to own the second ship of a quartet on order with which the New Zealand import/export trades were to establish OCL in the country's principal trades. Urgent attempts to get Ocean (Blue Funnel Line) to substitute at the last minute failed and, with apparent caution about the move into full containerisation apparent in amongst New Zealand's marketing boards, three of the four ships were cancelled and it was another four years before the revolution arrived.

As the ships of the Furness Withy fleet were sold off there were successive attempts to rationalise trades using chartered ships, often with cheaper crews. Several Royal Mail meat carriers ended their service in Shaw Savill colours and vice versa. The *Southern Cross* was sold in 1973; with the round-the-world passenger service ended there was a brief attempt to use the mechanically troubled *Northern Star* (24,756/1968) as a full-time cruise ship but, only 13 years old, she was sold for scrap in 1975. In 1970 Shaw Savill had bought Canadian Pacific's *Empress of England* (25,971/1957) and had her expensively modernised and renamed *Ocean Monarch* for a dual cruising role serving Australia, New Zealand and the UK. She was a failure and was also sold for scrap in 1975.

Manchester Liners' thoroughly planned move into containerisation focused envious foreign eyes on the company in 1974 which, by then, was a wholly-owned subsidiary of Furness Withy. This unwelcome and aggressive takeover bid was rejected by the Furness Withy board and became even more bitter when the Canadian company mounting it tried a flanking move by trying to buy control of Furness Withy, being eventually thwarted by the UK regulatory body which took two years to rule that neither takeover 'would be in the public interest'.

It was perhaps no coincidence that Furness Withy's Chairman at this time of pessimism and contraction was (Lord) Richard Beeching. His report of 1963, which caused the reduction of Britain's railway network by one quarter, historically associated his name with optimistic failure. Beeching's varied business career was reaching a conclusion at this time and he is remembered as contributing to OCL's early years by the size of his cigars and nothing else. It seems he had little knowledge of, or interest in, the history or the latent potential of the company of which he was the Chairman. By the time of an agreed take over by the C.Y. Tung Group in 1980, Shaw Savill was little more than a brass plate and the repository of tax advantages. The Tung Group may have bought Furness Withy to obtain their share of OCL but this was vetoed by the UK Government, conscious of the sensitive status of Hong Kong. It was the government of China that bailed out C.Y. Tung when it got into financial trouble in 1980, with Furness Withy being sold to Hamburg Sud in 1990 and eventually being wound up in 2005.

In 1882 the sailing ship *Dunedin* had successfully carried the first-ever cargo of frozen lamb from New Zealand to London. It was appropriate that the last ship to fly the flag of the Southern Cross was another *Dunedin* (18,140/1980-1986) that briefly operated in the trans-Pacific container trade with Andrew Weir's Bank Line.

Shaw Savill contributed at least three exceptional ships to Twentieth Century British maritime history: the *Dominion Monarch* of 1938, the *Gothic* of 1948 and this ship, the 20,204 grt *Southern Cross* of 1955. Belfast-built, twin screws and engines aft, 1,160 passengers and no cargo holds, she was the first merchant ship to be launched (on 17th August 1954) by a reigning British monarch. Thereafter she spent 49 years as a passenger liner and then a cruise ship until scrapped at Chittagong, Bangladesh from November 2003. *[Roger Martin/Russell Priest collection]*

The *Southern Cross* off the Overseas Passenger Terminal in Wellington harbour, towards the end of her Shaw Savill career. Note the screen with windows that has been added to her Lounge Deck above the stern. She is without her hull band. *[V.H. Young and L.A. Sawyer]*

The single screw, 18,140 grt *Dunedin* of 1980. A product of Swan Hunter (Shipbuilders) Ltd., Wallsend, she was the largest, fastest (at 19 knots) and last cargo vessel to be built for Shaw Savill. She was powered by a six-cylinder, two-stage, single-acting Burmeister and Wain diesel manufactured by Harland and Wolff Ltd. at Belfast, having an output of 20,500 BHP at 114 r.p.m. The *Dunedin* was employed on a service in conjunction with Bank Line's *Willowbank* (18,236/1980) between Australia, New Zealand, the Caribbean, central American and US Gulf ports. In 1986 she was sold to Hamburg Sud-Amerika, becoming *Monte Pascoal*, and was lengthened by 26 metres. After several name changes she was sold again in 2001 to become the *MSC Jessica*. On 6th June 2009 the former *Dunedin* was beached at Alang for scrapping. *[Russell Priest]*

MEMORANDA AND MEMENTOES FROM THE BIG ICS

Left: What is thought to be an original builder's model of the *Ceramic*, owned by the Otago Maritime Society of New Zealand and on display in the Maritime Hall, Otago Museum, Dunedin. *[Ian J. Farquhar collection]*

Below, left and right: long among the world's most famous model builders, Bassett-Lowke were commissioned by Furness Withy in 1953 to commemorate the *Gothic*'s service as royal yacht. In 2011 this model is displayed onboard HQS *Wellington,* moored on the Thames by the Embankment and headquarters of the Honorable Company of Master Mariners, London. Photo by courtesy of Captain Graham Pepper. *[Ambrose Greenway]*

D. Aitchison
MASTER

SS "ATHENIC"
SOUTHAMPTON
NETT. TONS
N.H.P

L. Burton

Autographs from the *Athenic's* maiden voyage in 1947. From top left Captain David Aitchison, Master; Thomas Henry Killingworth White, Chief Engineer; E. (Ted) Cordery, Purser; L. Burton (appointment not known); Arthur Edmond Smith, Second Officer; Alwyn Ernest Warren, Chief Officer. *[Brian Mountjoy]*

ROYAL COMMONWEALTH TOUR
1953/54.

EXCHANGE TELEPHONES

	No	STATION
P	1	H.M. The Queen's Day Cabin.
	2	H.M. The Queen's Sleeping Cabin.
	3	Royal Ante-Room.
P	4	H.R.H. The Duke's Day Cabin.
	5	H.R.H. The Duke's Sleeping Cabin
	6	Maid to Lady-in-Waiting.
P	7	Flag Officer—Royal Yachts.
	8	H.R.H. The Duke's Private Secretary.
	9	Australian Equerry.
	10	Press Secretary.
	11	Private Secretary.
	12	Director of Music.
	13	Equerry.
	14	Lady-in-Waiting I.
	15	Lady-in-Waiting II.
	16	New Zealand Equerry.
	17	Chief Clerk to Private Secretary.
	18	Surgeon Commander R.N.
	19	Clerk to Ladies-in-Waiting & Press Clerks Office.
	20	Australian Minister or Cypher Clerk.
	21	Exchange Telegraph Correspondent.
P	22	Commander R.N. Communications Officer.
	23	Commander R.N. Staff Officer Operations
P	24	Private Secretary and Assistant Private Secretary's Office.
	25	H.R.H. The Duke's Private Secretary and Clerks' Office.
	26	H.M. The Queen's Dresser.
	27	H.R.H. The Duke's Valet.
	28	B.B.C. Commentator.
	29	
	30	
	31	Ladies-in-Waiting Sitting Room
	32	Chief Steward.
	33	Senior Staff Smoking Room.
	34	Cypher Office.
	35	Royal Cypher Clerks' Office.
	36	Royal Cypher Clerks' Office.
	37	Royal Clerks' Office.
	38	Royal Clerks' Office.
	39	H.M. The Queen's Page.
P	40	Main Signal Office.
	41	Radio Office.
	42	Officers' Smoking Room.
	43	Call Box Promenade Deck.
	44	Captain.
	45	Chart Room.
	46	Chief Officer.
	47	Bureau.
	48	New Zealand Press Correspondent or Australian Tour Official.
	49	Clerk Accountant.
	50	Reuter Correspondent.
	51	Officer of Watch.

P *Denotes Telephone fitted with Privacy Equipment.*

WATCHES. For the purpose of discipline and to apportion the duties on board evenly, the Deck and Engine Room personnel are divided into three watches. The day commences at Noon and is divided as follows :—

Afternoon Watch	Noon	—	4.0 p.m.
First Dog Watch	4.0 p.m.	—	6.0 p.m.
Second Dog Watch	6.0 p.m.	—	8.0 p.m.
First Watch	8.0 p.m.	—	Midnight
Middle Watch	Midnight	—	4.0 a.m.
Morning Watch	4.0 a.m.	—	8.0 a.m.
Forenoon Watch	8.0 a.m.	—	Noon

The three Watches are now usually known as 12 - 4 Watch, 4 - 8 Watch and 8 - 12 Watch.

OFFICERS' WATCHES. The Officers keep a three-Watch system as follows :—

Chief and 4th Officers 2nd, 7th and 8th Engineers 1st Refrig. Engineer	... 4.0 a.m. ... 4.0 p.m.	— —	8.0 a.m. and 8.0 p.m.
2nd and 5th Officers 3rd, 6th and 9th Engineers 2nd Refrig. Engineer	... Noon ... Midnight	— —	4.0 p.m. and 4.0 a.m.
3rd Officer 4th, 5th and 10th Engineers 3rd Refrig. Engineer	... 8.0 a.m. ... 8.0 p.m.	— —	Noon and Midnight

TIME ON BOARD SHIP. Time on board ship is kept by means of a bell which is struck every half-hour.

Afternoon Watch	Second Dog Watch	Middle Watch	Morning Watch (contd.)
1 Bell 12.30 p.m.	1 Bell 6.30 p.m.	1 Bell 12.30 a.m.	5 Bells 6.30 a.m.
2 Bells 1.0 p.m.	2 Bells 7.0 p.m.	2 Bells 1.0 a.m.	6 ,, 7.0 a.m.
3 ,, 1.30 p.m.	3 ,, 7.30 p.m.	3 ,, 1.30 a.m.	7 ,, 7.30 a.m.
4 ,, 2.0 p.m.	8 ,, 8.0 p.m.	4 ,, 2.0 a.m.	8 ,, 8.0 a.m.
5 ,, 2.30 p.m.		5 ,, 2.30 a.m.	
6 ,, 3.0 p.m.		6 ,, 3.0 a.m.	
7 ,, 3.30 p.m.	**First Watch**	7 ,, 3.30 a.m.	**Forenoon Watch**
8 ,, 4.0 p.m.	1 Bell 8.30 p.m.	8 ,, 4.0 a.m.	1 Bell 8.30 a.m.
	2 Bells 9.0 p.m.		2 Bells 9.0 a.m.
	3 ,, 9.30 p.m.		3 ,, 9.30 a.m.
First Dog Watch	4 ,, 10.0 p.m.	**Morning Watch**	4 ,, 10.0 a.m.
1 Bell 4.30 p.m.	5 ,, 10.30 p.m.	1 Bell 4.30 a.m.	5 ,, 10.30 a.m.
2 Bells 5.0 p.m.	6 ,, 11.0 p.m.	2 Bells 5.0 a.m.	6 ,, 11.0 a.m.
3 ,, 5.30 p.m.	7 ,, 11.30 p.m.	3 ,, 5.30 a.m.	7 ,, 11.30 a.m.
4 ,, 6.0 p.m.	8 ,, Midnight	4 ,, 6.0 a.m.	8 ,, Noon

NOTE.—Seven Bells in the Morning and Forenoon Watches are struck 10 minutes earlier to allow the Watch next for duty to have their breakfast and dinner respectively.

One Bell is also struck at 3.45, 7.45, 11.45, a.m. and p.m., as warning to Watch below—i.e., off duty—to prepare to relieve the deck punctually at Eight Bells.

BADGES OF RANK. The Executive Officers of the vessel wear badges of rank as follows :—

Commander	Four bands ½" gold lace on cuffs. Gold leaves on cap peak.
Chief Officer	Three bands ½" gold lace.
Second Officer	Two bands ½" and one band ¼" gold lace.
Third Officer	Two bands ½" gold lace.
Fourth Officer	One band ½" gold lace.
Surgeon	Three bands ½" gold lace with scarlet cloth between.
Chief Radio Officer ...	Two bands ¼" waved gold lace with diamond of gold lace between.
Assistant Radio Officers ...	Two bands ¼" waved gold lace.
Chief Engineer	Four bands ½" gold lace with purple cloth between.
Second Engineer	Three bands ½" gold lace with purple cloth between.
First Refrigerating Engineer Third Engineer	... Two bands ½" and one of ¼" gold lace with purple cloth between.
Fourth Engineer First Electrical Engineer	... Two bands ½" gold lace with purple cloth between.
Fifth Engineer Second Electrical Engineer	... One band ½" gold lace on purple cloth.
Junior Engineers and Electrical Engineers	... One band ¼" gold lace on purple cloth.
Purser	Three bands ½" gold lace with white cloth between.
Assistant Purser	Two bands ½" gold lace with white cloth between.
Junior Assistant Purser ...	One band ½" gold lace on white cloth.
Chief Steward	Three bands ½" gold lace zigzag.
Second Steward	Two bands ½" gold lace zigzag.

When Officers are in white uniforms, similar stripes of rank are worn on the shoulder straps instead of on the sleeves of the jacket.

AUSTRALIAN SERVICE Via South Africa

without notice)

FARES — SHAW SAVILL LINE

FIRST CLASS: S.S. "ATHENIC," "CERAMIC," "CORINTHIC" and "GOTHIC"

	Brisbane to		Sydney to		Melbourne to		Adelaide to		Fremantle to	
	S.A.	U.K.	S.A.	U.K.	S.A.	U.K.	S.A.	U.K.	S.A.	U.K.
BOAT DECK	£	£	£	£	£	£	£	£	£	£
Single Rooms .. .. (per room)	138	183	135	180	132	177	129	174	123	168
† Double Rooms .. .. (per room)	254	336	248	330	242	324	236	318	224	306
† Double Rooms with Bath (per room)	284	386	278	380	272	374	266	368	254	356
PROMENADE DECK										
Single Rooms .. .. (per room)	131 / 138	173 / 183	128 / 135	170 / 180	125 / 132	167 / 177	122 / 129	164 / 174	116 / 123	158 / 168
Single Rooms with Bath .. (per room)	161 / 168	223 / 233	158 / 165	220 / 230	155 / 162	217 / 227	152 / 159	214 / 224	146 / 153	208 / 218
Double Rooms .. .. (per room)	231	306	225	300	219	294	213	288	201	276
† Double Rooms with Bath (per room)	284	386	278	380	272	374	266	368	254	356
Suite (for 1 or 2 Persons) (per room)	434	586	428	580	422	574	416	568	404	556

† CAN BE FITTED WITH PULLMAN BERTHS AND MADE AVAILABLE FOR FAMILIES AND PARTIES DESIRING 3-BERTH ROOMS AT APPROPRIATE RATES.

N.Z. TO UNITED KINGDOM
AND PACIFIC AND CARIBBEAN

FIRST CLASS
Via PANAMA and CURACAO.

GOTHIC, ATHENIC CERAMIC, CORINTHIC (15,900 tons).

From New Zealand—	To U.K.		To Curacao		To Panama	
	(‡Full Season)	(§Off Season)	(‡Full Season)	(§Off Season)	(‡Full Season)	(§Off Season)
Suite, for two persons	£770	£590	£610	£540	£590	£530
Single Room, with Bathroom	£305 & £320	£225	£242 & £254	£200	£232 & £244	£190
Single Room	£255 & £270	£200	£202 & £214	£175	£192 & £204	£165
Two Bedstead Room with Bathroom, (†) per adult	£285	£202/10/-	£225	£178	£215	£168
Two Bedstead Room, (†) per adult	£230 & £260	£180 & £190	£205	£165	£195	£155

†Most of the Double Rooms are fitted with a Pullman berth and these are available for families and parties desiring three berth Rooms.

‡Full Season: N.Z. to U.K., 1st January to 31st July.
U.K. to N.Z., 1st July to 28th February.

§Off Season: N.Z. to U.K., 1st August to 31st December.
U.K. to N.Z., 1st March to 30th June.

CARGO VESSELS
Accommodation is occasionally available in cargo ships from New Zealand to the United Kingdom. Most such vessels carry approximately 12 cabin class passengers usually in single or double cabins at rates from £155 to £170.

TOURIST CLASS

S.S. SOUTHERN CROSS (20,000 tons).
(All Cabins fully Air-conditioned.)

Via FIJI, TAHITI, PANAMA CANAL, CURACAO, TRINIDAD.

From New Zealand—	To U.K.	To Fiji	To Tahiti	To Panama	To Curacao	To Trinidad
Single Rooms	£205 & £215	£38	£75	£172 & £181	£179 & £188	£184 & £193
Two Bedstead Rooms	£180 to £215	£32 to £38	£67 to £75	£151 to £181	£158 to £188	£163 to £193
Two Berth Rooms	£175 to £190	£30 to £36	£63 to £72	£147 to £160	£154 to £167	£159 to £172
Three Berth Rooms	£160 & £185	£30 & £32	£63 & £67	£134 & £155	£141 & £162	£146 & £167
Four Berth Rooms	£150 to £160	£28 & £30	£59 & £63	£126 to £134	£133 to £141	£138 to £146
Six Berth Rooms	£145 & £150	£28	£59	£122 & £126	£129 & £133	£134 & £138
Supplement for Private Shower and Toilet	£30	£5	£10	£24	£26	£27

JECT TO ALTERATION WITHOUT NOTICE.

F SEASON RATES WHICH APPLY TO ALL ACCOMMODATION IN FIRST CLASS SHIPS.
31st DECEMBER, U.K. TO N.Z. 1st MARCH to 30th JUNE.

Opposite page top: HMRY *Gothic's* telephone directory. *[Terence Williams Collection; Voyager New Zealand Maritime Museum, ID 15799. T.J. Williams was HMRY Gothic's Second Electrician]*
Opposite page, bottom left and right: Extracts from a Shaw Savill 'Information for Passengers' booklet, 1961. *[Murray Robinson]*
This page, top: An extract from Shaw Savill's advertised fares, February 1953. *[Murray Robinson]*
This page, bottom: Fares and sailings from an undated brochure. *[Captain Graham Pepper, Shaw Savill Society]*

SHAW SAVILL LINE

SMOOTH, QUIET, FAST

A CHOICE of route, a choice of ship — but always smooth, quiet, fast travel. Those are among the features of travel the Shaw Savill way.

All Shaw Savill liners are one class — but you can select either a "first class" ship or a "tourist class" ship.

Expressly for tourist class are the "SOUTHERN CROSS" (20,204 tons) and the "NORTHERN STAR" (24,731 tons), modern ships which sweep you to England west via Australia and South Africa or east across the Pacific, through the Panama Canal and the colourful Caribbean.

These ships carry 1100 and 1400 passengers respectively. They're quiet, because they were designed with their engines aft; fast, because they carry no cargo; and smooth, because they're stabilised for passenger comfort.

A wide range of accommodation from 6-berth cabins to stateroom suites suits all budgets. Furnishings throughout are functional and tasteful. More deck space for fun-in-the-sun, magnificent public rooms for entertainment and relaxation and controlled air-conditioning make conditions pleasant for everyone.

At each port-of-call your ship's pursers' office arranges shore excursions for passengers so that you have splendid opportunities to see SYDNEY, MELBOURNE, FREMANTLE, DURBAN, CAPE TOWN, and LAS PALMAS if you travel via South Africa, or FIJI, TAHITI, ACAPULCO, PANAMA, CURACAO, TRINIDAD, BARBADOS and LISBON on the Panama Canal route. (Ports-of-call on this route vary throughout the year.)

1967 SAILINGS — N.Z.-U.K.
One Class
Mar. 9: "Northern Star" ex Wgtn via Panama.
Apr. 22: "Southern Cross" ex Wgtn via South Africa.
June 8: "Northern Star" ex Wgtn via Panama.
July 15: "Southern Cross" ex Wgtn via South Africa.

FARES:

"Southern Cross" via South Africa
N.Z.-UK.: Full Season from £187/-/- ($NZ374.00); Off Season from £150/-/- ($NZ300.00).
N.Z.-Cape Town: Fares from £127/-/- ($254.00).

29

"Northern Star" via Panama
N.Z.-U.K.: Full Season from £175/-/- ($NZ350.00); Off Season from £145/-/- ($NZ290.00).
N.Z.-Trinidad: Full Season from £146/-/- ($NZ292.00); Off Season from £115/-/- ($NZ230.00).

If you decide to travel on a "First Class" ship, either "GOTHIC" or "CERAMIC", both of which accommodate 70 to 80 passengers, will take you to England in really elegant comfort. Accommodation is in single and double bedstead rooms situated on the promenade and boat decks. Many of these cabins have their own private facilities.

1967 SAILINGS — N.Z.-U.K.
Apr. 7: "Ceramic" via Panama.
June 22: "Gothic" via Panama.

FARES:
N.Z.-U.K.: Full Season from £260/-/- ($NZ520.00); Off Season from £205/-/- ($NZ410.00).
N.Z.-Trinidad: Full Season from £210/-/- ($NZ420.00); Off Season from £200/-/- ($NZ400.00).

RETURN TICKETS are not only issued at a lower rate, but are interchangeable between all the ships and also between full and off seasons.

OFF SEASON rates apply between August 1 — December 31, N.Z.-U.K., and February 1 — June 30, U.K.-N.Z. (First Class vessels only).

For reservations see

RUSSELL & SOMERS LTD

Wide open spaces for fun in the sun are a feature of Shaw Savill service.

PROGRAMME OF DEPARTURE FROM JAMAICA.

Friday 27th. November.

0700	-	s.s."Gothic" shifts berth to Port Royal
0745	-	s.s. "Gothic" anchors Port Royal
0800	-	Dress ship out booms and gangways.
0830	-	On return from R.J.Y.C. Staff Barhe to be hoisted in.
1100	-	Army boat at Port Royal to bring heavy baggage. (Derrick to be rigged for hoisting in.)
1400	-	Boat at Port Royal for light baggage. Embarkation to be by port accommodation ladder.
1430	-	Royal Barge leaves ship. In boat booms.
1510	-	Her Majesty arrives Port Royal.
1545	-	Gothic ship's company, band etc., fall in. (details to be arranged)
1550	-	Her Majesty embarks in Royal Barge at Port Royal.
(approx) 1555	-	Her Majesty embarks in Gothic. Ceremonial arrival, introductions etc. Gothic breaks Royal Standard. Sheffield fires Royal Salute.
1605	-	Ship's Company fall out. Up Royal Barge. Hoist in all gangways. As soon as possible Gothic weighs and proceeds. Ship's Company fall in.Ceremonial Departure.
1700	-	Fly past by Aero Club.
1730	-	Drop Pilot - undress ship.

Above left: From a Russell and Somers Ltd. 'Holidays and Travel' brochure, 1967. *[Derek Ion]*
Above right: Arrival of HM Queen Elizabeth II aboard the royal yacht *Gothic*, 27th November 1953. *[Warwick Thomson]*
Below left: Wages from the *Athenic*. *[Neil S. Hudson]*
Below right: Music from the Band of HM Royal Marines. *[Warwick Thomson]*

2

ACCOUNT OF WAGES (Sec. 133, M.S.A. 1894) F.
Keep this Form as a Record of Your Nat. Insurance and Income Tax Deductions

NAME OF SEAMAN: HUDSON NEIL
Dis. A No. R629867

Name of Ship and Official Number	Class	Section	Income Tax Code	Rating	Ref. No. in Agreement
S.S. ATHENIC 167927 SOUTHAMPTON, NETT TON. 8759·70 N.H.P. 3700	U.	A or B	5	A.B.	15

Nat. Insurance No. ... Contributions commence Monday: F.D. (Date)

Date Wages Began	Date Wages Ceased	Total Period of Employment: Months	Days	Allotment Note given for: Amount	Date 1st Payment	Interval
10 OCT 1956	29 JAN 1957			£20	9-11-56	M

EARNINGS
Wages 3 months @ £31 per month
days @ £ per day
Increase in Wages (Promotions, etc.):
From to @ £ per mth mths days
From to @ £ per mth mths days
Overtime hours @ per hour
hours @ per hour
Leave and Subsistence brought fwd days
Voyage Leave days
Sundays at Sea
Total
Leave taken
Balance due days @ £ per day
Subsistence days @ £ per day
Delete as necessary: Carried forward to next voyage / Paid—to be shown in Earnings Column
Total Earnings
Less Reduction by £ p.m. mths days
Earnings
Deductions
Final Balance £ 27 7 4½
ADJUSTMENTS
Add
Deduct
£

DEDUCTIONS
Advance on Joining ... 15 —
Allotments ... 60
Fines
Forfeitures
Pension Fund No.
Income Tax
Union Contributions: weeks at
Nat. Insurance (Voyage): weeks at
Nat. Insurance (Leave): weeks at
Wireless Messages
Postages
Tobacco
Wines
Stores
Canteen
Cash
Total Deductions £
National Insurance paid to date wages ceased.
*National Insurance paid on leave to
*This line to be deleted if it does not apply.
Signature of Master
SEE OVER

PAID
OFFICE 29 JAN 1957 VICTORIA DOCKS

EIIR

PROGRAMME

1.	Overture	" Mirella "	Gounod
2.	Selection	" The New Moon "	Romberg
3.	Petite Suite		Debussy
4.	Waltz from	" Sleeping Beauty "	Tschaikowsky
5.	Entracte	" Cabana "	White
6.	Selection	" White Horse Inn "	Benatzky
7.	Intermezzo	" Running off the Rails "	Richardson
8.	March	" Liberty Bell "	Sousa

J. Vivian Dunn
Director of Music.

S.S. " Gothic "   December 9th,1953.

S.S. Athenic,
At Sea,
8th August, 1958.

Captain G.H. Heywood,
S.S. Athenic,
At Sea.

Sir,

We, the Trinidad contingent of your passengers on the S.S. Athenic now approaching England, wish to put on dutiful record our deep sense of appreciation of what this passage has meant to us.

Everything has combined to afford it the nature of an exhilarating pleasure cruise. The weather has been perfect, the ship has behaved admirably, but transcending these natural advantages has been the charm of unique friendship and gracious companionship which has united a group of distinct individuals into one happy family.

This exceptional circumstance, we are agreed, must be attributed almost wholly to the infectious graciousness so readily manifested by you, Sir, and the whole ship's complement under your inspiring leadership. Thoughtful consideration and the easy-going kindness and generous provision have all contributed to an uninhibited spirit of gaiety and sense of conscious well-being, never before experienced by us in any comparable circumstances.

This striking miracle of social integration will ever remain an unforgettable memory. But, when we convey thanks for this remarkable experience, we do so even more on behalf of the children, for whom this voyage must have built up an imperishable storehouse of enduring impressions. In this age of increasing social and national tensions lying immediately ahead, this memorable voyage may well constitute for them a land-mark of happy recollection and a beacon of inspiring incentive.

We could hardly conclude this testimony of grateful thanks, without mention of the characteristic spirit of sympathetic understanding and friendly accord which made the celebration of DISCOVERY DAY aboard ship possible. To have allowed it and then made ample provision for it was generous enough token of goodwill, but for the Officers to have joined so whole-heartedly in a celebration of such novel and unfamiliar character was at once a priceless gesture and feat of human graciousness.

There is but one last favour that we would request of you. It is, that you convey to your Head-Office in London our warm appreciation of this ship, and above all, for the stimulus of a ship's company of men and women who have served us so utterly, completely, nobly, and unselfishly.

We beg to remain, Sir
Yours very gratefully

A Gathering To Commemorate The Founding of the Shaw Savill Line

S. S. Athenic
Capt. G. H. Heywood

Port Chalmers — Tuesday, 28 October, 1958

RECEPTION 6.30—7 p.m. —Capt. G. H. Heywood, Mr. and Mrs. J. M. Ritchie and Mr. and Mrs. F. D. Harris will receive guests.

COCKTAILS 6.30 p.m. —will be served in the Smoke Room.

TOASTS 7.25 p.m.
—HER MAJESTY THE QUEEN — Capt. G. H. Heywood
—THE SHAW SAVILL LINE — His Worship the Mayor of Dunedin, Sir Leonard Wright
Response - - - Mr. F. D. Harris
—OUR GUESTS — Mr. J. M. Ritchie
Response The Very Reverend Walter Hurst, Dean of Dunedin

BUFFET DINNER 7.45 p.m. —in the Verandah Cafe and Smoke Room.

SHIPBOARD GAMES 8.30 p.m. —in the Smoke Room.

DANCING 8.30 p.m. —in the Lounge.

TEA 11 p.m. —will be served in the Dining Saloon.

TRIAL PROGRAMME.

Tuesday 27th. Oct.

1400 Vessel passes over D.G. Range. Prepare Stabd. Royal Gangway to "READY" position.

1600 Vessel moors to head buoy. (Two 3½" slip wires and two good ends manila.) 2nd. Officer and Bosun's Mate and party moor.
While vessel is mooring, 4th. Officer lowers starboard accommodation ladder.(Screens can be fitted in slow time later.) 4th. Officer and Saloon Deckmen and watch below Q.M.s then swing out port boat boom. Q.M's and Saloon Deckmen to be in uniform.

Chief Officer and party lower Stabd. Royal Gangway
When Stabd. Royal Gangway is ready with screens rigged etc., Party lower main aerials and rig festoon lighting.

Sunset:- Switch on festoon lighting.

Wednesday 28th. Oct.

0600 Prepare flags and downhauls for dressing ship. having previously lowered festoon lighting.

0900 Dress ship. Hoist out Staff Barge.

1030 Hoist in Staff Barge. Unrig Royal Gangway Unrig port boat boom

1130 Undress ship.

1300 Vessel sails for K.G.V. Dock.

1400 Exercise Transfer at Sea.

Thursday p.m. Arrive K.G. V. Dock with hands to Ceremonial Arrival Stations.

G. Anderson

Chief Officer.

Top left: Passenger plaudits for the master of the *Athenic*. Her chief officer on this voyage was J.O. Williams and her purser L.E. Northfield. F.W. White was chief engineer. *[David Green]*
Bottom left: trials and training preparatory to the royal voyage, HMRY *Gothic. [Warwick Thomson]*
Above: Well ordered hospitality aboard the *Athenic. [Murray Robinson]*

The New Zealand Company of Master Mariners

Wellington Branch

Annual Dinner on board the t.s.s. "Ceramic" at Wellington

Thursday 4th July 1963

Toast List and Procedure

The Wardens Opening Remarks	*Captain J. F. Holmes* D.S.O.
Our Guests	*Captain J. M. Mackay*
Reply by	*His Excellency The Govenor-General Sir Bernard Fergusson* G.C.M.G., G.C.V.O., D.S.O., O.B.E.
The Ship and Shaw Savill Line	*Captain H. C. McP. Douglas*
Replies by	*Captain N. S. Milne* *Mr J. D. MacMillan*
Absent Friends	*Reverend O. J. Mathews*

Grace — *The Reverend O. J Mathews*

Menu

Prawn Cocktail

Cream of Asparagus

Grilled Tay Salmon, Bearnaise

Escolopes of Veal, Holstein

Minted Garden Peas

Allumette & Croquette Potatoes

Babus au Rhum

Croute Eccosaise

Coffee

The Queen — *Captain N. S. Milne*

D I N N E R

Crayfish Mayonnaise

=

Roast Sirloin of Beef

=

Salad

=

Scotch Woodcock

S. " Gothic " January 30th, 1954.

LIST OF THOSE WHO WILL EMBARK IN
S.S. " GOTHIC " AT KINGSTON, JAMAICA.
ON FRIDAY, 27TH NOVEMBER, 1953

(A) HER MAJESTY THE QUEEN
HIS ROYAL HIGHNESS THE DUKE OF EDINBURGH

(B) HOUSEHOLD

The Lady Pamela Mountbatten (Lady-in-Waiting to The Queen)
The Lady Alice Egerton (Lady-in-Waiting to The Queen)
Major Sir Michael Adeane, K.C.V.O., C.B. (Acting Private Secretary to The Queen)
Lieut.-Commander M. Parker, M.V.O., R.N. (Private Secretary to The Duke of Edinburgh)
Lieut-Colonel The Honourable Martin Charteris, M.V.O., O.B.E. (Assistant Private Secretary to The Queen)
Commander (S) Richard Colville, C.V.O., D.S.C., R.N. (Press Secretary to The Queen)
Surgeon-Commander D. D. Steele-Perkins, F.R.A.C.S., D.L.O., R.N. (Medical Officer)
Captain Viscount Althorp (Acting Master of the Household and Equerry to The Queen)
Wing Commander Michael George Cowan, D.S.O., R.A.A.F. (Equerry to The Queen)
Lieutenant J. P. D. Hall, R.N.Z.N. (Equerry to The Queen)

(C) HOUSEHOLD OFFICIALS AND STAFF

Superintendent T. J. Clark (The Queen's Police Officer)
Inspector F. Kelley (The Duke of Edinburgh's Police Officer)
Miss Helen Gardiner, C.B.E., M.V.O. (Chief Clerk, Private Secretary's Office)
Mr. L. Treby, B.E.M. (Clerk Accountant)
Miss Felicity Irvine, M.V.O. (Clerk to Acting Private Secretary)
Miss P. Thomas (Clerk to The Duke of Edinburgh's Private Secretary)
Miss L. Hocking (Press Clerk)
Miss O. M. Short (Clerk to the Ladies-in-Waiting)
Miss M. Macdonald, M.V.O. (The Queen's First Dresser)
Miss E. MacGregor (The Queen's Second Dresser)
Miss F. Bramford (Lady Pamela Mountbatten's Maid)
Miss E. Holland (Lady Alice Egerton's Maid)
Miss P. Driscoll (The Queen's Sewing Maid)
Mr. J. MacDonald (The Duke of Edinburgh's Valet)

Top: Another example of the Big Ic liners as a venue for diverse social occasions, this one aboard the *Ceramic*. If the event happened to be in a different New Zealand port from where she or her sisters were at the time, cargo work would be halted, hatches closed and the ship made ready for sea. She would then proceed round the coast to where she was needed, then afterwards steam back to resume loading or discharge. *[Murray Robinson]*
Bottom left: Dining of a higher sort; the royal menu aboard HMRY *Gothic* the day she sailed from Bluff, New Zealand for the Tasman Sea and Australia. *[Ron Ingledew]*
Bottom right: Members of the Royal Household who accompanied the Queen and the Duke of Edinburgh on HMRY *Gothic*. *[Terence Williams Collection; Voyager New Zealand Maritime Museum, ID 15799]*

SHAW SAVILL LINE

ABERDEEN & COMMONWEALTH LINE

PASSENGER OFFICE

11A, LOWER REGENT STREET, LONDON, S.W.1.

TELEGRAMS:
SAVILL PICCY, LONDON
TELEPHONE:
WHITEHALL 1460

24th October, 1957.

FINAL EMBARKATION NOTICE

s.s. "GOTHIC"

Unforeseen circumstances have arisen which necessitate a slight alteration in the date of departure of the above vessel. Passengers will now embark at NO. 25 SHED, ROYAL ALBERT DOCK, LONDON, E.16., on WEDNESDAY, 6TH NOVEMBER, 1957 and not on the 7th November as originally arranged.

A special train conveying passengers to the above steamer will leave LIVERPOOL STREET STATION, LONDON, (Platform 5) at 2.30 p.m. on WEDNESDAY, 6TH NOVEMBER. The first-class rail fare is 3/3d. and tickets can be purchased at the Booking Office, Liverpool Street Station.

Passengers travelling independently should report for embarkation at NO. 25 SHED, ROYAL ALBERT DOCK, at 2.45 p.m.

AFTERNOON TEA WILL BE SERVED ON BOARD

The Company regrets the alteration in sailing and apologises for any inconvenience which it may cause to passengers. It is requested that the slip at the bottom of this notice be completed, detached and returned in the enclosed stamped addressed envelope.

CURRENCY WARNING:
Passengers are again warned that on embarkation all U.K. Currency Notes in excess of £10 per passenger may be confiscated by the Authorities and that the amount so confiscated is not recoverable.

FRIENDS:
The Company regrets that currency regulations and other restrictions imposed by the Customs and Immigration Authorities will not permit friends or relatives on board the vessel.

ITINERARY (Estimate Only)			Agents
Arrives Curacao	a.m.	18th November	S.E.L. Maduro & Sons, Inc.,
Leaves Curacao	p.m.	18th November	Curacao, D.W.I.
Arrives Cristobal	p.m.	20th November	W. Andrews & Co., Cristobal.
Leaves Cristobal	a.m.	21st November	- " -
Arrives Auckland	a.m.	9th December	Shaw Savill Line, 101 Queen St.

SHAW SAVILL & ALBION CO. LIMITED.

'Hurry along with packing my suitcase, dear, we're to leave a day early.' A hastening of departure times for the *Gothic's* passengers in October 1957. At least there will be afternoon tea at the end of the rush. [*Warwick Thomson*]

SHAW SAVILL & ALBION CO. LTD.—Continued.

Marine Superintendent: **Capt. A. E. Smith.**
Superintendent Engineer: **R. E. Evans.**
Cargo Superintendent: **Capt. A. R. Stephenson.**

Branch Manager:	*Town:*	*P.O. Box:*	*Telephone:*
G. Hawley	Auckland	3076	33-039
G. L. Almond (Asst.)			
Marine Supt. Capt. A. L. Turnbull			
E. W. Bryant	Christchurch	777	64-969
D. Manson (Freight).			
Agents:			
Levin & Co. Ltd.	Blenheim	44	89-299
National Mort. & Agy. Co. Ltd.	Dunedin	275	76-920
Common Shelton & Co. Ltd.	Gisborne	555	6748
Dalgety & N.Z. Loan Ltd.	Invercargill	850	84-169
Murray Roberts & Co. Ltd.	Napier	414	8412
Levin & Co. Ltd.	Nelson	71	6069
Newton King Ltd.	New Plymouth	244	5719
Dalgety & N.Z. Loan Ltd.	Tauranga	2193	84-159
Dalgety & N.Z. Loan Ltd.	Timaru	508	81-199
Levin & Co. Ltd.	Wanganui	447	5509

Top: A list of Shaw Savill's New Zealand agents in 1969. *[Ian J. Farquhar collection]*

'Yes sir, and would you like a cream-cheese bun to go with your cup of tea?' inquires the steward of the green-faced passenger as another huge sea explodes across the *Corinthic's* bow. She rises like a lift, white spray hurling and battering against the forward-facing lounge windows. 'Don't worry, sir,' continues the steward cheerfully, 'only another 30 days to London.' The date is June 1953 and every Merseyside rivet in the *Corinthic's* hull is being tested as she passes through the heads of Wellington to be embraced by New Zealand's wild Cook Strait. Barrett Reef, scene of a major shipping disaster 15 years later, is just astern on the liner's starboard hand. HMRY *Gothic* will grace these same waters in six months from the date of this photo. *[Ian J. Farquhar collection]*

INDEX

The Queen's night cabin aboard HMRY *Gothic*. Located in the after starboard corner of the deck house (renamed the Queen's House) on her Boat Deck, it was created by removing a fore-and-aft bulkhead between two twin-berth passenger cabins. An adjoining bathroom was extensively refitted and refurbished. After the royal tour of 1953-54 all of it was completely stripped out and returned to the way the two cabins had been when the *Gothic* was built. *[Wirral County Achive Collection]*

Persic. [Murray Robinson]

Runic. [Murray Robinson]